A Crown of Life:
The World of John McCrae

In Flanders Fields

In Flanders fields the poppies blow
Between the crosses, row on row,
That mark our place; and in the sky
The larks, still bravely singing, fly
Scarce heard amid the guns below.

We are the Dead. Short days ago
We lived, felt dawn, saw sunset glow,
Loved, and were loved, and now we lie
    In Flanders fields.

Take up our quarrel with the foe:
To you from failing hands we throw
The torch; be yours to hold it high.
If ye break faith with us who die
We shall not sleep, though poppies grow
    In Flanders fields

"Punch"
Dec 8 1915

John McCrae

A copy of 'In Flanders Fields' in John McCrae's handwriting, courtesy of National Archives of Canada C-26561

A Crown of Life:
The World of John McCrae

DIANNE GRAVES

Vanwell Publishing Limited
ST. CATHARINES, ONTARIO

Published in Canada by Vanwell Publishing Limited
St. Catharines, Ontario

Canadian Cataloguing in Publication Data

Graves, Dianne
  A crown of life : the world of John McCrae

Includes bibliographical references and index.
1. McCrae, John, 1872–1918. 2. Physicians –
Canada – Biography. 3. Soldiers – Canada –
Biography. 4. Poets, Canadian (English) –
Biography.* 5. Canada. Canadian Army –
Biography. 6. World War, 1914–1918 –
Biography. I. Title.

FC556.M42G72 1997   971.061'2'092   C97–931660–X
F1034.M42G72 1997

ISBN 1–55068–091–9

First published in the UK in 1997 by
Spellmount Limited
The Old Rectory, Staplehurst, Kent TN12 0AZ
UK

1 3 5 7 9 8 6 4 2
Typeset in Palatino by Palimpsest Book Production Limited,
Polmont, Stirlingshire
Printed in Great Britain by
TJ International Ltd, Padstow, Cornwall

Contents

Preface and Acknowledgements

It was on a warm summer evening in August 1992 that I first visited the site of John McCrae's dressing station near Ypres and listened to his famous poem, 'In Flanders Fields', being recited. That evening launched me on a long and eventful journey that would eventually take me to various parts of England, Scotland, France, Belgium and five times to Canada in search of the world of John McCrae. As I learned more about him, the people he knew and some of the events that linked their lives, I found myself fascinated to the extent of conceiving the idea of this book. It is the story of John McCrae and his world, the events he witnessed, and the generation of which he was a part.

A Crown of Life is an attempt to bring that lost world alive again. It is not a biography of John McCrae. That important task was admirably accomplished by John Prescott in his 1985 book, In Flanders Fields: The Story of John McCrae. Sir Andrew Macphail's book, In Flanders Fields, published in 1919, also contains an essay on John McCrae's character. My own efforts are built on the firm foundations first put in place by these two authors and I owe much to their work. I was fortunate to be able to meet with Dr Prescott and I would like to thank him for his interest and encouragement.

In the course of researching and writing A Crown of Life, many people have given generously of their time to assist me. First and foremost, I owe a very great debt of gratitude to John McCrae's surviving family. His niece, the late Mrs Margaret Gardner-Medwin, was most kind in not only allowing me access to family records but also in providing the hospitality of her home while I examined them. Her son, Dr David Gardner-Medwin, has been unfailingly helpful and supportive. Not only was he good enough to read my manuscript and make many amendments and suggestions, but also, despite his own very busy timetable, to answer queries and supply information. I am indebted to him.

The Canadian city of Guelph was John McCrae's birthplace and the people of Guelph have been unstinting in their assistance. I must make special mention of the help given me by the personnel of the Guelph Museums, to whom my thanks is heartfelt. The former Director of Guelph Civic Museums, Robin Etherington, was ready to assist from the start and enabled me to research at both McCrae House and Guelph Museum.

Bev Dietrich, Curator of McCrae House, has helped me in every way possible and I am extremely appreciative of all she has done. Both Val Harrison, the Museum's Program Assistant, and Kathleen Wall helped to provide information. Two former Curatorial Assistants, Charlotte Doud and Elizabeth Dagg, not only gave unselfishly of their free time but also shared with me their knowledge and enthusiasm. I am indeed grateful to both of them, and also express my thanks to Elizabeth, to Jennifer Burnell and to Hugh Macmillan, all of whom allowed me access to their research. Mrs Cynthia Macleod kindly gave me permission to quote from the unpublished manuscript of her father, C.L.C. Allinson, and Guy Goldston of the Guelph Collegiate Vocational Institute was good enough to send me material on John McCrae. A very special word of thanks and appreciation goes to Gloria Dent, who most generously shared with me a part of her research on Edward Johnson, enabling me to include in this book a hitherto unpublished episode in John McCrae's life.

In Montreal, where John McCrae worked for much of his professional life, I owe many debts of gratitude. June Schachter, History of Medicine Librarian at the Osler Library, McGill University, provided every assistance during my visits to the Library, readily responded to my various enquiries and came up with ideas and suggestions. I extend my most warm thanks to her, the Assistant Librarian, Wayne LeBel, and other members of staff. Christopher Parkinson, General Manager of the University Club of Montreal, welcomed me and gave me every assistance during my stay there. Herb Bercowitz of the Montreal General Hospital, Stella Aucoin of the Royal Victoria Hospital, Phoebe Chartrand and Robert Michel of the McGill University Archives, and Janice Paskey, Editor of *McGill News* replied helpfully and promptly to my requests for information, as did Anette O'Connell of the McCord Museum of Canadian History. Dr Harry Scott was good enough to provide information on his grandfather, the Venerable Archdeacon F.G. Scott. Dr Marian Kelen, daughter of Dr W.W. Francis, and her husband Andrew entertained me to lunch and spent time discussing my project with me.

Many other Canadians have assisted me. From the outset I received encouragement and helpful information from both Jim Lotz of Halifax and Major (Retd) Richard Malott of Ottawa. To them I offer my sincere gratitude for their interest and for all they have done. Others that I wish to thank are: Diana Tremain, granddaughter of Dr Henry Orton Howitt, who was kind enough to allow me to quote from her grandfather's article about John McCrae; the staff of the National Archives of Canada and the National Library; Stuart Sutherland, who generously assisted me in locating a number of sources; Jane Fox of *Legion* magazine in Ottawa; Anne Melvin, Librarian of the Royal Canadian Military Institute, Toronto; Captain J.R. McKenzie, Curator of the Museum of the Royal Military College of Canada, Kingston; Marilyn Bell of the Public

Archives of Prince Edward Island; Dr and Mrs Edgar Andrew Collard; Felicity Pope, Curator of the Canadian Museum of Health and Medicine; Peter Caissie, Department of Veterans' Affairs; Lloyd Jones of Regina; James Elliott of Hamilton; Francis Mozer of Hart House, University of Toronto; and Lagring Ulunday, Records Archivist at the University of Toronto Library. Douglas Hendry, Michael Whitby, Lieutenant-Commander William Glover RCN and Stan Dugdale assisted with aspects of my research. Violet Andras Peard, Noreen Young, Sandi Atack and other friends in Almonte have given their kind support in various ways.

In the United States, I am grateful to Dr Erwin Burke of Poquoson, Virginia; Prudence Taylor, Heritage Room Librarian of the Athens Regional Library System; and Timothy Field, President of Elliott & Fitzpatrick Inc., Athens, Georgia who very kindly supplied me with a copy of *The Miracle Flower* by Moina Michael. Ken Finland of the American branch of the Western Front Association published my request for information and I thank all those who responded.

In South Africa, Joan Abrahams of Bloemfontein was enthusiastic and helpful throughout, and Elaine Hurford kindly responded to my queries.

In France, I am greatly indebted to Guy Bataille of Wimereux, former editor of *La Voix du Nord* newspaper, who provided material from his own research, allowed me to quote from his article about John McCrae and guided me to specific locations associated with John McCrae's life from 1915 to 1918. Janine Watrin, Isabelle Condette of the Bibliothèque Nationale de Boulogne, John Munn of the Royal British Legion's Boulogne branch and Christian Devos of the Office Nationale des Anciens Combattants et Victimes de Guerre, all contributed information, and the Mayors of Lens and Doullens responded willingly to my enquiries.

In Belgium, I extend my most sincere thanks to the staff of the Stedelijke Musea, Ieper and the Documentatie-Centrum Dr Alfred Caenepeel; to Yvan Cauwelier, Yves Carton and Jan Louagie of Technisch Instituut Heilige Familie and all involved in Toerisme Heilige Familie, Ieper; and to Jacques Ryckebosch of Talbot House, Poperinge.

In Scotland, I appreciated the responses I received from the following people: Stephen Wood, Keeper of the Scottish United Services Museum and Edith Philip of the Museum's Library; Julian Small, Inspector of Ancient Monuments, Historic Scotland; Margaret Wilkes, Head of the Map Library, National Library of Scotland; Mrs Marigold MacRae, President of the Clan MacRae Society, Eleanor Stewart, its Honorary Secretary, and Fiona MacRae. *The Oban Times* kindly published my request for information and I was pleased to receive several replies. Finally, I wish especially to thank the staff of Eilean Donan Castle for the help and information they provided, and Elspeth Galbraith for her beautiful photograph.

In England, the staff of the Royal British Legion have been steadfast in their help and support. I thank most warmly the following people: Lieutenant Colonel (Retd) R.D. Hanscomb OBE, Assistant Secretary of the Royal British Legion; Major Tony Morgan, former Head of the Royal British Legion Poppy Appeal and Colonel Patrick Reger, the present Head of the Poppy Appeal; Robert Parkin, Chief Executive of the Royal British Legion Poppy Factory and his staff, in particular Ray Webb, who very kindly allowed me access to his own research; Jeremy Lillies, Head of Public Relations and Val Cooper, Public Relations Officer.

When I first set out to write this book, Tonie and Valmai Holt gave me encouragement and made many good suggestions. I am sincerely grateful to them and my former colleagues at Holts' Tours of Sandwich: Michael and Maureen Silver, the latter's assistance and contributions having been greatly appreciated; Lieutenant-Colonel Mike Martin and his wife Pat, who first had the idea of including John McCrae in the company's Ypres/Vimy/Somme tour; Isobel Swan, Sue Butler, Mary Rivers, Karen Ingleby, Pauline Dale, Michele Eren, Lieutenant-Colonel David Storrie OBE and Captain Paul Snook. Finally, I owe thanks and appreciation to Kevin Finucane, who willingly gave of his time to assist with research at various stages.

Peter Simkins, Senior Historian at the Imperial War Museum, gave me a number of suggestions to follow up. James Brazier, Editor of the Western Front Association's *Bulletin*, was consistently helpful and kind enough to publish my requests for information. I thank him and all the members of the Association who took the time and trouble to reply. In addition to the interest and support received from friends and family, I want to thank the following people who have assisted in a variety of important ways: Brigadier Peter Abraham FRCPsych, Julie Allum, Assistant Librarian at the Royal College of Physicians, John and Margaret Bell, Charles Beresford, Yvonne Brazier-Potter, Jean Burton, Cathryn Corns, Hill Harris, Tony Hole, Jill Lynch, John Marrin, Nicholas Martland, Margaret Sankey, Nita Schimscha, Yvonne Türkistanli, Linda Williamson and Charlotte Zeepvat. In conclusion, I wish to thank Betty Dancocks for allowing me to use her photograph, and Oxford University Press for allowing me to quote from *A Life of Sir William Osler*. If I have inadvertently omitted anyone, I hope they will forgive an honest oversight.

In the course of the five years it has taken to write this book, I not only acquired the many debts of gratitude that I have acknowledged above – I also acquired a family. Before I made my first research trip to North America, friends put me in contact with a Canadian historian, Donald E. Graves. In April 1994 I met Don for the first time in Guelph and it transpired that, like John McCrae, he was a former militia gunner from a town in southern Ontario. Our mutual interests blossomed and in due course we became man and wife. Don is a well-published author in his own right and, throughout the relentless task of completing this book, he provided the expertise in military history that I lacked and, on several occasions, was able to catch me before I fell into some of the yawning chasms that can open up before a neophyte author. The other member of the household who deserves a mention is what John McCrae would have called 'a little friend' – our tabby and white kitten, 'Wally' – who provided much-needed comic relief during the onerous process of editing this manuscript, and who turned out to be my harshest critic. On a memorable snowy January afternoon in Canada he quite literally tore part of my early draft to shreds.

Without the help and support I have received and the faith of my publisher, Jamie Wilson of Spellmount Limited, *A Crown of Life* could not have been written. I hope that everyone concerned will enjoy this book, made possible by their collective efforts.

Dianne Graves
St Valentine's Day, 1997

Every effort has been made to locate copyright holders. Any omissions are sincerely regretted and will be rectified when this book is reprinted.

List of Maps

Abbreviations Used in Notes

GM Papers   Diaries, correspondence and other papers in the possession of the Gardner-Medwin family

JM   John McCrae

MG   Manuscript Group

MH   Guelph Museums, McCrae House

Micro   Microfilm reel

MTRL   Metropolitan Toronto Reference Library, Baldwin Room

NAC   National Archives of Canada

OL   Osler Library of the History of Medicine, McGill University, Montreal

PCCA   Presbyterian Church of Canada Archives

RG   Record Group

UGL   University of Guelph Library

UTL   John P. Robarts Reference Library, University of Toronto

List of Plates

1. John McCrae as a baby. Courtesy of Guelph Museums, Guelph, Canada.
2. John McCrae (bottom left) with his mother Janet, brother Tom and sister Geills, circa 1881. Courtesy of Guelph Museums, Guelph, Canada.
3. Tom (left) and John McCrae, 1893. Courtesy of Guelph Museums, Guelph, Canada.
4. Guelph Christmas Market, 1896. Courtesy of Guelph Museums, Guelph, Canada.
5. John McCrae as a medical student at the University of Toronto, 1898. Courtesy of Guelph Museums, Guelph, Canada.
6. John McCrae relaxing at Mount Airy, Maryland, 1896. Courtesy of Guelph Museums, Guelph, Canada.
7. The Second Canadian Contingent at Halifax and about to depart for South Africa, January 1900. Courtesy of the Public Archives of Nova Scotia.
8. Major W G Hurdman (left), officer commanding D Battery, Royal Canadian Field Artillery, and Lieutenant Edward Morrison (right) at Green Point, Cape Town, February 1900. Courtesy of Guelph Museums, Guelph, Canada.
9. John McCrae in the mess dress of an officer of the Canadian Artillery, 7 March 1901. Courtesy of the McCord Museum, Notman Archives, Montreal.
10. Sherbrooke Street, Montreal, where it adjoins Metcalfe Street, winter 1896. John McCrae lived not far from this corner in the house of Dr Edward Archibald at 160 Metcalfe Street from October 1910 until the Great War. Courtesy of the McCord Museum, Notman Archives, Montreal.
11. John McCrae (centre) with Beatriz d'Arneiro (left) and Elizabeth Morrison (right), Paris, November 1906. The Edward Johnson Collection, Special Collections, University of Guelph Library.
12. Sir William Osler (centre front) and Lady Osler (far right) with a group of friends at 13 Norham Gardens, Oxford, 1907. Seated behind Lady Osler is Sir William's niece Amy Gwyn, who later married Tom McCrae. Courtesy of the Osler Library of the History of Medicine, McGill University, Montreal.

13. Members of Earl Grey's 1910 expedition outside the Wawaskkeski Clubhouse. John McCrae is seated left with Earl Grey standing behind him. Leo Amery is seated centre. Courtesy of Hudson's Bay Company Archives, Provincial Archives of Manitoba.
14. John McCrae circa 1908 with the daughter of a friend, possibly Dr Edward Archibald's daughter, Margaret. Courtesy of Dr David Gardner-Medwin.
15. Dr Tom McCrae with his sister Geills Kilgour and her children Margaret (standing left), Katherine (standing right), David (seated left) and Jack (seated centre). The photo is likely to have been taken either in the summer of 1914 or spring of 1915. Courtesy of Guelph Museums, Guelph, Canada.
16. Onlookers watching the arrival of the Canadian Expeditionary Force at Plymouth, 14 October 1914. Courtesy of National Archives of Canada PA-22708.
17. Top row from left: Lt Alexis Helmer, Dr Edward Archibald, Dr Lawrence Rhea, Capt. Lawrence Cosgrave
    Bottom row from left: Dr Herbert Birkett, Dr W.G. Turner, Professor J.G. Adami, Dr Francis Scrimger. Author's collection.
18. John McCrae seated on 'Bonfire', his faithful companion throughout the war, Boulogne 1916. Courtesy of Guelph Museums, Guelph, Canada.
19. Her Majesty Queen Mary visits No. 3 Canadian General Hospital (McGill), 3 July 1917. Accompanying the Queen are Matron MacLatchy (on her right), Colonel Birkett (turning to her right) and John McCrae (walking directly behind Matron MacLatchy). By kind permission of the Trustees, Imperial War Museum.

This book is dedicated to the late Margaret Gardner-Medwin, John McCrae's niece, who throughout its writing was a source of help, encouragement, kindness and support.

PROLOGUE

In the fields of Flanders, May 1915

Lieutenant Helmer was killed on the tenth day. The shelling had been heavy the previous night and it continued that morning when he left his dug-out to see how his section was faring. He died instantly when a German round exploded beside him.

There was little time to do anything about the body as the tenth day turned out to be a bad one. The Germans again attacked the French lines to the left with gas and the brigade went to 'quick fire' for ninety minutes to support the French. They were now down to twelve guns and these were being used so hard that their springs were going soft, the buffer oil in their recoil cylinders was beginning to boil and smoke, and the breeches had become so hot that the gunners had to cover their hands with sacking to load and fire.

When the firing died down somewhat, a detail went out to get the body. Helmer had been dismembered but the men collected what parts they could find, put them in sandbags, placed the bags in the form of a body on a grey wool army blanket and fastened the whole securely with safety pins. He had a picture of his girl with him when he was killed – a shell fragment had torn a hole through it but they put it in the blanket anyway.

After dark they buried Helmer in the little cemetery that the infantry had started. As the batteries were still in action, the colonel had to stay at the fire control post and most of the men had to be with their guns. The chaplains were busy with the wounded so the major who was second-in-command of the brigade led the small burial party that gathered around the open grave in the ground. The blanket and its contents were placed in the hole and the major spoke some words from the Church of England burial service. They then filled in the hole with shovels and used them to pound the plain wooden cross, lettered with the details of his name, rank, unit and date of death, into the ground at the head of the grave. Helmer was twenty-two years old when he died; he was a nice lad from Ottawa and everybody liked him. That night there was a lot of small arms fire but the German shelling was not as heavy.

Dawn was clear and bright but the good weather brought the German observation planes over and the enemy artillery became more accurate. At about 7:00 a.m. the brigade second-in-command looked out from his dug-out in the canal bank. He could see the little cemetery with wild flowers growing among the crosses and, in lulls between the shelling, he could hear birds singing in the sky above. He was a literary man, this major, and the sight of the cemetery roused something in him – he began to write a poem. In mid-morning, however, a report came in that the Germans were massing for another attack and Number Four Battery was ranged on their concentration area. The first round was one hundred yards short, but the second was on target and all four batteries then went to 'quick fire'. The forward observer reported good results but it provoked heavy German shelling that continued until nightfall. The eleventh day was also a bad one.[1]

NOTES

1.   JM Diary, 1, 2 and 3 May 1915; 1st Brigade Canadian Field Artillery War Diary; accounts of Sergeant-Major Cyril Allinson, Captain Lawrence Cosgrave and Lieutenant-Colonel Edward Morrison.

CHAPTER ONE

'From the lone shieling'[1]

1849–1872

On a chilly day in March 1849 the packet ship *Empress* edged her way cautiously through the array of small and large boats at anchor in the River Mersey to begin her journey across the Atlantic. As the tender pulled away bearing friends and relatives who had come to wave them off, the emigrants on deck had their last view of the smoking chimneys and busy wharves of the great port they were leaving. With the prospect of gales, storms, becalmings and icebergs ahead, not to mention the possibility of disease on board, people did not relish the long and invariably grim voyage under sail. Yet in the minds of some, any apprehension or fleeting sadness at their last view of Liverpool was far outweighed by the lure of the possible prize that awaited them, for this was the year of the California gold rush. The ship was bound for New York but not everyone was heading for America. Some had chosen Canada, among them Thomas McCrae and his family. Thomas was a man of enterprise and acumen, a stockbreeder and former shepherd who had built up a successful business in the town of Laurieston in south west Scotland. Now he wanted to try his luck in North America but his wife Jean, known to the family as Jane, was a woman of strong character descended from Ayrshire Covenanters[2] and did not readily agree to the move. It was only in the face of her husband's unrelenting enthusiasm for the proposed new adventure that she finally consented to make the three-thousand mile journey which would take them via New York and the Hudson River to the town of Guelph, located in one of the newly-settled areas north of Lake Ontario. The family group that set sail that early spring day comprised Thomas and Jean, their two children, David and Margaret, Thomas's parents, two brothers, two sisters and their families.

It was not the first time this particular family had left their home for a new destination. For centuries the territory of the Clan MacRae had been the Kintail Forest – an area of spectacular natural beauty within reach of the Isle of Skye that was also home to the golden eagle, the pine marten and the MacKenzies, the great clan of the north west Highlands. According to a later family account, Thomas's ancestor, Robert McCrae,[3] had forsaken Kintail in 1719, the year in which a battle had taken place

1

in which the MacRaes fought under Lord Seaforth, Chief of the Clan MacKenzie, against an English army. The MacRaes had always served the MacKenzies faithfully and supported them when Seaforth declared for the Pretender. The second Jacobite rising of 1719 ended when the battle of Glen Shiel was lost and the Highlanders disappeared into the mist of a June evening. Robert McCrae was reputedly among the clansmen who then decided to leave Kintail for a safer life in the Scottish lowlands. For one hundred and thirty years his descendants lived there peaceably enough but a spirit of adventure re-emerged in Thomas McCrae who now decided to cross the Atlantic to North America.

For Scots, and Highland Scots in particular, the new world exerted a powerful attraction. The final Jacobite defeat at Culloden in 1745 had brought with it harsh retribution and the end of the elaborate clan system which had endured for over a thousand years. Those who chose to remain in the Highlands struggled to eke out an existence in steadily deteriorating conditions. With the reduction in the status of clan chiefs, the land was turned over to flocks of sheep and their shepherd guardians. By the dawn of the nineteenth century, migration offered the only viable escape for many. Whole communities left the Highlands, taking with them their entire Gaelic way of life, language, inheritance and traditions. The cry of 'Dè cho fada's a tha gu Canada?'[4] could be heard at ports along the west coast of Scotland as people gathered to board ships heading across the great ocean. The deserted glens they left behind gradually took on an isolated beauty that to this day draws visitors from all over the world.

Robert McCrae's descendants settled contentedly among the dour and determined people who farmed in Ayrshire's gentle grassy hills and wooded dales. By the time Thomas McCrae was born, the family were farming farther south in Galloway, an area blessed by warmth from the Gulf Stream. Its beneficial effect along the Solway Firth coastline had given rise to rich, rolling pastoral country that supported red deer, abundant bird life, sheep and thickly-coated black and hornless Galloway cattle. For these Victorian McCraes, the move to the new world was born of a sense of enterprise and adventure rather than necessity. They were practical people whose knowledge and skills would be needed in the colony of Upper Canada, their chosen destination.

In the early years of the nineteenth century, this newly-proclaimed colony, later to become the Province of Ontario, was a rugged forest frontier where life for most inhabitants required continuous personal resourcefulness in order to maintain a level of survival little better than subsistence. Linking together settlers in this raw wilderness proved a long and arduous process and lack of mechanisation in undeveloped areas meant isolation. The clearing of land was desperately hard work. Farms and smallholdings were literally cut out of the forest and the battle against the elements was endless. Once established, towns and villages at least offered their inhabitants some social opportunities but they were often joined at best by rough and muddy tracks. The hardiness and honest pride of the Scottish emigrants who came to Upper Canada was to stand them in good stead, for it was no place for the indolent or those without practical skills.

During the War of 1812–1814 against the United States, all the resources of the infant colony were required to repel the American invaders. The vast majority of Upper Canadians remained loyal to the Crown and determined to protect themselves against insurgence and pillage. Inevitably they lost property and suffered war damage. This presented a problem since instructions from London had emphasised the need to economise and reduce the colony's financial dependence on Britain. An idea for a possible solution formed in the mind of one enterprising Scotsman, a man named John Galt.[5]

Galt was a novelist, poet and one of the leading literary figures of his day, but he was no sedentary writer. As a man of affairs, active in business both in Britain and overseas, he proposed the formation of a land company as a means to encourage settlement in Upper Canada. It would buy up, develop and settle Clergy and Crown Reserve land with proceeds from the sale of vacant lots, enabling the provincial government to pay off war claims and some of the administrative expenses. The government accepted the proposal and the new Canada Company was launched with capital of one million pounds subscribed largely by London merchants. Galt was appointed the company's agent and threw himself energetically into his new work. In the spring of 1827 he not only successfully disposed of the scattered Crown Reserves and much land in the Huron Tract, an area bordering Lake Huron, but he also set about founding new towns. For this, he used the concept of planning towns in advance of general settlement in order to stimulate land sales.

Guelph, the town destined to be the home of Thomas McCrae and his family, came into being on 23 April 1827, St George's Day. Galt had carefully selected the site and the official date of its founding, knowing it would always have a special significance for English settlers. Served by two rivers, the site was set in a healthy location at the centre of fertile tableland. As Galt and his party made their way in pouring rain through dense, virgin forest, his 'Warden of Woods and Forests' Dr William Dunlop, realised he had forgotten his compass. One of the most colourful figures in early nineteenth-century Upper Canada and already something of a legend in his own lifetime, Dunlop was not one to let such a trifling oversight concern him. After all, he had survived much worse as an army surgeon during the War of 1812. 'After wandering about like two pretty babes, without even the compliment of a blackberry', Galt wrote, they came across the home of an isolated Dutch settler who took them to the chosen place.[6]

The founding of Guelph was something of an occasion. Galt walked up a slope to a large sugar maple, took an axe and made the first stroke. 'To me at least', he later recalled, 'the moment was impressive – and the silence of the woods, that echoed to the sound, was as the sigh of the solemn genius of the wilderness departing for ever.'[7] A surveyor who accompanied the party declared the stump to be the centre of the prospective settlement, Dunlop pulled out his flask and all present drank a toast to the prosperity of the new town, which would take its name from the family name of King George IV. Five weeks later, Dunlop's cousin, Alexander, visited the area and left a vivid description of what he found:

> Travelling about twelve miles through rich and luxuriant country, we entered the forest of Guelph, containing about 50,000 acres . . . The road had only been cut through the forest four weeks before . . . Proceeding five or six miles we came to a hundred woodsmen . . . sent out as pioneers to cut the way open before us. The trees fell like enchantment before their resolute arms . . . The weather was beautiful . . . The blue sky gleamed through the green vista of the wood. . . giant elms, the maples, the cedars and the oaks, fallen from their high state, were crumbling into ashes or blazing into flames . . . We stalked through the avenue of burning trees, and descending towards a beautiful little stream about as large as the Doon, were received by his Guelphic Majesty (Galt) at the entrance of his Rustic Palace.[8]

Despite dense forest and cedar swamps, over five thousand settlers were living in the Huron Tract by 1841. Guelph's location, and the fact that it was blessed with some of the best agricultural soils in Upper Canada, was sufficient to attract men like Thomas McCrae of Galloway who saw its possibilities. A *Canadian Gazetteer* of this time described it as 'the district town of Wellington District' lying in 'the midst of finely undulating country . . . high dry and healthy.'[9] It was a town 'settled by respectable families from the old country, principally English, many of whom came from Suffolk and Norfolk, and who have some very fine farms.' The 'beautiful little stream' which had reminded Alexander Dunlop of Ayrshire's River Doon, was also a source of nostalgia for other Scots who settled in the locality.[10]

The McCraes prospered in their new home. In mid nineteenth-century Canada, timber was king and, after short spells working on a farm and as a bookkeeper, Thomas McCrae realised the potential of the lumber business. Within a short space of time the wood from the sawmill he had purchased was being used to build many of Guelph's shops and houses. In 1861, the outbreak of the American Civil War created a demand for clothing which American manufacturers were unable to meet, so he entered into a partnership to found a cloth mill making woollen garments and products. This company, Armstrong McCrae & Company, and later known as the Guelph Woollen Mills, was one of the town's most successful early businesses with a national reputation for excellence. Not content with this success, Thomas and his father decided to breed livestock. The knowledge and experience gained during their years in Kirkcudbright gave them a head start and it was not long before they were raising Cotswold and Southern sheep, Clydesdale horses and cattle. The latter brought them their greatest success and McCrae Shorthorns, Herefords, Polled Angus and Galloways won countless prizes at agricultural shows and exhibitions across North America.

The McCraes were a close-knit family who cared for each other and served their community. At the centre of their life was a strong Presbyterian faith; Thomas was an Elder of St Andrew's Church in Guelph and was actively involved in church affairs. Deeply religious and essentially modest, the family attended service several times each Sabbath and adhered to strict principles of duty, hard work and service to their fellow man. To this end, Thomas held various public offices that included serving as Chairman of Guelph's Board of Health and Justice of the Peace for Wellington County.

Thomas and Jean now had four children. The eldest, David, was a bright boy who loved the outdoor life and was as excited as any eleven-year-old boy would be when the first train steamed into Guelph in 1856. He was already showing promise as a sportsman, and over the next few years, became an enthusiastic lacrosse player who also enjoyed winter pursuits such as sleighing, skating and curling – a passion of his father's. In 1862, David entered the newly-founded Ontario Veterinary College and was a student on its first course. Upon graduation, he helped his father with the family businesses and his diary of that time described some of the many aspects of his work: the cutting of timber, his role in the running of the family mill, cattle inspections, the keeping of accounts and his journeys to Ottawa and Montreal to sell yarn.

David was to achieve fame and eclipse his father as a stockbreeder but, at heart, he was a military man and had been ever since he had first heard tales of the Highland Regiments and the Clan MacRae. In 1865, the twenty-year-old David learned that three-month training courses for militia (territorial army) officers were being offered, and appealed to his father to let him apply to attend one at Hamilton, the nearest centre. Seeing how keen he was, Thomas agreed and David passed the course. He soon found himself on active service when, in that same year, an Irish-American organisation known as the Fenian Brotherhood raided across the border into Upper Canada hoping to force a separation of Ireland from Britain. The small skirmishes that resulted demonstrated the need for artillery in the Canadian militia and, in 1866, David McCrae was one of the men who founded Guelph's first militia artillery unit. It was the start of a long tradition that would see Guelph contributing individual gunners, artillery units or sub-units to every campaign waged by the Canadian army for the next century.

As a militia officer, David McCrae was called out with his fellow gunners to take part in the celebrations in the summer of 1867 that marked the birth of the new Dominion of Canada under its first Prime Minister, Sir John A. Macdonald.[11] The date chosen, 1 July, was a brilliant summer day and crowds enjoyed lively parades, military reviews, fireworks and special illuminations that lasted late into the evening. Even without all the provinces that make up present-day Canada, it was a huge sprawl of a nation stretching from the naval and military station at Halifax, Nova Scotia to the great Niagara Falls of Ontario. The province of Ontario alone was three times the size of the British Isles including Ireland.

David McCrae was now twenty-two. His diary had from time to time mentioned social evenings and local dances where lively tunes on a fiddle kept everyone up into the early hours. Around this time it began to include numerous references to a young lady referred to as 'Jessie', the nickname of Janet Eckford, younger daughter of the Reverend John Eckford, a widower of Dunkeld, Bruce County, and formerly of Newbigging, Fife. The Eckfords had come to Canada with some friends two years after the McCraes and the area where they had purchased land was one of the last counties in western Ontario to be opened up for settlement. The land was of poor quality and John Eckford, no expert in land management or farming, became a pioneer in the true sense of the word. Having arrived with his son and two daughters during a very severe winter, he built his own cabin, split rails for fences, mended his own boots and grew his own wheat. Resourcefulness, self reliance and an unshakeable religious faith had seen him and his family through this tough beginning and in time their home 'Edenbank' was a happy, welcoming place full of children and pets.

Janet Eckford was a great reader. Since John Eckford's days at Edinburgh University, he had built up a good library and he encouraged her to make use of it. He read regularly to his children from an Edinburgh newspaper that a friend sent him, and told them stories that ranged from military tales to those of his own making. When romance came into these stories, the girls had to admit that they thought their father's love scenes were 'rather lacking in spice and ginger.'[12] Janet and her sister Annie went to school in Brant, the nearest settlement, but were taught Latin and Greek by their father. What the children did not have in material comforts was more than compensated for in educational and spiritual matters. All the family were singers and were much in evidence at church services where their father preached. Janet grew into an attractive young woman who loved literature, music and poetry. Her somewhat grave eyes belied the fact that she had a lively sense of humour, was a gifted mimic and enjoyed local amusements such as dancing, church soirées and band recitals. She and her sister were well liked and a cousin of their father described them as 'twa o' the maist lovingest girls he ever knew.'[13] This was the young woman who had caught the attention of David McCrae. Although it is not clear exactly when they first met, the romance blossomed and on 21 January 1870, David's twenty-fifth birthday, they were married at 'Edenbank'. As the staff of Armstrong McCrae & Company celebrated the event with an evening supper and dancing, Thomas McCrae and his wife welcomed the newlyweds back to Guelph.

Whether it was a sod hut, a log shanty or something grander, a home of one's own was the goal of every Canadian. David and Janet set up house in a simple but attractive limestone cottage that always provided kindly hospitality. It was here beside the River Speed that the couple's second son was born on St Andrew's Day, 30 November 1872. For Janet and David it was a happy coincidence that the new baby was born on the day of Scotland's patron saint. They already had a two-year-old son, Thomas, named after David's father; this second son would take his name from Janet's father, John Eckford.

NOTES

1. John Galt, 'Canadian Boat Song (The Lone Shieling)' in 'Noctes Ambrosianae, XLVI,' *Blackwoods Magazine*, September 1829.
2. The Solemn League and Covenant established Presbyterianism in England and Scotland in 1643. Covenanters were people who pledged themselves to defend the Presbyterian Church.
3. The spelling of Scottish Highland surnames varies, partly because they were spelled and spoken originally in Gaelic and then translated into English. The difference between Mc and Mac seemed to matter little until the twentieth century and there are numerous variants and sept names. The Clan MacRae Society today lists 34 official variants of the Clan of which McCrae is one, Mc for Mac being acceptable in all cases.
4. The translation reads: 'How far is it to Canada?'
5. John Galt (1779–1839), novelist and colonial promoter, was born in Irvine, Ayrshire, the son of a sea captain. He became a writer with a rare mastery of the Scots dialect and what is regarded as his best fiction deals with Scottish life.
6. Jennie W. Aberdeen, *John Galt* (London, 1936), p. 153.
7. Aberdeen, *John Galt*, pp. 153–154.
8. A.E. Byerly, *The Beginnings of Things* (Guelph, 1935), pp. 74–75.
9. William H. Smith, *Smith's Canadian Gazetteer* (Toronto, 1846), p. 42.
10. The Ayrshire Doon rises in McCrae country and several family homes were situated in the Doon valley.
11. Sir John A. Macdonald (1815–1891) emigrated to Canada from Scotland as a small child and became a lawyer and Q.C. He went on to become leader of

the Conservative Party of Canada and premier of Ontario in 1856. In 1867 he formed the first government of the newly-formed Dominion of Canada.

12. J.E. Gow, *John Eckford and his Family: Bruce Pioneers* (Quebec, 1911), p. 35.
13. 'Two of the most loving girls he had ever known'. J.E. Gow, *John Eckford and His Family*, p. 34.

CHAPTER TWO

'My little lad for a soldier boy'[1]

1872–1892

David McCrae had firm ideas about how to bring up his children. In what was a strongly religious age, counsel, example and prayer were judged to be of primary importance and the children grew up in a strict but affectionate home. From the time they were small, the two boys were expected to help Janet McCrae with simple tasks but, when these were done, they were free to play in the rambling garden behind the cottage. Although different in temperament, the brothers seldom quarrelled and were constantly in each other's company. Tom, the elder by two years, was a quiet, thoughtful and dependable boy who enjoyed being at home. John – Jack to family and close friends – was the livelier and more adventurous and needed a firmer hand as his aunt later remembered:

> John was a most loveable and affectionate child, but he certainly was a mischief. He was not disobedient. He only wanted to know the why and wherefore of everything. He used to pull all his toys apart to see what they were like inside.[2]

Small boys have a habit of getting into trouble and Tom and John found themselves occasionally receiving a good hiding from their father. Janet McCrae, while gently chastising them, would usually give them a sweet to lessen the misery of their punishment.[3] Although a cheerful and sincere boy, John had inherited his father's temper and when the two periodically clashed, Janet would tactfully find a way to separate them and soothe hurt feelings. Her composure and inner calm provided a natural balance to her husband's more volatile nature and the bond she formed with her children in the early years was never to be broken.

From an early age, the McCrae brothers' eager, enquiring young minds promised intelligence. David was keen to encourage his sons towards academic achievement and both were quick to learn. By the age of three, John had memorised the shorter catechism of the Church of Scotland before he could read. For one so young this was no mean feat and it was hard not to be captivated by the fair-haired, solemn-eyed little boy who could recite without error such phrases as 'the decrees of God are his eternal purpose – whereby he hath foreordained whatsoever comes to pass.'[4] When John was four, the family moved from their cottage to a larger house situated in a pleasant tree-lined street close to St Andrew's Church in the upper part of Guelph. This house had been the home of Thomas McCrae senior, who by now had purchased a farm outside the town. The prospect of regular visits to 'Janefield' as Thomas's country property was called, was something eagerly anticipated by both boys. John was always happy in the country and, from early in life, displayed the same love of animals and the natural world as his parents. His aunt later recalled that:

He was passionately fond of animals, especially dogs, cats and horses. Usually he owned at least three dogs and three cats. Once the family had reason to move to their grandfather's farm. Although no longer a small child, John refused to leave his cats to starve. After much trouble they were secured in a bag. Then everyone climbed in the carriage and started off. They had only driven a short way when the bag flew open and the cats jumped out with John after them. After an hour of hard work he recaptured them.[5]

Another story relates to the time he rescued the family bulldog from drowning after it had fallen through thin ice into the river. Taking off his coat, John wrapped the dog in it and braved the cold until he could warm the poor animal by the fire.

For this adventurous boy, the countryside presented the prospect of endless discovery. Guelph was typical of many towns and settlements in Canada which 'spread their square streets and their trim maple trees beside placid lakes almost within echo of the primeval forest'.[6] Nature was always close at hand and John became familiar with such animals as the striped skunk, the raccoon and the groundhog;[7] colourful birds that included the Eastern Bluebird, the rosy red Pine Grosbeak and the handsome, shy Wood Duck; wild flowers like the delicate red and yellow Wild Columbine, the Common Milkweed, staple fare of the Monarch butterfly, and the lovely three-petalled Trillium that covered the forest floor in springtime like a host of white stars. In local streams and rivers he could find bullfrogs, otters, giant water bugs and brilliant damselflies. Although Guelph was now a far cry from John Galt's clearing in the forest, large areas of woodland still lay beyond the fringe of civilisation. No great distance from Guelph was Lake Simcoe where Stephen Leacock, future academic, author and friend of John McCrae, was growing up on a farm. Leacock remembered his youth:

We lived in an isolation not known to-day even in the Arctic. The nearest village was four miles away, over rough roads and through cedar swamps. Newspapers we never saw. No one came and went. There was nowhere to come and go. And the stillness of the winter nights was as silent as eternity.[8]

The Canadian outdoors was something to be respected as survival might depend on knowledge of it and its changing conditions. David McCrae taught his sons the lore of the countryside and an appreciation of Canada's short, extreme seasons. Spring was a time to be relished. Rivers gushed with a transfusion of melted snow, trees suddenly took on a mantle of fresh green leaves and flowers bloomed with amazing rapidity in the moist, warm, sunny conditions. The approach of the long, hot days of summer was heralded by rapidly rising temperatures, humidity and an abundance of troublesome insect life. Relief could be expected at the start of September as work began on the harvest and the preparations for winter. Families went fruit and berry picking in countryside ablaze with the multi-coloured brilliance of maples. As cool gave way to cold and the magnificence of the white winter landscape, life revolved around home and neighbours stood ready to help each other in time of need. Like all young Canadians, John and Tom McCrae learned that life in Canada had a more intense pattern than in other more moderate climates.

John had just celebrated his sixth birthday when a third and final child was born to Janet and David McCrae. This time it was a daughter, Geills, and her arrival on 19 December 1878 must have made it a rather special Christmas that year. Though much involved with the new baby, Janet McCrae set aside time to introduce her older children to the delights of reading, poetry and music. She played the piano and encouraged them to sing with her. John developed a keen ear for music and also enjoyed his mother's favourite stories and poems.

While amusing her children with her mimicry, Janet also used this as an opportunity to teach them the importance of cheerfulness and a sense of humour. Her family's pioneering years had emphasised the need for these and other qualities like self reliance, duty and kindness to others[9]. In keeping with the Presbyterian tradition of 'plain living and high thinking'[10], Janet passed this legacy on to her children along with her cultured outlook. John had a close relationship with his mother. From the beginning, she was the spiritual anchor of his life and saw that beneath his extrovert, sociable exterior was a sensitive and imaginative soul. This duality of John's personality presented itself both in a love of group activities and of solitary, reflective pursuits such as drawing and writing.

Taught by their mother to read and to learn their multiplication tables by the time they reached school age, John and Tom attended the Guelph Central School. John was to prove a diligent pupil to whom all subjects came easily and whose favourite early reading consisted of fairy stories which took him on flights of imagination that he loved. Sundays in the McCrae home were devoted to church and the family never missed a service. The children were taught to study the Bible and to uphold the moral, social and spiritual code it contained. Sharing a pew in church with them were the local physician, Dr Henry Howitt, and his family. Dr Howitt's son, also named Henry, recalled visits to the McCrae house and the strict yet lively atmosphere that prevailed.

David McCrae followed his father's example by instilling into Tom and John his own principles of self discipline, honesty, directness and dissatisfaction with injustice and inequality. He taught them to take pride in their town, in which he was actively involved, their family heritage and their inheritance as Canadians within the British Empire. David's militia activities in Guelph and the fact that he was also serving as assistant-adjutant at the headquarters of the militia artillery in Ontario meant that the two boys were accustomed to seeing their father in uniform. He loved to recount the tales of military prowess that he had heard as a boy, and young Henry Howitt later remembered that 'Colonel David McCrae used to tell us stories, and taught us a great deal of history, mostly about battles, and that sort of thing'.[11]

While both boys enjoyed their father's stories, it was John who started to show a marked interest in military matters. Henry Howitt recalled that he could often be found with his head in a copy of the *Boys' Own Paper*, a popular magazine of the time filled with tales of heroism and adventure, of which there were plenty, both real and imaginary. History for John was no boring list of dates to be crammed but a living pageant of events and battles. Throughout his youth and young manhood, Queen Victoria's soldiers fought in wars, campaigns and uprisings. As her industrial might led to the expansion of her Empire, British authority on land and at sea guarded maritime trading routes, worked to combat illegal slavery and ignorance, and encouraged progress based on Christian principles. The popular hymn of the time, 'Onward Christian soldiers', conjured up images of soldiers tramping through jungle, snow, mountain passes and barren wastes. To the impressionable young John McCrae, the exploits of the 'soldiers of the Queen' ignited an interest that would never be extinguished and which would lead him ultimately to follow the call of battle. At this point in his life, however, all he could do was wait impatiently until he was old enough to join the local Guelph Highland Cadet unit.

In Canada, secondary education at that time was regarded as a privilege suited only to those destined for the professions. Men like John McCrae's grandfather, John Eckford, had been working to develop the provision of a quality educational system and David McCrae was a fervent believer in self improvement. As a director of the Guelph Mechanics' Institute[12] and the first Board of Management of the town's new Free Library, David was adamant that his sons should have the best possible education and both McCrae boys were sent to the Guelph Collegiate Institute. This institution provided secondary education of a very high standard and the unusually wide curriculum included Astronomy, Geology, Physiology, Greek, Latin and Divinity. John became a pupil at the age of twelve and came quickly to the notice of his new school principal and English teacher, Dr William Tytler. Tytler, who like David McCrae, served on the boards of the Library and Mechanics' Institute, found him a loveable boy and encouraged his interest in writing both poetry and prose. Another teacher, Mr Charlesworth, was impressed with 'the beautiful character of the boy'.[13] Already beginning to emerge were the personal characteristics that were to make John so popular and well regarded in the future. One of John's first letters to his mother was written in the summer of 1884 while he and Tom were staying with friends. It began a correspondence that was to last all his life.

Dear Ma

I am getting on pretty well here. I am lonesome where I have nothing to do. I caught a butterfly yesterday. This letter is written in a hurry. Please tell me if I am to write a French letter to Mr Albert. I think it would be a sort of a difficult matter without a dictionary. Mary and Tom go to school yet. They get their holidays on Monday. I tried to sketch the bridge the old mill and the old house the other day. I did not get on very well. I killed a snake yesterday. There are quite a lot of milk snakes around here . . . About ten men got off the train the other day here. I do not wash these mornings till about seven. I have given my head a wash every morning since I came. I was driving the horses in the wagon yesterday while they were loading the hay. They are cutting the hay to-day. I went to the bush yesterday with some salt for the cattle. I found them all right. They were in the berry patch. I have not much time just now. Love to all.

Your loving son.
J. McCrae[14]

In 1886, David McCrae decided that his younger son should accompany him on a business trip to Britain during the school holidays. The prospect of the journey and the new experiences that awaited him filled John with excitement and awakened in him 'a keen curiosity about ships and the sea'.[15] Canadians were very influential in the world of shipping. Samuel Cunard of Halifax had created a line that still occupies a position of world renown today, and a Canadian Scot, Hugh Allan of Montreal, had established the competing Allan Line. John and his father made their crossing on the *Etruria*, one of Cunard's new showpiece passenger steamships. Launched the previous year, it was fitted with the first refrigerating machinery ever installed in Atlantic liners; staterooms with hot water heaters; marble baths, steam and shower apparatus; a music room with a pipe organ; and a ladies' vestibule which provided scented baths and other modern comforts.[16]

On their arrival in London father and son walked the bustling streets of the Empire's capital and took in its sights and sounds: the traffic's rumble of wheels and clip of horses' hooves; the cries of the traders in Covent Garden market; and the tranquillity of the River Thames by moonlight. They also journeyed to Greenwich where, after admiring the architecture of the Royal Naval College, they spent time at an exhibition. John wrote an account of the model ships he saw and included an elaborate table of names, dimensions and tonnage. The eager thirteen-year-old remembered it all and could soon identify the house flags and funnels of all the principal liners. On any visit to a seaport in later life, John always made for the harbour first.

While in London, David took John to the public gallery of the House of Commons. The debate must have been lively that day as it incited the comment that, when a member 'is speaking no one seems to listen at all'.[17] Of all the famous landmarks John saw, the one that left the greatest impression upon him was Westminster Abbey. He retained vivid memories which he encapsulated six years later in an article entitled 'Reflections':

> Heartfelt is our awe as we stand beside lofty monuments, fit emblems of the aspirations that once warmed hearts, now forever at rest . . . Reverentially do we gaze at the tattered flags, drooping from the chancel-roof; speaking messages from far-off fields . . . Heroes have lived and died, thrones risen and fallen, empires grown old and decayed – but through all, unchanging in their majesty, those towers have kept steadfast watch – shone out cold and gray[18] in the misty dawn, gleaming a reflection to the morning sun, borne unmoved the glare of the dusty noontide and faded to dark vastness in the deepening twilight.[19]

For John McCrae, London was the beating heart of the British Empire and he was stirred by the sense of pride he felt at being a member of its family of nations. He was struck not only by its fine buildings, bustling thoroughfares and air of prosperity, but by all that it stood for.

Business on behalf of the Guelph Woollen Mills took David McCrae to the textile cities of Bradford, Halifax, Huddersfield and Nottingham. From there he and John travelled north to visit farming relatives in Galloway, where the teenager discovered another joy, fishing. When they reached

Edinburgh, John was immediately fascinated by its imposing castle and military installations. 'Saw "Mons Meg" big gun,' he wrote to his mother, 'I could crawl into her mouth easily.'[20] Throughout his journey John thought of the animals at home and asked about them in letters to his sister Geills. He kept mementos, newspaper cuttings and other keepsakes from the trip and, on his return to Canada, he started a scrapbook into which he was to paste his personal memorabilia: tickets and ships' passenger lists, illustrations from magazines, pictures of writers, newspaper articles and anything else that interested him.

In 1886, John turned fourteen and joined the Guelph Highland Cadet Corps. This renowned unit was commanded by Captain Walter Clark, physical education instructor, drillmaster for all the Guelph schools and a veteran of the Crimean War. Young McCrae was an enthusiastic cadet and became an officer in the Corps. He applied himself wholeheartedly, and, in 1887, was awarded a gold medal by the Ontario Ministry of Education for being the best drilled cadet in the province. The following year, at the age of sixteen, he became a bugler in his father's militia artillery unit.

Both brothers had done well at the Guelph Collegiate Institute and John was one of its best pupils. Gifted intellectually, he was also becoming a good pen and ink artist with an eye for intricate detail. But life was not entirely plain sailing for this talented young man. During his teenage years it emerged that he was asthmatic and Henry Howitt recalled that:

> Jack could never sleep in the 'Janefield' house without getting severe asthmatic attacks, so he slept at my father's home when in Guelph. Something at 'Janefield' caused an allergic reaction. It only caused it at night. Very likely the mattress, or pillows were filled with goose-feathers . . . So I have to thank goosefeathers for increasing a friendship that I will always treasure.[21]

Around this time, one of the world's great feats of engineering earned Canada international acclaim. A condition of British Columbia's entry into the new Confederation had been the completion within ten years of a railway crossing the country from Atlantic to Pacific. Upon the formation of the Canadian Pacific Railway Company in 1881, a group of far-sighted men, among them Donald Smith, a Scot who had risen to become Chief Commissioner of the Hudson's Bay Company,[22] had decided to back the project. That decision was to make them some of Canada's wealthiest men. Work on the railway began under the management of an American, William Van Horne and it was his energy, imagination, drive and experience that overcame the enormous challenges posed by the terrain of the Canadian Shield and the great natural bastion of the Rocky Mountains. Drilling, blasting and bridging their way through rock, forest and canyon, the hard-working teams of men had extended the line to British Columbia by November 1885 and Donald Smith had the honour of driving home the last gold spike. Travelling on that line would become one of the world's great railway journeys.

As 1887 dawned and Guelph contemplated its Diamond Jubilee, it was the beginning of a year that promised to be memorable for all the countries of the British Empire. Already, elaborate plans were in hand to mark the celebration of Queen Victoria's Golden Jubilee. After the death of her beloved husband Prince Albert in 1861, the Queen had retired from public life, leaving the Prince of Wales and his beautiful wife, Princess Alexandra, to become her popular representatives. The last few years, however, had witnessed her gradual re-emergence and now she was about to celebrate the fiftieth year of her reign. It was a period that had seen Britain rise to a pinnacle of wealth and power and brought Victoria unrivalled status as Queen over the greatest Empire the world had ever known. The Jubilee events, spread over several days, involved a Naval Review at Spithead, a Service of Thanksgiving at Westminster Abbey and a luncheon at Buckingham Palace. As a large gathering of European royalty assembled and made its way to the Abbey, the London crowds were treated to a dazzling spectacle.

For Queen Victoria, whose children and grandchildren had married into almost every European royal house, this was also an occasion for a family reunion. The German Kaiser Wilhelm I, now ninety years old and frail, was accompanied by his heir, Crown Prince Friedrich, husband of Queen Victoria's eldest daughter. Friedrich was a sick man and it began to look increasingly likely that his son, Prince Wilhelm, who had travelled with his parents to London, would soon be emperor. The young German prince was keenly interested in all things military and was a difficult person – even his mother described him as 'selfish, domineering and proud.'[23] The Prince of Wales with his flair for diplomacy saw the sense of keeping his demanding nephew happy for the sake of good future relations and, knowing Wilhelm's passion for military pageantry, ensured that there were many parades, reviews and regimental inspections to occupy his time. Wilhelm watched with great enthusiasm a demonstration of a new weapon – the Nordenfeldt machine gun. So impressed was he that he later procured this deadly new device of war for the German army which, by the time the new century dawned, would have more machine guns than any other army in Europe.

Reports of the Jubilee reached newspaper offices throughout the Empire. At the *Civil and Military Gazette* in Lahore, India, a young British journalist named Rudyard Kipling must have read them with interest as he prepared to return to England and an unknown future. Destined to achieve international fame as an author and poet, fate would also see his path cross thirteen years later with that of John McCrae. John, no doubt reading about the festivities and picturing the London of newspaper accounts as he remembered it from his visit the previous year, was soon to start his final year at the Guelph Collegiate Institute. He was keen to follow in the footsteps of his brother, Tom, who was now studying for a Bachelor of Arts degree at the University of Toronto, and worked hard during the winter of 1887–1888 in preparation for the entrance examination. When the date arrived, John was ready.

In Germany, Kaiser Wilhelm I died that spring and Crown Prince Friedrich, ill with throat cancer, began a reign that was to last just ninety nine days. As John McCrae awaited his final examination results, the world learned of Friedrich's death. Within hours of his passing, his vain, flamboyant, overbearing son had taken control and soon issued a decree making military uniform the official court dress. Crown Prince Rudolf, heir to the throne of Germany's ally, Austria-Hungary, voiced his concern that Wilhelm would soon 'engineer a great crisis in old Europe'. He regarded him as 'just the man to do it. He is supremely narrow-minded; and at the same time as vigorous and obstinate as a steer; he considers himself the greatest political genius of all time. What more do you want?'[24] The reign of Kaiser Wilhelm II had begun.

As Germany began to adjust to life under her new monarch, John McCrae heard that he had won a scholarship to the University of Toronto – the first student from Guelph ever to receive this honour. He began his undergraduate courses in the autumn of 1888 and was soon enjoying academic life at University College. The curriculum for a Bachelor of Arts degree was broad and included such subjects as English, French, German, Latin, Greek, Hebrew, Geology, Chemistry and Biology. John's schedule was busy but, like any undergraduate, he found time for other activities. Doubtless encouraged by David McCrae, he joined the Queen's Own Rifles, a Toronto militia infantry unit. Stephen Leacock, who happened to be a part-time student at the University in those years, later commented that, even then, John was 'a soldier of sorts'.[25] His good singing voice and love of music led him to become a member of the Varsity Glee Club, which took part in various concerts. His strong religious faith led him to debate against Darwinism and, in an overwhelmingly Protestant city where Sunday meant little else but church, he regularly attended services and missionary meetings.

As John got to know his way around Toronto, he saw at close hand a city that, in the last decades of the nineteenth century, was a bustling commercial centre with rail and maritime connections. With its solidly-built mansions, newly-completed provincial Parliament buildings and plethora of churches of all denominations, it had a serious but elegant ultra-Victorian air. Business was booming and streetcars clattered noisily up and down the bustling thoroughfares, yet the hustle of the city did not intrude into the relative calm of the University campus with its fine Romanesque-style buildings.

John's first year passed quickly. Although he was a good student, he complained like most undergraduates about his examinations, telling his mother that English was 'simply beastly'.[26] He need not have worried, for his results were very good. As he entered his second year in the autumn of 1889, he had already achieved academic excellence and acquired many friends. Fellow students found him kind, thoughtful and always ready to help them with both work-related and practical matters. He had a superb memory and was developing into a lively and gifted conversationalist, able to recount anecdotes in an amusing and entertaining way. With his capricious sense of humour, he kept a copy of *The Amenities of the Lecture Room: A Student's Handbook of Etiquette*, which suggested its readers should be 'affable with lecturers when you see them. Remember they have seen better days' and advised them that 'Sleeping is permissible during lectures, but no true gentleman will be guilty of snoring.'[27]

Photographs of John taken at this time reveal an open, sensitive face. The niece of Dr Angus Mackinnon, another doctor from Guelph with whom Tom McCrae had spent a great deal of time in early study, remembered the young undergraduate as 'a handsome, laughing, keen-witted young man'. She also described 'his personal charm, his gift for friendliness, his ready wit and quick sympathy, all allied with a good deal of true Scottish reserve'.[28] Henry Howitt's pen portrait of John depicted him as:

Tall, boyish, hair inclined to be wavy and fair; striking, sparkling eyes, teeth with hardly a filling in them, hard and of a pearly colour, the second incisors slightly tilted; all of which, strange to say, added to the attractiveness, and the infection of his smile. His smile was one of his greatest assets. His cheeks were inclined to be reddish; his head was well-formed; he had an excellent forehead. His expression changed frequently, but I think when smiling that he was most attractive.[29]

As far as dress sense was concerned, he apparently did not wear fashionable or particularly well-tailored clothes, tending to dress plainly and functionally and wear jackets that were too tight. A wing collar, a polka dot necktie and a silver watch and chain generally featured as part of his daily apparel.[30] John was already popular with the young ladies he met, according to a letter to his mother in March 1890 in which he described a social at the University YMCA attended by some seventy men and only ten women. It was an occasion when Darwin's famous theory came readily to his mind:

So you may imagine that there was 'competition' and it was a case of 'survival of the fittest' or perhaps 'survival of the luckiest'. I made the acquaintance of the whole ten, all of whom seemed very nice, especially – oh! no! I won't tell.

When the time came to see the young ladies home, John confessed to being one of the chosen few 'though the odds were large'.[31]

For all that university life offered stimulation and enjoyment, it also brought unexpected sadness. A fortnight later, John wrote to his mother with news of the death from typhoid of 'our girl-friend'.[32] This was a young woman he had known since he first arrived in Toronto and for whom he had clearly developed an affection. Her name was Alice McRae and John informed his mother that:

She was the sister of my class-mate, W.W. McRae and a daughter of Dr McRae who came here about three years ago. She was a very pretty girl, just nineteen, and, I am sure, with her disposition, was the light of the house. She and I had formed quite a warm friendship, and I feel very sorry at her death.[33]

John was one of the pall bearers at Alice's funeral and his first direct experience of death had a great impact on him. He poured out his feelings to his mother, telling her that 'Perhaps it is because I was brought into nearer connection with a death, than I have ever been before, that I think so much about it.'[34] Alice was buried at a place some distance from Toronto and his sensitive imagination pictured the scene 'where her grave will be, through the long nights, when "cold winds wake the grey-eyed morn" and when the sunless afternoons are deepening into the cheerless dark: when the summer rains drip from the trees; and the cold winter breaths sigh through the bare branches – through it all.'[35]

The memory of Alice and her death were to stay with John for several years to come. He had continued to keep the scrapbook begun after his visit to Britain in 1886. Now, among pictures of ships, soldiers, scenes from nature and literary figures of the day, began to appear phrases such as the 'hopes of Youth fall thin on the blast' and the occasional sad verse:

> In the cold moist earth we laid her
> When the forest cast a leaf
> And we wept that one so lovely
> Should have a life so brief.[36]

Through poetry and prose, the talented young man was to find an outlet for his creative imagination and some of his deeper feelings.

The University of Toronto magazine, *The Varsity*, sought contributions from students and John began to write short stories. Several of them, usually with a military theme and a moral point, began to appear in print.

However stimulating his life in Toronto, vacations in Guelph were always welcome breaks from study. John continued his links with the Guelph militia, becoming a gunner and later a quarter-master sergeant in the local artillery battery. He was also to be found at meetings of the Guelph Scientific Society. One of its members, a Mrs Browett, recalled a Saturday afternoon when the Society made a local expedition to collect plant specimens. After a pleasant outing and a singsong on the return journey to Guelph, Mrs Browett arrived home to find she was without a much-cherished cashmere shawl. As she was about to go to bed that night, her doorbell rang and she found John McCrae on her doorstep. With a merry twinkle in his eye and a hearty boyish laugh, he had, thoughtful as ever, called to return her lost property.[37]

The Howitt family remained close friends and invited John to go with them on a family holiday to Lake Ahmic, situated in an unspoiled area to the east of Georgian Bay, Lake Huron's eastern arm. The lake provided him with interesting subject matter for his sketchbook. In fine detail he drew scenes from woodland and water: a boat in a quiet creek; a heron in the shallows at twilight; a path through the forest; birds in flight. He was supposed to keep an eye on the younger boys, and Henry Howitt recorded that John was sent along with them, 'to keep us out of danger. We lived together fished together and hunted together for nearly three months, and when we returned, all of us in the pink of condition, he had endeared himself to everyone, especially to my friend and myself'.

Back in Toronto at the start his third year, John found his weekly timetable now had a strong scientific content and contained sixteen hours of 'Microscopical work'[38], five hours of Practical Chemistry and an hour and a half of Practical Mineralogy. Despite intermittent problems with his asthma, he was also playing rugby football for one of the University teams. As he pointed out to his mother, 'so you see I can't fool away much time!'[39] In fact, his interest in rugby had become something of an obsession and his letters around this time mention every match in which he and his brother played. No detail was spared, including injuries: 'I had a kick on the side of the head, and an eye nearly black, a skinned elbow and sundry bruises.'[40] Another bulletin informed his mother that: 'Tom plays in the scrummage & I on the wing . . . Tom was so black when we got home you would not have known him: his face [was] like a coal heaver's.' He had to confess that 'I can't think about anything but football.'[41]

A second YMCA social was in prospect, and this time the odds of forty-five men to fifteen young women were somewhat more favourable than at the previous gathering. John was able to relate with a certain degree of amusement and pride that 'Yours truly upheld the honor of the family in his usual able manner. Not "abel" manner for he did not get killed, though no doubt the rivals would have found it in their hearts so to do.'[42]

For all his light-heartedness, where the serious business of study was concerned, no effort was spared. After achieving the highest marks in his second year exams, John's course now involved more intensive study under Robert Ramsay Wright, the first of several outstanding men who were to influence him. Wright, the Professor of Biology, had been educated at Edinburgh University. In 1874 he had given up his position as a member of staff on the Challenger Expedition[43] to take up the post of Professor of Natural History at the University of Toronto. Three years later the University appointed him to its first chair in Biology. A gifted linguist, classicist and musician, Ramsay Wright was a genial, debonair, energetic and immensely talented man who placed great emphasis on laboratory teaching and developed a large teaching museum at the University. John McCrae was among the students who flocked to his superbly presented and illustrated lectures at which the ambidextrous professor intrigued his audience by being able to complete two blackboard drawings simultaneously. Those who studied under him were extremely fortunate for Wright was recognised as the outstanding figure in the development of biological sciences in Canada and one of the most memorable figures in the history of Canadian education. Hardly any wonder then, that John had written, 'I like Ramsay Wright's lectures best of all.'[44]

Despite his enthusiasm, John's years as an undergraduate continued to be marred by recurring asthma. The smoke from factories and homes, and the fumes from the petrol engines were polluting the air of the city. This was an unpleasant side-effect of a world in which the last decade of the nineteenth century was producing accelerated changes and developments in technology. However, most people were becoming accustomed to the modern inventions and amenities that were speeding up the pace of their lives to a degree hitherto unknown. Toronto's streets, houses, factories and public buildings were illuminated by electricity. Electric street cars were replacing horse-drawn vehicles. The use of the telephone was spreading quickly and people were getting used to typewriters, indoor toilets, central heating and linotype machines.

Having lived long enough to see these great changes and reflect on all that had happened in the forty-three odd years since he had left Liverpool on board the *Empress*, old Thomas McCrae died before the year 1892 was over. His grandchildren and their generation were coming to maturity in

a world that could not have been dreamed of by John Galt and the early
pioneers.

NOTES

1. From 'Isandlwana' by John McCrae, *The University Magazine* (Volume 9,
   No. 1, January 1910), p. 92. Micro mfm/AP/U577, UTL.
2. Mary Graesser, 'The Childhood of John McCrae', *Ontario Agricultural College
   Review* (Volume 37, No. 11, July 1925), pp. 420–421.
3. Author's conversation with Mrs Margaret Gardner-Medwin, 1 April 1995.
4. C.L.C Allinson, unpublished manuscript, 'John McCrae: Poet, Soldier Physician', p. 12, MH.
5. Graesser, 'The Childhood of John McCrae' p. 420.
6. Stephen Leacock, *Sunshine Sketches of a Little Town* (London, 1912), Preface p. xii.
7. The groundhog or woodchuck is a species of marmot, a large diurnal,
   burrowing rodent of the squirrel family, native to North America.
8. Stephen Leacock, *Canada: The Foundations of Its Future* (Montreal, 1941),
   p. xxiv.
9. John Prescott, *In Flanders Fields: The Story of John McCrae*, (Erin, Ont.
   1985), p. 11.
10. Prescott, *In Flanders Fields*, p. 11.
11. H.O. Howitt, 'John McCrae', *The Torch Yearbook of the Colonel John McCrae
    Memorial Branch 257* (Volume VIII, 1940), p. 13, MH.
12. In nineteenth-century North America, a 'mechanic' was a term for working
    man or labourer. Following the passage of a bill by the Parliament of
    Canada providing grants for Mechanics' Institutes, the Guelph Farmers'
    & Mechanics' Institute was created in 1850 to provide opportunities for self
    advancement in the community. Its objectives were '(1) the advancement
    of literature and the diffusion of knowledge amongst its members, (2)
    the formation of a library, (3) the delivery of lectures, which were to be
    illustrated as far as possible, (4) the organisation of classes for instruction
    and reading'. See Leo Johnson, *A History of Guelph, 1827–1927* (Guelph,
    1977), pp 141–145.
13. Undated article (c. 1918) from the *Guelph Mercury*, MH.
14. JM to Janet McCrae, 3 July 1884, MG 30, D209, Micro A-1103, NAC.
15. Andrew Macphail, *In Flanders Fields and other Poems by Lieut.-Col. John
    McCrae with an essay in Character* (Toronto, 1919), p. 88.
16. John M. Brinnin, *The Sway of the Grand Saloon: A Social History of the North
    Atlantic* (New York, 1971), p. 279.
17. Macphail, *In Flanders Fields*, p. 93.
18. John McCrae tended to use the American form of spelling words such as
    'grey', 'colour', 'honour', etc., in his letters and diaries. It also appeared in
    some, but not all, of his published articles. When his poetry was published,
    the English spelling of such words was generally used.
19. John McCrae, 'Reflections', *The Varsity* (Volume 11, No. 13, 9 February
    1892), p. 178. mfm LH/V377, UTL.
20. JM to Janet McCrae, 28 May 1886, MG 30, D209, Micro A-1103, NAC.
21. Howitt, 'John McCrae', p. 13.
22. The Hudson's Bay Company was incorporated in England in 1670 to seek
    an Arctic west passage to the Pacific Ocean, to occupy the lands adjacent to

Hudson's Bay and to carry on any profitable commerce with those lands. It engaged in the fur trade during the first two centuries of its existence and is still active today as a commercial trading company involved in real estate, merchandising and natural resources. *Canadian Encyclopaedia*, Volume II, pp. 843–844.

23. Alan Palmer, *The Kaiser: Warlord of the Second Reich* (London, 1978), p. 14.
24. John Van der Kiste, 'Two Imperial Heirs', *Royalty Digest* (October 1995), p. 112.
25. Article 'In Flanders Fields' by Stephen Leacock, *The Times*, 18 February 1921.
26. JM to Janet McCrae, 17 May 1889, MG 30, D209, Micro A-1103, NAC.
27. John McCrae's Scrapbook, MH.
28. Mae Stuart Clendanan, *The M'Craes of Carsphairn*, (Reprinted from the Gallovidian Annual, 1938) p.10.
29. Howitt, 'John McCrae', p. 7.
30. Howitt, 'John McCrae', p. 7.
31. JM to Janet McCrae, 3 March 1890, MG 30, D209, Micro A-1103, NAC.
32. JM to Janet McCrae, 15 March 1890, MG 30, D209, Micro A-1103, NAC.
33. JM to Janet McCrae, 15 March 1890, MG 30, D209, Micro A-1103, NAC.
34. JM to Janet McCrae, 15 March 1890, MG 30, D209, Micro A-1103, NAC.
35. JM to Janet McCrae, 15 March 1890, MG 30, D209, Micro A-1103, NAC.
36. John McCrae's Scrapbook, MH.
37. Article by Jarvis Flora Maclean Browett, 'The Late Lt.-Col. M'Crae', 14 February 1918, unnamed newspaper, MH.
38. JM to Janet McCrae, 22 October 1890, MG 30, D209, Micro A-1103, NAC.
39. JM to Janet McCrae, 22 October 1890, MG 30, D209, Micro A-1103, NAC.
40. JM to Janet McCrae, 27 October 1890, MG 30, D209, Micro A-1103, NAC.
41. JM to Geills McCrae, 5 November 1890, MG 30, D209, Micro A-1103, NAC.
42. JM to Janet McCrae, 22 October 1890, MG 30, D209, Micro A-1103. NAC. John is referring to the Old Testament story of the brothers Cain and Abel.
43. The Challenger Expedition was the first worldwide oceanographic expedition and was intended to investigate (1) the distribution of animal life in the deep ocean and (2) to seek to understand how oceans circulated. Under the patronage of the Royal Society and with the financial support of the British government, HMS *Challenger*, a ship modified especially for oceanographic research, voyaged the Atlantic, Indian, Pacific and Southern oceans between December 1872 and May 1876. Among other things, it provided new information about the oceans, their temperature, salinity and specific gravity, and identified hundreds of previously unknown animal species. The voyage gave impetus to other Western European nations to undertake worldwide exploration in later years. *The Canadian Encyclopaedia*, Volume I, p. 313.
44. JM to Janet McCrae, 9 October 1888, MG 30, D209, Micro A-1103, NAC.

CHAPTER THREE

'Amid my books I lived the hurrying years'[1]
1892–1897

As 1892 came to a close, Canadians looked back on an eventful year that had marked the twenty-fifth anniversary of the Dominion and the adoption of the Red Ensign as the country's official flag.[2] From a collection of disparate colonies in the summer of 1867 a nation stretching from Atlantic to Pacific had emerged and Canada stood on the threshold of an exciting age. Tourism by train was now a reality and William Van Horne of the Canadian Pacific Railway was sending members of the Royal Canadian Academy of Art out west to paint the Rockies and to promote rail travel. Work had also begun on the elegant château-style railway hotels, the first of which was to be the imposing Château Frontenac in Quebec City. Canadians now had time for leisure. The bicycle had become the latest craze and the country's first professional theatre companies were launching coast-to-coast tours that provided a taste of things to come. Although it was a time in which respectability and gentility were still of the utmost importance, the 'nineties', as a history of the period notes, 'witnessed the sunset of the Victorian ethic, the passing of a time when the role and importance of God, the Queen, the flag, duty, honour, virtue and family life were all clearly defined.'[3]

Toronto's industrial spread had increased the amount of pollution in the city and, by the end of his third year at university, John McCrae's asthma was so bad that the only sensible solution was to take a year out. To someone of his motivation this was a blow, but he resolved to make the best of things and obtained a teaching post at the Ontario Agricultural College where courses consisted of theoretical instruction and 'hands on' experience at its model farm. Unfortunately, all was not well at the College. In addition to external resentment from the Ontario farming community, which generally felt that a college education contributed little or nothing to practical success in farming, there was internal friction between the College president and the farm superintendent.

In this troubled atmosphere, John's appointment as Assistant Resident & Mathematical Master was unpopular from the start in certain quarters. He was resented for his lack of experience and found himself with the unenviable task of teaching students of his own age or older subject matter that was of no interest to them. It was not long before they began to make life difficult for him and a campaign was started against him on the grounds that it was possible to ask questions in class that he could not answer. Matters came to a head one day when John arrived late in the Mess Hall to preside at dinner. Some rather loutish students who had already been guilty of certain misdemeanours tossed food around the Mess Hall, overturned tables and finally threw John in the campus pond. Although not responsible for the disturbance, as Resident Master, John was taken to task and the incident was regarded as a reflection of his inability to maintain discipline. Matters intensified when five students complained officially about John's 'inability to teach, ignorance of the subject taught, and negligence in preparing his work.'[4] At this point, David McCrae intervened. John's father had been partly responsible for the founding of the College and was a stolid supporter of its battery of artillery. Now a top stockbreeder who had been invited to be an expert judge at that year's World's Fair in Chicago,[5] he knew the Ontario Minister of Agriculture personally. After meeting with him, David told the College students in his characteristically forthright manner that if his son could not do his job properly he would have to leave, but that he must be justly treated.[6] John was suspended while a commission of inquiry was set up to investigate the affair.

Despite this unhappy situation, John's health had sufficiently improved by the summer of 1893 to enable him to attend a militia artillery officer's course at the lakeside town of Kingston. With its attractive waterfront distinguished by martello towers from an earlier era, Kingston was the home of Canada's Royal Military College and School of Artillery. Applying himself with his usual dedication, John passed the course and, on 9 August 1893, donned the blue uniform with scarlet facings worn by a second lieutenant of artillery. In a photograph taken at the time by a Kingston photographer he looked every inch the young officer. A week before he was due to return to Guelph, he wrote to Laura Kains, a friend he was corresponding with, that, 'I do just think of what a time I shall have when I am back to the O[ntario]. A[gricultural]. C[ollege]. but thank you, under present conditions, I am not desirous of going back, though I must.'[7] When the commission of inquiry announced the results of its investigation into the Ontario Agricultural College and Model Farm, John was exonerated. It had, nevertheless, been an unpleasant business that must undoubtedly have left its impression upon him. He resigned his teaching job and, in the autumn of 1893, returned to the world of higher learning and the familiar smile of his favourite professor.

Tom McCrae was by now working towards a degree in medicine and the brothers decided to share a house on Huron Street in Toronto. They seemed happy in their new lodgings and found a local restaurant that fed them to their satisfaction. John was soon able to report to his mother that, 'Tom and I are well: our appetites are much larger than of yore, under Powell's Restaurant grub.'[8] As the Biology course work progressed, Ramsay Wright began to do more than a little to encourage John to follow in his brother's footsteps. Together with his good friend, Dr William Osler, the brilliant new Physician-in-Chief at Johns Hopkins University, Baltimore, Wright had visited a number of European universities in recent years and attended Louis Pasteur's lectures in Paris. His pursuit of his own research and thirst for new knowledge was infectious and brought out the best in his bright young student. John began seriously to contemplate a career in medicine.

With pressure on him to make up lost time and complete his final year, spare time activities were a welcome contrast. He helped out behind the scenes at one of the University's drama productions and his liking for music took him to hear a recital by Sousa's[9] band. Where sport was concerned, although fencing was a new interest and he was working out at a gymnasium, rugby continued to be hot favourite. In one of the matches that October, John injured a finger and broke his nose, reassuring his mother in his next letter that having been inspected by the doctor, the damage would 'not disfigure the appendage at all'.[10] His asthma still recurred intermittently but he had learned to cope with it positively and seemed more concerned that it should not interrupt his singing practice for a forthcoming Glee Club tour.

Whenever he had a spare half hour John continued to write. Although he did not question his religious faith, the problem remained of interpreting its meaning in the light of the temptations, pleasures and hardships of earthly life. Death – whether from disease, misadventure, severe weather or wild animals – was an inevitable and accepted part of that life. The impact of Alice McRae's loss lingered in John's mind as he grappled with the theme of death as a release from the struggles of life. A short story, entitled 'My Day Dreams', was the first of a number of essays and poems that pursued this subject:

> She is gone, and I wake to the sad reality; and as I look out at the long, gray horizon, broken only by the old church tower standing gloomily out against the fast-darkening sky, with a throb of pain I remember that the winds of forty winters have raved in the bare tree tops, and the sorrows have come and gone since we laid our little darling with her short-lived six years beside the old tower by the river. And one dark, misty morning our soldier boy, spared longer to me, gave up his life in the bleak Crimea. The smoke of battle was his only pall, the rattling volley his requiem.[11]

In one of his sketchbooks there is an unpublished poem that concerns young lovers parted in death. The poem is illustrated by some of his own drawings and, although undated, its style, theme and the fact that it is accompanied by small pencil sketches – most of which John completed in the period 1892–96 – indicate it is likely to have been written around that time.

> In the dim old garden the branches sway
> With the passing breath of the dying day,
> She walks alone, and her steps are slow
> For her lover went, as she bade him go
> (That summer evening, long ago!)
>
> She looked so gentle, and sweet and fair,
> (With the sunbeams kissing her golden hair),
> 'We cannot part,' said his eager glance,
> 'We must,' she answered, 'It is for France!'
>
> In the garden fair, where the roses grow
> Two lovers parted, long, long ago,
> On a summer eve when the world was bright,
> With the radiant glory of sunset bright.
>
> The stars look into her saddened eyes,
> 'We shine to-night where thy lover lies';
> And the night-wind whispered (and went its way)
> 'I tossed the grass on his grave, to-day'.
> But the white moon pitied the maid's mischance,
> And whispered softly 'It was for France.'[12]

In view of what the future held, the poem's references to fighting for France lent it something of an air of premonition.

As studies, sports and social life continued apace, *The Varsity*, magazine of the University of Toronto, published John's latest short story,'A Love Affair', in December 1893. The following year, his first two published poems reflected the inner turmoil that had resulted from the untimely ending of his friendship with Alice.

The Hope of my Heart

Delicta juventutis et ignorantius ejus, quaesumus ne memineris, Domine[13]

> I left, to earth, a little maiden fair,
> With locks of gold, and eyes that shamed the light;
> I prayed that God might have her in His care
> And sight.

Earth's love was false; her voice, a siren's song;
(Sweet mother-earth was but a lying name)
The path she showed was but the path of wrong
And shame.

'Cast her not out!' I cry. God's kind words come –
'Her future is with Me, as was her past;
It shall be My good will to bring her home
At last.'[14]

A Song of Comfort

'Sleep, weary ones, while ye may –
Sleep, oh, sleep!'
Eugene Field

Thro' May time blossoms, with whisper low,
The soft wind sang to the dead below:
'Think not with regret on the Springtime's song
And the task ye left while your hands were strong.
The song would have ceased when the Spring was past,
And the task that was joyous be weary at last.'

To the winter sky when the nights were long
The tree-tops tossed with a ceaseless song:
'Do ye think with regret on the sunny days
And the path ye left, with its untrod ways?
The sun might sink in a storm cloud's frown
And the path grow rough when the night came down.'

In the grey twilight of the autumn eves,
It sighed as it sang through the dying leaves:
'Ye think with regret that the world was bright,
That your path was short and your task was light;
The path, though short, was perhaps the best
And the toil was sweet, that it led to rest.'[15]

For the prospective young medical student, the dreaded final examinations were now not far off. Ramsay Wright was considering recommending John for a Fellowship in Biology and was keen that he should attend a summer field course in marine biology at Wood's Hole in Massachusetts – already a centre of oceanographic study. Although David McCrae offered to pay for the course, John felt he would rather earn the necessary money from his writing. Either way, if Wright's recommendation depended upon his completing the course, John told his mother, 'I would feel as if I were breaking faith in not going.'[16] The last few weeks before the exams were very pressured. John wrote home that this 'is a wicked one sided life to be leading, I know, but it won't last very much longer'.[17] Having an older brother who had already been through the ordeal was a help, and by the time the examinations started, John was ready. He passed easily and in later years a friend wrote that John never regretted taking his first degree course with its Arts component. It had been the perfect preparation for a young man who had a natural love of letters and a wide outlook on the world.

When the summer vacation started, John gladly accepted his father's offer to pay for the course at Wood's Hole and set off by train to Boston. From there he proceeded down the coast to Cape Cod, passing quaint towns and villages with white-steepled churches, tidy clapboard cottages and sea captains' houses with their distinctive 'widows' walks'.[18] Wood's Hole looked across to the nearby Elizabeth Islands, to Martha's Vineyard, and to the more distant former whaling centre of Nantucket Island with its secluded beaches, peaceful byways and historic mansions. Any views John might have hoped for on arrival, however, were obscured by a heavy sea fog which presaged the arrival of high pressure and warm weather. On settling in, he found he was one of a number of Canadians and kept his mother fully and regularly informed of his progress. Within a few days he was able to report that 'I have the anatomy of my beasts pretty well into my head.'[19] John must already have been formulating his ideas about what made a good lecturer, for he declared that one of his teachers was monotonous and did not emphasise his points.[20] Attention to dress was required even in the warmth of summer, and a comparison of his own with that of other students led to the amused comment that 'I am wearing out all my old collars – styles which Columbus may have introduced.'[21]

The Cape proved to be an area of natural beauty with scenic harbours, tranquil inlets and an unspoilt sandy coastline of striking desert-like dunes. Inland exploration revealed to the enthusiastic young naturalist bird nesting grounds, cranberry bogs, marshes, rivers and areas of forest and scrub. In their free time, the students went swimming and sailing. John made the most of the clear, hot, New England summer days. He enjoyed bathing in the six-foot rollers and took his sketchbook to the beach, drawing yachts and coastal scenes. There were several boat excursions: one to Martha's Vineyard with its very attractive shoreline, and another when John and a few other students rowed out to a nearby island one evening. He remarked on the beautiful phosphorescence, describing how, 'every dip of the oar was a mass of silver'.[22] Another free day, described by John as 'one of the pleasantest days of my life',[23] offered the chance of a leisurely cruise by yacht to a place along the coast called Penkase. The yacht passed dozens of schooners and fishing smacks as it made its way down Vineyard Sound, and near one cove John saw 'three or four three-masters anchored, and a lighthouse surmounting it all'.[24] The sights and sounds – the thousands of shrieking terns and gulls, the light on the water, the wrecks that were visible above the surface, the wonderful names like Tarpaulin Cove and Buzzards Bay – John loved it all. He was in buoyant mood as he finished off a letter to his mother, explaining to her that the students were going to sing in a church service dedicated to sailors and proudly announcing that her son was to be part of a quartet consisting of tenor, soprano, alto 'and myself BASSO. See me gloat! . . . We are going to sing "Intercession" – you know it . . . and "Melita".'[25]

On his return to Toronto, John was told he had been awarded his three-year Fellowship in Biology. The question of future study now became acute. His enjoyment of the summer course at Wood's Hole prompted a discussion on the possibility of postgraduate work with Dr Archibald Macallum, another of his lecturers, but Macallum urged him to study medicine, for, as John explained to his father,

> If science does not turn out as I expect, or if anything untoward turns up, I could fall back on practice, in which he [Macallum] says I would surely succeed. That, he says, is almost a necessity; that is, to have a saver to fall back upon: then it will enlarge the field of my chances 20 times . . . in any case the Medicine will render the Science of much more value and vice versa.[26]

Macallum recommended Johns Hopkins University, Baltimore, not only because it had a large financial endowment at its disposal but also because it was to be 'the centre of Medical work on the continent'.[27] After further discussion with Ramsay Wright, however, John decided to remain at the University of Toronto. As he became a medical freshman in October 1894, his brother Tom was entering his final year and put his skills to work on his younger brother when John developed a cough. 'Tom . . . went over me thoroughly,' wrote John to his father, 'and says that my heart and lungs are perfectly sound.' As if to dispel any lingering doubt, he added, 'I am feeling splendid, and have an appetite like a horse.'[28] One advantage of a Biology Fellowship was that it entitled the holder to tutor other students. In John's case this helped him to pay for his medical studies since the Guelph Woollen Mills had now been sold and the McCraes were not as comfortably off as they once had been.[29] One student remembered John's kindly approach as a tutor who not only 'always had time to aid a student' but 'was quick to see a student's difficulty and point out to them the way to overcome it.'[30]

Life at this time was a round of medical studies, militia and other social activities but John continued to write poetry and his years as a medical student were also his most prolific as a poet. His output of correspondence, diaries and compositions was not unusual at that time, for there were far fewer diversions and entertainments available than today, and consequently more time in which to put pen to paper. In the Victorian age as a whole, gentility, respectability, duty and obedience to a code of behaviour were placed above the mere indulgence of personal feeling. John's poetry enabled him to commit to paper thoughts that the constraints and rigid social norms of the time made it almost impossible to voice. Although he had not had the traditional British boarding school upbringing of emotional isolation, tough sports and somewhat spartan conditions, he nevertheless lived by the strict code of his Presbyterian upbringing. Such was his self-discipline, that not a moment must be wasted and rather than idling away his spare moments with limericks or doodles, he sketched and wrote poetry.[31]

As an avid reader of the works of many writers, John also enjoyed collecting poetry and copying it into a series of notebooks. A superbly retentive memory meant he had already acquired a general knowledge and appreciation of literature rare in a young man of his age, and often wrote to his mother or sister about books he had read. A number of magazines were now becoming interested in publishing his work, the foremost of which in Canada at that time was *Saturday Night*. In late 1894 it ran a short story competition and much to his delight, John was the winner.

Tom McCrae obtained his medical degree the following year and was offered a post at Toronto's General Hospital. He needed to be close to his place of work and the two brothers found a new house to rent nearby. They corresponded as regularly as ever with their parents and sister, especially during the early part of 1895 when there was a smallpox epidemic in Guelph. Mercifully the McCraes escaped the illness. When Tom decided to move into quarters at the hospital that autumn, John remained alone in the rented house, deciding he would probably get more work done by himself. His commitment to his studies was such that tempting social opportunities to dine with friends or take part in Glee Club concerts could only be fitted in at intervals. It was, as John put it, like 'a very thin slice of meat sandwiched in between some very thick slices of biological bread'.[32] However, in choosing medicine, it was clear from his motivation and high marks that the future Dr McCrae had made the right decision.

Eager to gain experience, the young medical student spent the first of several vacations helping Dr Howitt with his busy practice in Guelph. It was the beginning of a path that was to bring him, both as a doctor and later as a soldier, into daily contact with life's tragedies and hazards. While John was staying with the Howitts that year he composed a poem entitled 'Eventide'. The scene it described might easily have been harvest time at the family farm, 'Janefield', where David and Janet McCrae now lived. Although mainly concerned with livestock breeding, David grew some crops and his fields looked westwards across the valley of the River Speed to Guelph. In later years, Henry Howitt recollected that this was not the only composition John completed while he was a guest of the family and that a 'number of his poems were written while he sat on a seat in the bay window at the front of my house.' However, Henry particularly remembered the writing of 'Eventide' and the fact that John had allowed him to see it before it was completed.[33]

Eventide

The day is past and the toilers cease;
The land grows dim 'mid the shadows grey,
And hearts are glad, for the dark brings peace
At the close of day.

Each weary toiler, with lingering pace,
As he homeward turns, with the long day done,
Looks out to the west, with the light on his face
Of the setting sun.

Yet some see not (with their sin-dimmed eyes)
The promise of rest in the fading light;
But the clouds loom dark in the angry skies
At the fall of night.

And some see only a golden sky
Where the elms their welcoming arms stretch wide
To the calling rooks, as they homeward fly
At the eventide.

It speaks of peace that comes after strife,
Of the rest He sends to the hearts He tried,
Of the calm that follows the stormiest life –
God's eventide.[34]

Another poem written that year echoed the feelings Alice McRae had awoken and the inner conflict that had resulted.

Unsolved

Amid my books I lived the hurrying years,
Disdaining kinship with my fellow man;
Alike to me were human smiles and tears,
I cared not whither Earth's great life-stream ran,
Till as I knelt before my mouldered shrine,
God made me look into a woman's eyes;

And I, who thought all earthly wisdom mine,
Knew in a moment that the eternal skies
Were measured but in inches, to the quest
That lay before me in that mystic gaze.
'Surely I have been errant: it is best
That I should tread, with men their human ways.'
God took the teacher, ere the task was learned,
And to my lonely books again I turned.[35]

Outwardly John could always be relied upon to appear cheerful and to present the lighter side of his nature in his daily dealings with the world at large. Underneath his friendly, outgoing exterior, however, he looked at everyday life through the consciousness of a personal spiritual dimension. A reflective sadness pervaded much of his writing and one could muse over whether he had inherited his race's 'half-mystical preoccupation with the dead'[36], but his belief in the ultimate peace that followed the travails of life never waivered.

The young Canadian was by now a firm admirer of the work of Rudyard Kipling, who celebrated the Empire in prose and verse and who served as its unofficial poet laureate. At this time, Kipling was living with his American wife on her family estate in Vermont and finding the New World an antithesis to his years in India. There were no peasants, castes or pretences of old loyalty in America and he enjoyed its vitality and eagerness for growth, change and innovation. Kipling had been watching with interest as the march of European civilisation continued to spread across Asia and Africa. He was both a patriot and an imperialist who recognised the problems of formulating colonial policy and communicating over such great distances. While he admired what he saw as the qualities that had made Britain great, he also recognised that the attitudes of people in the mother country were not always in touch with those actively engaged in the business of empire. As he offered both encouragement and counsel through the medium of his prose and poetry, Kipling's heart went out to the men who day by day faced the hazards and dangers of life in the foothills of the Himalayas, the tundra of northern Canada or the disease-ridden African jungle. The British soldier, whom he had come to know and love from his years in India for his tenacity, maturity and sense of humour, was to Kipling both the foundation and the human side of the Empire.

The final domain for imperial expansion was Africa. In December 1895, international attention focused on the south of the continent, where the drive for that expansion sought to bring about a political union of earlier settlers known as the Boers, and more recent British immigrants. The Boers, who were descended from Dutch, Flemish, German and French Huguenot stock, were devoutly religious, independent and suspicious of all change. In search of freedom from British control, the most determined had trekked a thousand miles across the veld in 1836 and 1837 to form two small independent Boer republics, the Orange Free State and the Transvaal. Having recognised them, the British government reversed its decision in 1877 and formally annexed the Transvaal. Three years later the Boers revolted and defeated British troops at Majuba Hill in 1881. With their own way of life and beliefs firmly established, the majority of the Boers wanted nothing to do with the British Empire but the discovery of diamonds along the Orange River in 1867 and huge reefs of gold in the southern Transvaal nearly twenty years later had led to economic transformation and social conflict. The influx into the Boer republics of what the local people called 'Uitlanders' – foreign miners and investors, a large number of whom were British – was perceived as a challenge to the Boer culture. The Uitlanders, who paid most of the taxes, were disenfranchised and allowed no rights of citizenship.

Discontent grew and when talk of an armed uprising against the Boer government started to spread among the Uitlanders, a name often mentioned was that of Cecil Rhodes, imperialist and immensely wealthy Prime Minister of the Cape Colony. Rhodes had built up substantial interests in the Rand gold industry and put his fortune to work in the cause of the British Empire. In his eyes, the Boers were a considerable obstacle to his dreams of expanding the Cape Colony to the north, constructing a railway from the Cape to Cairo and establishing a federation of South African states within the British Empire. British troops could not be used in any possible rising against the Boers but Rhodes had a private body of troopers in the service of his British South Africa Company. He also had, as his best friend and assistant, Dr Leander Starr Jameson, a Scot who had abandoned medical practice to share in making 'the whole of southern Africa British at last'.[37]

Representatives of the Reform Movement, a revolutionary movement among the Uitlanders, visited Rhodes in Cape Town to discuss their situation and, in the months that followed, plans for a possible uprising emerged. In mid-October 1895, Jameson began to assemble a force on the Transvaal's western frontier and, after weeks of delay and deferral, took the decision to ride into the Transvaal Republic with almost five hundred men on the night of 29 December 1895. Tailed by Boers almost from the beginning, he and his men came to within striking distance of Johannesburg but were skilfully coerced around the outside of the city and surrounded. With, as it turned out, only half-hearted support from the Uitlanders, they fought until they were almost out of ammunition. When he realised his mission had failed, Jameson surrendered on the morning of 2 January 1896. He and five officers were handed to the Cape government and sent to England for trial. The captured raiders were found to be carrying copies of cipher telegrams proving Rhodes' complicity in the preparations for the raid. The Cape Colony's premier tendered his resignation and was later reprimanded following a House of Commons Select Committee enquiry.[38]

The British government publicly condemned the raid and there was concern over Germany's reaction, given that German influence in the Boer republics was substantial. To Kaiser Wilhelm II in Berlin, the uprising was further evidence of what he perceived as 'a deliberate British policy of patronizing and ignoring German interests and the German Emperor.'[39] In a state of great agitation and always one for the grand gesture, he began to visualise sending troops to the Transvaal and establishing a German protectorate, but was persuaded by his aides to confine his actions to a congratulatory telegram to President Paul Kruger acclaiming the fact that the independence of the Transvaal had been successfully safeguarded. The message, sent despite a warning from the British Ambassador in Berlin that Germany's public encouragement of the Boers would harm Anglo-German relations, deeply offended people in Britain. Once again Wilhelm's rather heavy-handed involvement in international affairs had created difficulties and Queen Victoria herself decided to write to the grandson whose faults she regarded as stemming from 'impetuousness as well as conceit'. She received a deferential, evasive, reply.[40]

The Kaiser was ambivalent towards Britain and found himself both fascinated and at the same time envious of her global Empire and naval power. Grand Admiral Alfred von Tirpitz, Chief of Staff to the German High Command, had already been commissioned by his sovereign to develop a strategy for a German High Seas Fleet, and the day after Jameson's surrender, he handed Wilhelm a memorandum calling for a flagship and two squadrons of eight battleships that would cause 'even the greatest sea state in Europe' to adopt a more conciliatory approach to Germany.[41] To those whose political antennae were finely tuned, the signs were worrying.

One man who had begun to watch Germany with interest was the Empire's unofficial poet laureate, now preparing to leave Vermont and return to England. As Rudyard Kipling sailed for home, the summer of 1896 saw a general election in Canada in which the Liberals swept into power and with them, Canada's first French-Canadian Prime Minister, Wilfrid Laurier. Laurier, already an eloquent voice for liberalism based on justice, tolerance and most importantly, national unity, was to lead his country into a new era and hold the reins of power for the next fifteen years. Driven by a vision of integrating new immigrants and bringing together all his country's diverse elements, he took up office convinced that the next century belonged to Canada.

As Laurier began his term, John McCrae was just completing his second year of medical studies and had gained second place overall in the end-of-year exams. Some of the University's students, John among them, were sent to gain further practical experience at a summer convalescent hospital for sick children in Maryland. After a lengthy train journey he arrived at the Robert Garrett Hospital, Mount Airy, which he later described as follows:

> Away up in the hills of Maryland, where there is little but sunshine, storms, fresh air and glorious views, is a hospital, maintained by the generosity of one of America's most benevolent women, where the children of the poor are carried away during the summer months to receive such attention as the most careful system of nursing makes possible. None but sick children are admitted.[42]

John quickly made friends with the staff, patients and the resident animals, a tabby kitten called 'Bill' and two mongrels, 'Christopher' and 'Sport'. The camera was an invention he favoured and he had brought one with him. Photographs showed him with some of his small patients, and relaxing off duty on the hospital's verandah where he liked to sit with his current reading matter – *Lorna Doone* as it happened. He left an account of his time there, entitled 'The Comedy of a Hospital.' Full of humour and pathos, it was later published in *The Westminster*, a Canadian Presbyterian magazine. No doubt wishing that diseases could be cured at the speed at which modern invention was now producing the first petrol-driven cars and moving pictures, John sought to find a silver lining to the cloud that he faced daily on the hospital wards, commenting that 'the casual visitor is not likely to note the vein of comedy that underlies the tragedy of suffering children, but it is there'. As an example, he cited:

> A small paralytic, accused by the head nurse of having 'cursed' a little girl, defends himself thus: 'I didn't curse to-day. I cursed yesterday, but I hain't cursed to-day'. Surely this is a new interpretation of 'Sufficient unto the day'.[43]

Having brought his sketchbook, John took it with him on walks and bicycle rides. He put it to good use by producing a collection of drawings under the title 'A Maryland Summer'. There was much to catch his eye in the surrounding countryside. He sketched corn stooks and fields at twilight; delicately etched trees, leaves and grasses; undulating hills and woodland scenes; and views of the nearby Chesapeake Bay, an area of great natural beauty stretching some two hundred miles from Norfolk Virginia almost to Pennsylvania. More than forty rivers and thousands of streams flowed into it from sources originating almost as far north as Vermont, out across the Blue Ridge Mountains into West Virginia and south from the outer limits of North Carolina.

More of John's poems and another story found their way into print that

Pen and ink drawing by John McCrae of boats at anchor in a quiet inlet.
From his sketchbook 'A Maryland Summer', 1896.
Courtesy of Guelph Museums, Guelph, Canada

year. His story, entitled 'How the Twenty-Third Paid Forfeit,' concerned
the love affair of a Dorothy Churchill, 'the sweetest girl that ever disturbed
a man's peace of mind,'[44] and a Captain Richard Callonby-Byton of His
Majesty's Twenty-Third Light Dragoons. Of three poems he published in
1896, 'Then and Now' had the sense of a love poem and conveyed in its
final lines a feeling of self-conciliation.

Then and Now

> Beneath her window in the fragrant night
> I half forget how truant years have flown
> Since I looked up to see her chamber-light,
> Or catch, perchance, her slender shadow thrown
> Upon the casement; but the nodding leaves
> Sweep lazily across the unlit pane,
> And to and fro beneath the shadowy eaves,
> Like restless birds, the breath of coming rain
> Creeps, lilac-laden, up the village street

When all is still, as if the very trees
Were listening for the coming of her feet
That come no more; yet, lest I weep, the breeze
Sings some forgotten song of those old years
Until my heart grows far too glad for tears.[45]

John's next poem, 'In Due Season', seemed to mark the end of his period of soul searching.

In Due Season

If night should come and find me at my toil,
When all Life's day I had, tho' faintly, wrought,
And shallow furrows, cleft in stony soil
Were all my labour: Shall I count it naught

If only one poor gleaner, weak of hand,
Shall pick a scanty sheaf where I have sown?
'Nay, for of thee the Master doth demand
Thy work: the harvest rests with Him alone.'[46]

The year 1897 was one to remember around the Empire, for as the industrious medical student continued his studies, Canada and her fellow member countries stirred in anticipation of the Diamond Jubilee of their Queen. All eyes were turned towards Britain. There was to be an important Naval Review at Spithead and a procession through the nation's capital, more dazzling than anything ever seen before. People converged on London from all over the world and those Canadians determined to be a part of the commemorations booked their passage. As the longest reigning monarch in English history and sovereign over lands that now covered a quarter of the earth's surface, Queen Victoria's sixty years were being celebrated as a festival of imperial unity, strength and splendour.

On 22 June 1897, the Empire's premiers, each with a body of his own troops, took their places in the fifty-thousand strong cavalcade that would start and end at Buckingham Palace. London was packed with cheering, flag-waving crowds who could hardly hear themselves above the ceremonial drumming, church bells and gun salutes. The fashionable and wealthy had expensive seats in stands or balconies along the route whilst the poorer folk donned their best clothes and saw what they could among the great mass that lined the pavements. The effect of thousands of men in a wondrous assortment of costumes and uniforms was stunning. Among representatives as diverse as richly-attired Indian princes, New South Wales cavalrymen, tribesmen from Borneo and Hong Kong policemen in coolie hats, was Canada's Prime Minister, Wilfrid

Laurier, with an escort of Canadian Hussars. In the midst of it all was the Royal landau, the Queen herself wearing a black and grey dress and shaded by a white silk parasol from the intermittent sunshine. The great procession paused to allow her carriage to stop at the foot of the steps of St Paul's Cathedral, where a service of thanksgiving was held.

This magnificent celebration was to leave the British public with a much greater sense of unity and belonging than before. Traditionally rather vague and indifferent about their Empire and lulled into a sense of security by the Pax Britannica, the peace which dozens of small wars and conflicts had failed to dislodge, the whole panoply of Empire had caught them up in a climactic moment in the nation's history. Not everyone, however, was swept along in the flood tide of elation. Some already saw that the world was changing and Britain's ascendency could not last much longer. America posed economic challenges while those of Russia and France were diplomatic. Above all, Germany, whose Kaiser was attending the Spithead Review, was a nation on the rise, intent on levering itself from continental mastery to world power. It already had Europe's most powerful army and was about to construct a High Seas Fleet. Rudyard Kipling, now approaching the height of his fame, was already convinced of the German threat and sounded a warning note about the dangers of over-confidence in his poem, 'Recessional'. Five months later German marines occupied the Chinese port of Kiaochow, transferring it on a 99-year lease to Germany and demonstrating German aggression in her search for overseas possessions.

For now, however, the overwhelming mood in June 1897 was one of rejoicing in a moment of greatness at the end of a triumphant century for Britain. Queen Victoria herself, much moved by what she had seen, sent a short message by telegraph to all corners of her Empire. It said simply: 'From my heart I thank my beloved people. May God bless them.'[47]

NOTES

1. From 'Unsolved' by John McCrae, *The Canadian Magazine of Politics, Science, Art and Literature* (Volume 5, May–October 1895), p. 550, MTRL.

2. Although Canada was authorised a Blue Ensign similar to those of Australia and New Zealand in 1865, in 1892 Canadian merchant ships were permitted to fly the British Red Ensign with a distinctive Canadian coat-of-arms on the fly. For nearly three-quarters of a century this flag, which really only had official status on merchant vessels, also served as Canada's national flag. In 1965, after much debate and controversy, the Canadian government adopted the current flag which consists of a red maple leaf on a white background. This adoption took place in the face of considerable opposition from Canadians who thought that the Red Ensign, having been used in four wars as Canada's flag, was good enough.

3. Peter C. Newman, *Canada 1892: Portrait of a Promised Land* (Toronto, 1992), p. 11.

4. A.M Ross, *The College on the Hill: A History of the Ontario Agricultural College, 1874–1974* (Toronto, 1974), p. 11.
5. Jennifer Burnell, 'The McCraes of Guelph: Urban and Rural Development in Nineteenth Century Canada' (Guelph, 1992), p. 17. The 1893 World's Columbian Exposition was the first world's fair ever held in the Americas and marked the recognition of the United States as a major industrial power. The six-hundred acre fair site contained some 150 neoclassical buildings designed for the occasion and clad in white marble. There were exhibitors from over 72 countries and the fair attracted 27 million visitors. See Alexis Gregory, *The Gilded Age* (London, 1993), pp. 14–15.
6. Prescott, *In Flanders Fields*, p. 16.
7. JM to Laura Kains, 4 August 1893, MH. Laura Kains came from a part-English, part-Scottish family and her grandfather, Thomas Kains, had been a paymaster on H.M.S. *Victory*. The author is grateful to Hugh Macmillan for supplying this information.
8. JM to Janet McCrae, 21 January 1894, MG 30, D209, Micro A-1103, NAC.
9. John Philip Sousa (1854–1932), American bandmaster and composer of military marches. In 1868 he enlisted in the U.S. Marine Corps and during the Great War, having enlisted in the U.S. Navy, he took charge of the band training centre at Great Lakes Naval Base, Illinois. Following the success of 'In Flanders Fields', Sousa set the poem to music.
10. JM to Janet McCrae, 16 October 1893, MG 30, D209, Micro A-1103, NAC.
11. John McCrae, 'My Day Dreams' *Saturday Night* (Volume 6, No. 16, 11 March 1893), p. 9. Micro mfm/AP/S388, UTL.
12. Untitled poem by John McCrae, 1896 Sketchbook, MH.
13. The translation reads: 'The sins of the youth and his ignorance we beg you not to remember, O Lord.'
14. *The Varsity* (Volume 13, No. 16, 21 February 1894), p. 3, Micro mfm/LH/V377, UTL.
15. *The Varsity* (Volume 13, No. 13, 31 January 1894), p. 3, Micro mfm/LH/V377, UTL.
16. JM to Janet McCrae, 12 April 1894, MG 30, D209, Micro A-1103, NAC.
17. JM to Janet McCrae, 12 April 1894, MG 30, D209, Micro A-1103, NAC.
18. New England houses of the period often had at the top a central single room that served as an observation point and was surrounded by a balcony. It was said that the wives of sea captains would walk there as they watched for their husbands' ships.
19. JM to Janet McCrae, 15 July 1894, MG 30, D209, Micro A-1103, NAC.
20. JM to Janet McCrae, 15 July 1894, MG 30, D209, Micro A-1103, NAC.
21. JM to Janet McCrae, 15 July 1894, MG 30, D209, Micro A-1103, NAC.
22. JM to Janet McCrae, 9 August 1894, MG 30, D209, Micro A-1103, NAC.
23. JM to Janet McCrae, 12 August 1894, MG 30, D209, Micro A-1103, NAC.
24. JM to Janet McCrae, 12 August 1894, MG 30, D209, Micro A-1103, NAC.
25. JM to Janet McCrae, 12 August 1894, MG 30, D209, Micro A-1103, NAC.
26. JM to David McCrae, 20 October 1894, MG 30, D209, Micro A-1103, NAC.
27. JM to David McCrae, 20 October 1894, MG 30, D209, Micro A-1103, NAC.
28. JM to David McCrae, 31 October 1894, MG 30, D209, Micro A-1103, NAC.
29. Prescott, *In Flanders Fields*, p. 17.
30. Edward H. Craigie, *A History of the Department of Zoology up to 1962* (Toronto, 1966) p. 89: Appendix D, W.H. Piersol, 'Memories of Long Ago'.
31. Leacock, 'In Flanders Fields'.
32. JM to Janet McCrae, 25 October 1895, MG 30, D209, Micro A-1103, NAC.

33. Howitt, 'John McCrae', p. 13.
34. *The Canadian Magazine of Politics, Science, Art and Literature* (Volume 6, May–October 1896), p. 343, MTRL.
35. *The Canadian Magazine of Politics, Science, Art and Literature* (Volume 5, May–October 1895), p. 550, MTRL.
36. D.K. Broster, *The Flight of the Heron* (London, 1925), p.16.
37. Jan Morris, *Heaven's Command* (London, 1979), p. 516.
38. Robert K. Massie, *Dreadnought: Britain, Germany and the Coming of the Great War* (New York, 1991), pp. 218–219, 229.
39. Massie, *Dreadnought*, p. 222.
40. Massie, *Dreadnought*, pp. 226–227.
41. Massie, *Dreadnought*, p. 169.
42. John McCrae, 'The Comedy of a Hospital', *The Westminster: a paper for the home* (Volume 1, No. 3, 11 September 1897), p. 182. Micro mcfm T3W4, PCCA.
43. John McCrae, 'The Comedy of a Hospital', p. 182.
44. John McCrae, 'How the Twenty-Third Paid Forfeit,' *The Varsity* (Volume 13, No. 20, 22 March 1894), p. 4. Micro mfm/LH/V377, UTL.
45. *Massey's Magazine* (Volume 2, No. 1, August 1896), p. 96. UTL.
46. *The Westminster* (Volume 2 No. 1, January 1897), p. 13. Micro mcfm T3W4, PCCA.
47. Dorothy Marshall, *The Life and Times of Queen Victoria* (London, 1972), p. 214.

CHAPTER FOUR

'Yet couraged for the battles of the day'[1]
1897–1900

By that summer of imperial splendour, John McCrae had completed his third year of medical studies. He passed almost the entire long, hot season at the Robert Garrett Hospital in Maryland, enjoying his work and free time spent riding, reading and going for long walks. He remembered those months for the young patients he came to know and love, a brief working visit to Johns Hopkins Hospital, Baltimore, the 'corking thunderstorms'[2] and occasional expeditions by steamer down the Chesapeake Bay, returning at twilight when all seemed to him to look its best. In September, the time came to return to Canada and his all-important final year at the University of Toronto. Despite the problem of his asthma, John continued to show exceptional ability and dedication. When the results were announced the following year, his performance was outstanding. Not only did he graduate with an Honours Degree in Medicine but as top student overall, he won a Gold Medal and a scholarship in Physiology and Pathology. The University of Toronto, with its very full and thorough preliminary training in science, was turning out high-calibre graduates who would in time become some of the leading doctors in North America. Years later, it would be written of John and Tom McCrae and some of the other medical students who graduated around that time that 'No school of this generation in North America can claim quite so brilliant a band of physicians and pathologists as original alumni.'[3]

John was about to enter a profession which was undergoing profound change. The advances made by men like Louis Pasteur in France and Joseph Lister in Scotland enabled Canadian doctors, who had a chance to train under them, to return home armed with the techniques of aseptic surgery. Post-operative infections could now be linked to micro-organisms and measures taken to prevent infection. German scientists had been particularly effective in identifying specific germs as the causes of particular diseases. The germ theory had been gradually accepted and laboratory work was now an integral part of medical studies. As doctors sought to trace the source of epidemics, new vaccines were gradually being produced to help combat infectious diseases. In the last years of the century, doctors enjoyed a position of high prestige and large, modern hospitals were the sign of a progressive community.

Dr John McCrae's first year as a doctor was spent, as his brother's had been, as a Resident House Officer at Toronto General Hospital. During this time he was invited to return for a short period to teach Zoology at the Ontario Agricultural College. With the unhappy events of five years earlier well behind him, he accepted. He continued to write poetry in his spare time and introduced his love of the sea into two of his poems that year. One, 'The Harvest of the Sea', was published in *The Westminster* in May 1898 accompanied by one of his own pen and ink drawings of sailing ships.

At this time, the best medical graduates of the University of Toronto were given the chance to undertake a period as Resident House Officers at Johns Hopkins Hospital in Baltimore.[4] As July 1899 approached, John looked forward to returning to the hospital he had briefly visited the previous year and where Tom McCrae, now engaged in further study at Göttingen, Germany, had been on the staff since 1895. Once more he set off for Maryland, but this time his visit would draw him into the orbit of one of the great figures in the history of modern medicine – Dr William Osler.

William Osler was the son of a Cornish minister who had emigrated to Canada. In the year John McCrae was born, he had graduated with a degree in medicine from McGill University in Montreal, and after further research in London, Germany and Austria – the latter two countries being at the leading edge of research and medical teaching at that time – had returned to Canada greatly impressed with what he had seen. Osler was just twenty-five years of age when he was offered the post of Professor of the Institutes of Medicine at McGill University. The next ten years, devoted to teaching pathology and physiology, were to lay the foundations of a career that would bring him international renown as the great teaching physician of the late nineteenth century.

When the new Johns Hopkins Hospital was built at Baltimore, funded by a legacy from a local Quaker businessman, Osler, by then Professor of Clinical Medicine at the University of Pennsylvania, was invited in 1889 to become its Professor of Medicine. He decided to accept, attracted not only by the high calibre of staff but also by the fact that for the first time in an English-speaking country, the hospital would be organised into separate clinical units. In setting up the hospital's medical school, it was Osler's intention that it should offer the best possible tuition and be run along the lines of those he had seen in Germany. His innovative approach brought teaching into hospital wards by decreasing the amount of lecturing and increasing the time students spent with patients. They were taught to combine laboratory work with bedside observation and practice.

Osler's success as a teacher could be attributed not only to his extraordinary talent and command of his subject, but also to the fact that he had a thorough understanding of human nature. His message to his students was simple: hard work was essential to success but the toughest phases of medical training and practice could and should always be lightened by a happy and broad outlook, a love of life and an interest in art and literature. He emphasised the importance of equanimity, cheerfulness and kindness in dealing with patients; of taking lots of notes and keeping up to date with the latest developments; of keeping emotions 'on ice';[5] and, when considering marriage, of avoiding a life of 'soul wasting struggle with worldly annoyances'[6] that had been the fate of Dr Tertius Lydgate, the medical character in George Eliot's novel, *Middlemarch*. Osler's own capacity for hard work was remarkable and he inspired the same in others.

William Osler's lovely sense of humour, lightness of heart, charm and compassion endeared him to one and all. Nobody who knew him could ever forget his merry, dark eyes and constant flow of warmth, jokes and anecdotes. This was no superficial veneer, for underneath he was as unselfish, generous and kind as he appeared. Under his leadership, Johns Hopkins Medical School became the best in North America and Osler's superlative teaching was to produce many fine doctors and earn him a place of honour in the medical profession. Indeed, by the turn of the century William Osler was probably the best-known physician in the English-speaking world. Yet he always remained a modest and charming man.

Tom McCrae was already a close associate and regular visitor to the beautiful ivy-covered house on the corner of Baltimore's West Franklin Street where Osler and his wife Grace lived with their three-year-old son, Revere, and where he had written a large part of his magnum opus, *The Principles and Practice of Medicine*. Next door lived Dr Harvey Cushing, Assistant Resident in Surgery at Johns Hopkins, and several medical students, among whom was Osler's godson, Bill Francis. 'The Chief' and 'Mrs Chief' – as the Oslers were affectionately known – entertained students to dinner most Saturdays. At discussions over biscuits, cheese and beer, Osler talked not just about medicine, but also about his favourite authors and poets. Tom McCrae's younger brother found a warm welcome awaiting him.

John soon came to know Baltimore, a 'homely, homespun sort of a town'[7] of picturesque cobbled streets, unpretentious housing and somewhat primitive sanitation. Humid in summer and raw in winter, it was a busy place where streetcars toiled up and downhill and old-fashioned markets regularly overflowed with produce from the farms on the eastern shore of Chesapeake Bay. It is not hard to imagine the excitement of being at America's leading medical school and having the privileged company and teaching of a man like William Osler. There was also the prestige and challenge of belonging to an élite band of young doctors at the very centre of great changes now taking place in their chosen profession. In his free time, John once again found much to lure him away from the town environment: the rolling Maryland hills and meadows scattered with fragrant wild blue, red and purple morning glory; rambles through fields of pumpkins and maize near inlets of the Chesapeake Bay; the rich bird and aquatic life of its shoreline; and the fascinating variations in light and colour brought about by the constant progression of time and weather. His sketchbook began to fill up with more land – and seascapes of the area.

The Bay was a veritable paradise for naturalists. Its shallow creeks and inlets bordered an area of fresh and salt water wetlands that were the home of oysters, bald eagles, river otters and dozens of species of fish and wildfowl including crayfish, blue crabs and great blue herons. As fishing boats busily harvested the seafood, transport steamers daily ferried their passengers the length and breadth of the Chesapeake. That John at some point made the trip as far south as the Virginian capital of Richmond is evidenced by his sketches of the James River approaches to the city. He also drew other aspects of the Bay and a delightful set of head and shoulders profiles of his fellow passengers on the S.S. *Virginia*. They included a bearded minister with dog collar and straw boater, a young woman wearing a hat elaborately decorated with fruit and an elderly sleeping gentleman.

The young doctor's interest in pathology and physiology undoubtedly met with the wholehearted support of William Osler, who believed that a good grounding in pathology was vital to success in medicine. John applied for and was awarded the Governor's Fellowship in Pathology being offered by Osler's old university, McGill. When the time came to leave Baltimore after his two-month stay, he had established the foundations of a lifelong friendship with the Oslers and would later show evidence of Osler's influence, both in his attitude to his patients and colleagues and in his dealings with his friends.

The idea of a university in Montreal had first been conceived early in the nineteenth century by a Scot who was at that time living on his estate in pleasant countryside near the bottom of the mountain that overlooked the town. James McGill had come to Canada in the late eighteenth century after completing his education at Glasgow University. Attracted by stories of fortunes to be made from the fur trade, of which Montreal was the centre, he carved out a life that led ultimately to both wealth and position. As a successful businessman and politician, McGill believed strongly in the value of education and decided that his adopted land should have an institution after the style of his own Scottish university that would play a significant role in the life and development of Canada.

Accordingly, he made a bequest of money, buildings and forty six acres of his estate, conditional upon a university or college being established within ten years of his death. In 1813, eight years after McGill's passing, his vision was realised.

By the time John McCrae arrived in September 1899 to take up his Governor's Fellowship, McGill University had survived years of struggle to achieve ultimate success. Generous donations had enabled it to increase and improve its facilities and its reputation was now attracting leading scientists of the calibre of the unassuming New Zealander, Ernest Rutherford. Having become McGill's Professor of Physics at the young age of 27, Rutherford, a future Nobel Prize winner, conducted his research and made some of his most fundamental discoveries in one of the best-equipped laboratories to be found anywhere. Thanks to the generosity of Sir Donald Smith, now elevated to the peerage as Lord Strathcona and serving as Canada's High Commissioner in London, a brand new medical wing was nearing completion. It was here that John was to meet the third of his influential teachers.

The first impression of George Adami, McGill's Professor of Pathology, was of a short, moustacheoed, dapper figure dressed, with the elegance that characterised the university's senior teaching staff, in morning coat, pin-striped trousers and waistcoat. Lancashire-born and bred, he was yet another brilliant, cultured man who had achieved much in a short time. In his formative years he had travelled widely throughout Europe in the company of his art-loving father, and time spent among the treasures of museums and galleries had helped to develop a highly refined artistic taste and love of objets d'art and beautiful paintings. Having gained a First Class honours degree in Natural Sciences at Cambridge, he had decided to make his future in medical research and, while working at his old university as a Demonstrator in Pathology, Adami had won a much-cherished scholarship to study under Dr Louis Pasteur in Paris. By the time he learned of the vacancy for a Professor of Pathology at McGill, he was Director of Studies in Natural Sciences at Jesus College, Cambridge. The Canadian position offered great challenges and Adami's enthusiasm overcame his reservations. He was on holiday in the Swiss Alps in 1892 when he received a telegram advising him that he had been selected.

Pathology in Canada at this time was virtually an untouched field and a long way from being regarded as a discipline in its own right. George Adami knew that what lay before him was a great opportunity to interest others in his subject. Again, largely due to the generosity of Lord Strathcona, funds became available for a Chair of Pathology, a Medical School extension and new pathological laboratories at the city's Royal Victoria Hospital, where Adami was Pathologist. During the next few years he developed and built up his department. He always remembered his study in Paris with gratitude and established two fellowships along identical lines, of which John McCrae would now be one of the holders.[8] Adami's own special blend of energy and geniality made him a popular lecturer whose students delighted in his fascinating and stimulating classes. As one of a brilliant group of young professors who helped to develop McGill's social life, he had many friends and those invited to his home found it a meeting ground for cultured people. When John McCrae arrived to study under him, there were reckoned to be few men in Montreal who had a wider knowledge of literature or finer artistic taste than George Adami.[9] It soon became apparent that John and the professor had much in common and were going to get along both in and out of the laboratory. Yet within a few months, John was to find himself thousands of miles from academic life in Montreal.

By 1898 the British in southern Africa were settled into three colonies – Natal, the Cape Colony and Rhodesia. The intervening years since the disastrous Jameson Raid had been uneasy ones for both Boers and British. Paul Kruger, president of the Transvaal, had signed an offensive-defensive alliance with the Orange Free State and treatment of the 'Uitlanders' within his republic had become more severe. Rudyard Kipling had been following events with interest and decided to see the Cape Colony for himself. Late in 1898 he took passage for Africa and arrived after a pleasant voyage at the sleepy port of Cape Town. The decision to explore his surroundings led to a chance meeting with Cecil Rhodes, an invitation to Groote Schuur – his Cape Dutch mansion – and a discussion of the vision both men shared of a unified country where the British could settle and make their fortunes.

A new High Commissioner had been appointed to the Cape Colony the previous year whose brief was to negotiate with the Boers. Sir Alfred Milner, a German-trained lawyer and diplomat, was a New Imperialist who recognised before many of his contemporaries that in due time Britain stood to be eclipsed by the growing power of countries like the United States and Germany. Milner approached his task with no preconceptions and only after lengthy and careful analysis did he come to the conclusion that the Uitlander grievances were real and serious. In late May 1899, a conference opened at Bloemfontein at which Milner met Paul Kruger. It was now fairly obvious that, if agreement was not reached to secure a better deal for the Uitlanders, war was a strong possibility. Milner's proposals and Kruger's counter-proposals could not be matched and although negotiations continued, relations deteriorated.

With 'British ambitions all over Africa reaching a peak of energy and fulfilment'[10] Britain's Colonial Secretary, Joseph Chamberlain, regarded the issue as one of British prestige. At home, many people were against the idea of forcibly incorporating the Boer republics into the Empire. However, for those intent on developing the vast material resources of South Africa as a whole, there could be no place for anachronistic opposition. *The Times* sent a young journalist, Leo Amery, to report on the 'peaceful political settlement which they believed in sight'.[11] He met both Milner and Rhodes, finding Milner convinced that Kruger meant war and Rhodes equally convinced that Kruger would back down if the British stood firm. Intent on hearing the Boer viewpoint while there was still time, Amery set out for the Orange Free State. As he crossed the Karoo by train, he marvelled at 'the exhilarating fineness of the pure upland air, the fragrant scent of the crushed herbs underfoot, the vivid blue of the distant peaks, the glories of sunrise and sunset, and the sense of boundless space.'[12] It was a country for horsemen and the Boers were masters in the saddle.

After being assured that the presidents of both Boer Republics desired peace, Amery was given an introduction to the Transvaal Commander-in-Chief, General Piet Joubert. For the next week, he shared the life of his camp and saw that Joubert had potentially 'a very formidable force'.[13] Amery's concern was reinforced when Joubert told him that although he hated war as much as some of the policies of his own people, he would do his duty. As hopes for a peaceful settlement faded, Boer mobilisation began and British troops were moved up to the Transvaal border. Kruger issued an ultimatum on 9 October 1899 demanding their immediate withdrawal. It expired on 11 October and that day, Britain found herself at war with the Boer republics. As Boer commandos crossed the frontier to lay siege to the towns of Ladysmith, Kimberley and Mafeking, Leo Amery squeezed onto the last train carrying refugees to Cape Town. There, he found a cable from *The Times* appointing him their chief war correspondent.

One Canadian watching the build-up to war with considerable interest was William Osler. In England that September of 1899, he and his family were almost at the end of a most enjoyable two-month holiday on the Dorset coast. Osler had visited Britain regularly over the years and was a good friend of Lord Strathcona, who was to fund and give his name to a new Canadian regiment, Lord Strathcona's Horse, that would take part in the coming conflict. Like his illustrious friend, Osler was a strong imperialist who believed that as far as South Africa was concerned, the stake was worth the sacrifice. In Canada, the English-speaking press reported in great detail the events that had led to the outbreak of war. It was in favour of Canadian participation.

The problem facing the British administration in South Africa was that there were few British troops there and those that were found themselves woefully unprepared. Back in Britain a large force was hurriedly assembled and sent on its way to South Africa within the week. The majority of British people viewed the affair as a minor disturbance – as almost all the others in their lifetime had been – that would be over by Christmas. In command of the expeditionary force was General Sir

Redvers Buller, who had won a Victoria Cross in the Zulu War of 1878. After a century of victories won mainly in small colonial conflicts, the British were confident of success and the spirit in which they were going to war was nonchalant. As the troop transports made their way through the heat of the South Atlantic, Buller was amused when another ship signalled him, asking not for news from South Africa but for horse racing results from England.[14] Buller had only 5,000 cavalry under his command, even though the British were aware of Boer prowess on horseback. His regulars, however, were veterans of several previous campaigns and were confident of success. On the face of it, the odds against the Boers were enormous.

By the time the main British force arrived in the Cape at the end of October, the Boer Generals Cronje and Joubert had seized the initiative. The British garrisons in Kimberley and Mafeking were surrounded and Joubert had occupied the whole of Natal north of the Tugela River. At Ladysmith, just two British battalions stood between the Boers and the coastal port of Durban. Leo Amery, who was now in the area, managed to send *The Times* the report of a colleague in the beseiged town of Ladysmith that constituted the first real news of the siege.[15] Buller decided to divide his force into three parts. About half remained under his command and set off for Natal while a contingent under the command of General Lord Methuen was despatched to relieve Kimberley. The remainder, including most of the cavalry, were ordered to contain the threat of a Boer invasion of the Cape Colony.

The Boers, well-armed, daring and fighting on home terrain, proved from the outset to be far tougher opposition than expected. Their army consisted of irregulars – mostly farmers, hunters and trekkers – undisciplined but bound together by a sense of purpose, brotherhood and religious faith. These excellent horsemen were also first-class marksmen using smokeless powder and small-calibre, high-powered magazine rifles. Boer scouts spotted the massive columns of British infantry marching across country. Using the art of concealment and the element of surprise, the Boers inflicted slaughter on the advancing British in sudden and unexpected attacks. What had worked on the Indian frontier proved of little use now and during the first few months the British sustained heavy losses. Shock waves reverberated around a nation that, jingoistic and proud, believed itself to be the strongest in the world.

Britain requested assistance from Australia, New Zealand and Canada. While English-speaking Canadians responded positively out of a sense of duty to the Empire, most French-Canadians regarded it as no concern of theirs and saw it as a kind of British plot to subdue them as a minority people. Prime Minister Wilfrid Laurier's Liberal government, dependent upon French-Canadian votes for its political survival but, at the same time under great pressure from its English-speaking population, was split. Things came to a head when the contents of a telegram from the British Colonial Secretary, Joseph Chamberlain, thanking Canada for its offer of troops, was leaked to the press. Canada had, in fact, not offered troops but the telegram forced the government's hand. After a lengthy cabinet session, the decision was made to raise a force of one thousand Canadian volunteers. Since they would be maintained at British expense, Parliamentary approval was not required and Laurier assured French-Canadians that the decision would not create a precedent for the future. Recruiting appeals met an enthusiastic response and by early November, the 1,155 men who made up the newly-organised 2nd (Special Service) Battalion of the Royal Canadian Regiment were on their way by ship to Cape Town.[16]

With their services excluded from an infantry battalion, the men of Canada's militia, cavalry and artillery units watched the departure of the Royal Canadian Regiment with envy. John McCrae, almost twenty-seven years old and on the brink of his medical career, was unable to rest as he followed events. Despite every prospect of a distinguished future at McGill, he could think of little else but the war. Fired up by his urge for adventure, his sense of duty and his desire to put his military training to the test, he waited impatiently to see if a second contingent would be despatched that would include artillery and cavalry. The possibility that he might miss out left him feeling utterly wretched and he confessed to his mother that:

> ever since this business began, I am certain there has been no 15 minutes of my waking hours that it has not been in my mind . . . I don't suppose you can quite understand it and I'm certain the pater doesn't – he might have, at my age . . . One campaign might cure me – but nothing else ever will, unless it should be old age . . . I am ashamed to say I am doing my work in a merely mechanical way . . . For goodness sake; if there is any way to be devised by which I could get out there, tell me what it is! . . . My position here I do not count as an old boot beside it, nor anything else much, as I think now.[17]

In fact, demands for a second Canadian contingent arose before the first had left. With a federal election in prospect, Canadian politicians decided to use the public's imperialistic fervour to their advantage. The English-language papers in Canada advocated a more substantial contribution to the war and the *Montreal Star* warned that if 'England is crushed, Canada is lost . . . Nothing we can do, no sacrifice we can make, will be one jot too great . . . This is our war'.[18] Any loss of British world power as a result of a defeat in South Africa would leave Canada open to the threat of American imperialism. Canada's concern, both at a possible American invasion and the fact that Britain was not producing the anticipated quick victory in South Africa, led to increased support for a second contingent.

In South Africa, meanwhile, events took a dramatic turn. As 1899 drew to a close, the British suffered three defeats in one week at Magersfontein, Stormberg and Colenso. The events of those disastrous days became known as 'Black Week' and British pride suffered a terrible knock. Leo Amery happened to be a guest at a lunch party being given in Cape Town by Sir Alfred Milner on the day on which news of Colenso was received. Although Milner had been making light of the reverses, this latest blow caused the mask of cheerfulness to disappear.

Buller was replaced as Commander-in-Chief by the 67-year-old Lord Roberts of Kandahar with Lord Kitchener of Khartoum, newly arrived from his posting as Governor General of the Sudan, appointed to be his Chief of Staff. The British government had already declined to accept more Canadian troops, but the devastating effects of 'Black Week' made them reconsider and Joseph Chamberlain informed the Canadian Governor General, The Earl of Minto, that the British government had changed its mind. Two months of fighting the Boers had brought home the need for small, mobile units composed of mounted men who were very good shots with a rifle. The Canadian Chief of Staff was a British officer, General E.T.H. Hutton. He was particularly proud of the Canadian artillery which was often complimented by British officers for being the most efficient arm in the tiny military establishment and he pressed Ottawa to despatch a force of cavalry and artillery to South Africa. On 21 December the government announced that it would send three squadrons of mounted rifles, a brigade of field artillery and a squadron of mounted scouts with a total strength of some 1,230 men, 1,124 horses and eighteen artillery pieces.

John McCrae received the news with a mixture of excitement and relief. Encouraged by his medical colleagues and with the blessing of Professor Adami, who arranged for his Fellowship at McGill to be postponed for a year, he set off for Guelph. The town had now grown into a city and its recruiting centre was busy. The second contingent's brigade of artillery was under the command of Lieutenant-Colonel Charles Drury, an officer in the small regular Canadian army. A militia order was issued on 29 December 1899 naming the officers selected for the new contingent and Lieutenant John McCrae was assigned to command the right section of D Battery. The local paper decided that 'McCrae – both from his proficiency as a soldier and knowledge and skill in medicine – should make a model officer for service in South Africa.'[19] The three batteries of the artillery brigade, C, D and E, mobilised at Kingston, Ottawa and Quebec respectively. Fifty-four men from Guelph, many of them chums, former classmates, working colleagues and relatives, joined D Battery under Major W.G. Hurdman, a militia officer from Ottawa. Once the men had been mustered and organised into batteries, they spent two weeks being drilled and trained in rifle shooting and horsemanship. Drury directed his officers to provide themselves with maps and recommended books on South Africa, emphasising that it 'is a matter of the greatest importance for Officers to understand thoroughly the history and characteristics of the inhabitants, and the nature of the country in which warlike operations are being undertaken.'[20]

When the day of departure arrived, the Mayor of Guelph proclaimed a half-holiday and the local people turned out to give their men a huge send-off. John paraded them and, after having their photograph taken, listening to the inevitable speeches, receiving copies of the New Testament and watching John being presented with a set of field glasses, the volunteers set out for the railway station. Guelph was immensely proud: the streets were decorated with bunting, fireworks were let off in the town square and a great bonfire lit on the frozen river near the station. An official procession accompanied the volunteers for South Africa who had difficulty reaching the station through the throng of well-wishers. The gunners of Guelph could not have asked for a finer display of support.

On 15 January 1900, seen off from Ottawa by The Earl of Minto and large crowds, the 174 men and six guns of D Battery, Royal Canadian Field Artillery[21] left for the Nova Scotian port of Halifax. The train that carried them was cheered at every point along its route and, on their arrival, Halifax did its best to give the men of the second contingent an equally warm welcome. John and some of the other officers were billeted in the comfort of the Queen's Hotel. Large, rambling and well appointed, its shaded roof garden offered a commanding view of the harbour and its excellent cuisine made it a popular haunt for visiting politicians. The lieutenant-governor[22] of the province held a reception and the Methodist Church sponsored a turkey dinner for all ranks. The following evening while the officers dined at the Royal Artillery Mess, the men attended a smoking concert at the town's new Armoury, now being used as headquarters for the South African volunteers. Local people soon became used to the sight of the khaki or dark blue serge uniforms and pillbox hats of the artillery. Dress uniform for the mounted troops consisted of a blue coat with a standing collar trimmed with white facings and dark crimson sleeve braid, long tight trousers, a stetson hat, puttees, ankle boots and spurs. The whole effect helped to create a popular image of fearless frontiersmen and rough riders, but in reality the majority of men were largely eastern urban blue and white collar workers.

The task of loading men, guns, horses and equipment onto the three ships that were to take them on their transatlantic voyage was considerable. John and D Battery were to sail on the *Laurentian*, a former passenger liner belonging to the Allan Line. The gunners were inspected and addressed by the lieutenant-governor, senior officers and the Minister of Militia before they marched past the crowds lining the route to the docks. Travelling with them were four Canadian nurses, among the first to serve overseas as members of the new Canadian Nursing Service. In a crowd of wellwishers, the men from Guelph were pleased to see one of the city's prominent businessmen, Mr J.G. Sully of the Raymond Manufacturing Company. Sully, who was a friend of David McCrae, chanced to be in Halifax on business and went on board the ship. John wrote a last letter to his mother before the *Laurentian* sailed:

My dear Mater,
We had a great send off & are all on board. The Leinsters & the Garrison bands played us off with 'The girl I left behind me!' & 'Auld Lang Syne' and 'God Save the Queen'. I can't exactly describe it all: it is such a jumble, but here we are. Gen[eral]. Hutton said to me this a.m. re my section 'You have a very fine body of men there'. The Armouries were packed to see us off: I had one or two old friends on hand – the Randolphs from Fredericton.

We have Ewan on board, I am glad to say: we have foregathered already, on the strength of his knowing father: we have 1 chaplain, 4 nurses (that rather breaks up the mess, a bit).

I got pater's telegram, & others from the Mayor, (Nelson), the Nelsons of Montreal, Walter Gow: Miss Stanley (of Lucan, Ont[ario]) a friend of Mrs. Craig, Miss Taylor from Vancouver (a far cry): the [Johns] Hopkins Canadians & old Tom.

I shall go in for news later: for I want to get several notes off tomorrow by the pilot.

We have had very hard work here & we are glad to see the last of Halifax. I am glad to say I am as fit as can be: & I know you will be glad. Heavy rain to-day: misty: a very poetical scene, as the boat moved off . . . Thank Geills for her last letter. One from Hattie Chaplin got me on the boat. Everybody has been so good.

Good-bye, dear Mother. Love to pater & Geills. I shall write Tom.
Yours lovingly
Jack[23]

That day, John's family was very much on his mind. With his letter, he sent his mother a sealed envelope marked 'to be opened if anything unforeseen should happen'.[24]

An excellent diarist, John kept a detailed account of the voyage. The ship was soon christened 'The Rolling Polly' on account of the fact that it 'swaggered along in a very unladylike style' rather like 'a giddy old maid in her first bathing suit.'[25] As a consequence there was widespread seasickness. John managed to avoid it but became concerned about the welfare of the many fine horses. Poor ventilation and overcrowding was a constant problem and despite best efforts, some two dozen animals were lost during the voyage. Shipboard life was very busy and once calmer waters were reached, the officers and men settled into an active if monotonous shipboard routine of drill, signal practice, lectures, sentry duty and other tasks. Major Hurdman organised talks on gunnery, ammunition, signalling, husbandry and the South African campaign to date. John's own duties included orderly officer, officer of the day, supervision of stable duty, drills, signalling practice and work on the guns. There were also social functions to organise – sports, attendance at church parades and afternoon tea on deck every afternoon at five, at which the nurses in their long skirts, high-necked blouses and straw boaters, presided. With 'the best piper of the Royal Scots on board' and 'a small orchestra who play not badly but sing better', evening concerts also proved popular.[26] One of the first orders issued on board ship was that there was to be no shaving. After a week everyone was looking so disreputable that jokes at the mess table were frequent and it 'was suggested by Lieut[enant]. McCrae that we all shave our upper lip a la Kruger, before landing at Cape Town'.[27]

As John had mentioned in his letter to his mother, the second contingent was accompanied by John Ewan, a reporter from the *Toronto Globe* newspaper whom David McCrae knew personally. There was also another non-combatant on board – a monkey named 'Jacko' who was the battery mascot and whose antics were irrepressible. John noted in his diary on 26 January 1900 that 'Jacko' is 'getting to be a great nuisance and appears everywhere making havoc,' including chewing 'the book of Jeremiah out of Major Hurdman's Bible and various other pranks.'[28] Lieutenant Edward Morrison, a fellow officer and future life-long friend of John, also recorded 'Jacko's' antics:

He got down the major's field glasses, took them out of the case and is alleged to have been peering out of the porthole with them when apprehended. He also developed a taste for military literature, and digested portions of the Queen's regulations and several drill books.[29]

The nights were now often warm enough for the officers to sleep on deck and several sat up to observe the Pole Star and the Southern Cross. John's diary for 27 January 1900 recorded a

Beautiful sunset tonight at sea: all the bugles blow Retreat at sundown, giving a very pretty effect. Stars are exceedingly bright . . . I have just been out taking the picket. In the stables, the long row of heads in the half darkness, the creaking of the ship, the shivering of the hull to the vibration of the engines. Then up on deck forward – the sky half covered with scudding clouds, the stars bright in the intervals . . . and looking aft, the funnel with a track of smoke trailing off into the darkness on the starboard quarter . . . the masts drawing maps across the sky . . . if you have ever been there, you know it all.[30]

On the night of 29 January he saw 'a magnificent meteor' which 'was in view for fully 15 seconds – quite the biggest I ever saw. The S[outhern]. Cross came into view last night.'[31] John also recorded phosphorescence, whales and flying fish.

Despite winds and high seas, the *Laurentian* made good time. On 31 January she called at the coaling station on the Cape Verde Islands, described by John Ewan, the *Toronto Globe* reporter, as 'savage, solitary and enchanting'.[32] A view of the islands from the sea featured among the several sketches John had time to produce on the journey. Crossing the Equator involved the usual shipboard fun, but as the ship approached the Cape, the pace of work speeded up in preparation for arrival. At 5.00 a.m. on 16 February, John awoke to his first sighting of Table Mountain. The *Laurentian* docked in Table Bay alongside over a hundred ships, many of which sounded their whistles and steam sirens in greeting. The local people sent fruit on board and the nurses received bouquets of carnations and roses. As the Canadians came ashore, they found an atmosphere of excitement over the news that the day before, Kimberley, where Cecil Rhodes had been sequestered in his own diamond fields, had been the first of the three towns under Boer siege to be relieved.

John's first impressions of Cape Town were of a town that hummed with excitement. The Canadians found it to be a picturesque, quaint old place with buildings of many architectural styles and streets of hard-packed dried mud. Edward Morrison observed that along these streets the 'people stroll in shoals . . . and are a brilliant throng even in the moonlight, with their white dresses, red and yellow turbans and fezs. All the hansom cabs are gorgeously painted and gilded and bear such names as "Dashing and Bold", "Napoleon the First", "Swift and Sure".'[33] John and Morrison spent a pleasant hour on the cool verandah of the City Club looking down over the city and harbour. The docks were continually full of vessels bearing the colours of most of the world's major shipping lines. 'The harbor as I see it from my seat . . . is a perfect picture of colour,' John wrote, 'it is just sunset & I see 8 steamers, with splashes of color on their stacks & white hulls & spars,' while the 'surf beats constantly so that one can hear it, and the breeze from the sea is delightful.'[34]

Soldiers from all corners of the Empire crowded Cape Town's busy streets by day and night and D Battery was given a great ovation as it marched through the town centre. Social functions were frequent and the chance to mingle with some of the famous British regiments gave John a sense of comradeship and exhilaration at being part of the great machine of Empire. Away from the town, the Cape was an area of rich vegetation. Under the brilliant blue sky palm trees thrived and orchards were lush with peaches, quinces, mangoes and other fruits. Gardens burgeoned with gaudy flowers and the air carried the aromatic scent of pine and eucalyptus. In the brightness of the day or the night sky turned brilliant with stars, Canada seemed a world away.

The Canadian Artillery units moved into camp just three hundred yards from the seashore at Green Point under Table Mountain, where they were to spend the next two weeks while the horses recovered from their sea voyage. Colonel Drury lost no time in preparing his men for action and they worked so hard that sleep was a positive luxury. Off duty, John and his fellow officers continued to cut quite a dash in their stetsons. The Canadian gunners were especially popular with the locals who warmed to their quiet, businesslike approach and admired both their horsemanship and their large horses. Many of the inhabitants of Cape Town turned out to watch a military sports afternoon in which the gunners' powerful tug-of-war team beat the sailors from the fleet.[35] Despite the hard work and lack of creature comforts, John took to his new life. He wrote to his mother about the long hours of preparation they were undergoing:

> You have no idea of the <u>work</u>. Section commanders <u>live</u> with their sections, – the right way. It makes long hours & I never knew a softer bed than the ground is these nights . . . I really enjoy every moment though there is anxiety. We have lost all our spare horses and have enough to turn out the battery and no more.[36]

The British blunders and defeats that had characterised the first part of the war were now being reversed by Lord Roberts' second phase. With a completely new strategy and new troops, he had drawn up a plan to assemble an army on the Modder River, advance northwards outflanking the Boer General Piet Cronje's commandos at Magersfontein, and invade the Transvaal and Orange Free State. Buller and his troops would remain on the defensive in Natal. Using tactics that had included the sending of false messages, Roberts and his force succeeded in surprising Cronje and caught up with him at Paardeberg Drift. With Cronje in a defensive position along the river bank awaiting reinforcements, the British began a frontal attack on 18 February that was to last for the next ten days. Eight days later six companies of the Royal Canadian Regiment made a night attack, and amid casualties and some confusion, four companies retreated. The two that remained saw at first light next day that the Boers were ready to surrender. Their part in this victory helped to establish the Canadian soldier's reputation as a fighting man.

As Lord Roberts continued towards Bloemfontein, in Cape Town John McCrae's path was about to cross that of a man who had become one of his heroes. With the Boers 'in their last encampment' and the British 'at the apogee of their imperial advance',[37] war in South Africa was something Rudyard Kipling had anticipated for some time. He was optimistic of a quick British victory and hopeful that his country would seize this golden opportunity to rehearse for the war with Germany that he could already visualise. Accompanied by his wife, two children, a nanny and a governess, he set out once again for Cape Town. They stayed at the busy Mount Nelson Hotel and soon found themselves table companions of Leo Amery. Lord Roberts invited Kipling to join the staff of *The Friend*, a newspaper for the troops containing news, army notices and articles of fiction. With the job came a pass to go anywhere he liked and this was used to good effect. In an effort to boost morale and find out about conditions at first-hand, he went to some of the military hospitals with supplies of tobacco for the soldiers.

On the day before the military sports afternoon, his bespectacled figure could be seen around the lines of the 1st Brigade, RCFA. Most of the officers and men were so busy that they didn't notice him but one of the drivers recognised Kipling from newspaper photographs and told his officer. To John McCrae and many of the other Canadians, the chance to meet one of the most famous men in the Empire was not something that any of them wanted to miss. After the sports had finished, Edward Morrison, Chaplain Cox, the padre, and John set off on horseback to try and find 'the little great man'[38] at the Mount Nelson Hotel.

Set in beautiful gardens, the Mount Nelson had opened just six months before the outbreak of the war and was to all intents a 'bit of London in South Africa'.[39] Offering the latest facilities and lavishly furnished with an eye for artistic detail, it presented the atmosphere of an elegant country retreat, 'an oasis of quiet dignity and gracious living'.[40] After tethering their horses in the hotel courtyard, the three Canadians found themselves in a reception hall with cosy settees, flowering plants and a supply of the latest British and colonial newspapers and magazines. A glance into the splendid dining room with its striking art nouveau ceiling, revealed white-gloved, turbanned waiters and a tailcoated maître d'hôtel moving unobtrusively among the potted palms. The war had put the hotel firmly on the map and it was thriving, booked solid with 'journalists, sightseers, adventurers, wives, sweethearts and all manner of camp-followers'.[41] It was also a great gathering place for millionaires, politicians, war correspondents and writers, such as the one John McCrae and his colleagues were seeking.

As they strolled around, the Canadians discovered a young subaltern relaxing in the rotunda, who turned out to be Lord Woolverton. He told them he was personally acquainted with Kipling and would be happy to introduce them, but on this particular occasion they had missed him by half an hour. Since the three were due to return later to dine with Ewan of the *Toronto Globe*, they decided to take a ride around the city. Just as they were leaving, they learned that Kipling had unexpectedly returned and was in the hotel office. Edward Morrison later recalled the scene as they found him, immediately recognisable and dressed in a khaki-coloured suit. 'We Canadian gunners stood afar off and devoured him with our eyes as we thought of all the good half-hours he had given us reading his works,'[42] but, after a friendly glance was cast in their direction, the Canadian with the most nerve approached him to explain that they had missed seeing him the previous day. Kipling laughed:

'That is all right,' he said. 'I heard you cursing considerable' (he did not know one of the trio was the chaplain because the latter was wearing a lieutenant's uniform) 'and I could tell you were up to your eyes in work licking things into shape to get to the front and not wanting to be bothered with visitors, so I did not wish to interrupt.'[43]

John McCrae's diary for 22 February 1900 recorded the meeting with the man whom he described as 'the high priest of it all':[44]

He told us a few things about up country. He is charmingly free and easy – says up country is Hell! Asked a good deal about our corps. Said he had been up in camp but thought from our appearance we were not 'receiving'. He was dressed in kharkee [sic], is short & rather round faced – with the glasses on as usual. We were all delighted to meet him.[45]

Kipling had already seen the poor sanitary arrangements for the soldiers and was appalled at the numbers who were dying of disease. A great advocate of preventive measures, he advised the three Canadians to 'look out for the water and don't drink any that has not been first boiled. The worst difficulty you will have is in keeping your men from it. The only way to do it is to fine them.'[46]

Their memorable meeting ended with Kipling wishing them well and saying he would probably see them at Kimberley. He knew about the kind of country they were going to be fighting in. It was a world of hazy blue skies and distant rifle fire; of hot days and bitter cold nights;

of drought, deluges, sandstorms, hunger and disease. A few days later D Battery received orders to move up to the front.

NOTES

1. From 'The Warrior' by John McCrae, *The University Magazine* (Volume 6, No. 4, December 1907), p. 454. Micro mfm/AP/U577, UTL.
2. JM to David McCrae, 21 August 1897, MG30 D209, Micro A-1109, NAC
3. J.G. Adami, 'Obituary of John McCrae', *British Medical Journal*, 9 February 1918, pp. 190–191.
4. Prescott, *In Flanders Fields*, p.25.
5. Harvey Cushing, *The Life of Sir William Osler* (Oxford, 1925), Volume I, p. 461.
6. Cushing, *Sir William Osler*, Volume I, p. 463.
7. John F. Fulton, *Harvey Cushing* (Springfield, Illinois, 1946), p. 118.
8. Prescott, *In Flanders Fields*, p. 43.
9. Marie Adami. *J. George Adami: A Memoir* (London, 1925), p. 149.
10. Jan Morris, *Farewell the Trumpets* (London 1979), p. 67.
11. L.S. Amery, *Days of Fresh Air: Being Reminiscences of Outdoor Life* (London, 1939), p. 120.
12. Amery, *Days of Fresh Air*, p. 126.
13. Amery, *Days of Fresh Air*, p. 134.
14. Morris, *Farewell the Trumpets*, p. 64.
15. Amery, *Days of Fresh Air*, p. 143.
16. In order to placate French-Canadians who were largely set against what they regarded as a British 'adventure', the Canadian troops sent to South Africa were all officially classified as volunteers and not part of either the permanent or militia components of the Canadian military establishment. In actual fact, most of the units raised for service in South Africa had a stiffening of regulars and drew the bulk of their recruits from existing English-speaking militia units. Calling them 'special service' volunteers that were not officially part of either the permanent or militia force was a convenient fiction and a classic Canadian compromise to ameliorate the quite different attitudes of the francophone and anglophone segments of the Dominion.
17. JM to Janet McCrae, 8 November 1899, MG 30, D209, Micro A-1109, NAC.
18. Carman Miller, *Painting the Map Red: Canada and the South African War*, 1899–1902 (Ottawa, 1993), p. 154.
19. Undated (circa 29 December 1899) newspaper article, assumed to be *Guelph Mercury*, Boer War Ledger, MH.
20. Orders by Lieutenant-Colonel F.G. Stone, Commanding Brigade Division. Field Artillery for Special Service. Kingston 4 January 1900. Section 5, 'Books'. RG9, IIA3, Vol. 32. Micro T-10404, NAC.
21. In 1899, the regular units of the Canadian artillery were designated either Royal Canadian Horse Artillery (actually field artillery) or Royal Canadian Garrison Artillery (coast artillery). The militia units, which did not win the 'Royal' prefix until the First World War were designated Canadian Field Artillery or Canadian Garrison Artillery. D Battery, nominally a volunteer unit raised for special service not belonging officially to either the regular or militia organisation was designated Royal Canadian Field Artillery.
22. In provincial Canadian government, the office of lieutenant-governor carries

59

with it 'all the formal, prerogative and discretionary powers exercised by the monarch or Governor General'. The appointment is made by the Governor General upon the advice of the Prime Minister. The usual term is five years but this is often extended. (*The Canadian Encyclopaedia*, Volume II, p. 1006).

23. JM to Janet McCrae, 20 January 1900, GM Papers.

24. Undated letter (circa 1919) from Janet McCrae to Sir Andrew Macphail, MG 30 D150, NAC.

25. Edward W.B. Morrison, *With the Guns in South Africa* (Hamilton, 1901), p. 26.

26. JM to Janet McCrae, 25 January 1900, MG 30, D209, Micro A-1102, NAC.

27. Morrison, *With the Guns*, p. 29.

28. JM Diary of South African War, 26 January 1900, MG 30, D209, Micro A-1102, NAC.

29. Morrison, *With the Guns*, p. 31.

30. JM Diary of South African War, 27 January 1900, MG 30, D209, Micro A-1102, NAC.

31. JM to Janet McCrae, 30 January 1900, MG 30, D209, Micro A-1102, NAC.

32. Article by John Ewan, *Toronto Globe*, 1 February 1900, Boer War Ledger, MH.

33. Morrison, *With the Guns*, p. 47.

34. JM to Janet McCrae, 3 March 1900, MG 30, D209, Micro A-1102, NAC.

35. Morrison, *With the Guns*, p. 51.

36. JM to Janet McCrae, 25 February 1900, MG 30, D209, Micro A-1102, NAC.

37. Jan Morris, *Farewell the Trumpets*, p.68.

38. Morrison, *With the Guns*, p.52.

39. Elaine Hurford, *The Mount Nelson: In Grand Tradition* (Cape Town, 1992), p. 17.

40. Hurford, *The Mount Nelson*, p. 9.

41. Hurford, *The Mount Nelson*, pp. 18-19.

42. Morrison, *With the Guns*, p. 53.

43. Morrison, *With the Guns*, p. 54.

44. JM to Janet McCrae, 25 February 1900, MG 30, D209, Micro A-1102, NAC.

45. JM Diary of South African War, 2 February 1900, MG 30, D209, Micro A-1102, NAC.

46. Morrison, *With the Guns*, p. 54.

CHAPTER FIVE

'That day of battle in the dusty heat'[1]
1900–1901

On Saturday, 4 March 1900, the centre and right sections of D Battery left Cape Town by train, their departure having been delayed by a shortage of rail trucks. Cape Town was jubilant at news of the long-expected relief of Ladysmith and spirits were high at the station as the Canadians watched the arrival of Boer prisoners of war. The first part of their journey took them past the familiar whitewashed Cape Dutch farmhouses, orchards and vineyards and into mountain scenery that grew finer and bolder. Crowds welcomed the train at every stop plying the soldiers with fruit, but gradually these demonstrations of enthusiasm ceased and the population farther along the route became more sullen as the train moved onwards into pro-Boer territory. The mountains finally gave way to a vast, flat landscape of stone and scrub, where the distant, rocky, cloud-topped hills looked as if they had been painted a subtle shade of blue and the heat haze made everything seem even more remote.

The battery's initial destination was Victoria Road, a station about four hundred miles north east of Cape Town on the railway line from the Cape to Kimberley. The relief of Kimberley and now Ladysmith, the capture of Cronje's men and Lord Roberts' successful advance on Bloemfontein had intimidated many Boers into returning to their farms. There were, however, still some two thousand armed Boers in the region looting and destroying property. The need to protect the rail link was vital and Colonel Sir Charles Parsons had been charged with leading one of three columns intended to suppress a Boer force just west of the De Aar-Belmont section of the railway. Parsons' column, comprising Imperial Yeomanry and troops from New Zealand, Australia and Canada, was ordered to approach from the south. The route would take them from Victoria Road west to the town of Carnarvon and thence to the town of Kenhart – a distance of 280 miles in total. With two other columns closing in from the centre and north, the British planned to drive the Boers into a net.

Under an escort of New Zealand Mounted Rifles, the men of D Battery and 'Jacko' the monkey reached Victoria West on 6 March to find that the five hundred Boers said to have been there a few days earlier were now some twenty miles farther away. They spent the next

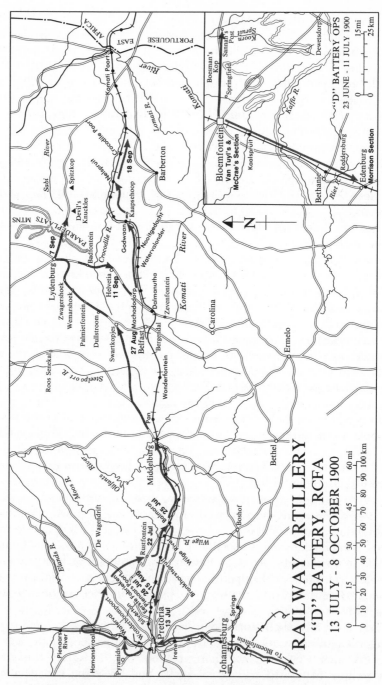

'D' Battery, Royal Canadian Field Artillery operations,
13 July–8 October, 1900

six days in this pleasant farming village in a valley, where the worst they encountered was a dust storm, lizards, alligator-like beetles and the nocturnal signalling of Boers in the hills. News reached them that the centre of the three British columns had been repelled by a Boer attack and Lord Kitchener himself had set out in force to stamp out the problem. D Battery, meanwhile, prepared to cross the Karoo on the next leg of its journey to Carnarvon. With oxen and mules pulling the supply wagons, the column could average little more than three miles per hour. Fortunately for the officers and men, they had been issued with goggles which proved to be a godsend when they encountered a blinding sandstorm. On 13 March, John recorded in his diary that he had seen 'Wonderful clouds of millions of locusts, looking like dust at a distance . . . Clouds lasted for an hour or more and could be seen lining the horizon.'[2] Edward Morrison described them as so thick 'they looked like a rusty fog.'[3]

John Ewan, the journalist from the *Toronto Globe*, caught up with the column as it reached Carnarvon on 17 March, exhausted and short of water. The British flag was much in evidence. Houses and public offices were decorated with bunting and the women of the district had prepared 'gallons of tea and mountains of cake'[4] for the hungry and thirsty troops. The soldiers learned that their advance was having an effect and the rebels were fleeing. 'Before we came,' Ewan wrote, 'we were told by the real loyalists of Carnarvon that rebel feeling was gaining headway, but the sight of these guns, with the husky fellows seated on the limbers, had a distinctly tonic effect.'[5] A compulsory church parade was held next day in the worst of the heat. John had to confess to his mother that it was 'a hot business standing up in [a] hollow square in the blinding sunshine' and as for attempting to keep clean, he told her that, 'a sight for the gods, was Eaton[6] and myself bathing in a puddle that would compare with any stagnant puddle you ever saw.'[7]

The rebels were now reported to be heading up country towards Kenhart and Parsons decided to divide his troops into two columns. A small flying column consisting of a squadron each of Canadian Mounted Rifles, New Zealand Mounted Rifles, West Australian Mounted Infantry and John's right section of D Battery was ordered to hurry towards Kenhart. Here it would hopefully surprise the rebels and join up with the centre column. The remaining troops and supplies would follow on as quickly as possible.

The misery of a dust storm that blew down tents and covered everything – including food – in a thin layer of sand, was just the start of two gruelling weeks for the flying column. In the Karoo, changes in the weather happened with great speed and blistering sun gave way to sheet lightning and torrential rain for the next three days. Streams were transformed into rushing cataracts and roads into rivers of mud.

The column had to halt for a day as the transport wagons floundered through water courses. Forage for the horses became scarce and with accommodation at a premium, the officers had to spend the night in a local jail. On 21 March, the column reached the deserted settlement of Van Wyk's Vlei, from which the elusive rebels had once again flown a day or two before. Consisting of a dozen or so flat-roofed, mud-brick buildings spread over the base of a barren valley, it reminded Edward Morrison of 'the sun baked bottom of a dry mud puddle.'[8] The officers used a local house as their Mess and had a singsong round the piano that evening. In this remote place it seemed strange to John to hear 'waltzes; . . . in a room lit by a candle stuck in a jam tin; I could not refrain from remarking . . . that it was a far-cry to the Yacht Club Ball.'[9] He described his march to his cousin, Walter Gow:

Here I am with my first <u>command</u>! Each place we strike is a little more God-forsaken than the last – and this place wins up to date . . . Jack, my horse is doing well, though he is thin. The night before last on the road we halted, & I dismounted for a minute. When we started to go on, I pulled on the reins but no answer. The poor old cuss was fast asleep in his tracks, and in about thirty seconds too.

It really is <u>awful</u>ly hard work this continuous marching. The men on every halt just drop down on the road & sleep till they are kicked up again in 10 minutes. Poor devils! they do it willingly, too. I am C[commanding]. O[fficer]., adjutant, officer on duty, & all the rest since we left the others. Talk about 'the army in Flanders'! You should hear this battery. I always knew soldiers could swear, but you ought to hear these fellows.[10]

In his next letter dated 24 March 1900 he was daydreaming of the good things of home: 'wouldn't I just like to sit down to tea with you all: I think of Geills' whipped cream and strawberry jam and <u>lots</u> of bread & butter. Hooray! Some day it will come.'[11]

Two days later, John's diary recorded that 'there is a bad swamp just ahead of us. Guide says this is worst rain in 10 years.'[12] When the column reached De Naauwte near the Olifantsvlei River, it was forced to wait, with no shelter, for the rain to cease. When the hot sun re-appeared, the streams dried as quickly as they had formed but it still took seven hours to get horses, men and equipment across the swamp which was some fifteen hundred yards wide. John rode back and forth helping the men and, on one occasion, had a narrow escape:

Jack stumbled & fell on top of me, with my leg below him. Three times I tried to struggle out. I got put under each time & though the water was not more than 1½ or 2 feet deep I couldn't get up. Finally 2 C[anadian]

M[outed] R[ifles] men got me & pulled me on my feet and another held up Jack's head till he got his wits & could get up . . . I am very thankful that we both escaped. I was pretty well mired up when I got free. Jack got a good fright & fairly quaked the next time he came through.[13]

According to Edward Morrison, John had come close to drowning but, typically, he refused to rest and continued his duties as if nothing had happened.[14] When there was work to be done, no matter how unpleasant, John McCrae was there to help and encourage his men.

Although short of rations, the Canadians were cheerful. By marching at night the flying column was averaging anything up to thirty miles a day. The images that stayed with John were of vivid sunsets and soft dawns; the night sky bright with a myriad stars; the misty purple groove of the hills; the flickering of bivouac fires; the steady plodding of the oxen and the scurrying of khaki figures. He observed the Karoo's native bushes interspersed with a succulent, bitter tasting shrub and the creatures which lived in this barren region: jackals, hyenas, small brown lizards, scorpions, herds of goats and snakes, such as puff adders and an occasional deadly black mamba. The area's moods and effects fascinated him, particularly the 'mirage of the African desert' which 'we often saw; it is a strange shimmering light, far off toward the horizon, which resembles a huge lake . . . With evening, the desert seems, if possible, more silent than by day; the stars come out with beautiful clearness.' John particularly enjoyed the dawn, those 'hours of the morning, at day-break' which 'make one glad of life, and a thousand bits of light and shade, of plain or kopje,[15] recall, by glorious contrast, days when one dwelt in cities and knew not if the sun shone by day, or the moon by night.'[16]

The supply column which followed had fallen badly behind. On minimal rations and suffering a dysentery epidemic, it had to endure a further ten days of torrid heat and drenching rain at Van Wyk's Vlei before the river subsided sufficiently for it to cross. Approaching Kenhart, meanwhile, the flying column was running short of food and starting to lose some of its exhausted horses. The area round Kenhart had been annexed by the Boers as part of the Orange Free State but, as the column entered the town at 5.00 p.m. on 31 March 1900, there was not a Boer to be seen. After a rough and rainy night, Sir Charles Parsons formally raised the Union Jack the following morning marking the re-annexation of the Kenhart district to the Cape Colony. The troops presented arms and gave three cheers for Queen and Empire. The loyalists, who now felt safe, thought that the brass 'RCFA' flash on the gunners' uniforms, which stood for Royal Canadian Field Artillery, actually meant 'Rebel Chasers from America'.

The hardships of marching now began to catch up with D Battery. They had become accustomed to drinking 'brown scummy water (to be drunk while holding the breath, for obvious reasons)' and eating 'wheat crushed on flat stones, and made into saltless flapjacks' and 'mutton, boiled two hours after killing.'[17] John admitted he had grown very tired of his monotonous fare, added to which 'the stench of dead horse when the wind falls at night' was not, he decided, 'a pleasant accompaniment to one's meals'.[18] There was a lot of rheumatism among the men and twenty-five of them became ill with dysentery because the Canadians could not get sufficient utensils to boil all their water. Morale was also suffering for, although they were in rebel country, they were getting no real opportunity to fight. Some of the men got drunk and had to be confined to camp after looting broke out in the town. Yet in spite of the hardships and problems John was enjoying himself. He wrote in a letter to his father that, although it was impossible to keep clean, his uniform was dirty and he had been unable to shine his boots for weeks, he was finding it, 'a great life . . . I am as brown as a berry – brown-black in fact; and weighed a week ago 162½ so I am pretty fit.'[19]

Kitchener's efforts to drive the rebels into the arms of the northern column and prevent their escape across the Orange River had not been successful and when the central and northern force met up, the net was empty. With his supplies almost exhausted, General Settle, commander of the northern column, was persuaded by his Canadian Intelligence Officer, Colonel Sam Hughes, to march north to pick up supplies at Upington. The intrepid, resourceful Hughes and a group of scouts engineered a further Boer retreat by fooling the enemy into thinking there was a large force immediately behind them.

April in the southern hemisphere is the harbinger of colder weather. The supply column and main force of the flying column were ordered back to the base camp at De Aar but sickness, food shortage and the pitiful condition of the horses were to make it a gruelling journey. D Battery was now split up: Morrison and the left section remained with the main part of the flying column; the centre section was despatched to the Orange River while John McCrae's right section was ordered to Victoria Road Station to guard the railway line. Setting off under a blazing sun, John wrote to his mother on 10 April that:

> We shall certainly have done a good march when we get to the railroad, 478 miles through a country desolate of forage . . . For two days running we had 9 hours in the saddle without food . . . My throat was very sore & swollen for a day or two, and I felt so sorry for myself at times that I laughed to think how I must have looked – sitting on a stone . . . drinking a pannekin of tea . . . and eating a shapeless lump of brown bread (don't show me brown bread when I get home); my one 'hank' tied around my neck, – and serving as a bandage alternately . . . it is miserable to have a head like a buzz saw, – and the sun good and

hot, and 'gargle' in one's water bottle . . . It is after nightfall that the thirst really seems to <u>devour</u> one – it actually gnaws then: and I think of all the cool drinks I could get at home, and the good things to eat. Cold roast beef cut thin aggravates me very frequently: I can almost smell it.[20]

By 13 April, Good Friday, they had passed through Carnarvon again but it was now raining hard and there was little shelter from the weather for several nights. For the horses and mules, the going was very hard but through John's care, his section lost fewer horses than other units. John and his men arrived at Victoria West on 17 April and settled into their new camp. It was to be a life characterised by guard duty, cold nights and the continuous smell of camp fires for which the universal fuel was sheep manure with its 'very strong, unpleasant odor – that is simply infernal.'[21] Like their daily routine, their diet continued to be monotonous, described by John as 'soup, tough mutton, bread without butter, and tea or coffee.' He confessed to his mother that 'Two nights ago I dreamt I ate a first class breakfast right through.'[22]

Nevertheless, the life still appeared to suit him. He was physically fit and his asthma had evidently not re-appeared for he informed his mother: 'My old enemy has never even hinted his presence since I left home and he scarcely ever crosses my mind now.'[23] A few days later, John relayed to his mother that:

Since I last wrote, we have been at Vict[oria]. Road . . . hoping for orders to move, but they have not yet come. Most of the other troops have left. D Squadron C[anadian]. M[ounted]. R[ifles]. my messmates for the past 5 w[ee]ks, have left and I am an orphan . . . They, (in the kindness of their hearts) say that if I get stranded, they will do the best they can to get a troop for me in the Squadron or some such employment. Impracticable but kind. I have no wish to cease to be a gunner, however.[24]

Reports came back down the line that E Battery of the Canadian artillery, part of a force chasing the Boers north of the Orange River, had acquitted themselves extremely well when caught in a surprise attack at the Battle of Faber's Put. The young Canadian gunners had kept their cool under fire, encouraged by the daredevil Colonel Sam Hughes, who not long before the battle had paid a visit to John's section of D Battery and informally inspected their camp. At Faber's Put, with seeming disregard for his own safety, Hughes fired point-blank at the enemy and passed along E Battery's line with the shout: 'Never mind me, boys; give them beans',[25] and the gunners had done just that. This time however, his forays in search of Boer prisoners and his publicised comments on the conduct of the battle were to land him in trouble. Although his fellow countrymen in South Africa admired Hughes, their enthusiasm was not shared by senior British commanders, particularly after, having been charged with a mission to search for the commando of the Boer leader, De Villiers, and negotiate nothing less than its 'wholly unconditional surrender', Hughes returned having captured only part of it.[26] He was ordered to the Cape to explain his actions and within a short time, the controversial freelance Canadian was on his way home. In later years, his obvious talents, bellicosity and impetuous approach were part of the drive that would carry him to prominence.

At Victoria Road, John McCrae continued to work his men hard, believing firmly that it benefited both morale and discipline. He was a hero to one young gunner in his section, Walter Bapty, who was to follow his example and become a doctor. Bapty's memories of John were of 'a slim studiously minded young lieutenant' whose subordinates loved him for the 'friendly, warm-hearted man' that he was. John was always quick to provide medical care for his men – Bapty recalled that on 'on one occasion I called upon his surgical training to remove a deeply embedded needle from my hand. This he did skilfully but gently and with understanding.'[27] Time spent guarding the railway line gave John an opportunity to study the system in operation with its Dutch engines that he described as resembling '"shunters", in that they carry the coal in the cab, and the water-tanks on the boiler.'[28] While the Canadians could only watch and wait, trains passed by carrying other troops and such noteworthies as Lady Roberts and the Duke of Norfolk. John's letters home left his mother in no doubt of what he thought about his posting. He spent a good deal of time alone in what he termed 'this villainous little roost'[29] where he decided 'it is a great thing to be on speaking terms with yourself'.[30]

Any break in routine was welcome and one duty required of an officer was his participation in courts martial. On 18 May, John had to attend several taking place at Beaufort West and it made a pleasant change to be travelling seventy miles down the line on one of the trains he so often saw passing by. Although most Canadians behaved well in the Karoo, some of the British soldiers did not and, to ensure the utmost fairness, British wrongdoers were tried by a panel of Colonial officers. Edward Morrison had been summoned to the same court martial and the two Canadian friends swapped news. Morrison shared John's sense of frustration at the lack of action.

While the Empire rejoiced at the news of the relief of the town of Mafeking on 17 May 1900, John and his men were beginning to despair of ever seeing any action in their remote and somewhat primitive location. Far from being glorious, the right section of D Battery, Royal Canadian Field Artillery, was discovering the essential truth about military life –

that it was mainly unrelieved drudgery brightened, in this case, only by the weekly mail delivery. Their routine of guard duty, daily work, drills, church parades and practical necessities such as shoeing horses or the issue of new jackets, almost reduced eager John McCrae to a state of depression. Queen Victoria's birthday on 24 May brought a day of celebration that lifted everyone's spirits. After firing a twenty-one gun salute, the section took part in a march past and a sports afternoon at which it carried off most of the prizes. The cold nights of the approaching southern winter were now telling. John recorded: 'I gathered a snowball of hoarfrost . . . Of course we are 4175 feet above the sea & this is one of the highest points around, which explains the matter.' With sunset around 4.45 p.m. followed by bleak, dark evenings, he confessed 'It isn't much fun to lie in one's tent under the blankets to read old newspapers & sleep is a desirable relief.'[31] His morning baths had become something of an ordeal and he told his mother that the 'tub is a corker – the sponge I always have to melt out first.'[32]

The nurses who had travelled on the *Laurentian* were working at No. 10 General Hospital in Bloemfontein. One of the four, Sister Margaret Macdonald, whom John described as 'a mighty good sort'[33] sent him a parcel of chocolates, tobacco, novels and 'a hot water bag'[34] for which he was extremely grateful. He learned that one of the other nurses was ill with typhus and wrote every day to cheer her up, explaining to his mother that although he did not know her very well, 'I thought South Africa was quite sufficient excuse for an over-riding of the conventionalities so I scraped up all the funny things I knew and sent them & I got a very wavering note of appreciation.'[35]

As always, John took an interest in the animals he encountered. Apart from 'Jacko', the mischievous monkey, the gunners had also now acquired four pups and various other pets including a bulldog who particularly amused John with his 'puffing & grunting & worrying all the time'.[36] He was also fond of his horse, 'Jack', who had earned 'a reputation for deep thinking – by his sober appearance & thoughtful looks',[37] and later admitted that 'I shall be sorry to part with the old rascal.'[38]

Finally, a long-awaited order arrived on 19 June 1900 for D Battery to concentrate at De Aar, in preparation for a move to Bloemfontein. While John and his men had been at Victoria Road, British fortunes had continued to rise. Sir Redvers Buller had broken the last Boer resistance in Natal and Lord Roberts had led his army into the Transvaal, capturing Johannesburg on 31 May and Pretoria on 5 June. As the right section of D Battery set off for Bloemfontein by train John calculated that they had marched over seven hundred miles. At De Aar, a seven-hour stop enabled him to visit the hospital. Although the dry terrain and the absence of germs made wounds easy to treat, the lack of clean drinking water was a source of a great deal of illness. Kipling, who commented that the army had brought disease to the otherwise sterile sun-baked South African veld, had been correct in his warnings about boiling water. De Aar was a most unhealthy place where funeral parades took place with unnerving regularity. John had heard about it from Edward Morrison and had already told his father that, 'I am glad I am not a med[ical officer]. out here: no thank you. No R[oyal]. A[rmy].M[edical]. C[orps]. or any other M[edical]. C[orps]. for me.' When he saw the hospital for himself he was appalled at the poor sanitation and declared that 'for absolute neglect & rotten administration, it is a model'.[39]

Hardly had the three sections of the battery re-united at Bloemfontein, 'happy as clams'[40] to see each other again, than Morrison's section was sent south to Edenburg to guard the railway line from Bloemfontein to the coast. Although the city did not offer much of interest, the gunners welcomed the prospect of being able to get what they regarded as luxury items after their time in the Karoo. Essential repair and maintenance work having been completed at their camp outside the city, they could enjoy some well-deserved leisure time. John visited some of the hospitals and, at No. 10, met up again with the nurses from the *Laurentian*. He also went to a service in the city's Cathedral and a performance of the play, 'Charley's Aunt', staged by what he described as a 'frightfully third-rate company – play funny enough, but acting was fearful'.[41] A culinary treat came in the form of an evening with the officers of the ammunition column and 'an excellent little dinner – roast carved on the table and plum pudding'.[42] On one of his rides into the city, John noticed the contrast between the funeral of an officer and the funeral of a common soldier that were taking place in a churchyard. Despite the full military honours of the one and the poor simplicity of the other, death was the great leveller for, when all was said and done, 'they live in far-varying degrees of society, but they die alike handsomely.'[43]

His long exile over, Lieutenant McCrae's spirits returned to their normal cheery level. He told his sister that 'I certainly do like soldiering' and that 'it is a very self respecting kind of life, and really requires lots of thinking to do it well.'[44] The next orders received required D Battery to proceed to Pretoria. Just before he left Bloemfontein, John paid a final call on the nurses at their billet. He was glad of the opportunity for feminine company as his correspondence with Canadian girls back home had tapered off since his arrival in South Africa. As he complained to his brother Tom, it seemed he was 'pretty completely out of all my Canadian damsels' hearts. I scarcely ever get letters except from one or two . . . Out of sight etc. – it is sad but apparently true.' John had been missing the ladies and found it 'a great lack never to see a woman to talk to; except at rare intervals'.[45]

In a state of buoyant anticipation, D Battery set off on 11 July to join Lord Roberts' field force. A forty-hour train journey brought them to their destination. On the way they passed through countryside that bore the marks of fighting in gutted buildings and blackened vegetation, wrecked bridges and stations, freshly dug graves and dead animals littering the roadside.[46] As they neared Pretoria, the sound of gunfire brought them in contact with the reality of the war. They were sent to Wonderboom, five miles to the north, where they were too late to assist in the town's defence. In the city itself, Lord Roberts' raising of the Union Jack outside the city's Parliament Building had been a moment to savour for the Imperial troops, but the fight was far from over. Farther up country the Boer General Louis Botha was maintaining a firm hold on the railway line that linked Pretoria to the port of Lourenço Marques. Lord Roberts now decided to mount another operation involving three columns that would advance on the railway line from the south, north and central area. Command of the northern column was given to General Sir Ian Hamilton, whom John was later to refer to as 'an ideal soldier'.[47] D Battery was to form part of this column's advance guard which, together with the column in the south, would speed forward to intercept the railway line either at Belfast or Middelburg. Hopefully, the Boers would be forced, like butterflies, into the waiting net of Lord Roberts.

With a transport line six miles long, the column of 4,500 infantry, D Battery's 12-pdr field guns, two pompom guns and some larger artillery pieces set out from Wonderboom on 18 July 1900. Marching across country in clear, sunny conditions, they saw flashes from the heliographs of Boer signallers in the distance and the winking of their lights at night. A few long-range Boer shells were a reminder of their presence and on the second day, some fifty Boer marksmen, hidden in a wooded bluff, ambushed Hamilton's scouts and caused panic. D Battery, unlimbered at the time and watering its horses, was caught off guard. As the Canadian Mounted Rifles set off in pursuit of the enemy, the artillery found itself unable to return fire for fear of hitting its own men. A Boer patrol continued to shadow the column and everyone was alert to the danger of night incursions. Its vulnerability also increased after Sir Ian Hamilton's guide led the column off course and it was forced to retrace its steps.

On 21 July at De Wagen Drift, the Boers seized their opportunity. During the night they placed several guns on a kopje overlooking the British camp and next morning, opened fire on the rear of the column, killing two transport drivers and several mules. With assistance, the centre section of D Battery was able to silence the enemy but the Boers were determined to try again. The long procession was now crossing open countryside and some four miles farther along its route, it was fired on again from another kopje. Moving its horses well out of range, D Battery took cover behind some remaining stubble in a newly-ploughed cornfield. Unable to get an accurate range on the Boer position, the Battery fired 96 shrapnel shells into the kopje at a range of about four thousand yards. A passing regiment of infantry yelled 'Give it to 'em, Canydians!' [sic][48] in encouragement. Although it had been joined by other guns, D Battery had been the first to get into action that day and was later officially complimented on its performance.

John recorded the day:

> Our baptism of fire . . . They opened on us from the left flank . . . Their first shell was about 150 yards in front – direction good. The next was about 100 [yards] over; & we expected we were bracketed . . . One shrapnel burst over us & scattered on all sides of us. I felt as if a hail storm were coming down, & wanted to turn my back, but it was over in an instant . . . The whistle of a shell is <u>very</u> unpleasant. You hear it begin its scream; and it gets louder and louder, and seems to be coming exactly your way – and then you realize that it has gone over . . . Our position was quite in the open. The greater majority of the shells fell between our guns & wagons.[49]

John added a further note that, 'the Boers fired 5 or 6 shells around the battery. The last one a shrapnel burst over us in front and the pieces flew over our heads.'[50] As the march continued through the cold winter days and Hamilton's column joined Lord Roberts' main column at Bronkhorstspruit, it hit bad weather. A bitter wind and torrential rain turned the dust to mud and the dry streams into raging torrents. On 25 July the march was brought to a halt and the troops, without food or tents, were forced to spend a miserable night under guns or limbers, protected only by their greatcoats and waterproof sheets. John described the conditions:

> The day was like a Dec[ember] afternoon and the rain was fearfully chilly. When we got in about dark, we put the lines up, and then found that the transport could not get in – and it had all our bankets and coats. I had my cape and a rubber sheet for the saddle, both soaking wet. Being on duty . . . I bunked out, supperless like everyone else, under an ammunition wagon; it rained most of the night, and was bitterly cold. I slept at intervals . . . I kept the same position all night, both knees in a puddle and my feet being rained on. It was a mighty long night.[51]
>
> At morning I had a puttee round my head as a night cap and wore the other. My cape was wet and muddy, and altogether I was not handsome . . . I never knew such a night; and with decent luck, I hope never to see such another.'[52]

Getting to Balmoral next morning was a relief. On arrival, the men had their first sighting of their commander-in-chief, Lord Roberts, and his chief of staff, Lord Kitchener. 'Bobs', as Lord Roberts was affectionately known by the troops, inspected D Battery and asked to have the officers called out, John McCrae thus having the opportunity to shake hands with another of his heroes. Before Roberts set off to Pretoria to consolidate his position, Major Hurdman succeeded in persuading him that when he resumed the march, D Battery would accompany him.

The Canadians, meanwhile, had to return once more to the necessary but tedious work of guard duty. John McCrae and Edward Morrison were ordered to take their sections to Pienaars Poort, some twenty miles east of Pretoria. Here, they were to guard a narrow gorge with a ten-mile view across the surrounding countryside. The prospect sounded more exciting than guarding a railway line but in the event, the most arduous part of the work proved to be the climb up to the gun positions. Each man took it in turns to man the rock sangars for forty-eight hours with a detachment of gunners. Morrison described the amusing sight of them going up the mountain with 'blankets, grub, pans, kettles and all the rest of it on our backs' like 'a party of prospectors going up the White Horse pass in the Yukon.'[53]

When not on duty and scanning the horizon with binoculars, the gunners slept, read books, wrote letters and enjoyed the dietary delights of sweet potatoes and peanuts – luxuries they had not tasted in a long time. A man for statistics, John recorded that they had now marched a total of 760 miles in all. Light relief was offered by the chance to join a local contingent of The Connaught Rangers and Royal Irish Fusiliers for some organised fun that included a gymkhana, side shows, band music, races and a sing-song. John continued to sketch and to add to a unique collection he had started, as Morrison remembered:

> Lieut[enant]. McCrae is of a philosophic turn of mind, and has a love for the curious and unique in art and nature. He is engaged in making a collection of gems of profanity, scintillations of genius evoked by the conditions and trials of war from the Canadian intellect. Whilst on detachment up Kenhardt [sic] way he acquired a most interesting nucleus for his collection . . . There was one troop sergeant-major of the cowboy push who was a veritable gold mine for the young collector.[54]

He was good company too. One freezing night, Morrison remembered him 'lying on his blankets on the other side of the tent singing "Drink to Me Only With Thine Eyes,"' and added that such 'allusions are painful and unnecessary in view of the present chronic condition of our mess hamper. Besides we have nothing to smoke but that rancorous Boer tobacco.'[55]

They were allowed a short period of leave and John took his in Pretoria. Its Grand Hotel offered comfortable accommodation and he greatly enjoyed the luxury of sleeping in a bed for the first time since he had arrived in South Africa. Nursing Sister Margaret Macdonald and her Canadian colleagues had by now been attached to the staff of the Irish Hospital, located in the city's Palace of Justice. They had kept in touch and were pleased to see the young lieutenant, confessing that their hardest work had involved enteric fever and dysentery cases. In the weeks that followed, there were few signs of any Boer presence near Pienaars Poort apart from an occasional sighting. On 15 August Edward Morrison and his section were moved to a new post thirty miles away and with his friend gone, John went exploring in his free time. He found a small valley in the vicinity with a stream, beautiful butterflies and trees – one nearly forty feet high – with 'no leaves but bright scarlet flowers'.[56] The time of inactivity was almost at an end, however. Three weeks later John received orders to return to Balmoral, where General Louis Botha and another Boer leader had established a new headquarters.

On arrival at Erstefabrieken, John reported to Colonel William D. Otter, officer commanding the First Canadian Contingent, and then loaded his guns and horses onto the train that was to collect Edward Morrison and his section along the way. No sooner had they reached Belfast station than they found themselves under fire. The left section of D Battery was immediately directed to a line of trenches two hundred yards from the station. The gunners had arrived in time for the final stages of a four-day battle that was soon over. After being inspected for a second time by Lord Roberts, John proudly noted in his diary that:

> We were presented to him in turn: he spoke a few words to each of us, asking what our corps was, and our service. He seemed surprised that we were all Field Artillery men – I dare say the composition of the other Can[adian]. Corps had to do with this . . . He asked a good many questions about the horses, the men, the spirits of the men particularly and altogether showed a very kind interest in the battery.[57]

Botha and his men had been dislodged but not, as yet, captured and still commanded part of the railway line. Lydenburg, the Boer's northern supply depot, was situated about fifty miles north of Belfast in rugged mountainous country accessible via steep, tortuous and heavily guarded mountain tracks. Lord Roberts issued orders for the destruction of Botha's base and Sir Ian Hamilton's column joined General Sir Redvers Buller and his troops to form part of the force charged with this difficult task in terrain that gave every advantage to the enemy. On 1 September 1900, the right and centre sections of D Battery were attached to the column with two batteries of the Royal Horse Artillery. Ten miles north of Belfast they came under Boer fire but the enemy was driven off. With the artillery and mounted infantry constantly on watch to combat Boer snipers and long-range guns, they progressed with caution. Most of the third day, 3

September, was spent struggling to move their guns and equipment up steep hills under continuous fire.

On the approaches to Lydenburg, enemy resistance increased and the battery had to dispel Boer snipers from two positions. A mile outside the town itself, the column was subjected to intense fire that the short-range British guns could not get within range to silence. Although the British force gained entry to Lydenburg, Boer gunners continued to harass them for two days. On 7 September D Battery, a section of the Royal Horse Artillery and the 18th and 19th Hussars fought Boers outside the town until relieved. John McCrae's diary recorded that:

> The Boers opened on us with 5 guns – 4 on the crest, & one advanced on the face of the hill at about 10,000 yards, their shells being accurate from the first. They shelled us till dark, over 3 hours; a shell about every 2 or 3 minutes, often two together. The gun on our left fired for a long time on Buller's camp – the one on the right on us & we could easily tell which it was. They burned powder, & we could see the smoke and flash; then a soul-consuming interval of 20 to 30 seconds, then we heard the report, and about 5 sec[onds]. after, the burst. Many (about 15 or 18) in succession burst over ourselves . . . The shrapnel burst all around us. – I picked up a no. of falling pieces within a few feet of us. It was a trying afternoon, . . . and we stood around & wondered if we would be hit.[58]

Continuous, accurate Boer shelling forced the British to move their troops and transport out of range. To end this annoyance, an attack was planned for the following morning, 8 September, under cover of long-range artillery fire. In a fortuitous early mist the British made good progress before being spotted by the enemy, and managed to establish a position for their artillery whence the guns could shell the Boers in preparation for a final infantry assault. John recalled D Battery's part in the battle:

> At last we got the order to advance, just as the big guns of the enemy stopped their fire. We advanced about 4 miles mostly up the slope, which is in all about 1500 feet high, over a great deal of rough ground and over a number of spruits. The horses put to their utmost to draw the guns up the hills; it was terrific. As we advanced we could see artillery crawling in from both flanks, all converging to the main hill, while far away the infantry and cavalry were beginning to crown the heights nearer us . . . As the field guns came up to a broad platform, section after section came into action, and we rained shrapnel, pom-poms and lyddite from the 5″ howitzers on the crests ahead and to the left. Every now and then a rattle of Mausers and Metfords would tell that the infantry were at their work, but practically the battle was over . . . The

wind blew through us cold like ice as we stood on the hill; as the artillery ceased fire, the mist dropped over us chilling us to the bone.[59]

Botha, who had foreseen the outcome, escaped into the mist with his men. When it was all over, John felt Lydenburg had been hard but instructive and his training had served him well.

Leaving General Sir Redvers Buller to complete the operations in the north, Lord Roberts now turned his attention to Boer activity farther south. For the right section of D Battery, camped just to the north of Lydenberg, there was time to enjoy their surroundings. Their officer observed 'weeping willows . . . all a beautiful light green; the apple trees (or some trees like them) in blossom, and the most beautiful Canada-like spring smell everywhere – the first time we have had Canada brought back so strongly.'[60] On 15 September, John and his men were moved to Godwaan station and once more resumed guard duty. Somewhat ragged and dirty by now, they resigned themselves to their situation and their staple, if meagre repast of 'hard tack, bully & jam'.[61] John found some very amenable company in the person of a staff officer of the King's Own Scottish Borderers, who had fought at Magersfontein. The two men shared a sense of humour and John enjoyed his new friend's Mark Twain-style stories interspersed with extremely funny comments.[62]

In the weeks that followed, he and his section made three expeditions against the Boers. At times they passed through beautiful surroundings and while camping at Kantoor Spruit, they found themselves in a lovely valley where two streams rushed down rocks into deep pools and almost tropical vegetation made it 'a regular Eden for greenness.'[63] At Eland's Kop, they had their most significant engagement since Lydenburg, opening fire on Boers scurrying for the crest of a hill. By now, John was beginning to think of home and decided that, in terms of clothing, he would need a 'refit before I can go into society'.[64] The war had become a matter of 'mopping-up' operations that belonged, more properly, to the British. Back in England, the British government decided it was no longer willing to pay the cost of keeping the Canadian troops in South Africa. It was just as well, as most of the second Canadian contingent had no desire to continue the fight now that their term of service was over. As Edward Morrison wrote, 'Roses and lilies and lilacs are blooming here, but I don't think any of us will be sorry to exchange them for the nice, clean, beautiful snow of old Canada.'[65]

The other two sections of D Battery had been having a more active time. The centre section helped to clear the country of Boers along Lord Roberts' route to his headquarters at Nelspruit and Edward Morrison's section was involved in a rearguard action at Leliefontein which resulted in three Canadian VC's. Morrison himself was awarded the DSO. Many Boer farmhouses in the Belfast area housed secret supplies of weapons and the decision was made to torch them. Morrison and his men formed part of the force, led by General Horace Smith-Dorrien, that undertook the task. Morrison called it a 'burning trek'[66].

For the remainder of their time in South Africa, the three sections of the battery went back on railway guard duty, their routine broken by occasional encounters with snipers and enemy patrols and aggravated by sickness, snakes, boredom and deteriorating physical conditions. By 23 November 1900, all active men of the Canadian contingent had been recalled to join their units in Pretoria in preparation for the return to Canada. The Colonial commanders organised a huge dinner and the Canadian officers were dined out by the Gordon Highlanders, who lined the railway tracks to wave them off. John McCrae had been in hospital at Pretoria since 24 November with a bout of fever and did not take part in the leaving celebrations. He was discharged on 8 December and caught the mail train from Bloemfontein, reaching Cape Town at 9.00 a.m. on 12 December in time to assist with the task of loading guns and equipment onto the return ship, the *Roslyn Castle*. The Canadians found they were sharing a camp with about five hundred returning Australians. All the colonials were determined to enjoy their last night in the city and despite the efforts of their officers, sentries and military police, over a thousand men left the camp that evening. Before the night was out, they had drunk the bars and hotels dry.

The *Roslyn Castle* sailed at 4.30 the following afternoon. John kept a log of the ship's position and daily progress, noting that they crossed the Equator on 23 December. As the 'indefatigable secretary'[67] of the ship's social committee, he helped to arrange nightly concerts and the Christmas festivities. Despite rough weather after New Year, the men were in good shape as their ship approached the Nova Scotian coast on 9 January 1901 and there were cries of delight at the sight of the snow-covered tug which came alongside in the darkness to put the medical officer aboard.[68] Almost a year after John's departure, the *Roslyn Castle* dropped anchor in Halifax harbour and he sent his father a two-word telegram which said simply: 'Arrived safely.'

A journalist from the *Guelph Mercury*, who had travelled to meet the city's gunners, was given a hearty welcome as he came on board the ship. He reported that:

> I went aft to meet Lieut[enant]. McCrae. Here again the welcome I had to give seemed poor indeed to the warmth of the one I received, for, although a stranger to the gallant officer who had so nobly upheld the honour of his native city, I was given a greeting no less hearty than might have been tendered an old friend.

Thanking the newspaper for its reception, John sent greetings to the people of Guelph and told the reporter that their march in the Karoo had been described by Lord Roberts as the 'wonderful, incredible march of these Canadians.'[69]

The following day, 10 January 1901, D Battery marched with the other returning troops through Halifax before boarding the train at 10.00 p.m. for the two-day journey to Guelph. After a reunion with his parents at a station just outside Guelph, John and his men reached their destination at midnight on 12 January 1901. Despite the late hour, the city was in a state of high excitement: crowds of citizens turned out to cheer their boys, bands played and fireworks were let off as the gunners marched through the streets. The shops along their route were decorated with flags and bunting and had left their lights on at the request of the Mayor. John, the recipient of a hometown hero's welcome, was shouldered all the way to the Winter Fair Building where the Mayor formally greeted the returning gunners and told them of Guelph's pride in them and the fact that 'Our beloved Queen has no more loyal defenders and British supremacy no more loyal supporters than the men of the right section of D Battery.' Ever modest, John replied simply that, 'For myself I have nothing to say, but I do feel like paying tribute to the unselfish and soldierly qualities of the men whom I had the honor to command.'[70]

There is no doubt that John McCrae had proved an inspired leader. His men had come to love and admire him for his generous conduct and his companionship as he shared their rations, hardships and frustrations. On many an evening in camp he had kept them cheerful when there was nothing much to smile about. Although he was an authority figure, he had the rare gift of being able to step down and become one of them without losing their respect. Their toasts and well-deserved tributes to him on the train journey to Guelph had moved him. The commanding officer of D Battery, Major W.G. Hurdman, was full of praise: 'Of L[ieutenan]t. McCrae I wish to speak in special commendation. He is an exceptionally clever officer and a perfect gentleman.'[71]

Exactly two weeks after John's return to Canada, Queen Victoria died and the Empire mourned her passing. For John, looking back on his part in the war and still coming to terms with his feelings, it was a time of restlessness and conflicting emotions. His service in South Africa had left him fit and experienced. He had realised his ambition to fight, felt the flow of adrenalin from coming under fire and earned his Queen's Medal with three clasps for his service in the Cape Colony, the Orange Free State and Belfast. Although he believed firmly in the need to fight evil, he had seen the miseries, privations, death, disease and wasteful destruction that war brought to civilians and soldiers alike. John did not talk about his experiences, but his private reflections later produced a poem and an article. Now the time had come to put the war behind him and return to medicine. Relinquishing the trappings of war, it was a dark-suited Dr John McCrae who boarded a train that winter of 1901, bound for Montreal and McGill University.

NOTES

1. From 'The Unconquered Dead' by John McCrae, *The McGill University Magazine*, (Volume 5, No. 1, December 1905), p. 97. Micro mfm/AP/U577, UTL.
2. JM Diary of South African War, 13 March 1900, MG 30, D 209, Micro A-1102, NAC.
3. Morrison, *With the Guns*, p. 71.
4. Thomas G. Marquis, *Canada's Sons on Kopje and Veldt* (Toronto, no date given), pp. 352–3.
5. Undated article (circa 17 March 1900) by John Ewan, *Toronto Globe*, Boer War Ledger, MH.
6. Captain D.I.V. Eaton, second in command of D Battery.
7. JM to Janet McCrae, 18 March 1900, MG 30, D209, Micro A-1102, NAC.
8. Morrison, *With the Guns*, p. 80.
9. JM Diary of South African War, 21 March 1900, MG 30, D209, Micro A-1102, NAC.
10. JM to Walter Gow, 22 March 1900, MG 30, D209, Micro A-1102, NAC.
11. JM to Janet McCrae, 24 March 1900, MG 30, D209, Micro A-1102, NAC.
12. JM Diary of South African War, 26 March 1900, MG 30, D209, Micro A-1102, NAC.
13. JM Diary of South African War, 26 March 1900, MG 30, D209, Micro A-1102, NAC.
14. Morrison, *With the Guns*, p. 117.
15. In Afrikaans, the word 'kopje' meant a small hill.
16. John McCrae, 'Builders of Empire,' *The McGill University Magazine* (Volume 1, No. 1, December 1901), p.69. Micro mfm/AP/U577, UTL.
17. John McCrae, 'Builders of Empire', p. 68.
18. JM to Janet McCrae, 29 April 1900, MG 30, D209, Micro A-1102, NAC.
19. JM to David McCrae, 4 April 1900, MG 30, D209, Micro A-1102, NAC.
20. JM to Janet McCrae, 10 April 1900, MG 30, D209, Micro A-1102, NAC.
21. JM Diary of South African War, 18 April 1900, MG 30, D209, Micro A-1102, NAC.
22. JM to Janet McCrae, 10 April 1900, MG 30, D209, Micro A-1102, NAC.
23. JM to Janet McCrae, 19 April 1900, MG 30, D209, Micro A-1102, NAC.
24. JM to Janet McCrae, 23 April 1900, MG 30, D209, Micro A-1102, NAC.
25. Marquis, *Canada's Sons*, p. 364.
26. Miller, *Painting the Map Red*, p. 204.
27. Walter Bapty, From 'Letters to the Editor', *Canadian Medical Association Journal* (Volume 88, 30 March 1963).
28. John McCrae, 'Builders of Empire', p.70.
29. JM to Janet McCrae, 11 May 1900, MG 30, D209, Micro A-1102, NAC.
30. JM to Janet McCrae, 11 May 1900, MG 30, D209, Micro A-1102, NAC.
31. JM to Janet McCrae, 28 May 1900, MG 30, D209, Micro A-1102, NAC.
32. JM to Janet McCrae, 11 June 1900, MG 30, D209, Micro A-1102, NAC.
33. JM to Janet McCrae, 4 June 1900, MG 30, D209, Micro A-1102, NAC.
34. JM to Janet McCrae, 4 June 1900, MG 30, D209, Micro A-1102, NAC.
35. JM to Janet McCrae, 11 June 1900, MG 30, D209, Micro A-1102, NAC.

36. JM to Janet McCrae, 4 June 1900, MG 30, D209, Micro A-1102, NAC.
37. JM to Janet McCrae, 18 June 1900, MG 30, D209, Micro A-1102, NAC.
38. JM to Janet McCrae, 31 August 1900, MG 30, D209, Micro A-1102, NAC.
39. JM to David McCrae, 20 May 1900, MG 30, D209, Micro-A-1102, NAC.
40. Morrison, *With the Guns*, p. 139.
41. JM Diary of South African War, 30 June 1900, MG 30, D209, Micro A-1102, NAC.
42. JM Diary of South African War, 29 June 1900, MG 30, D209, Micro A-1102, NAC.
43. John McCrae, 'Builders of Empire', p.66.
44. JM to Geills McCrae, 1 July 1900, MG 30, D209, Micro A-1102, NAC.
45. JM to Tom McCrae, 22 August 1900, MG 30, D209, Micro A-1102, NAC.
46. Miller, *Painting the Map Red*, p. 211.
47. John McCrae, 'Builders of Empire', p. 72.
48. Morrison, *With the Guns*, p. 157.
49. JM Diary of South African War, 21 July 1900, MG 30, D209, Micro A-1102, NAC.
50. JM Diary of South African War, 23 July 1900, MG 30, D209, Micro A-1102, NAC.
51. JM Diary of South African War, 25 July 1900, MG 30 D209, Micro A-1102, NAC.
52. JM Diary of South African War, 26 July 1900, MG 30, D209, Micro A-1102, NAC.
53. Morrison, *With the Guns*, p. 170.
54. Morrison, *With the Guns*, p. 122.
55. Morrison, *With the Guns*, pp. 196–7.
56. JM Diary of South African War, 10 August 1900, MG 30, D209, Micro A-1102, NAC.
57. JM Diary of South African War, 30 August 1900, MG 30, D209, Micro A-1102, NAC.
58. JM Diary of South African War, 7 September 1900, MG 30, D209, Micro-A-1102, NAC.
59. JM Diary of South African War, 8 September 1900, MG 30, D209, Micro A-1102, NAC.
60. JM to Janet McCrae, 11 September 1900, MG 30, D209, Micro A-1102, NAC.
61. JM to Janet McCrae, 11 September 1900, MG 30, D209, Micro A-1102, NAC.
62. JM to Janet McCrae, 19 October 1900, MG 30, D209, Micro A-1102, NAC,
63. JM Diary of South African War, 20 September 1900, MG 30, D209, Micro A-1102, NAC.
64. JM to Janet McCrae, 22 October 1900, MG 30, D209, Micro A-1102, NAC.
65. Morrison, *With the Guns*, p. 291.
66. Morrison, *With the Guns*, p. 274.
67. Morrison, *With the Guns*, p. 302.
68. Miller, *Painting the Map Red*, p. 286.
69. Article, assumed to be from the *Guelph Mercury*, 11 January 1901, Boer War Ledger, MH.
70. Article, assumed to be from the *Guelph Mercury* dated 11 January 1901, Boer War Ledger, MH.
71. Article, assumed to be from the *Guelph Mercury*, dated 11 January 1901, Boer War Ledger, MH.

CHAPTER SIX

'Labour hath other recompense than rest'[1]
1901–1904

Montreal, the city that was to be John McCrae's home for the next fourteen years, was a centre of shipping, manufacturing and finance. Since the time when John Molson, an early settler from Lincolnshire, had established a brewery in 1786, launched Canada's first steamboat and set the local economy on the road to prosperity, it had grown and flourished. The modern metropolis that was Montreal in 1901, was far removed from the walled town familiar to James McGill, founder of the university which had taken his name. The majority of Montreal's leading businessmen were hard-working Scots. Great commercial dynasties had grown up through families like the Molsons; William Dow from Perthshire with his interests in brewing, insurance and shipping; Hugh Allan and his brother Andrew, sons of a Glasgow shipowner, who had created a major shipping line; and John Redpath, a stonemason from Berwick who built churches and the locks on Canada's Lachine Canal.

Their wealth had created beautiful homes where, in the time of James McGill there had been mainly farms. Into this new English-speaking élite had come others – men like George Drummond from Edinburgh who became president of the Bank of Montreal; Robert Reford who developed an ocean shipping business; and the men who had supported and built the Canadian Pacific Railway – Lord Strathcona, his cousin Lord Mount Stephen and William, later Sir William, van Horne. Bringing with them wealth and prestige, they had also initiated financial help for McGill University and donated money for new amenities such as the city's Royal Victoria Hospital. By the turn of the century, these leaders of Canada's commercial life were among its richest and most influential citizens and were concentrated in a fairly small area that covered roughly one square mile adjacent to McGill University on the lower slopes of Mount Royal. In their enclave well above the general noise of Montreal's centre, the 'merchant princes'[2] who controlled some two thirds of Canada's wealth had built fabulous homes. It was an exclusive neighbourhood that exuded power and had much in common with London's Knightsbridge or Edinburgh's New Town.

Traditionally clannish, the main social life of the Scots of Montreal

revolved around the church and the St Andrew's Society. The Society
had come into being some sixty-five years earlier to honour Scotland's
patron saint and to dispense charity to Scots in Montreal, many of whom
arrived from Britain in a sickly and destitute state. As nineteenth-century
civilisation had flowed into the New World, it had opened the door to
an altogether more graceful age. The St Andrew's Day Ball, inaugurated
in 1848, was now a splendid affair held at the city's Windsor Hotel and
almost always attended by Canada's Governor General. Débutantes or
'belles' were presented and, after an evening of dancing, midnight
signalled the piping in of the haggis and the start of a sumptuous
supper. As dawn broke the last dance ended and hands were joined in
'Auld Lang Syne.'[3] This important annual occasion was the highlight of a
social calendar that included supper parties and summer garden parties;
holidays spent at elegant summer homes on lakes and islands; winter
activities such as curling, ice skating and sleighing; and an annual winter
carnival with 'Fêtes de Nuit' and a spectacular Ice Palace that resembled a
fairytale fortress. As torches and fireworks lit up the sky, the dark winter
days were transformed and Montreal was likened to St Petersburg. Into
this world, where learning brushed shoulders with opulence, stepped
John McCrae.

As soon as he was settled, John wrote to the Dean of the Faculty of Medicine at McGill thanking him for having granted the postponement of his
Fellowship in Pathology. The stimulus of working again with Professor
George Adami became a daily delight. Now in his tenth year at McGill,
Adami had fulfilled his ambition to build a School of Pathology. Like
William Osler, he had made use of European teaching from Cambridge
and Paris and the McGill Pathological Laboratory was by now a point of
reference for researchers and practitioners across Canada. Adami insisted
on the British tradition of clinical training and his lectures sparkled with
humour and originality. Here was someone who had the gift of making
difficult topics enjoyable and easily understood – something at which
John McCrae was later to prove equally adept. Adami insisted on the
need for research and personal experimental work, constantly sharing
with his students the fruits of his work as Pathologist at the nearby Royal
Victoria Hospital, his membership of the Montreal Medico-Chirurgical
Society and his contributions to the *Montreal Medical Journal*. With a love
of books that rivalled Osler's, Adami paid for a medical library and gave
his students full access to his own books and pathological specimens. He
also founded the Lister Club, a medical group which met regularly to
discuss scientific problems and participate in open discussions. In many
ways, George Adami's encouragement of the pursuit of knowledge and
research echoed the work of his predecessor, William Osler.

The first year after South Africa was one of unrelenting hard work, but
there was also time to make new friends and enter into university life.

Henry Howitt, John's young friend from Guelph, arrived as a freshman in Medicine and the two frequently met in the Medical Building and sometimes at dinner with friends. They also belonged to the same Greek Letter Society and nearly every Saturday evening John would appear at the Zeta Psi House. Although older, he was popular for showing a lot of interest, giving wise advice and telling stories 'as only he could tell them'.[4] While Henry was doing his first-year work he attended John's weekly Pathology demonstrations, at which case studies and findings were explained. He recalled that these sessions were very popular and no student ever missed them. Already John was developing a talent for communicating in a way that could be easily understood and remembered. In Henry's words, it 'was the reputation which he created at those Saturday demonstrations that largely influenced his future'.[5]

The work of Fellow in Pathology involved research at McGill and post-mortem examinations at Montreal General Hospital. It was here that John met Dr Wyatt Johnson, the General's brilliant pathologist and another talented former student of William Osler. The hospital's post-mortem reports were recorded in an autopsy book and one of John's tasks was to keep this record up to date. In 1901 he added the following brief inscription:

> Our lyfe is but a Winter's Day.
> Some only breakfast, and away.
> Others to Dinner stay, and are fulle fedde.
> The oldest man but suppes, and goes to bedde.
> Large is his dette, y lingers out the day.
> He that goes soonest hath the least to pay!![6]

With his pleasing personality, his respect for learning and authority and his drive for excellence, John adapted easily to the life of the 'polite, civilized and class conscious'[7] Montreal medical community. Professionally, George Adami recognised in his young protégé an ability and a dedication that promised much. Socially, they had a good deal in common. Both were charming, humorous and cultured, made friends easily, had a wide knowledge of literature and shared a love of travel. Adami's wife was related to Lord Strathcona, and while Adami had an entrée to Montreal high society, he also had other friends from many walks of life. John was introduced to 'men of science, of letters, of music, of the cloth, adventurers from the home-land discovering Canada, artists of the new and old schools, men of finance or ne'er-do-wells. . . . These evenings were never dull.'[8]

Among medical colleagues and students alike, the charming professor was appreciated for his many qualities, not the least of which was the combination of his own brand of sophistication and humour. Everyone went to him for advice, whether at his breakfast table where he gathered friends on Sunday mornings, or to splendid dinners at his home where the atmosphere was 'infused with enthusiasm for scientific advancement'.[9] With a man like George Adami to inspire and encourage him, John McCrae understandably enjoyed those first months back at McGill.

In South Africa, meanwhile, the war had still not come to an end and had entered a new and unhappy phase. Lord Kitchener had adopted a strategy of dividing the country into sections using wire fences and blockhouses into which he would sweep Boer commandos. In its early and dramatic phases, the war had aroused great excitement. Now, the rise in taxation needed to fund Kitchener's plan had turned public opinion in Britain against it, even more so when it became known that thousands of Boer families, whose homes had been destroyed, were being housed in a new kind of detention centre, known as a 'concentration camp', where disease was rife. By the time the Boers finally capitulated, both sides were bitter and exhausted. On 31 May 1902 a peace treaty was signed at Vereeniging, under which the Boers were very well compensated for the devastation of their lands and eventually given full equality within a self-governing South African union of the four European colonies. In the view of some people, Rudyard Kipling among them, the Boers lost the war but won the peace.

Many British soldiers returned home with a deep respect for their adversaries as fighters who had held off an enemy more than four times their number. Taking victory and defeat with the same air of sobriety, the Boers in their turn also admired some of the qualities of their victors. Both sides had treated prisoners and wounded decently. The worst killer had been disease – of some four hundred thousand soldiers who had fought under the British flag, an appalling twenty-two thousand had died mostly from disease. It had started as another imperial 'adventure' but, in the end, the war in South Africa dispelled Britain's old zest for such 'adventures'.

For Canada, as for the other Dominions that fought in the war, South Africa had been a testing ground. At Paardeberg, Leliefontein, Bloemfontein, Mafeking and elsewhere, Canadians had acquitted themselves very well and shown a stamina and initiative that were well matched to the Boer style of fighting. More than 7,000 Canadians had served in South Africa and the experience they had gained was to stand them in good stead.[10]

On 18 September 1901, John and other Montreal veterans who had served in South Africa were presented with their war medals at a special ceremony outside the city's main railway station. The streets were lavishly decorated and John reported that 'the town quite turned itself inside out – and really looked very pretty'. In keeping with such occasions, the hospitals had 'the usual harvest of fireworks casualties, people falling off arches etc'.[11] His social calendar was filling up. He described riding, walking on Montreal Island during the lovely autumn afternoons, an invitation to a Hunt Club Ball, a ticket for a performance of the opera 'Carmen' and a clutch of dinner parties and dances. On 1 November, John attended a reception given by Lord Strathcona at the impressive residence where he had hosted the future King George and Queen Mary just a few months earlier. This splendid occasion turned out to be 'a crush' but John still managed to gain an impression of His Lordship's home and pronounced it 'a very beautiful house – luxurious in a marked degree for Canada'.[12]

With the onset of another Canadian winter came the sight of skaters in the parks and on the frozen St Lawrence River, sleighs in the snowy city streets and Christmas trees bright with their festoons of lights. It was all a great contrast to John's previous shipboard Christmas in the warmth of the South Atlantic. Despite his 'habitual modesty'[13] in not talking about his war experiences, he had continued to follow the progress of the conflict in South Africa and, when invited to speak to the Royal Canadian Military Institute on 'Artillery and Its Employment in South Africa', his lecture was well received. The announcement of the first edition of a new publication, *The McGill University Magazine*, motivated him to submit an article about the war entitled 'Builders of the Empire'. It was printed in the first edition and enabled him both to set down his thoughts and impressions of South Africa, and to reiterate the price paid by 'men whose message goes to the Empire, by the voice of a new colony that they have won by blood, -"O stranger, go thou and tell our people that we are lying here, having obeyed their words".'[14]

The following year, 1902, brought John a study trip to Europe, a disappointment and the consolation of a promotion. He had decided to study for the Licentiateship of the Royal College of Physicians, no doubt encouraged by George Adami with his British background, training and firm belief in the critical link between Pathology and Clinical Medicine.[15] John's plans would take him to Prague for a period of study, returning via London to sit his examinations. By this time the age of mass travel was in full cry and the company founded by Thomas Cook, the Englishman whose first venture had been a day's train trip from Leicester in 1841, was now selling thousands of tickets covering millions of rail and steamship miles. For those who could afford it, colourful travel posters offered railway journeys around Europe and North America; Nile, Mediterranean and Arctic Circle cruises; new winter sports holidays; and organised tours to far-flung destinations. For North Americans, the business of getting to Europe was becoming a pleasure in contrast to the ordeal it had once been. Britain, America, Canada and Germany – in its surge to the forefront of maritime power – competed to build transatlantic ships of the most extravagant luxury. With their sumptuous interiors and tall funnels, these floating palaces had come to be seen as emblems of national power and status.

John left New York in that spring of 1902 bound for Naples. He found he was one of only a dozen or so English-speaking passengers on board his ship, the majority being Mexicans on a pilgrimage to Rome. All too soon they hit bad weather, prompting John to comment with humour that:

> Mexican habits of costume are picturesque, but unsuited for sea-sick weather. From careful observation, it may be concluded that the neatest wear for those who do not care to spend much time upon the ceremony of dressing is a tight-fitting tailor-made gown and a rubber bathing cap. The mantilla is most effective, when not worn.[16]

As the ship entered the Mediterranean on a clear evening, John's account of his journey made particular mention of the famous Rock of Gibraltar standing out against the glow of the deepening sunset. After docking at Naples, he took a train northwards, adding with more humour that, if 'you have to see Naples and die, arrange your demise that it may occur subsequently to a visit to Pompeii'.[17] During his visit to the famous ancient site, he saw the flower that, unbeknown to him, was to bring him fame and immortality. Pompeii was a peaceful place with 'streets and courtyards paved with stone, the rooms carpeted by short grass, the walls topped by verdure, with an occasional poppy, the blue sky above it and smoking Vesuvius just over the walls.'[18]

Having enjoyed Rome, Venice and a spectacular train journey through the Alps to Vienna, John arrived in Prague for a six-week stay. His sightseeing there included some of the city's palaces and he was especially fascinated by the medieval City Hall clock which seemed to have a mind of its own since, 'no modern clockmaker has been able to read the riddle of its mechanism, and it goes in a disjointed haphazard way. The times at which it strikes its erratic hours are announced on a placard close by.'[19] John had come to study Pathology at Prague's Deutsche Universität, the oldest university in central Europe. His journey each day from his lodgings involved walking through a pleasant park full of spring flowers where 'the birds can run riot'.[20] A Wagner festival was being staged and he managed to secure tickets to 'Tristan & Isolde' and 'Tannhäuser'. One night the sky was ablaze with fireworks marking a religious festival.

Unfortunately, Prague proved to be an unhealthy place for the keen student. He contracted bronchitis and was obliged to cut short his study programme, making for the Bohemian health resort of Teplitz with its dozen or so large bath houses and verdant parks. Here, John read avidly during his period of recovery, bathed in the hot springs, attended outdoor concerts and mingled with the throngs of people enjoying the sociable atmosphere. As soon as he was fit, he took a train to Berlin where his observation of some of the German customs and national traits led him to conclude that 'there is no one more thoroughly imbued with the sense of Germany's national greatness than her own people, and the calm assurance of superiority is often exasperating'.[21] After pausing at Potsdam to see the tomb of Frederick the Great, John proceeded across the North German plain into Holland. The young traveller found he enjoyed the quaint untidy streets of Amsterdam and quiet canals where 'fat barges unload straw-packed crockery, where market gardens flourish on the fore-decks of pug-nosed rafts, and where the well-fed cat sits in the sun on the roof of the deck-house.' It was a country he could relax in, and 'for a charming half day I mooned around Delft, sat in the sunshine on the edge of the canal, kicked my reflective heels, watching the barges and the windmills and the green fields.'[22]

On arrival in London, John took lodgings at 19 Montague Place, Bloomsbury. The examinations were approaching and he discovered he was one of a number of Canadian doctors all there for the same purpose. On 11 July 1902 he wrote to his mother that, despite the long hours of preparation, he had managed to attend a Sunday service at St Paul's Cathedral, to meet acquaintances and to take in some of the atmosphere of a city growing livelier under Britain's new King, Edward VII. A particularly strong cast was playing in Shakespeare's 'The Merry Wives of Windsor' and John went to see it with a Miss von Eberts, afterwards reporting that among the performers had been:

Ellen Terry,[23] who really looks as sweet as ever, and I think acts better: the two Kendals[24], Beerbohm Tree[25] – all splendid: the whole thing was excellent. A few days ago I saw Sir Cha[rle]s Windham in 'David Garrick' – which was also A1; a very pretty play and he an extremely good player. These are quite among the best things going in town.[26]

Two days later, John learned he had passed Medicine but failed Obstetrics & Gynaecology. Another letter to his mother explained the situation:

I got ploughed, sure enough! 'Referred' for 3 months they call it: last night I finished the orals in Med[icine]. & Midwifery (inc. Gynecology) [sic]. The man in Gynec[ology]. found a weak spot in my paper, took me on it, kept on it and never left it . . . I am truly sorry for the sake of you at home, to be playing 'ugly duckling' to the family . . . I got thro' medicine – so I am not entirely shamed. Tomorrow & Tues[day]. comes Surgery, but I feel quite careless about it, and am only hoping for the best.

I am not sure that a chastening like this is not a good thing: I was getting to think that I was too good.[27]

Despite his failure he was not despondent and took comfort from several pleasant hours spent browsing through some of London's many second-hand bookshops. His mother wrote reassuring him that he had not disgraced himself and John replied, relieved that 'it doesn't seem to have broken one heart in the whole family'.[28] He was later to pass his Obstetrics and Gynaecology at the second attempt, and be awarded his LRCP qualification in 1904. Before he sailed for Canada, news reached him of the untimely death of Wyatt Johnson at the age of forty-two and on his return to Montreal Dr John McCrae was appointed to the vacant position of Pathologist at the Montreal General Hospital.

In the country he had just left, the pen of the man John had last seen at the Mount Nelson Hotel was now hard at work. Both Rudyard Kipling and the journalist, Leo Amery, had returned from South Africa concerned at what they had seen. The British defeats of the early months of the war had revealed cracks that were beginning to form in what had hitherto seemed an invincible Empire. Amery believed that a great international struggle lay ahead and was convinced that if the British army was to function properly, it was in urgent need of major reforms. Kipling worried over the army's performance in South Africa and, while filled with admiration for the courage of the individual British soldier, he felt soured by the ineptitude of some British senior officers and distressed by the high rate of disease and non-combat deaths.

As far as Kipling was concerned, there were serious lessons that needed to be taken to heart as the very nature of armed conflict had changed dramatically. Well-informed and intuitive, he continued to pinpoint what he saw as the German menace. New thinking and new technology were required for the future and he was convinced that a programme of compulsory military service should be swiftly implemented to help build an army that would be equal in size to that of Germany or France. From 'Batemans', his peaceful home in Sussex, he started a campaign to alert the British to the growing danger of European militarism, set up a movement to encourage Rifle Clubs in villages, and presented his nearest club at Rottingdean with a Nordenfeldt, the same machine gun that had caught the Kaiser's eye a few years earlier. In a letter to a journalist friend, Kipling expressed his deep concerns: 'We in England are just camping comfortably on the edge of a volcano . . . Meanwhile the Teuton has his large cold eye on us, and prepares to give us toko when he feels good and ready. We ought to see in a few years now.'[29]

He also began to write poetry warning of danger from an external enemy and from lack of action within the country. His poem 'Before a midnight breaks in storm' prophesied terrible violence and stressed that there was still time to make the necessary preparations. Over the next few years Kipling was to emphasise the social gains of conscription, to remonstrate against self satisfaction, to attack all classes and aspects of

English life and to warn of the trivia standing in the way of national awareness and preparedness. As he pointed a finger towards the deficiencies of Britain's military system, across the North Sea, the Kaiser was intensely concerned with his own.

Before leaving England after the funeral of his grandmother Queen Victoria, Kaiser Wilhelm II had talked of an alliance between the two nations – one in which the British would have command at sea and the Germans on land. 'With such an alliance,' Wilhelm had announced at a luncheon in his honour at Marlborough House, 'not a mouse could stir in Europe without our permission.'[30] Despite this declaration, he was still much involved with the role and build-up of Germany's new High Seas Fleet, attributing his strange passion for the Navy in no small way to his 'English blood'[31] and boyhood memories of visits to Osborne, Queen Victoria's home on the Isle of Wight. It was generally accepted that his country now had the best army in Europe, but she had not previously sought to challenge British domination of the seas. In this respect, Britain was alert. Kipling had no need to warn the Admiralty, who were aware of the growing threat of German naval rivalry.

For reasons of state and family connections, Kaiser Wilhelm made periodic visits to Britain. The grandmother, who had on one occasion described him as a 'hot-headed, conceited, and wrong-headed young man'[32] but who had nevertheless tolerated him with a fondness reserved for her eldest grandchild, had gone. In her place on the throne of Great Britain sat an uncle who made no secret of the fact that he had little time for his nephew and was relieved when his visits were over. King Edward VII was already looking not in the direction of Germany, but of France. A confirmed francophile who spoke almost faultless French, he loved Paris and felt at home there. For him, there was so much to enjoy in the brilliance and elegance of Paris society, the city's superb restaurants, the horse racing at Longchamps and Auteuil and the variety of its theatre.

Edward had ascended the throne at a difficult and complex time politically. Within continental Europe there was a common dislike of Britain and a sense of unease at the great power she wielded. The South African War had left her unpopular and isolated; it was now imperative to acquire some friends and allies, particularly in view of the potential hostility of Germany. The King's long apprenticeship as Prince of Wales enabled him to bring to the throne a great breadth of experience. He delighted in diplomacy and his inbuilt common sense combined with tact, charm and a genial disposition, made him a natural ambassador. He was gregarious and mobile by nature. He loved to travel and be seen, and his people loved him the more for it. Somehow he managed to combine a regal dignity and strong regard for form with a total lack of any unnecessary pomposity.

The European tour Edward undertook in 1903 led him first to Britain's oldest ally – Portugal, and thence to Italy, Gibraltar, Malta and France. This final visit was aimed at helping to settle outstanding colonial disputes between Britain and France and establishing better relations. A special train brought the King to Paris on a perfect spring afternoon for the start of a three-day visit that, after a difficult beginning, was to end an unqualified success. Having identified himself with the cause of Anglo-French friendship, he quickly won the sympathy of the French people and by the time he left Paris to the cries of 'Vive le Roi!' and 'Vive le bon Edouard!', he had laid the foundation for reconciliation and the beginning of the strange relationship that was subsequently to develop between the two countries and bring them to fight side by side eleven years later. In London, rumours of the Anglo-French rapprochement were followed by more alarming rumours of German intentions. It was a theme picked up successfully by South African War veteran and novelist, Erskine Childers, in his famous book *The Riddle of the Sands*, by far the most popular summer holiday reading that year.

For John McCrae, the summer of 1903 meant another short period at Johns Hopkins, Baltimore, which he found to be 'a great brushing up on the clinical work'.[33] He enjoyed seeing the Oslers once again in the absence of his brother Tom, who was away in Europe. Baltimore sweltered in temperatures well into the nineties, and while John was there, the city suffered damage from a tornado. Nevertheless he survived well on a combination of work and a readily available supply of peaches and cold drinks. He also set aside time that summer for the annual Canadian militia training camp activities. Once a year, the militia attended a two-week session of training with occasional demonstrations for the benefits of spectators. Socially, a militia commission opened doors and offered pleasant friendships outside a man's occupation or profession. Since South Africa, John had been promoted to the rank of major and, together with lst Brigade Canadian Field Artillery, he proceeded to camp at the town of Deseronto on Lake Ontario. As an officer, John now presented the appearance of a tall, handsome man, resolute, widely experienced and mature. Punctuality, discipline, unquestioning obedience, detestation of slackness and the complete fulfilment of one's duties were all cardinal virtues to him. He adhered to them in his military, professional and personal life, and looked for them in other people.

Deseronto would have been an enjoyable break from his medical work and a chance to see old friends, but the train transporting the main militia contingent jumped the track in the early hours of 9 June 1903 injuring one or two of the men, killing one horse and smashing some of their equipment. Thankfully John, along with most, escaped what could have been a dreadful disaster. The remainder of his vacation time saw him engaged in quieter pursuits. Friends with a summer home at Kennebunkport on the Maine coast had invited him to join them for a week in September. It proved to be a delightful rest, during which he 'contrived to have the very best possible time – canoeing, sailing, driving and so on, ad infinitum.'[34] The 'ad infinitum' also included a delicious clam and lobster supper and happy hours spent reading Robert Louis Stevenson's *The Master of Ballantrae* on the verandah to the sound of Atlantic rollers just fifty yards from the doorstep.

With the start of another academic year in prospect, John returned to Montreal. His professional life now became more demanding as he and three other members of the McGill medical teaching staff took on additional work as Special Professors at the University of Vermont Medical College. This meant an early start on his day off from McGill and a train journey through the pleasant hills and wooded valleys of New England to the town of Burlington on the eastern shore of Lake Champlain. Along its 120-mile length could be seen all manner of sailing boats, fishing craft and ferries plying their way back and forth. It was a long day for the doctor and he was rarely back in Montreal much before midnight or even the early hours on occasions. During the eight years he was to teach at Burlington, John came to be regarded as the most senior of the visiting professors. Although his main role was to lecture in Pathology, his medical knowledge was so wide-ranging that if one of his colleagues failed to appear, he could substitute admirably.[35] Never wasting a minute, he used the train journey to and from Burlington to write letters and prepare notes for the following day's lectures.

Both at Burlington and McGill, where he was now teaching Bacteriology and Pathology, John was already becoming popular and proficient in the lecture room. He found he had the ability to fasten knowledge in the mind of a student with picturesque, clear phrases, and emulated his own teachers by illustrating his lectures whenever possible. The students were well-taught, entertained by his witticisms and philosophical observations, and given the impression that their tutor took of genuine personal interest in each one of them. The temper inherited from his father showed on occasions when John came across carelessness or lack of professional standards, but for the most part he was kind and patient with the honest plodder, visibly enthusiastic over the brightest and keenest, and supportive overall. In later years after Henry Howitt became a general practitioner and succeeded his father as Guelph's Medical Officer of Health, he recalled the help John had given him at McGill:

In my third year he demonstrated in Histology and Bacteriology . . . I am forever grateful for the assistance Jack McCrae gave me in making easy, a subject which at first was very difficult for me. To be able to do so was his great gift'.[36]

The high standards John set himself and his student were prompted by his belief in the duty of a physician to attend human distress in all walks of life, and to do the job to the very best of his ability. One young man who greatly admired John's example and followed it, was Francis Scrimger, another McGill third-year student who lived, ate and breathed medicine. He and his teacher were to remain friends and were later to serve at the same hospital in France.

Away from medicine, John enjoyed mixing with members of the other McGill faculties and around this time, he met Stephen Leacock. Having come to academic life by the hard route of a degree earned through evening study, Leacock had just completed his doctorate at the University of Chicago. A Fellowship in Political Economy had given him an entrée to McGill and he was now a member of the new Department of Economics and Political Science. With a shared love of humour and writing, the two men were to get to know each other well and the young doctor always enjoyed his invitations to the Leacock home for, as he later wrote 'Stephen is good company'.[37] John was becoming no less well-known as a humorist than Stephen Leacock would ultimately be, the difference being that he used his humour to enhance his teaching while Leacock employed his in the writing that was to bring him fame. Someone else destined for literary success was also about to visit Montreal, and John found himself with an invitation to attend 'an At Home to meet W.B. Yeats whoever he is: he is a writer "of sorts" I think, as the Englishmen say.'[38]

The snowy Montreal streets were busy with shoppers as John caught the train home to Guelph for a family Christmas that year. On his return, the popular doctor seemed to enter an extremely busy period professionally and socially, as he explained in a letter to Janet McCrae:

Thurs[day]. was the Nervous diseases class, Friday I cut the Medico Chi[rurgical Society]. being weary of medical things, and played bridge at the Hays' with a nice little party of eight. Saturday I was at Miss Sally Stephens' theatre party to The Country Girl – after a good dinner. Sunday I purposed as a day of rest – made my visit early at the R[oyal]. V[ictoria]. H[ospital]. & went to Church: did the routine work in early aft[ernoon]. . . . Then I went to church again, and had supper at Norah Craig's aunt's – and so to bed . . . Monday – medical reporting club until 11 p.m. So you can see work is busy: the daily visit at the R[oyal].V[ictoria]. H[ospital]. is rather wearing, & I am giving 2 4th year clinics per week in Medicine, besides my Path[ology]. teaching. Between times I have my Tropical Med[icine]. paper for April 10; a life of Bichat[39] (for the Mont[real]. Med[ical]. Jour[nal].) for March 7th, two case reports for the Medico Chi[rurgical Society]. March 4th; then I go to Ottawa (D[ivisional]. A[rtillery]. A[ssociation].) Friday – but I cannot stay over to the Gov[ernor]. Gen[eral]'s dinner on Saturday as

I have to lecture to the nurses at the M[ontreal]. G[eneral]. H[ospital]. on Sat. ev[enin]g.[40]

His description of life being 'a very constant rush'[41] seemed entirely appropriate, but no matter how late the hour or how much work awaited him, John always made time to attend St Paul's Presbyterian Church in Montreal. His religion, broadened by his experiences in South Africa, remained a focal point in his life.

On 8 April 1904 the formal signing of the much-hailed Anglo-French Entente Cordiale took place. The Germans had known for some time that an agreement was imminent and in private, the German Foreign Ministry regarded it as a major diplomatic defeat. However, nobody seriously believed the new rapprochement between the two old enemy nations would survive very long. Besides, Kaiser Wilhelm had other things to occupy his mind. That February, Japan had attacked the Russian Fleet at Port Arthur and started a war that changed the strategic balance of the Far East. The Kaiser supported Russia and noted the effectiveness of the modern quick-firing artillery used in the conflict. The German general staff speculated on the effectiveness of the Russian army in a future European war and profited materially from the Russo-Japanese conflict, concluding a valuable trade agreement in Russia that July. The Chief of the German General Staff, General Graf Alfred von Schlieffen, was now convinced that if war came to Europe, Germany would gain a rapid victory in the West. Although the German Naval High Command was not ready for battle, the first British war plan for operations against the German fleet was drawn up that June by the Director of Naval Intelligence, Rear Admiral Prince Louis of Battenburg.

Such matters seemed far removed from the life of the average Canadian, whose country had been enjoying unparalleled prosperity under Prime Minister Wilfrid Laurier's government. As a new Governor General settled into Rideau Hall, his official residence, he was greatly encouraged by what he saw. Albert, 4th Earl Grey, regarded his appointment as an opportunity to forge stronger links of empire in a country that in recent years had witnessed, among many things, the discovery of gold in the Klondike and the opening up of the Prairies to thousands of newcomers. Rising world prices and cheap shipping had created a world market for Canadian wheat and production had increased enormously. The vast plains where it grew were now connected into the greater transport system by a network of railway branch lines. The charming, patient Laurier had maintained his deep commitment to national unity and was re-elected in 1904 by a big majority. Canada's rising fortunes and the buoyant international environment in which the gold standard supplied a universal mode of exchange, led him to reiterate his firmly-held belief that 'the twentieth century belongs to Canada'.[42]

Those days of unimpeded trade and travel brought a freedom of movement and a flood of migration. A busy Canadian immigration campaign in Europe caused complaints from Berlin to Downing Street about the 'attempt to lure our fellow countrymen to this desolate, sub-arctic region'.[43] Nevertheless the human flood tide continued up to 1914, creating truly cosmopolitan communities, especially in Alberta and the Prairies. Moving west was now a popular option.

At McGill, the term of John's McCrae's Fellowship in Pathology came to an end and a new encumbent arrived. Dr Oskar Klotz was a recent graduate of the University of Toronto and was later to succeed John as Assistant Pathologist at the Royal Victoria Hospital, or Royal Vic. as it was otherwise known. John took Oskar under his wing and the two men became close friends. As part of their Pathology teaching work, they performed autopsies with George Adami giving the commentary. Years later, Klotz remembered that John was very helpful at such times, since

> he possessed a direct and logical mind, and a snappy comment which savoured of Carlyleism[44] . . . McCrae's interests were partly clinical and in training pathological; he could visualize the clinical events and then from our findings he would bring some co-ordination of the several views . . . Those of us who had the opportunity of being a party to these occasions were indeed fortunate.[45]

Like Henry Howitt, Klotz also praised John's teaching style:

> John McCrae was a born teacher . . . I have repeatedly met students who sat under him and they never stinted their praise of his teaching. The students loved him for the interest he always displayed in their difficulties and because he showed the human side of medicine. They learned from him the unselfish duty of the physician to human distress in all walks of life. They loved him, too, because he never feared to step from the dignity of the teacher to the level of the student.[46]

In that first decade of the twentieth century, the doctors carving out their medical careers in Canada were a notable group. Nearly every department in the profession was represented by enthusiastic and highly-motivated young men who had completed extensive post-graduate training in Canada and overseas.[47] Typical of this group was another of John's medical friends, Dr Edward Archibald, a surgeon at the Royal Vic. Just a few months older than John, Archibald was a fluent French speaker who had spent part of his Arts degree course at the Universities of Montpelier and Freiburg before studying medicine and graduating from McGill to undertake extended further training in Breslau, Berlin, Göttingen and London. John McCrae, Edward Archibald and their friends, Doctors Bill Turner, Campbell Palmer Howard and Bill Francis – William Osler's

94

godson who was now completing his internship at the Royal Victoria – all became members of the Krausmanian Club. They gathered on a monthly basis at Krausman's restaurant in Montreal and debated social, practical and philosophical topics late into the night. George Adami occasionally joined them, one of the few senior members of the Faculty to do so, as he enjoyed their frank, open exchanges. John's genial personality, stimulating conversation and highly developed humour made him a popular member of this circle.

The staff of the Royal Vic. had been expanding and in 1904 it was decided to create a new level of position between a physician or surgeon and the more junior clinical assistant in each speciality. Among the first new appointments, John was made an Associate in Medicine and Edward Archibald an Assistant Surgeon. The familiar sight of the tall, handsome Dr McCrae with his buoyant stride, winning smile and kindly approach endeared him to staff and patients alike. His success both on and off the wards was growing and brought him an invitation from the University of Vermont to give the opening address at the start of the 1904-5 session of the Medical Faculty. He entitled it 'The Privileges of Medicine', and in it summarised his main ideals and his faith, emphasising his belief that it was the duty of a good doctor to serve his poor patients every bit as much as his wealthy ones.

As 1904 came to a close, John could look back with satisfaction on twelve months of achievement that included the publication of two further poems in *The McGill University Magazine*. One of them returned to his theme of death as a release from the battle of life, a theme that had been heightened by his experiences in South Africa.

Upon Watts' Picture, 'Sic Transit'

'What I spent I had; what I saved, I lost; what I gave, I have'

But yesterday the tourney, all the eager joy of life,
The waving of the banners, and the rattle of the spears,
The clash of sword and harness, and the madness of the strife;
To-night begin the silence and the peace of endless years.
(One sings within).

But yesterday the glory and the prize,
And best of all, to lay it at her feet,
To find my guerdon in her speaking eyes:
I grudge them not, – they pass, albeit sweet.

The ring of spears, the winning of the fight,
The careless song, the cup, the love of friends,
The earth in spring – to live, to feel the light –
'Twas good the while it lasted: here it ends.

Remain the well-wrought deed in honour done,
The dole for Christ's dear sake, the words that fall
In kindliness upon some outcast one, –
They seemed so little: now they are my All.[48]

To some, John McCrae's lesser-known poems are seen as charming, if on occasions somewhat sombre, examples of Victorian and Edwardian verse. Others perceive in them a mystical quality. His second 1904 poem, 'The Dying of Père Pierre', has been cited as one such example.

The Dying of Père Pierre

' . . . with two other priests; the same night he died, and was buried by the shores of the lake that bears his name.'

Chronicle

'Nay, grieve not that ye can no honour give
To these poor bones that presently must be
But carrion; since I have sought to live
Upon God's earth, as He hath guided me,
I shall not lack! Where would ye have me lie?
High heaven is higher than cathedral nave:
Do men paint chancels fairer than the sky?'
Beside the darkened lake they made his grave,
Below the altar of the hills; and night
Swung incense clouds of mist in creeping lines
That twisted through the tree-trunks, where the light
Groped through the arches of the silent pines:
And he, beside the lonely path he trod,
Lay, tombed in splendour, in the House of God.[49]

The recurrence of the theme of death in John's poetry was at odds with his outward demeanour, which one friend described as:

one of continuous laughter. That is not true, of course, for in repose his face was heavy, his countenance more than ruddy; it was even of a 'choleric' cast, and at times almost livid, especially when he was recovering from one of those attacks of asthma from which he habitually suffered. But his smile was his own, and it was ineffable. It filled the eyes, and illumined the face. It was the smile of sheer fun, of pure gaiety, of sincere playfulness, innocent of irony; with a tinge of sarcasm – never.[50]

Stephen Leacock may have given another clue to the serious nature of much of John McCrae's poetry when he wrote that 'If a man has a genuine sense of humor he is apt to take a somewhat melancholy, or at least a disillusioned view of life. Humor and disillusionment are twin sisters.'[51]

NOTES

1. From 'Recompense' by John McCrae, *The Canadian Magazine of Politics, Science, Art and Literature* (Volume 7, May–October 1896), p. 142. MTRL.
2. Donald Mackay, *The Square Mile: Merchant Princes of Montreal* (Vancouver, 1987), Title page.
3. Edgar Andrew Collard, *Montreal Yesterdays* (Toronto, 1963), pp. 215–219.
4. Howitt, 'John McCrae', p. 9.
5. Howitt, 'John McCrae', p. 9.
6. Autopsy Book 1902–3, inside cover, MS 264, OL. The verse is from 'Horae succisivae, or spare hours of meditations', written in 1631 by Joseph Henshaw, who became Bishop of Peterborough in 1663. In John McCrae's version, the spelling has been modernised and there are other changes, including the last two lines, which may or may not have been composed by him.
7. Elizabeth Dagg, 'A Race of Passionate Men: The Lives of John McCrae and Norman Bethune' (Guelph, 1993), p.11.
8. Adami, *J. George Adami*, p. 165.
9. Adami, *J. George Adami*, p. 166.
10. Miller, *Painting the Map Red*, p. 4. The Canadian units that fought in South Africa were: 2nd (Special Service) Battalion, Royal Canadian Regiment; D, E and F Batteries, Royal Canadian Field Artillery; 1st Battalion, Canadian Mounted Rifles (re-designated the Royal Canadian Dragoons in 1900); 2nd Battalion, Canadian Mounted Rifles; and Lord Strathcona's Horse. The 3rd, 4th, 5th and 6th Battalions, Canadian Mounted Rifles were recruited and sent to South Africa but arrived after the war had ended. Finally, twelve troops of the South African Constabulary were also recruited in Canada and some did see action during the war.
11. JM to Janet McCrae, 20 September 1901, GM Papers.
12. JM to Janet McCrae, 1 November 1901, GM Papers.
13. JM to Janet McCrae, 19 October 1901, GM Papers.
14. John McCrae, 'Builders of Empire', p.74.
15. Prescott, *In Flanders Fields*, p. 43.
16. John McCrae, 'Hasty Notes and Judgements', *The McGill University Magazine* (Volume 2, No. 1, December 1902), p. 108. Micro mfm/AP/U577, UTL.
17. John McCrae, 'Hasty Notes and Judgements', p. 111.
18. John McCrae, 'Hasty Notes and Judgements', p. 111.
19. John McCrae, 'Hasty Notes and Judgements', p. 115.
20. JM to Janet McCrae, 23 April 1902, GM Papers.
21. John McCrae, 'Hasty Notes and Judgements', p. 116.
22. John McCrae, 'Hasty Notes and Judgements', p. 118.
23. The English actress Ellen Terry (1847–1928) was one of the most popular stage performers in Britain and North America. She played many great Shakespearean parts during the 24 years that she worked as the leading lady of Sir Henry Irving, the celebrated actor and theatre-manager. Their partnership, one of the most famous in the history of the British theatre, had just ended in 1902 when she appeared in 'The Merry Wives of Windsor'.

24. William (1843–1917) and Dame Margaret (1849–1935) Kendal were an English husband and wife team of actor-managers whose theatrical company trained many performers who later attained eminence. 'Madge' Kendal was a brilliant actress who overshadowed her husband on the stage, but William Kendal was an astute businessman with a fine artistic sense.

25. The actor-producer Sir Herbert Beerbohm Tree, who was the half-brother of caricaturist and writer Sir Max Beerbohm.

26. JM to Janet McCrae, 11 July 1902, GM Papers.

27. JM to Janet McCrae, 13 July 1902, GM Papers.

28. JM to Janet McCrae, 16 August 1902, GM Papers.

29. From a letter written by Kipling to H.A. Gwynne in 1908, Lord Birkenhead, *The Life of Rudyard Kipling* (New York, 1978), p. 252

30. Massie, *Dreadnought*, p. 303.

31. Massie, *Dreadnought*, p. 150.

32. Massie, *Dreadnought*, p. 107.

33. JM to Janet McCrae, 4 August 1903, GM Papers.

34. JM to Janet McCrae, 14 September 1903, GM Papers.

35. Neville Terry, *The Royal Vic: The Story of Montreal's Royal Victoria Hospital 1894–1994* (Montreal, 1994), p. 68.

36. Howitt, 'John McCrae', p. 11.

37. JM to Janet McCrae, 25 February 1910, GM Papers.

38. JM to Janet McCrae, 17 December 1902, GM Papers.

39. Marie-François-Xavier Bichat (1771–1802), was a French anatomist and physiologist whose systematic study of human tissues helped to found the science of histology.

40. JM to Janet McCrae, 24 February 1904, GM Papers.

41. JM to Janet McCrae, 24 February 1904, GM Papers.

42. Réal Belanger, 'Sir Wilfrid's Sunny Ways', *Horizon Canada* (Volume 7, No. 77, August 1986), p. 1829.

43. Stephen Leacock, *Canada*, p. 205.

44. John McCrae read and enjoyed the works of the Victorian philosopher, Thomas Carlyle.

45. Adami, *J. George Adami*, p. 163.

46. Adami, *J. George Adami*, p. 163.

47. Prescott, *In Flanders Fields*, pp.45–46.

48. *The McGill University Magazine* (Volume 3, No. 1, December 1903), p.32, Micro mfm/AP/U577, UTL.

49. *The McGill University Magazine* (Volume 3, No. 2, April 1904), p. 67, Micro mfm/ AP/U577, UTL.

50. Macphail, *In Flanders Fields*, p. 85.

51. David M. Legate, *Stephen Leacock: A Biography* (Toronto, 1970), Preface, p. 2.

CHAPTER SEVEN

'The careless song, the cup, the love of friends'[1]
1905–1908

On 6 April 1905 a train on its way from Calais to the south of France made a special stop three quarters of an hour from Paris. The white-haired elegantly dressed gentleman who boarded was afforded every courtesy and swiftly escorted to a private carriage. As he entered, a distinguished bearded figure rose to welcome him. After an initial exchange of pleasantries, the two settled down to a discussion over cigars and refreshments as the train sped on towards the French capital.

In the wake of the Entente Cordiale, King Edward VII of Britain and President Emile Loubet of France had established a good relationship that the King took every opportunity to foster. On arrival at Paris's Gare du Nord, the two men parted having sanctioned an exchange of naval visits during the coming summer. Thus, one hundred years after the Battle of Trafalgar, British ships sailed peacefully into the French port of Brest in July 1905 and everyone cheered. A month later it was the turn of Portsmouth to play host to the French Northern Squadron. King Edward presided over a formal dinner on board the royal yacht *Victoria and Albert III* and more than a thousand people streamed into Portsmouth Naval Barracks for a lavish ball. The Royal Navy had spared no expense to entertain their French visitors: the dance floor was fringed by banks of palms, hydrangeas and marguerites and half the main hall was transformed into a conservatory with baskets of flowers hanging from the ceiling. In the city of London the French were honoured guests at a special Lord Mayor's banquet at the Guildhall. To great applause, the French Admiral Caillard spoke of the English Channel being not a barrier but a bond.

Germany, meanwhile, had continued to build up its own fleet and King Edward's arrival at the Kiel Regatta the previous summer had prompted Kaiser Wilhelm to have every German warship on display. With his full support, the introduction of a new German Navy Bill in March 1905 proposed expenditure of more than £185 million over the next twelve years. In a grand speech in Bremen, Wilhelm emphasised that every German warship launched was one more guarantee of peace and that 'Our Lord and God would never have given Himself such pains with our German Fatherland and its people if He had not predestined it to something great.'[2] The vision of a procession of German battleships taking to the seas was much in the mind of Britain's First Sea Lord, Admiral Sir John ('Jacky') Fisher who, throughout his term in office, was to be convinced of the inevitability of war with Germany. It was not something Fisher wanted but, in these times of growing tension and danger, his clear priority was to ensure that Britain had the best, most efficient and most powerful fleet. Even before he had taken up office the previous October, Fisher had been working on the drastic reforms he intended to impose on the navy. In December 1904 he had announced, as part of his overall plan, the intention of building a fast battleship to be known as H.M.S. *Dreadnought*.

Some ten days before King Edward's meeting with President Loubet, the Kaiser boarded the steamer *Hamburg*, and headed through the English Channel and Bay of Biscay towards the Mediterranean. With his habitual love of ceremonial occasions, he anticipated with pleasure a visit to Gibraltar and the opportunity to wear his uniform as an honorary Admiral of the Fleet. When he decided to make what appeared to be an impromptu visit to the Moroccan port of Tangier there was much consternation, for Morocco was a trouble spot. In 1880 Germany, Britain, Italy, Spain and France had been the signatories of the Treaty of Madrid, specifying that before any one power were to consider seizing political and economic power in Morocco, it must consult with the other signatories. Germany had never displayed any such intentions, but France had a long-held ambition to possess Morocco. The kidnapping the previous year of two British and American civilians by a local chief in rebellion against the Sultan of Morocco, had convinced the expatriate community that law and order could no longer be maintained in the country. The fact that France had offered to assist in reorganising the Moroccan army and demanded that the Sultan should hand over his police, army and customs houses to French officers and officials, had caused Sultan Abdul-Aziz to ask the German ambassador to confirm whether France 'spoke for Europe'. The reply had been one of unequivocal and continued support for Morocco's independence. Germany's Chancellor, Prince Bernhard von Bülow, sensing the possibility of an eventual Anglo-French-Russian entente and worried about the balance of power in Europe, now saw his opportunity to humiliate France. The Kaiser's short visit, far from being impromptu, was designed to thwart French plans and 'foster our economic interests in Morocco'.[3]

The Germans had underestimated British sensitivity to any suspicion of German intriguing against their Entente partner so near to their vital trade routes. At around the time King Edward and President Loubet were having their meeting, Wilhelm arrived at Gibraltar to a very cool reception. He less than tactfully told Prince Louis of Battenburg, commanding the British Second Cruiser Squadron, that 'we know the road to Paris and we will get there again if need be. They should remember no fleet can defend Paris'.[4] Exchanges between France and Germany continued during the coming weeks and led ultimately to the resignation of the French Foreign Minister and to German demands for an international conference on Morocco. Concerned observers must have watched this German diplomatic offensive with growing unease and well they might, for in Berlin, von Schlieffen, Chief of the German General Staff, was formulating a plan to defeat France in a thirty-one-day campaign.

As events on the international stage ran their increasingly troublesome course, the tasks laid before a busy doctor like John McCrae seemed unending. The steady progression of his medical career was bringing with it yet more demands as he engaged in 'the heroic struggle by which a man gains a footing in a strange place in that most particular of all professions'.[5] He was now invited to take on additional work as an examiner in Clinical Medicine, Pathology and Bacteriology, and as Pathologist to the Montreal Foundling and Baby Hospital. John's round of 'outdoor clinics, laboratory duties, post-mortems, lecturing, teaching, demonstrating, visiting patients in hospital and at home, meetings, conventions, papers, lectures, editing, reviewing' was 'enough to appall the stoutest heart.'[6] He sometimes felt the strain but seldom gave that impression, and was normally seen going about his work 'gaily, never busy, never idle'.[7] Stephen Leacock later recalled that 'no man in our circle worked harder than did John McCrae. Yet he seemed to find time for everything, and contrived somehow to fill in the spare moments of a busy life with the reveries of a poet.'[8]

These 'reveries' had produced another poem. 'The Pilgrims' returned to the theme of death as a reward for a life of toil and John submitted it to the editor of *The McGill University Magazine*, Dr Andrew Macphail. Macphail was at that time a lecturer in Medicine at Bishop's University in Montreal and had known John for several years. He was very taken with his latest offering and wrote to John pronouncing it to be 'the real stuff of poetry. How did you make it? What have you to do with medicine?'[9] Acknowledging their shared Scottish roots, he ended his letter with the Gaelic salutation 'slainte filidh', or in English, 'Hail to the poet'.[10] From a man like Andrew Macphail, this was praise indeed.

The Pilgrims

An uphill path, sun-gleams between the showers,
Where every beam that broke the leaden sky
Lit other hills with fairer ways than ours;
Some clustered graves where half our memories lie;
And one grim Shadow creeping ever nigh:
And this was Life.

Wherein we did another's burden seek,
The tired feet we helped upon the road,
The hand we gave the weary and the weak,
The miles we lightened one another's load,
When, faint to falling, onward yet we strode:
This too was Life.

Till, at the upland, as we turned to go
Amid fair meadows, dusky in the night,
The mists fell back upon the road below;
Broke on our tired eyes the western light;
The very graves were for a moment bright:
And this was Death.[11]

Although poetry was something John tended to compose in his spare half hours, he regularly allocated time to writing medical articles and by 1914 would have published a total of forty-six. Some of these were the result of his own research and some were written in collaboration with colleagues. John's pieces included subjects as wide-ranging as 'Recent Progress in Tropical Medicine', 'An analysis of two hundred autopsies upon infants' and 'Some Literary Physicians'. The latter enabled him to introduce his love of history and literature, taking among his subjects, Rabelais,[12] Smollett[13] and Oliver Wendell Holmes.[14] According to Andrew Macphail, these articles were more a testament to 'his industry rather than to invention and discovery, but they have made his name known in every text-book of medicine'. Macphail's view was that John was no experimental investigator and had 'neither the mind nor the hands'[15] for laboratory work. Instead, he preferred to let nature do its own work, believing that, if 'one begins with humility, there is Nature, eager at every hand to teach us things'.[16] Overall feelings of optimism in the future of the Empire embraced the belief that disease and other forms of human suffering would be conquered by modern science, and doctors like John McCrae worked on the treatment of infectious diseases such as typhoid and scarlet fever. Around this time, he joined three other doctors setting up a private practice in Montreal. It was known among themselves and their friends as 'The Bull Pen', but he disliked the chore of sending out accounts and admitted to having made little money during the first year of the new practice.

Dr McCrae was now in great demand socially. Writing to his mother early in 1905, he listed his recent activities: attendance at a dance, dinner with friends, a snow shoe walk with a small group, supper with George Adami who wanted to show him some new art acquisitions, and a walk over Mount Royal. He continued:

Dr. Adami entertains the Path[ology]. staff to-morrow evening, generous man! On Sat. I am to dine with the Bells . . . I am having an awful time dodging invitations: I don't like to have to seem to pick my friends, but the pace is too great. I really think I have about twice as many invitations of all sorts as there are days: I don't like to seem a society man at all – but it fairly pours upon one. Yet it does not involve late hours, which is one great advantage. The outdoor sports, though, I take as they come, as I think that, at least is entirely advantageous.[17]

In terms of his popularity, John seems to have been a victim of his own success. Andrew Macphail later remarked that:

Wherever he lived he was a social figure. When he sat at table the dinner was never dull . . . His contribution was merely 'stories', and these stories in endless succession were told in a spirit of frank fun. They were not illustrative, admonitory, or hortatory. They were just amusing, and always fresh. This gift he acquired from his mother, who had that rare charm of mimicry without mockery, and caricature without malice.[18]

Montreal society hostesses, not unnaturally, competed to invite John to their tables and he received many invitations to make up parties for dances and balls, which had grown more and more splendid in recent years. Although he was a popular guest, John never aspired to be one of the prestigious élite, many of whom were recorded for posterity by the sons of William Notman, a renowned Canadian photographer with a Montreal studio never short of society commissions.

For a non-materialistic man who nevertheless appreciated art and beautiful things, it must have been a fascinating experience to be invited into the magnificent 'Square Mile' residences of the wealthy set in their large gardens ablaze with colour from spring to the first frost of autumn. Each was built entirely to the taste of its owner and architectural styles were extraordinarily diverse. One might encounter a Tudor manor house or a Scottish castle; a French château or an Italian villa. Expert craftsmen were often brought from Europe to create lavish interiors with marble flooring, intricate woodwork or ornate ironwork for the great conservatories where tropical plants flourished in the winter months. Rooms were filled with lush soft furnishings, custom-made and antique furniture, and valuable objets d'art. Sir William Van Horne in particular was a noted collector of Japanese porcelain and had amassed an impressive private art collection that attracted interest from around the world.

Formal dining in such splendid surroundings was an elaborate affair. As much care was generally taken with the table arrangements, garnishings, place settings and floral displays as with the food itself. By the light of ornate chandeliers and candelabra, guests could look forward to a sophisticated menu and, if the hostess had planned her guest list well, conversation would sparkle. Given the strict code of social etiquette of the time that forbade discussion of certain topics, John proved a consummate entertainer whose amusing stories were a welcome relief in what could be a social minefield. Anyone meeting him at that time would have encountered a tall, slim, alert, clean-shaven man with a delightful smile denoting the humour that was so often just below the surface. He looked younger than his years and was often mistaken for a student. Despite his time in the militia, he did not have a particularly military bearing but his manner of speaking was positive and succinct. This man who delighted social gatherings never lost interest in the humblest of his patients, nor failed to keep in touch with his boyhood friends in Guelph.

For all the glitter of Montreal society, London was yet more dazzling. King Edward and Queen Alexandra presided over a lively and fashionable Court into which the King introduced a fascinating mix of people from many backgrounds and walks of life. Débutantes were presented, and made a graceful tableau as they waited in line to curtsey to their sovereign. Splendid formal dances were held in an atmosphere fragrant with jasmine or tuberoses, and alive to the strains of such popular waltzes as Lehar's 'The Merry Widow'. Leading figures of the day attended dinners at fashionable London venues like the Trocadero in Piccadilly with its potted palms, elegantly lit tables and stylish clientele. The King's summer diary of 1905 included a ball hosted by the Duchess of Devonshire, at which the great ladies were on show, bejewelled and decked with flowers; an inspection of cadets at the Royal Military College, Sandhurst; a cruise; a visit to the Newmarket races; Cowes Week and the Royal Garden Party at Windsor. From country house parties with their traditional leisurely pursuits, to the delights of the music hall, the fair and Hampstead Heath – known to Londons as ''appy 'Ampstead'; from journeys along the Thames by boat and tea on riverside terraces to weekends at the seaside by train or paddle steamer; from shooting parties after 'the glorious Twelfth' to bicycling through the country lanes and walking in the hills and dales that bordered Britain's industrial British heartland – rich or poor, this was the stuff of an Edwardian summer.

The short Edwardian period has often been likened to a last age of innocence, an Indian summer, a time of carefree light-heartedness between the long Victorian age and the terrible war that was to come. The glories of the English countryside were recorded in *Nature Notes of an Edwardian Lady* by Edith Holden, the gifted writer and illustrator, and in a series of essays by the writer Edward Thomas, who was later to win fame as a war poet. Both authors evoke a peace and beauty that many were wistfully to remember as a lost paradise. The poppy was a flower that caught their interest, as it had that of the Victorian aesthete, Dr John Ruskin, who described it as,

All silk and flame: a scarlet cup, perfect-edged all around, seen among the wild grass far away, like a burning coal fallen from Heaven's altars.[19]

The poppy is painted glass; it never glows so brightly as when the sun shines through it. Wherever it is seen – against the light or with the light – always, it is a flame, and warms the wind like a blown ruby.[20]

Although the land, like Ruskin's poppy, seemed to glow 'with a splendour which suggested serenity . . . seismic faults had developed below, and the Edwardian age is characterised by a rapidly accelerating process of economic, social and political disturbance'.[21] Britain's imperial greatness was under threat from the rise to 'great power' status of Germany, the United States and Japan. At home, the ruling families still maintained their splendid houses and estates, but now 'they counted for less'.[22] The catholic tastes of King Edward had opened up fashionable society to many who, a generation earlier, would never have been able to enter it and, although it was a prosperous time, 'the increasing parade of luxury involved the growing discontent of the poor'.[23] Notwithstanding the depressing towns and urban poverty resulting from industrialisation, the standard of living for the working classes had been improving. With the spread of education and a new feeling of class-consciousness, people were becoming impatient for social change.

Social conditions and the erosion of the countryside by industrial progress were factors influencing the work of writers around that time, but some among them were more concerned with what they perceived as external dangers to their country. Rudyard Kipling continued to try and awaken Britain to what he had foreseen since the South African War, and Sir Arthur Conan Doyle was another prominent writer who did likewise. Already known for his Sherlock Holmes stories, Conan Doyle was an expert in military affairs who had also written a history of the South African War. As an outspoken critic of the government, he tried to raise the alarm about the inadequacies of the British armed forces. Thomas Hardy had written with honesty about the South African War and was now working on *The Dynasts*, his epic treatment of the Napoleonic War. Although set a hundred years earlier, 'it impacted with an almost contemporary insight into the nature of wholesale international military conflict'.[24] Hardy's description of the 1809 battle of Talavera 'seemed to foreshadow the whole mythology of what was to come in Flanders a few years later'.[25]

As the summer of 1905 moved into autumn and John McCrae's star continued to rise steadily in the firmament, he learned of his promotion to the position of Assistant in Medicine at the Royal Vic. George Adami, whose daughter John was now tutoring, encouraged him to apply for the vacant Chair of Medicine at Galveston, Texas, but John was not keen to uproot himself. Someone who had, however, just left his Baltimore home for pastures new, was Dr William Osler. A vacancy had arisen for the position of Regius Professor of Medicine at Oxford and Osler's name had been put forward. From an imperial point of view, the university felt it would be a splendid thing to have a professor who was a Canadian by birth and held in the highest international esteem by his profession. When news broke of Osler's appointment, it produced a huge outpouring of congratulations and good wishes from colleagues everywhere.

While William and Grace Osler were enjoying the first autumn days in Oxford, the trees in Ottawa had already taken on their striking red, orange and gold tints. Among the students enrolling at the city's Lisgar Collegiate that year was thirteen-year-old Alexis Helmer. Although he still had much studying ahead of him, young Helmer was already actively interested in the world of the military. He had no way of knowing that he was now embarking on a road that would lead him to university, the Royal Military College and the battlefields of the Western Front; nor that he would have an enduring link with a doctor in Montreal whose poems were, as yet, unknown to him.

For John McCrae the last months of 1905 passed rapidly and shortly before Christmas, he returned to Guelph. It was not just the traditional festivities that drew him home to 'Janefield', where his parents now lived and where his father David continued to breed cattle with great success. On 21 December 1905, the farm was the scene of a happy family occasion as the pretty, vivacious twenty-seven-year old Geills McCrae married James Kilgour, a barrister whose family were friends of the McCraes. According to a local newspaper account, the bride wore,

> a gown of white crêpe de chine over white silk with embroidered chiffon, and carried a bouquet of white roses. The bridal veil, which was not worn over the face, was fastened with pearl pins and white heather; the bride wore a pendant of pearls and diamonds, the gift of the groom.[26]

Geills and her husband were going to begin a new life in Brandon, Manitoba, not far (in local terms) from Winnipeg, the financial and commercial centre of the west.

As the Canadian winter held the country in its customary icy grip, across the sea in Portsmouth dockyard, work had been proceeding at record pace to build the first of Admiral Sir Jacky Fisher's new ships. On the damp morning of 10 February 1906, a huge gathering of dignitaries and guests assembled at the yard to await the arrival of their King. Towering above them was the hull of the vessel he had come to launch, its bow garlanded with red and white geraniums. On his arrival, King

Edward VII, wearing the uniform of Admiral of the Fleet, made his way to the rostrum erected for the occasion. In time-honoured fashion he took a bottle of wine from a nest of flowers in front of him and swung it against the bow of the new vessel. With the words: 'I christen you Dreadnought'[27] echoing around the official enclosure, the ship glided down her slipway into the water and the band played 'God Save the King'. Fisher surveyed her with pride, for this was the ship that would revolutionise naval warfare. He knew she had the speed to enable her to choose the range at which she wished to engage the enemy and great guns that would enable her to stay out of range of lesser opposition. With her arrangement of guns and turrets, her turbine engines and five thousand tons of armour plating, her power was impressive in relation to the ships that had preceded her. In fact, Dreadnought made obsolescent every battleship previously constructed. The Germans, their curiosity heightened by the unusual amount of secrecy surrounding the building of the new vessel, went into a state of near panic when they received confirmation of her specifications. Fisher's opposite number, Grand Admiral von Tirpitz, took the decision to build ships of the Dreadnought type and to enlarge the Kiel Canal to accommodate them. The two nations were embarking in earnest on a naval arms race.

During those early months of 1906, John McCrae's whirligig of socialising, teaching, private practice, visits to Vermont and work at the hospitals showed no sign of slowing. His many social engagements included a charity ball and 'a pleasant interlude on Friday when Lady Drummond gave a Musicale at the Art Gallery . . . the audience was very swell and presumably select'.[28] One of the numerous dinner parties he attended in Montreal was at the invitation of Marguerite Gault, wife of Hamilton Gault, a dashing English-born millionaire from a textile and property family. John would be their guest on a number of occasions over the next few years and in this instance, after a splendid meal at the Gaults' elegant home, the select gathering went to a performance of Shakespeare's 'As You Like It'. Among John's friends, it seemed set to be a year of marriages, so much so that 'there is a universal groan beginning to be heard through the land,'[29] John later professed. He was now an eligible and very presentable bachelor of thirty-three and although not wealthy, no doubt regarded as a good marriage prospect. Although essentially a 'man's man', it seems that 'somehow or other he made an equal appeal to the fairer sex'[30] but despite his or their charms, marriage still seemed to be far from John's mind and his letters revealed little more than an occasional intriguing nickname for his female acquaintances, such as 'Miss Snowball' or 'The Domestic Art Lady'.[31]

When not attending weddings or hunting for suitable nuptial gifts for his friends, the talented doctor enjoyed the opportunities that now seemed to present themselves to mix business with pleasure. At lunch with Dr Herbert Birkett, future Dean of Medicine at McGill, or William Caldwell, Professor of Philosophy, John could discuss university affairs and his current reading matter. Dining with Dr John Todd, who had recently returned from several years in Africa, he was able to share his interest both in travel and tropical diseases. At supper with his ex-student Francis Scrimger, who was a keen violinist, the two men combined medical topics with their love of music. Scrimger, a new addition to the surgical staff of the Royal Vic., displayed a single-minded devotion to his work and would later show a similar dedication to duty that would single him out on the battlefield.

High standards and professional zeal were things John had always encouraged in his students, demonstrating at the same time a great humanity and his extraordinary charm and humour. Just as he himself continued to follow William Osler's advice to young doctors to put their emotions 'on ice', he liked to quote to his own students the legend from his poem 'Upon Watts' Picture, "Sic Transit"', inspired by what he regarded as 'the most suggestive picture in the world'. It read, 'What I spent I had; what I saved I lost; what I gave I have.'[32] John told his young charges that it 'will be in your power every day to store up for yourselves treasures that will come back to you in the consciousness of duty well done, of kind acts performed, things that having given away freely you yet possess.'[33] Although John's students were aware from such references that he wrote poetry in his spare time, it came as a surprise to their teacher to discover from Stephen Leacock that his reputation had reached illustrious circles. Following a visit to Government House in Ottawa, Leacock reported that the Governor General, Earl Grey 'speaking of the poets of Canada, . . . said "we haven't mentioned McCrae of Montreal"' and 'Leacock spread this about as an excellent bon mot.'[34]

'McCrae of Montreal' was about to find a new friend and publisher for his poetry in the man who had complimented him the previous year. In 1906 a chair in the History of Medicine was established at McGill and Andrew Macphail was appointed to the post. In coming to McGill, Macphail, a physician, former school teacher, editor and playwright, was something of a Renaissance man returning to his alma mater. He was keen to continue his editorship of *The McGill University Magazine* and willing to guarantee it financially. From the following year until after the war, the re-named *University Magazine* set a standard of excellence in English-speaking Canada under Macphail's rigorous direction. He introduced distinguished contributors and included many of his own unpaid articles on political comment and social criticism. He also published all John McCrae's poems up to 1914 and invited him to be a member of the magazine's editorial committee. John had been reading with interest *The Times History of the War*, written and edited by Leo Amery in the years following his return from South Africa, and had found 'Spion Kop . . . a bad chapter to read'.[35] His poem, 'The Unconquered Dead', may possibly have been inspired by the account of Spion Kop or by the Boer victory over the British at Magersfontein.

The Unconquered Dead

' . . . defeated, with great loss.'

Not we the conquered! Not to us the blame
Of them that flee, of them that basely yield;
Nor ours the shout of victory, the fame
Of them that vanquish in a stricken field.

That day of battle in the dusty heat
We lay and heard the bullets swish and sing
Like scythes amid the over-ripened wheat,
And we the harvest of their garnering.

Some yielded, No, not we! Not we, we swear
By these our wounds; this trench upon the hill
Where all the shell-strewn earth is seamed and bare,
Was ours to keep; and lo! we have it still.

We might have yielded, even we, but death
Came for our helper; like a sudden flood
The crashing darkness fell; our painful breath
We drew with gasps amid the choking blood.

The roar felt faint and farther off, and soon
Sank to a foolish humming in our ears,
Like crickets in the long, hot afternoon
Among the wheat fields of the olden years.

Before our eyes a boundless wall of red
Shot through by sudden streaks of jagged pain!
Then a slow-gathering darkness overhead
And rest came on us like a quiet rain.

Not we the conquered! Not to us the shame,
Who hold our earthen ramparts, nor shall cease
To hold them ever; victors we, who came
In that fierce moment to our honoured peace.[36]

As the summer of 1906 drew to a close, the industrious doctor was preparing to sit for the Membership examination of the Royal College of Physicians in London. After a brief hunting trip with his brother, Tom, and friend Dr Bill Turner, during which the three men went in search of the peaceful haunts of Quebec Province and the chance of pheasant or wood duck, John left for London on 5 October. On the way to England, he commented enthusiastically in a long letter to his mother that his modern Canadian liner, *The Empress of Ireland*, was 'a beauty' with tasteful fittings and woods 'as fine as I ever saw them'.[37] He enjoyed a comfortable passage in very pleasant company, the only exceptions being 'two full grown specimens of the genus bore on board'. The chance to relax was 'a great relief after work' and John confessed that, for the voyage at least, the 'lazy life has suited me excellently'.[38] The Oslers had invited him to their hospitable home in Oxford, known to friends as the 'Open Arms', and after his Clinical examination at Charing Cross Hospital, John heard Sir William Osler give that year's Harveian Oration[39] at the Royal College of Physicians. Over the next few days, he told Janet McCrae that he revisited both Westminster Abbey and 'my old friend the Tate Gallery'[40] with its Turner collection, new since his last visit. On his travels around the city, he noted the electrification of the London underground and the fact that the motor bus 'has become a factor' in modern life.[41]

John passed his examination and received a telegram of congratulations from the Oslers. Before returning to Canada he had decided to enjoy a well-earned break in Paris with an old school friend and was soon on his way to the city whose flourishing community of artists, musicians and writers gave it an added fascination in the early years of the century. Harry Higinbotham, who ran the city office of the Sun Life of Canada, was the son of a former Mayor of Guelph and militia officer friend of David McCrae. He lived in a pleasantly furnished apartment on the Avenue de l'Opéra and had a wide circle of acquaintances. A few months earlier, Harry had played host to another young man from Guelph, Edward Johnson, who had known both Harry and John at Guelph Collegiate Institute.

With his fine tenor voice, Edward was already a promising singer who had performed with the New York Symphony Orchestra and, during the summer of that year, had come to Paris for additional lessons and auditions. Harry had not only welcomed him but arranged a tea party to show off Edward's voice to some of his friends. When Edward sang, he was accompanied on the piano by Beatriz d'Arneiro, the daughter of a Portuguese diplomat and composer who had left Portugal for Paris and was making a modest living as a répétiteur or singing coach. The more the young Canadian tenor and the accompanist talked, the clearer it became that Beatriz could help Edward with his career and, although she was the elder by seven years, they became attracted to each other. When Edward returned to New York to fulfil work commitments, Beatriz, the better correspondent of the two, wrote long and frequent letters to him.

On his arrival, John McCrae found his friend Harry 'walking out' with a young American named Elizabeth Morrison, also in Paris to take singing lessons. Aware that Beatriz d'Arneiro was alone, Harry invited her to meet John. Beatriz, who was known to her friends as 'Bebe'[42], was a striking woman of aristocratic bearing, small and slender with dark brown eyes, luxuriant auburn hair and beautiful hands. She was also a charismatic personality adept at wit and mimicry, who did not suffer fools gladly. In a letter to Edward Johnson, Beatriz described her first impression of the Canadian doctor:

November 4th 1906 – Sunday night
At 6 the party came in.- Dr. McCrae did not strike me as very congenial at first, but he was only reticent as I found out afterwards. He is tall & quite young apparently, although he must be between 30 & 35 – We started a conversation on the subject of the separation of the church & the state in France, then went over religious questions on a general scale, & gradually the ice thawed & I found out he is clever & very well read. – At 8 we went to dinner to the Taverne Royale[43], I walked with him all the way, & when we got to the Taverne we felt as if we had known each other a long time.- At dinner, we all started joking & laughing, & the thing went on crescendo to such an extent that we had the whole place aghast at our hilarity![44]

Yet again, John's great ability as a story-teller helped to make the evening enjoyable for everyone as:

Story succeeded story, repartee parried repartee. I warmed up, Harry warmed up, & we were in fits for 4 solid hours, for we left at 12 p.m. Dr. McCrae had an endless stock of stories, some of them the best I've ever heard, & he tells them very well. – Half way through the evening I noticed E.[Elizabeth Morrison] & H.B [Harry Higinbotham] whispering to each other, looking at me & Dr. McCrae & laughing.- Ça y est. E. has just told me, that both she & H.B are convinced I've made a hit & that McCrae has a dead crush on me!
We drove home in a cab the four of us. – At the door H.B kissed me as usual. Dr. McC[rae] said: 'Did he kiss you? If I only could too!' Reckless as usual, I answered: 'Why help yourself' – never dreaming he would take me at my word, & before I could wink he had planted a kiss on my cheek, what a kiss! – It certainly [was] meant to last a time, hadn't I regained my wits & torn myself away. – My cheek actually smarted on my way upstairs – I was flabberghasted! [sic] – I think he did it for fun, but all the same it was a surprise![45]

After that successful first evening, John, Beatriz, Harry and Elizabeth spent time together every day for the next ten days. The Paris season was in full swing, and with it, 'crowds of people, life & hustling all round. Outside the cold air, the rain; inside brightness, warmth, music, pretty women, pretty gowns, furs, violets, all that can make the moment attractive.'[46]

On 5 November they went to the opera to see Jules Massenet's new offering, 'Ariane', and afterwards had supper at the Café de la Paix 'where we all piled like a pack of wolves none of us having had any dinner in order to be at the opera in time to get the front seats in the box.'[47] The following day after spending time in the city centre and having tea at Harry's flat, John saw Beatriz home in a cab. 'He is very nice & charming,' she confessed to Edward and 'we had quite a serious conversation on the way home, on life & different views of it.'[48] At Harry's apartment the next evening, all four launched into song around the piano: 'I began to look over "Ariane", then Elizabeth sang, Harry sang, Dr. McCrae sang, I sang, well! we all sang; & it was a quarter to 10 when we thought about dinner.'[49]

The Salon d'Automne offered an exhibition of current painters and John accompanied Beatriz, who afterwards described works by Manet, Monet, Courbet,[50] Carrière[51] and an interesting section devoted to Russian art. Later that evening after dinner, the four friends went ice skating to the Palais de Glace before finishing the day with a drink at Fouquet's famous restaurant[52]. Beatriz had become quite fond of John, telling Edward,

Dr. McCrae has quite adopted me. He is [an] awfully nice boy, reminds me of you, in some of his ideas. We are quite chummy and, of course, he falls to my lot – H.B being too occupied. I haven't had a chance to speak to him alone once, & I would so love to talk about you.[53]

At dinner the next evening, however, the young ladies were silent as the men 'talked of trout-fishing, baseball & sports in general.'[54] Later, after they had returned to Harry's flat and listened to an impromptu recital by Elizabeth, John and Beatriz were left alone to discuss history, poetry, literature and life, on which,

of course, we did not agree – The first stumbling block was Oscar Wilde's work – I claim he is one of the greatest poets of the age – Dr. McCrae can't disassociate his work from his private life . . . Subject led to subject and, as Dr. McCrae seemed puzzled about me, curious to know what had [made] me what I am, I ended by talking about myself . . . We came home in a cab still discussing difficult matters, & parted on the understanding of his coming around tomorrow to get me to go to Napoleon's Tomb.[55]

The debate continued at the next opportunity and Beatriz reported to Edward Johnson that, 'we chatted & laughed, I landed some outrageous theories as usual against all legalized institutions, marriage included'. When discussion moved to books and plays, Beatriz discovered that John had 'read a lot of the french authors, & therefore we got interested and forgot the time.'[56]

With the weekend in prospect, Harry suggested a visit to the Moulin Rouge but finding it closed for rehearsals, they made their way instead to Montmartre and a restaurant with Spanish guitarists and dancers. After a good meal, the sight and sound of a nearby fair drew them into its midst, Beatriz admitting that 'H.B & I have a common weakness for merry-go-rounds.' They tried their hand at shooting and enjoyed other rides like the 'toboggan' on which 'each person sits on a rug & you come down flying corkscrew fashion, rounding curves at a great rate, from the height of four floors'. After the fun of the fair, everyone 'adjourned to Pezon's Menagerie & witnessed a very good show of wild beasts'. It was now 11.30 p.m. and Beatriz thought,

> it would be giving Dr. McC[rae] a treat to go to the 'Bal Tabarin.' It is a sort of winter 'Jardin de Paris' but far more lively. The place was packed; – all sorts & conditions of people. – As for cocottes,[57] I believe they were all there. Dance succeeded dance . . . Dr. McC[rae] thought there was an atmosphere of <u>hell</u> about the place. To me it suggested only the low part of human nature.[58]

For someone of John's background, certain aspects of Paris night life were hard to take but he was fascinated next day by his visit to Napoleon's Tomb, which had been postponed from a few days earlier. After tea and whisky at Harry's flat, John, Beatriz, Elizabeth and Harry went out for a late dinner at the Taverne Royale. It was almost the end of John's stay in Paris and seeing Beatriz home to her door that evening:

> He kissed me on the cheek & said, 'Bebe, I may never see you again, so I must have something better,' & tried to get my lips. – The others were laughing – I shook him smilingly, but determinedly, & said: 'That's all I can give you' – He did not insist – he is really very nice. Six months ago I would have thought nothing of it & should certainly have allowed him to give me a kiss on the lips. Now it is different.[59]

Having understandably enjoyed his time in Paris, John sailed for Canada feeling rested and 'mentally invigorated to a great degree'.[60] He had been missed during his absence and found a pile of invitations and a warm welcome from his landlord on his return to Montreal. For some three years, John had been living on the top floor of the house belonging to Edward Archibald. He enjoyed a warm relationship with Archibald and his wife Agnes, who had not long presented 'Eddie' as John called him, with the first of four daughters. The annual St Andrew's Ball was looming and John, who had decided to attend that year, cut a dashing figure in his militia uniform. As Christmas 1906 approached, he spent a happy evening among friends at a dance held at 'Ravenscrag', the beautiful home of Sir Montagu and Lady Allan. On another cold winter night, he took a sledge through Montreal's snowy streets to the palatial residence of the millionaire, James Ross, afterwards waxing enthusiastic about the excellent dinner and the 'the magnificent lot of pictures in the house'.[61] As far as his work was concerned, he could only ask his mother to imagine 'the list of memos on my pad at home',[62] assuring her that 'the idle streak in the family gets no chance.'[63] Letters from his brother or William Osler often told a similar story.

Osler had now been at Oxford nearly two years and was held in great esteem by all who had come to know him. Despite his exalted professional reputation, people always found him warm, energetic and remarkably modest. His magnetism and human touch left a deep impression on everyone and the students enjoyed his lightness of step and spirit. He was never too busy to help anyone in trouble, as was the case during the spring of 1907 when disaster came to McGill. A fire destroyed the medical building, including the Department of Pathology and George Adami's private library. People refused to be discouraged but money was desperately needed for a new building. When William Osler heard the news, he immediately jumped to the rescue and spoke to his friend, Lord Strathcona, about raising the necessary funds.

At Osler's home, 'The Open Arms', the professor and his wife entertained on an almost continuous basis. His niece, Amy Gwyn, spent time with her uncle and his family in Oxford in 1907 and Tom McCrae arrived during her stay. As well as assisting Osler to write a major new seven-volume work, *A System of Medicine*, Tom was in England to be admitted to the Fellowship of the Royal College of Physicians. Quieter by nature than his brother but equally brilliant as a doctor, Tom was now thirty-seven years old and well established in his career as Assistant Professor of Medicine at Johns Hopkins. Amy Gwyn was a pretty, slender young woman with lovely violet eyes and fair hair worn up in a style that gently framed her face. When they announced their betrothal, the Oslers were delighted. Tom had evidently not confided in his brother, who first heard the news after returning from a visit to the parents of his friend, Dr Bill Turner. It came as something of a revelation and, although very pleased, John divulged to his mother that 'I have an indefinable feeling of loneliness, as if I had lost a friend, but I suppose the remedy is in my own hands'.[64]

The American writer, Mark Twain, and Rudyard Kipling were among other guests at 'The Open Arms' that summer, the Oslers much enjoying the lively company and bubbling good humour of the latter. Oxford University's award of honorary degrees to both men came in a year of honours for Kipling, who in a matter of months was to learn that he had been awarded the Nobel Prize for Literature for 'the great power of observation, the original conception and also the virile comprehension and art of narration that distinguish his literary creations'.[65] His third accolade of 1907 came in the form of an honorary degree awarded by McGill University and, after the presentation ceremony on 17 October, the students unhitched the horses of his carriage and whisked a slightly bemused Kipling through the streets of Montreal. To mark the visit, Sir William Van Horne offered a private Pullman car on the Canadian Pacific Railway, enabling the Empire's most famous writer to travel in style across Canada.

Before he left Montreal, Kipling handed Andrew Macphail an article and gave a lecture at McGill in which he voiced the concern he continued to feel for his country: 'It must be hard,' he said, 'for those who do not live there to realize the cross between canker and blight that has settled on England for the last couple of years. The effects of it are felt throughout the Empire, but at headquarters we taste the stuff in the very air.'[66] Sitting in the audience was John McCrae, who told his mother that Kipling had given 'an easy, well spoken address' and that afterwards, 'I had a handshake, and recalled the last time we met – when in Capetown.'[67] At the end of the year when Andrew Macphail published Kipling's article in *The University Magazine*, John McCrae's latest poem, 'The Warrior', appeared directly beneath it.

The Warrior

> He wrought in poverty, the dull grey days,
> But with the night his little lamp-lit room
> Was bright with battle flame, or through a haze
> Of smoke that stung his eyes he heard the boom
> Of Blücher's guns; he shared Almeida's scars,
> And from the close-packed deck, about to die,
> Looked up and saw the *Birkenhead's* tall spars
> Weave wavering lines across the Southern sky:
>
> Or in the stifling 'tween decks, row on row,
> At Aboukir, saw how the dead men lay;
> Charged with the fiercest in Busaco's strife,

> Brave dreams are his – the flick'ring lamp burns low –
> Yet couraged for the battles of the day
> He goes to stand full face to face with life.[68]

While Kipling was seeing Canada by train, William Osler was preparing to attend the presentation of another honorary Oxford degree. This time the recipient was the man who personified all that so deeply concerned his delightful houseguest of a few months earlier. The presentation was to take place in the splendour of Windsor Castle and Osler recalled donning his robes at the town's White Hart Inn and being driven in a carriage to the Castle. The Master of Ceremonies showed the eminent professors to a reception room hung with pictures by the Dutch painter Van Dyck where they waited in a semi-circle to be introduced.[69] As one of a deputation of sixteen of Oxford's most distinguished men, Osler, to his immense fascination, found himself meeting and shaking hands with Kaiser Wilhelm II.

Happy with his latest visit to Britain and the programme of events arranged in his honour, the Kaiser, for once, was diverted from his usual sabre-rattling and began to think of ways to restore harmony between the two nations. Lord Morley, then Secretary for India, who saw much of him at Windsor and elsewhere, reported that the general verdict from people well qualified to judge, found him 'superficial, hurried, impetuous, badly balanced' but that for all that, 'he appears to have left in the mind of everybody . . . that he does really desire and intend peace.'[70]

At home in Germany, however, Admiral von Tirpitz was putting plans to the German parliament to speed up the modernisation of the German fleet by twenty-five per cent each year. The plans called for new battleships of the 'Dreadnought' or 'Super Dreadnought' class and posed a serious threat to the Royal Navy for, ironically, by launching the *Dreadnought*, Britain had rendered obsolescent most of her main battle fleet. As Britain's *Dreadnought* construction programme continued, Admiral Sir Jacky Fisher's conviction about a coming war grew stronger. The only question was when? As the German Chancellor, von Bülow, had anticipated, Britain now had formal alliances with both France and Russia. The Anglo-Russian Entente, primarily concerned with Asian affairs, had effectively settled differences between the two countries. The Russians had realised that they could not afford to be part of any arms race and, at their behest, a second peace conference had been convened earlier that year in The Hague with an agenda to reduce expenditure on armaments and produce collective pledges to limit weapons and warship construction. Talk as they might, however, with Germany, Austria-Hungary and Italy tied into the Triple Alliance and Britain, France and Russia now effectively linked together and spurred on by their fear of an expanding German fleet, the two great European power blocs were formed and heading for a collision.

NOTES

1. From 'Upon Watts' Picture, "Sic Transit"' by John McCrae, *The McGill University Magazine* (Volume 3, No. 1, December 1903), p. 32. Micro mfm/AP/U577, UTL.
2. Sir Richard Holmes, *Edward VII, His Life and Times* (London, 1910), p. 567.
3. Massie, *Dreadnought*, p. 356.
4. Palmer, *The Kaiser*, p. 112.
5. Macphail, *In Flanders Fields*, p. 125.
6. MacPhail, *In Flanders Fields*, p. 126.
7. Macphail, *In Flanders Fields*, p. 126.
8. Leacock, 'In Flanders Fields'.
9. Macphail, *In Flanders Fields*, p. 51.
10. Macphail, *In Flanders Fields*, p. 51.
11. *The McGill University Magazine* (Volume 4, No. 1, January 1905), p.82, Micro mfm/ AP/U577, UTL.
12. François Rabelais (1483–c.1553) was a French writer who to his contemporaries was an eminent physician and humanist. He is best known as the author of the comic and satirical masterpieces *Pantagruel* (1532) and *Gargantua* (1534).
13. Tobias Smollett (d. 1771) was an English satirical novelist. Smollett attended anatomical and medical lectures at the University of Glasgow but left without a degree. He served as a surgeon's mate in the Royal Navy and later set up as a surgeon in London. Among his most famous novels is *The Expedition of Humphrey Clinker*.
14. Oliver Wendell Holmes (1809–1894) was an American physician notable for his medical research and teaching. Holmes was Professor of Anatomy & Physiology at Harvard but achieved his greatest fame as a humorist and poet.
15. Macphail, *In Flanders Fields*, p. 122.
16. John Prescott, 'The Extensive Medical Writings of Soldier-Poet John McCrae', *Canadian Medical Association Journal* (January 1980), p. 110.
17. JM to Janet McCrae, 11 January 1905, GM Papers.
18. Macphail, *In Flanders Fields*, p. 125.
19. John Ruskin, *Proserpina, Studies of Wayside Flowers Part I.* (Orpington, 1875) p. 79.
20. Ruskin, *Proserpina*, p. 86.
21. Philip Magnus, *Edward the Seventh* (London, 1964). Author's note, p. xiii.
22. John Buchan, *The King's Grace* (London, 1935), p. 28.
23. Buchan, *The King's Grace*, p. 29.
24. Robert Giddings, *The War Poets* (London, 1988), p. 7.
25. Giddings, *The War Poets*, p. 7.
26. Undated account (circa 21 December 1905), in *Guelph Mercury*, MH.
27. Massie, *Dreadnought*, p. 480.
28. JM to Janet McCrae, 20 January 1906, GM Papers.
29. JM to Janet McCrae, 6 September 1906, GM Papers.
30. Howitt, 'John McCrae', p. 15.
31. JM to Janet McCrae, 11 January 1905, GM Papers.

32. *The McGill University Magazine* (Volume 3, No. 1, December 1903), p.32.
33. Macphail, *In Flanders Fields*, p. 140.
34. JM to Janet McCrae, 1 April 1906, GM Papers. 'Bon mot' means witty saying.
35. JM to Janet McCrae, 15 January 1906, GM Papers. The British had suffered a major defeat at Spion Kop involving the famous Highland Brigade.
36. *The McGill University Magazine* (Volume 5, No. 1, December 1905), p. 97, Micro mfm AP/U577, UTL.
37. JM to Janet McCrae, 5 October 1906, GM Papers.
38. JM to Janet McCrae, 11 October 1906, GM Papers.
39. The Harveian Oration was founded by the benefaction of William Harvey (1578–1657), distinguished physician and discoverer of the circulation of the blood. Harvey was elected Lumleian lecturer (see Chapter 15, endnote 46) at the College of Physicians in 1615 and the Harveian Oration was first given in 1656. It took the form of an annual feast for the Fellows of the Royal College of Physicians and on the same day, a Latin oration (given in English after 1865) commemorating Harvey and other benefactors of the College, an exhortation to follow their examples and another exhortation to Fellows and Members 'to search and study out the secrets of nature by means of experiment'. It remains the highest ranking and most prestigious of the annual College lectures and is always given the title of an Oration.
40. JM to Janet McCrae, 19 October 1906, GM Papers.
41. JM to Janet McCrae, 30 October 1906, GM Papers.
42. Pronounced Bébé.
43. The Taverne Royale was a café-bar on the Rue Royale.
44. Beatriz d'Arneiro to Edward Johnson, 4 November 1906, Sunday night, Edward Johnson Collection, UGL.
45. Beatriz d'Arneiro to Edward Johnson, 4 November 1906, Sunday night, Edward Johnson Collection, UGL.
46. Beatriz d'Arneiro to Edward Johnson, 6 November 1906, Sunday night, Edward Johnson Collection, UGL.
47. Beatriz d'Arneiro to Edward Johnson, 6 November 1906, Tuesday morning, 2 a.m., Edward Johnson Collection, UGL.
48. Beatriz d'Arneiro to Edward Johnson, 6 November 1906, Tuesday morning 2 a.m., Edward Johnson Collection, UGL.
49. Beatriz d'Arneiro to Edward Johnson, 6 November 1906, Tuesday night, Edward Johnson Collection, UGL.
50. Gustave Courbet (1819–1877) was of the romantic but realistic school of painters.
51. Eugene Carrière (1849–1906), was a symbolist who interpreted the dreams of other poets.
52. Fouquet's was an elegant and expensive restaurant situated on the Avenue des Champs-Elysées.
53. Beatriz d'Arneiro to Edward Johnson, 7 November 1906, Wednesday night, Edward Johnson Collection, UGL.
54. Beatriz d'Arneiro to Edward Johnson, 8 November 1906, Thursday night, Edward Johnson Collection, UGL.
55. Beatriz d'Arneiro to Edward Johnson, 8 November 1906, Thursday night, Edward Johnson Collection, UGL.
56. Beatriz d'Arneiro to Edward Johnson, 9 November 1906, Friday night, Edward Johnson Collection, UGL.
57. Cocottes were the fashionable Parisian prostitutes of the demi-monde.

58. Beatriz d'Arneiro to Edward Johnson, 11 November 1906, Sunday 2 a.m., Edward Johnson Collection, UGL.
59. Beatriz d'Arneiro to Edward Johnson, 11 November 1906, Sunday 2 a.m, Edward Johnson Collection, UGL. Beatriz and Edward later married and lived in Florence until Beatriz's death in 1919. Edward and their daughter, Fiorenza, then returned to America where he became one of the New York Metropolitan Opera Company's most acclaimed singers and later its general manager.
60. JM to Janet McCrae, 2 December 1906, GM Papers.
61. JM to Janet McCrae, 12 December 1906, GM Papers.
62. JM to Janet McCrae, 12 December 1906, GM Papers.
63. JM to Janet McCrae, 9 December 1906, GM Papers.
64. JM to Janet McCrae, 26 August 1907, GM Papers.
65. From Rudyard Kipling's Nobel Prize citation on display at 'Batemans', Burwash, East Sussex.
66. Rudyard Kipling, *Letters of Travel, 1892–1913* (London, 1920), p. 127.
67. JM to Janet McCrae, 23 October 1907, GM Papers.
68. *The University Magazine* (Volume 6, No. 4, December 1907), p. 454, Micro mfm AP/U577, UTL.
69. Note by Sir William Osler entitled 'Degree to the Emperor of Germany at Windsor', dated 15 November 1907, Acc. 326/2, Box 7, OL.
70. H.M. Wilson, *The Great War*, Vol. 10 (London, 1917) p. 558.

CHAPTER EIGHT

'We lived, felt dawn, saw sunset glow'[1]
1908–1910

Against a background of international politics, life went on. After a busy winter in which John McCrae delighted in his periodic walks around Mount Royal and the sight of 'masses of heavy white frost, and the sun dazzlingly bright'[2] the spring of 1908 brought the great Italian tenor, Enrico Caruso, to Montreal. Tickets were at a premium but John was among the select audience who greatly enjoyed his performance. It was an occasion when he could put work to the back of his mind but not for long, for he was about to take up a new appointment as physician to the Royal Alexandra Hospital for Infectious Diseases. The study of this area of medicine interested him, and as well as documenting the cases of scarlet fever referred to him in his new work, he presented a paper at that year's conference of the Canadian Maritime Medical Association, describing cases of the disease among his young patients. In his own inimitable way, he managed to make it humourous, recounting the ordeals of a child aged three and a half who,

> came in with diphtheria, caught scarlet fever, had chicken pox, got edema of the glottis, was intubated a number of times, coughed up the tube one night, it rolled under the bed and could not be found; it was supposed she had swallowed it and a tracheotomy saved her life; she developed bilateral otitis and mastoiditis, had her mastoids trephined, and finally departed on the 116th day cured, but disconsolately wailing. The hospital staff bore the separation well.[3]

A timely glance at a newspaper that summer would have informed John of London's magnificent Franco-British exposition and the 1908 Olympic Games held at the city's impressive new stadium; of King Edward VII's visit to Russia – the first by a British monarch and the first meeting with his nephew, Czar Nicholas II, in seven years; and of the King's subsequent visit to Kaiser Wilhelm to protest against the growth of the German navy. As the days began to mellow, John left his duties to perform the happy task of acting as best man at the September wedding of Tom McCrae and Amy Gwyn.

Hardly had the newlyweds begun to settle down to life together in Baltimore, than events in central Europe produced more drama. Early in October 1908, the daily routine of the courtly, punctilious Emperor Franz Joseph of Austria-Hungary was interrupted by news that two Balkan provinces of the Ottoman Empire, Bosnia and Herzegovina, had been annexed into his domain. From his desk in Vienna's Hofburg palace, Franz Joseph held sway over fifty million subjects of such diverse nationalities as Magyars, Czechs, Slovaks, Croats, Serbs, Slovenes, Italians, Romanians and Poles. All were 'artificially bound together by accidents of history and the authority of the Habsburg dynasty'.[4] Franz Joseph was not the only sovereign interested in the Balkans. Each year the Ottoman Empire, 'the sick man of Europe', which had until recently held sway over the Balkans, was becoming more decrepit and Czar Nicholas II of Russia visualised the possibility of extending his empire's territory southwards. If Russia could gain control of the city of Constantinople and the Dardanelles Straits, she would have access to the Mediterranean. If she also established herself as a protector of the largely Slav population of the Balkans, she would become the leading power in the area. In the midst of this intense rivalry, the Austro-Hungarians completed their annexation. The Austro-Hungarian Foreign Minister believed he had struck a secret bargain with his Russian counterpart that would permit the annexation, and give Russia concessions over the right to move her warships through the Dardanelles and the Bosphorus. Unfortunately the Austrians acted before the Russians had completed the diplomatic negotiations needed to change the status of the Dardanelles. Russia was indignant at what it perceived as an Austrian trick and there was talk of mobilisation of the armies of both countries. A flurry of letters between the Czar, the Emperor and the Kaiser failed to pour oil on troubled waters.

Oxford's Regius Professor of Medicine had not long returned from a pleasant summer holiday in the Lake District and Scotland when the crisis broke. For William Osler, it was the first time in thirty years that he had been able to award himself a three-month sabbatical and the holiday had marked the start of it. Consequently, he had done little else but read, walk and enjoy the chance of some peaceful fishing with his teenage son, Revere, whose passion for rod and line warranted his father's affectionate nickname of 'Ike', short for Izaak Walton.[5] Now Osler was in Paris, and with his interest in international affairs, no doubt followed this latest situation closely. In Berlin, meanwhile, Kaiser Wilhelm was anxious to avoid war. Austria-Hungary was Germany's one reliable ally and he saw his chance to lessen the threat of encirclement as neither Britain nor France had any direct interests in Bosnia-Herzegovina. By the end of February 1909, the crisis came to an end after Germany, siding more closely with Vienna, issued Russia with something like an ultimatum. Czar Nicholas, whose empire had managed to survived an internal rebellion in 1905, was in no position to wage war and he was forced to back down and agree to Austria's annexation. He did not, however, forget his humiliation and began to prepare for a possible conflict against both Austria-Hungary and Germany. The European cauldron had begun to bubble.

William Osler's return to Oxford to continue his important campaign against diseases like typhoid and tuberculosis, occurred during a period of considerable unease in Britain. People were apprehensive about German intentions and anti-British statements made by Kaiser Wilhelm in an interview published a few months earlier in the *Daily Telegraph* had astonished Europe. Early in 1909 King Edward donned his diplomatic mantle and decided to pay his nephew another visit in the interest of Anglo-German relations. The Kaiser played down the crisis over Bosnia-Herzegovina in his uncle's presence but, as a precaution, authorised the Chief of his General Staff to exchange letters with his Austro-Hungarian opposite number so that the two armies could cooperate in the event of war in Europe.

As King and Kaiser journeyed through Berlin in an open carriage, they were surrounded not only by cheering onlookers, but by the architecture of a new city. The public buildings, main streets and square of the German capital had been built or rebuilt since 1870 in a heavily pretentious style. With its imposing Reichstag, Arch of Triumph at the Brandenburg Gate and its mile-long avenue, 'Unter den Linden', it spoke of national grandeur with a spotless and orderly efficiency. The Prussian nobility dominated the army and the army, in turn, dominated the German empire. The life of the Kaiser's highly-ordered court included immense state dinners and other formal functions, and he took a strong personal interest in music and the arts. Nothing was spared to impress any Royal visitor, especially Edward VII.

A few months later in July 1909, the English Channel that had always given Britons a sense of protection, was flown for the first time by a Frenchman, Louis Blériot. Rudyard Kipling, keenly interested in the potential of powered flight, had already written a story entitled 'With the Night Mail' in which he foretold of an airliner guided by radio services and allotted safety levels and landing priorities. During his visit to McGill University in 1907, he had informed his fascinated audience that travelling the world would eventually be no more difficult than travelling within one's own neighbourhood and Blériot's flight was a further step towards the realisation of Kipling's vision. Things were moving at such a pace that, as one historian later put it:

In a single generation came the motor car, wireless telegraphy and the conquests of the air and of the world under the sea. Such inventions and the application on a colossal scale of older processes of steam and electricity, were actually transmuting the economic, social and international fabric before it had time to solidify.[6]

King Edward entering Berlin in state with the Kaiser, February 9, 1909

To a man like Rudyard Kipling, all this came as no surprise. During the South African War, his journalist colleague, H.A. Gwynne, had published a series of articles in *The Friend* newspaper entitled 'Is the Art of War Revolutionised?'. Kipling had for some time anticipated the form that future land battles would take as the human mind applied modern science to warfare. Scientific knowledge, lateral thinking, visualisation and application were all it took to put creative invention to destructive use and, for what he believed lay ahead, Kipling more than once used the word 'Armageddon'. Another author, H.G. Wells, used the same term in a series of books in which he gave a terrible insight into the kind of assault that the increasing power of technology could wield over the frail human form. In 'A Dream of Armageddon', published in 1911, Wells presented a very explicit picture of a war fought using flying machines as well as ground troops and artillery. Sir Arthur Conan Doyle began writing about the form of a future war and the clear danger posed by submarines to Britain's maritime lifeline.[7] Such ideas, however, were seldom taken seriously for few yet realised that man's 'very command over Nature, so admirably and marvellously won, had become his greatest peril.'[8]

In Montreal, the light in John McCrae's study continued to burn late into the evenings during 1909. In addition to his various posts and his work as a lecturer in Pathology at McGill, the University had also appointed him lecturer in Medicine. Utilising the odd half hour to good effect as always, the material John had been gathering on cases of scarlet fever encountered in his work at the Royal Alexandra Hospital was, he decided, sufficient for him to be writing a thesis for his M.D. degree, which he hoped to complete by the end of the year. He had a good deal of writing to do that year, William Osler and his brother, Tom, having prevailed upon him to contribute several chapters to their joint ten-volume work, *A System of Medicine*[9], yet John also still found time for other medical articles. One such, entitled 'The Pirates of Medicine', attacked the charlatans of the medical world and, with his nautical partiality, John concluded that: 'We are not all line-of-battle ships, but a little one gun sloop with the ensign is more honourable than a 40-gun frigate that is a buccaneer.'[10]

Socially, John was now included in the vice-regal circle and since the previous autumn had attended several functions in Ottawa and Montreal at the invitation of Earl Grey, Canada's Governor General, or his daughter, Lady Evelyn, who was described as 'young and quite pretty, with fresh rosy cheeks and her father's dark eyes'.[11] After dinner on one occasion, John and Andrew Macphail were invited to join His Excellency for 'a smoke and a chat and we went to the library and had the affairs of the nation out until midnight.'[12] Amid a round of balls, dances, suppers and parties, the Scottish music hall star Harry Lauder[13] came to Montreal to give a concert. John had a chance to meet him afterwards at Montreal's University Club, and found Lauder pleasant and unaffected.

The idea of a gathering place for graduates of all universities had come about at a lunch John had attended with Stephen Leacock, and when 'some of the leading University graduates of the City'[14] had been asked if they were in favour of establishing such a club, the response had been immediate and positive. The University Club had opened its doors in the spring of 1908 to a rapidly increasing membership, popular, among other reasons, for the fact that its 'jealously guarded masculine atmosphere served as an escape from the flightier affairs of town and gown.'[15] As founder members, John and Leacock, who had returned from a year's tour of the Empire lecturing on 'Imperial Organisation and Development', were following its progress with interest and for the man who confessed to having become 'rather stale on work',[16] the company and the stimulus of meeting others outside his own professional circle was something he appreciated.

Both John and his humorous friend were also active members of another very exclusive body known as the Pen and Pencil Club. This met fortnightly at the Montreal studio of Edmond Dyonnet, a teacher and academician of the Royal Canadian Academy of Arts, and was described by Leacock this way: 'Such literary life as there has been in English-speaking Montreal has centered round various little organizations past and present, of which the Pen and Pencil Club is without doubt the most venerable and the most notable.' With its members assembled 'in the half-light of a studio, falling asleep over essays read to it, and waking up to look at pictures or drink scotch and soda', it had, according to Leacock, 'developed a life and character of its own.' Although it numbered those of a literary persuasion among its members, 'it lived rather on brush than on ink. The pencil was mightier than the pen.'[17]

A collection of photographs of club members taken by the studio of William Notman around that time would seem to bear out the fact that art dominated letters at the Pen and Pencil Club.[18] It included a couple of lawyers, several writers like John, Stephen Leacock, Andrew Macphail and another new colleague from McGill, John Macnaughton, who had just arrived from Queen's University in Kingston to teach Classics. They were outnumbered, however, by artists and those with a strong interest in art like Sir William Van Horne. According to Leacock, it was 'in this little circle that Jack McCrae's poems first came before the world'.[19]

Among John's medical friends, Oskar Klotz was the closest. In the intervening years since John had eased him kindly into his new work at McGill, Oskar had done well and as 1909 drew to a close, John and his medical colleagues hosted a farewell party for Dr Klotz, soon to be Professor Klotz. The University of Pittsburgh had been seeking someone to fill the chair of Pathology and Bacteriology, and Oskar had been appointed to the position. The two men soon started up a lively correspondence, for Oskar was clearly a confidant and someone to whom he could express his more private feelings. As letters found their way to and from Pittsburgh, John addressed his friend variously and affectionately as 'you old blister'[20], 'old cock'[21] and 'my ancient'.[22]

Soon after church bells had rung in the new year of 1910, it was clear that this was to be a year in which exploration and invention claimed the world's attention. A Frenchman, Jean Charcot, was voyaging in Antarctica and the German Geographical Society decided to honour Ernest Shackleton, discoverer of the magnetic South Pole. Preparations were already under way for the expedition of Captain Robert Falcon Scott, due to leave England in June to begin its attempt to reach the South Pole ahead of a Norwegian team, led by the polar explorer, Captain Roald Amundsen. Thomas Edison, the American genius of technology who had invented the phonograph and the first commercially successful incandescent lamp, demonstrated his latest development – talking motion pictures – and it was reported that X-rays were proving useful in detecting lung disease. In the midst of these newsworthy ventures, a new Director of Pathology arrived at the Montreal General Hospital. This was Dr Lawrence Rhea, with whom John McCrae was to work for most of the next eight years. All who came to know Rhea soon realised that beneath his dry humour and dispassionate outward demeanour was a sterling character of great kindness and humanity. Another welcome arrival was Dr Bill Francis, returning from study in Europe to set up in practice in Montreal and to work as a Demonstrator in Pathology assisting Dr Maude Abbott, the Curator of the McGill Medical Museum.

In Oxford, William and Grace Osler had two excited young women staying with them at 'The Open Arms' during the spring of 1910, to the distraction of the Rhodes scholars. Ottilie Wright was the daughter of one of Osler's old friends and Nona Gwyn, the younger sister of Tom McCrae's wife Amy. Both were to be presented at Court and questions of protocol and dress were much in their minds when everything was changed by the death of King Edward VII on 6 May 1910. After years of being monarch-in-waiting, his reign had lasted barely a decade. Bronchitis had been followed by a series of heart attacks, and the bulletin announcing his death was signed by four doctors, one of whom was his Physician-in-Ordinary, Dr Bertrand Dawson, whom John McCrae would come to know well within a few years. Edward had been a very popular monarch and messages of sorrow poured in from all over the world. Sir Wilfrid Laurier telegraphed on behalf of the Canadian people that the King had won not only the respect of all his British subjects, but, by his efforts towards international harmony and goodwill, he had become universally recognised as a great peacemaker.[23] On Sunday 8 May 1910, churches throughout the Empire were full as people mourned his loss. His body was taken to Westminster Hall and for the first time in British history, a King lay in state so that his subjects could pay their respects.

Both Emperor Franz Joseph and Kaiser Wilhelm were among the multitude of European monarchs and statesmen who attended the sad but splendid funeral. The uncle who had never seen eye to eye with his German nephew had predicted before he died that 'I have not long to live. Then my nephew Willy will make war.'[24] Despite their differences and the 'strange and mischievous mixture of rivalry and contempt'[25] that Wilhelm had felt for his uncle, he genuinely mourned the King's passing and *The Times'* report of the funeral described him as looking 'so noble that England has lost something of her old kindliness if she does not take him back into her heart today'.[26] Wilhelm rode beside the young King George V in the procession that followed the coffin. Presiding over the most powerful nation on the Continent and with his uncle gone, he could now lay claim to being Europe's leading monarch. As they slowly made their way through London's streets, the incredibly splendid and impressive array of kings, emperors, crown princes, archdukes and grand-dukes seemed to mark a high point in the history of European royalty. It was the concluding royal pageant of an era already on the wane. Never again would there be such a regal gathering, for Europe was entering a danger zone. Behind the kings in the procession rode the Austro-Hungarian archduke whose death four years later would sweep away the old order forever.

Events, both national and international, continued to occupy the attention of the British journalist, Leo Amery, and the intervening years since the South African War had been as busy for him as for John McCrae. Amery had continued his work for *The Times*, been admitted as a Barrister of the Inner Temple and completed his seven-volume history of the South African War. With his irrepressible energy, ardour and spirit of adventure, Amery was someone who enjoyed the chance to travel to remote places, and when an invitation arrived from the resident representative of the Crown in Canada, it was one he was only too happy to accept.

Earl Grey, whose father had been Private Secretary to both Prince Albert and Queen Victoria, was now in his penultimate year as Canada's Governor General. During his illustrious career, he had served as a Member of Parliament, as Administrator of Rhodesia and, prior to the Canadian appointment, as a Director of the British South Africa Company. The Earl was a warm and inspiring man in his late fifties, whose imperialism was part of his humanity. To him, the British Empire was everything and, without being jingoistic, he felt immensely proud of what it had achieved. In his mind, the Union Jack stood for 'Justice, Honour, Freedom, Duty and Disinterested Service'.[27]

Canada was undoubtedly the jewel in the crown of his career and he had loved every moment of his time there. Struck by the country's potential and the magnificence of her scenery, he wanted to see his young colossus achieve the highest things and concentrated his efforts on making Canada aware of the sense of greatness of her destiny as a full partner of the Empire. He spoke with animation of his hopes for an imperial parliament in London and advocated the building of a Dominion House that could help to increase Britain's awareness of her Empire. Like Kipling, he perceived a national apathy in some areas which he knew he would not find in Germany, commenting that, if 'I had been a German, and gone with this idea to the Kaiser, every telephone bell in the palace would have been ringing in five minutes, and the thing would have been accomplished.' Instead, he encountered a 'lack of imagination. People talk of the difficulties of doing things. They prefer to go along in smooth ruts.'[28] During his time in Canada, Earl Grey had done much to encourage national unity and the development of Canadian talents in the fields of art, music, dance and architecture. Anyone fortunate enough to be invited to his brilliant, animated receptions and dinner parties at Government House and on his travels across the Dominion, found him a wonderful host who made each guest feel important and deserving of his undivided attention.

For years public opinion in the Canadian west had been clamouring for a direct rail link to the outside world via a port on Hudson's Bay. It was argued that by virtue of the curvature of the earth, the distance from such a port to Liverpool was less than from Montreal. In earlier times, the entire north-western portion of Canada had been opened up by a route established by the Hudson's Bay Company. What had been possible by canoe and sailing ship should clearly be both possible and profitable by rail and steamship and Earl Grey was keen to see for himself. He believed that an expedition would help to focus public opinion in Canada upon the situation and his idea soon became reality.

Responsibility for planning the journey was given to a Royal North West Mounted Police superintendent, Major John Moodie, a Scot who had spent most of his years of service exploring and working in some of the remotest parts of Canada. A few years earlier, Moodie had sent a team of dogs to Roald Amundsen during his long, icebound sea voyage through the North West Passage. Now, Amundsen was on his way to the South Pole but for Moodie and his travellers, the point of departure was to be Norway House at the northern end of Lake Winnipeg. The route they would be following led via a series of lakes and rivers to York Factory, the old Hudson's Bay Company headquarters on the western shore of the Bay, where a Canadian government steamer would be waiting to transport them back to eastern Canada via Labrador, Newfoundland and the St Lawrence. In addition to Major Moodie, four of his staff, a cook and two servants, the Governor General's party would consist of his cousin George Grey, brother of Sir Edward Grey, Britain's Foreign Secretary; Major Trotter, aide-de-camp; Professor Reginald Brock, Director of the Geological Survey of Canada; Leo Amery; and two men from

McGill University. One was John Macnaughton, Professor of Classics and the other, filling the position of expedition doctor, was John McCrae.

In the weeks leading up to the date of departure, the air age came to Montreal. There was enormous excitement when, at 6.00 p.m. on Saturday 2 July 1910, the sound of a motor in the sky brought people flocking from their houses. Evening shoppers and clerks deserted the shops and streetcars stopped to allow impatient passengers onto the sidewalks. What they all wanted to see was the first aeroplane flight over the city by the intrepid aviator, Count Jacques de Lesseps, who a few weeks earlier had flown the English Channel in his monoplane,'Scarabee'. It had been just six and a half years since the American brothers, Wilbur and Orville Wright, had achieved the first flight in a heavier than air machine. Now the Count's exploits had brought him to Canada and thrilled the populace of Mount Royal, McGill University and the central part of the city.

John McCrae's journey to Manitoba to join his fellow travellers gave him the opportunity to spend some time with his sister Geills, who now had a growing family. Her eldest daughter, Margaret, thought her Uncle Jack was great fun as he gave her books and they shared fun and laughter. Many years later, she would recall that there seemed to be no generation gap between her and her thirty-seven-year old uncle. With his great gift for story-telling John dreamt up wonderful adventures and would finish each day's instalment at a moment of anticipation that kept her in eager suspense until the next.[29]

John could always be relied upon to keep a detailed record of important

Sketch of Norway House by John McCrae, from his diary of Earl Grey's 1910 expedition. Courtesy of Guelph Museums, Guelph, Canada

events in his life and the 1910 expedition was no exception. A notebook and a camera were packed in his travelling bag and his account began on the day the train from Winnipeg took him to Selkirk where he boarded *The Wolverine*, a very comfortable boat which ran to Warrior's Landing at the mouth of the Saskatchewan River. A small steamer then took members of the party to Norway House where flags, decorations and 'a reception by Indians and double-barrelled guns awaited us'.[30]

The first night's camping caused John to comment enthusiastically on the equipment they had been issued by the Mounted Police: 'The kit is great. Each man has a green silk-mix tent, with inside fly-tent: a waterproof holdall (M[ounted]. Police), an eider down in bag (mattress if necessary): blanket, waterproof sheet, all strapped together for a load.'[31]

Having indeed been well provided for, the entire personnel of the expedition were to travel in twelve canoes, each paddled by two Cree Indians. Everyone was prepared for an early start but they awoke next day to rain and strong winds. While waiting for the weather to improve, the animal-loving John noted in his diary that 'There are 5 black pups here about 6-7 weeks old, which are the most playful family I ever saw. They would delight the soul of anyone less than 80 years of age.'[32] Finally, on the afternoon of 8 August, a large crowd that included Earl Grey's wife and daughter watched the twelve freshly painted and varnished canoes get under way. As the cavalcade splashed and pushed its way into the rough water they were heading towards the area described by Stephen Leacock as 'lands forlorn', that in summer were 'carpeted with grass and humming with a myriad insects, with wide lakes, a glare of day that hardly knows sunset, fast rivers that cannot linger, and in winter the starlit desolation of arctic snow.'[33]

They made their camp at the end of the first day on 'a beautiful rocky promontory opposite an unusually well-wooded shore lying in the evening light and soon in the soft glow of a fine sunset'.[34] From the start, Earl Grey was the life and soul of the party and 'his infectious enthusiasm, merry humanity, and complete selflessness, irresistibly carried one along with him'.[35] Soon after leaving at 6.00 a.m. next day, John bagged two mallards – he was a good shot as he was to prove more than once over the next ten days. After some small rapids, the canoes left the Nelson River for the Etchimamish River, an Indian name which meant, according to John, 'stream running both ways'.[36] Each canoe had paddles, sculls and a sail if required. A further couple of hours brought the picturesque flotilla into Hairy Lake, where they were able to hoist their sails and glide past endless stretches of yellow water lilies and fringes of reeds. That night they were forced to camp on marshy ground amid high grass, which proved to be a gathering place for mosquitoes. Protective nets were absolutely necessary for, as John noted: 'A bare hand gets a dozen in a minute.'[37]

After entering wooded country and the waters of the Hayes River, the journey grew more difficult with an increasing number of port- ages.[38] Although some were a matter of a mere thirty yards over flat rock, nevertheless the amount of baggage involved a lot of loading and unloading. The Indians proved to be devout Methodists and sang hymns along the way. John was sharing a canoe with Leo Amery and doubtless enjoying the opportunity to discuss aspects of *The Times History of the South African War* with its author. The association of two exceptional raconteurs and vigorous minds was a guarantee that there would be few tedious moments during the trip. Amery remembered John as 'the most lovable of men' and the fact that 'as a storyteller I have never met his equal . . . every night in our mess tent or round the camp-fire he would pour out his anecdotes – and never repeated himself'.[39] On clear nights, the sky was particularly fine. Leo and John, who enjoyed smoking a pipe, would sit outside their tent for hours 'unable to tear ourselves away from the ever-shifting, radiant play of the Aurora Borealis and the warm, velvety stillness of the night'.[40] George Grey proved to be an accomplished fisherman and their staple foods of soups, jam, cheese and fruit were supplemented by pike and other fish. On the approaches to Oxford Lake, the Indians demonstrated their skills as they negotiated three sets of rapids and two portages over considerable falls of water. As dusk was falling on 12 August, the expedition reached Oxford House, an old Hudson's Bay station on the lake. John noted in his diary that it consisted of 12-15 scattered houses, and also that there were,

no white people except at the present moment 3 fire rangers. The howl of huskies fills the air at odd times . . . Crowds of squaws and children, the former in bright shawls . . . The youngest papooses wrapped up in the familiar way (with dried moss by way of a diaper). Two infected arms among the party Indians, and a small boy of the village on whom a bag of flour fell constitute the patients for the day. His Ex[cellency]. held a pow-wow with the Indians thro' an interpreter. The Indians had a dance in the store house, doing jigs to a fiddle which played tunes strongly reminiscent of Scotch airs; then, the 'Lancers' – a very banal performance.[41]

As they progressed farther, the Indians continued to show incredible prowess on the water and, as everyone set up camp by the picturesque Trout Falls the following evening, the more adventurous among the party discovered some welcome additions to their diet:

Berries are abundant – red currants, . . . black ones . . . gooseberries, small red & a little more acid than the tame one, blueberries, raspberries

& occasional strawberries. Mr. Grey got some good pike with a spoon, but nothing w[oul]d rise to the fly. . . . Everybody thoroughly well burnt, but getting into good physical shape.[42]

Another few days of rivers, lakes, rapids and frosty nights brought them down the Hayes River on the final leg of their journey to York Factory. They had reached the eastern edge of the pre-Cambrian Canadian Shield and 'a splendid run of rapids: 9 portages, mostly short and running 30 or 40 rapids'.[43] Lunch was eaten using 'a canoe sail for the tablecloth on a big rock by the water'.[44] John found it thrilling to watch the Indians' skill at shooting the rapids, describing it as the true 'sport of Kings'.[45] As the Hayes River cut its way through the clay soil around the southern and western shores of Hudson's Bay, the party encountered quicksand, mosquitoes, blackflies and sandflies. However, the last part of the journey was made in good time and all the canoes had reached York Factory by 7.00 p.m. on Friday 19 August 1910, eleven days after they had set out. At this, the oldest settlement on Hudson's Bay, Earl Grey's arrival was met by a salute from an ancient cannon.

The steamer *Earl Grey*, anchored some fifteen to twenty miles offshore, looked, according to John McCrae 'like a private yacht'[46] and was 'much the biggest ship that has ever been in Hudson's Bay'.[47] The captain and first mate were standing by with a motor launch to ferry the party and its supplies out to the ship, which had just sufficient coal on board to make Gaspé at a speed of ten knots. After viewing a possible site for a port at the terminus of the proposed railway, the *Earl Grey* began the long homeward journey.

The weather was beautiful and John wrote in his diary: 'It is strange to be going over practically uncharted seas.'[48] The following day, in almost Mediterranean warmth, everyone was up early and 'on deck in our pyjamas at 6.30 having coffee'[49] off Churchill, the other alternative possible port farther up the Bay's western shore. After exploring the area and passing an Eskimo camp, the ship continued its journey. By Thursday 25 August it had crossed Hudson's Bay and was in Hudson's Straits, a stretch of water rarely open before the end of July and risky to attempt after mid-September. The weather continued to be warm enough to sit on deck in the sun without a coat and enjoy wonderful views. This particular area could pose navigational problems for a future shipping route for, as John described:

The compasses went off their heads (due probably to the proximity of the magnetic pole, which is only a couple of hundred miles away). All the time, no stars could be seen & the moon was overcast, & 2 short circles made by the ship did not move the needle at all. After half an hour it righted.[50]

During the course of a short diversion north east to Baffin Island, John spotted quite a number of walrus and 'ice in considerable quantity, bergs probably 25-30 in sight at a time'.[51] To Leo Amery they looked 'dazzling white, except where, near the water's edge, they reflected the blue of the surrounding sea'.[52] Until now, John's medical work had been light but, on 27 August, 'Mr. Grey ruptured a muscle in his leg . . . and it now needs some little attention to justify my existence.'[53] After skirting a glacier, the ship headed south east, anchoring for the night against bad weather at Port Burwell, a settlement close to the northernmost point of Labrador, where they were able to take on coal left there by Major Moodie sometime earlier. At the settlement's Moravian Mission, a tiny European colony of Germans and English were living amid Eskimos and an all-pervasive smell of blubber. With fog accompanying their journey down the Labrador coast, the *Earl Grey*'s passengers enjoyed reading, conversation and games of bridge. Much to his delight, John had found a good library on board.

After visiting St Anthony, headquarters of Dr. Wilfred Grenfell, medical missionary of the National Mission for Deep Sea Fishermen, the steamer entered calmer waters. John McCrae's diary for Monday 5 September 1910 reads, 'a beautiful clear morning, sea moderate, wind fairly strong, bright sunshine. Running down the W[est]. Coast of N[ew]f[oundlan]d. 4 or 5 miles out. The shore is high & rocky, but no details are to be made out in the light that prevails.' The ship was now passing through the Belle Isle Straits towards the tree-clad Bay of Islands. Newfoundland was not part of Canada at this time and the decision had been made not to visit St John's, the capital, lest it should incite possible rumours of its annexation. Instead, the *Earl Grey* moored off the west coast and the vice-regal party took a train to Grand Falls. Here a new pulp and paper factory and township had been established through the energy of Lord Northcliffe, the British publishing magnate, who was waiting to greet them. After their adventures in the Canadian wilderness, the sight of Lady Northcliffe's English-style country house was a welcome one. Lord Northcliffe's dynamic mind was constantly at work on new projects and, in Newfoundland, he had built 'a model town'.[54]

Lord Northcliffe, like Leo Amery, Rudyard Kipling, Sir Arthur Conan Doyle and H.G. Wells, was a man convinced that Britain was unprepared to fight the major war that he believed was coming in the near future. Five years before, he had corresponded with the retired Field Marshal Lord Roberts who had been warning that, despite her navy, Britain lay open to foreign invasion. Northcliffe, farsighted enough to realise the truth behind this idea, had conceived the idea for a novel on the subject and hired a writer, William Le Queux, to produce the book. Carefully researched with help from Lord Roberts and entitled *The Invasion of 1910*, the book appeared in 1906 and had been serialised by the *Daily Mail*. In the plot, a German army assembles and proceeds to invade England from much the same area of the Frisian coast described by Erskine Childers in his earlier novel with a similar theme, *The Riddle of the Sands*. The moral of Le Queux's story is clearly pointed out by one of the characters in the book who states: 'Had we adopted his [Roberts'] scheme for universal service, such dire catastrophe could never have occurred.'[55] In the minds of some, Lord Northcliffe, through the views expressed in his newspapers, 'played an important role in shifting the interest of Great Britain from Germany to France and in policy leading to the First World War'.[56] *The Invasion of 1910* was an overwhelming success but Britain's War Secretary, Richard Haldane, was disgusted at 'the entire spy-invasion mania'[57] it had created and believed that Lord Roberts' 'repeated statements that we are in danger of invasion and are not prepared to meet it'[58] were doing 'a good deal of mischief'.[59] For now, Northcliffe was glad to welcome the vice-regal party to his Newfoundland residence.

Nearing the final phase of its sea voyage, the *Earl Grey* steamed for the mainland. The surviving portion of John McCrae's diary finishes on 5 September 1910 and Leo Amery's account describes the remainder of the homeward journey: a day on a modern whaling boat, an inspection of coal mines and iron works at Sydney, Cape Breton Island, where Lady Grey and her daughter were waiting to rejoin the party, some sailing and a visit to the ruins of the former great French fortress of Louisbourg. The last port of call provided the chance to set foot upon the distinctive red soil of Prince Edward Island. The quiet inlets, woods, meadows, farms and plentiful orchards that made up its gentle, pastoral landscape, were an enjoyable contrast to the rugged northern vistas, and with the prospect of autumn colours and good food in view, the expedition could look forward to a pleasant couple of days. Andrew Macphail had grown up on the island and was waiting to welcome the vice-regal party to 'Orwell', his family homestead. Through Macphail, Earl Grey had also sent a request that he very much wished to meet another prominent islander – Miss Lucy Maud Montgomery – whose book, *Anne of Green Gables*, had been published the previous year to great acclaim. The *Earl Grey* moored in the harbour of the island's tiny capital, Charlottetown and, on Tuesday 13 September, Earl Grey and his companions proceeded by train and carriage along the rust-coloured dirt roads to Andrew Macphail's door.

The island was in a state of excitement over the visit and Lucy Maud Montgomery was anxious about what dress she should wear for the occasion. Described as 'short and slight . . . with delicate aquiline features, bluish-grey eyes and an abundance of dark brown hair',[60] she appeared neat and attractive in 'pretty brown silk'[61] as she presented Earl Grey with autographed copies of her books. Following afternoon tea, the Governor General and the author walked in the garden as they discussed her heroine, Anne. They seemed to like each other and Lucy Maud Montgomery described Earl Grey as a 'tall, genial, elderly man with a frank, pleasant face and a most unaffected "homely" manner'.[62] Having met all the members of the expedition, she stayed for dinner served at tables that spilled from Andrew Macphail's dining room onto a covered verandah. The following evening Earl Grey returned the hospitality when Macphail and Lucy Maud Montgomery were rowed out to a formal dinner on board the steamer. For the latter, the worst part of the evening was curtsying backwards out of the vice-regal presence and she confessed that she had 'narrowly escaped falling over the high doorstep and my train combined'.[63] Leo Amery, meeting Andrew Macphail for the first time, found him a 'most original and argumentative of political philosophers', when not practising medicine or growing 'record potatoes'.[64] Macphail knew John McCrae enjoyed fishing and took him to a stream running through a deep ravine which broadened out under alder trees. The sea trout were running that afternoon and he gave John a fine rod to try, which 'excited his suspicion,' and led him to demonstrate that he was no novice at the art of fly fishing.[65] The visit to Prince Edward Island, and in particular the last evening, was a great success. When the returning adventurers parted company at Quebec, it marked the end of what had been for John 'an ideal trip'[66] and for Leo Amery, 'two of the pleasantest months I have ever spent'.[67]

John and Amery had enjoyed each other's company and John subsequently sent his companion photographs of the expedition. The following year, Leo Amery was elected as the Conservative Member of Parliament for what later became Birmingham Sparkbrook, and began a long political career. The two men were to meet again, unexpectedly and sooner than they might perhaps have imagined. A short time after the expedition had finished, John received a letter from Earl Grey, which indicated that his sparkling form and his warm, witty, stimulating company had won him yet another fan:

> It was a great pleasure to have you as one of my party, and I am very grateful to you for the very real contribution you made to my own individual and to the general enjoyment of the trip. You were able to beat the record of the Arabian nights, for I believe the 3000 miles of our travels were illumined by as many stories![68]

The journey cemented a continuing friendship between the two men. The Hudson's Bay route was subsequently opened up and, by the time Leo Amery wrote his account of the expedition in 1939, he could already foresee that, in line with Kipling's prediction of 1904, it would not be long 'before the high speed passenger 'plane does the journey from England to Winnipeg or Edmonton in the day'.[69]

NOTES

1. From 'In Flanders Fields' by John McCrae, *Punch* magazine, 8 December 1915.
2. JM to Janet McCrae, 4 December 1907, GM Papers.
3. John McCrae, 'Scarlet Fever; Some Observations upon Three Hundred and Twenty-Five Cases', *Maritime Medical News* (20:335, 1908).
4. Theo Aronson, *Crowns in Conflict: The Triumph and The Tragedy of European Monarchy 1910–1918*, (London, 1986), p. 68.
5. Izaak Walton (1593–1683) was an English biographer who wrote *The Compleat Angler*, a classic idyll on the stratagems and pleasures of fishing.
6. Professor G.M. Trevelyan, as quoted in H.V. Morton, *Pageant of the Century* (London, 1933) p. 8.
7. Peter Buitenhuis, *The Great War of Words* (London, 1989), p. 3.
8. Professor G.M. Trevelyan, as quoted in Morton, *Pageant of the Century*, p. 8.
9. *A System of Medicine* was the title preferred by Sir William Osler and Dr Tom McCrae and was used by British publishers. *Modern Medicine* was the title used by publishers in the United States of America.
10. John McCrae, 'The Pirates of Medicine', *Montreal Medical Journal* (38:523:1909).
11. Mary Rubio & Elizabeth Waterston, *The Selected Journals of L.M. Montgomery*, Volume II (Toronto, 1987), Friday 16 September 1910, p. 14.
12. JM to Janet McCrae, 20 December 1908, GM Papers.
13. Harry Lauder (1870–1950), was a very popular Scottish music-hall comedian who composed simplehearted Scottish songs. Later knighted, he sang to the troops during the First World War and gave many concerts for war charities.
14. 'History of the University Club of Montreal' by Edgar Andrew Collard, written for the University Club in 1977 and revised in 1992, p. 1.
15. Legate, *Stephen Leacock*, p. 47.
16. JM to Janet McCrae, 14 April 1909, GM Papers.
17. Stephen Leacock, *Montreal – Seaport and City* (New York, 1942), p. 311.
18. The photographs form part of the William Notman Collection, McCord Museum of Canadian History, Montreal.
19. Leacock, 'In Flanders Fields', *The Times*, 18 February 1921.
20. JM to Oscar Klotz, 11 January 1910, MG 30, B61, Klotz Papers, NAC.
21. JM to Oskar Klotz, 13 March 1911, MG 30, B61, Klotz Papers, NAC.
22. JM to Oscar Klotz, 24 February 1911, MG 30, B61, Klotz Papers, NAC.
23. Holmes, *Life of Edward VII*, p. 607.
24. Edward VII to Countess Greffulhe, a leader of Parisian society. Quoted in Alexis Gregory, *The Gilded Age: The Super-Rich of the Edwardian Era* (London, 1993), p. 217.
25. Winston S. Churchill, *Great Contemporaries*, (London, 1937), p. 24.
26. *The Times*, 7 May 1910.
27. Harold Begbie, *Albert, Fourth Earl Grey: A Last Word* (Toronto, 1917), p. 123.
28. Begbie, *Albert, Fourth Earl Grey*, p. 136.
29. Author's conversation with Mrs Margaret Gardner-Medwin, 1 April 1995.

30. JM Diary of 1910 Expedition, 6 August 1910, MH.
31. JM Diary of 1910 Expedition, 6 August 1910, MH.
32. JM Diary of 1910 Expedition, 7 August 1910, MH.
33. Leacock, *Canada*, p. 127.
34. Margery Hinds, 'A Governor General Goes North', *The Beaver* (Summer, 1971), p. 16.
35. Amery, *Days of Fresh Air*, p. 285.
36. JM Diary of 1910 Expedition, 9 August 1910, MH.
37. JM Diary of 1910 Expedition, 9 August 1910, MH.
38. A 'portage' is a Canadian term that means the carrying of boats, supplies, etc. overland between navigable waterways. It can also mean the route used for such transport.
39. Amery, *Days of Fresh Air*, p. 286.
40. Amery, *Days of Fresh Air*, p. 289.
41. JM Diary of 1910 Expedition, 13 August 1910, MH.
42. JM Diary of 1910 Expedition, 13 August 1910, MH.
43. JM Diary of 1910 Expedition, 17 August 1910, MH.
44. JM Diary of 1910 Expedition, 17 August 1910, MH.
45. JM Diary of 1910 Expedition, 17 August 1910, MH.
46. JM Diary of 1910 Expedition, 20 August 1910, MH.
47. JM Diary of 1910 Expedition, 21 August 1910, MH.
48. JM Diary of 1910 Expedition, 21 August 1910, MH.
49. JM Diary of 1910 Expedition, 21 August 1910, MH.
50. JM Diary of 1910 Expedition, 24 August 1910, MH.
51. JM Diary of 1910 Expedition, 26 August 1910, MH.
52. Amery, *Days of Fresh Air*, p. 292.
53. JM Diary of 1910 Expedition, 27 August 1910, MH.
54. JM to Janet McCrae, 5 September 1910, GM Papers.
55. Massie, *Dreadnought*, p. 635–636.
56. Harold Innes, as quoted in Buitenhuis, *The Great War of Words*, p. 1.
57. Massie, *Dreadnought*, p. 637.
58. Massie, *Dreadnought*, p. 637.
59. Massie, *Dreadnought*, p. 637.
60. Molly Gillen, *Lucy Maud Montgomery: The Wheel of Things* (Toronto, 1975), p. 85.
61. Rubio and Waterston, *The Selected Journals of L.M. Montgomery*, Wednesday 7 September 1910, p. 12.
62. Gillen, *Lucy Maud Montgomery*, p. 83.
63. Rubio and Waterston, *The Selected Journals of L.M. Montgomery*, Friday 16 September 1910, p. 16.
64. Amery, *Days of Fresh Air*, pp. 296–7.
65. Macphail, *In Flanders Fields*, pp. 128–9.
66. JM to Janet McCrae, 5 September 1910, GM Papers.
67. Amery, *Days of Fresh Air*, p. 297.
68. Earl Grey to JM, 26 September 1910, MH.
69. Amery, *Days of Fresh Air*, p. 293.

CHAPTER NINE

'They do not see the shadows grow'[1]

1911–1913

John returned to Montreal in September 1910. Earl Grey's expedition was a talking point at the university but work beckoned and the adventurer was soon occupied, not only professionally, but also in helping to administer the sale of the family farm, 'Janefield'. For almost half a century it had been the headquarters of the famous McCrae herd of Galloway cattle, but now, David McCrae's advancing years and the fact that his sons had chosen another career prompted his decision to put it on the market. As the year drew to a close, John and the Archibald family moved to a new house in Montreal's Metcalfe Street and he received confirmation that he had been granted an M.D. degree from the University of Toronto for his thesis, 'A study of 850 cases of scarlet fever with more particular consideration of 71 fatal cases'.

1911 was to be a year of more changes and innovations, but as far as one existing invention was concerned, John McCrae along with other busy doctors, found it both a blessing and a curse, complaining that the 'telephone goes these days something cruel'.[2] He was contemplating how he could fit in another professional writing project, George Adami having invited him to share in producing a new medical work entitled *A Textbook of Pathology for Students of Medicine*. This was to be a shortened version of Adami's standard two-volume text, *The Principles of Pathology*, and intended to make the contents of the latter accessible to the general student. As the pace of life continued to speed up, so for John, it seemed, did his work schedule.

William Osler, on the other hand, found himself with rather more time than usual to appreciate his surroundings. After having fulfilled a professional obligation to visit hospitals in Cairo, he was travelling in Egypt that February with his brother. Transport both on land and water was becoming increasingly sophisticated, with more powerful motor vehicles and a luxurious train, the Orient Express, operated by the Belgian, Georges Nagelmackers, and his Compagnie Internationale des Wagons-Lits. As he journeyed down the Nile to visit the ancient sites at Luxor and Karnak, Osler was perfectly happy with his thoroughly modern river boat that enabled him to study the ceaseless panorama of

Egypt's legendary river. He wrote of the desert and mountain scenery; of old fishing craft with their 'curved prows and remarkable sails'[3]; of his visit to the Khedival Library with its enormous and superbly illustrated editions of the Koran. There would be much to relate on his return. William and Grace Osler were again expecting the arrival of their two Canadian charges, Ottilie Wright and Nona Gwyn. Delayed by a year, the girls' presentation at Court was scheduled for 25 May and they arrived in Oxford full of excitement.

The spring of 1911 was marked by good weather. As preparations were being made for his Coronation, King George V welcomed his cousin Kaiser Wilhelm to the unveiling on 16 May 1911 of Sir Thomas Brock's new statue of their grandmother, Queen Victoria. Although King George was very British by nature and was keenly interested in his country and her Empire, he recognised that Britain was now well and truly involved in Europe. Unlike his father, he was well disposed towards the Kaiser and relations between the two were cordial. The unveiling ceremony took place outside Buckingham Palace amid cheering crowds, gun salutes and the music of military bands. One of the invited guests at the brilliant gathering that sunny spring day was Grace Osler, who was staying at Mayfair's Brown's Hotel with Ottilie and Nona in anticipation of their presentation at Court. When the big day finally arrived, Grace described the scene in their room: 'Behold three females – one aged . . . grey-haired lady, and two beautiful young girls . . . sitting on a bed waiting for dresses to arrive to go to Court . . . I look like <u>Katherine of Aragon</u>, the girls like angels.'[4] One of the 'angels' had already caught the eye of John McCrae's friend, Dr Campbell Palmer Howard, who would undoubtedly have approved of her beautiful off-the-shoulder presentation gown with its train, veil and headdress of feathers.

As Canadians bought flags and prepared to celebrate the Coronation, the Medical Faculty of McGill University was also looking forward to an important event. After the disastrous fire four years earlier, McGill's new medical building was now complete, thanks to insurance funds and a generous bequest from Lord Strathcona. The official opening on Monday 5 June 1911 was to be carried out by Earl Grey, now in his last months as Governor General. When the day arrived all went well, and at a rather grand garden party held in the grounds of the nearby Royal Victoria Hospital, guests from the university, the medical profession and Montreal society mixed and mingled to the sound of an orchestra playing light classical and operatic pieces such as 'La Bohème', 'The Blue Danube' and the 'Chocolate Soldier'. Elaborate hats, lace-trimmed parasols and exquisite dresses of the prettiest fabrics and shades moved among dark suits that sunny afternoon. Later, at Montreal's elegant Windsor Hotel, the Dean, Professors and members of the Medical Faculty's teaching staff gave a dinner for the university's medical graduates. Lord Strathcona, the

1. John McCrae as a baby.

2. John McCrae (bottom left) with his mother Janet, brother Tom and sister Geills, circa 1881.

3. Tom (left) and John McCrae, 1893.

4. Guelph Christmas Market, 1896.

5. John McCrae as a medical student at the
University of Toronto, 1898.

6. John McCrae relaxing at Mount Airy, Maryland, 1896.

7. The Second Canadian Contingent at Halifax and about to depart for South Africa. January 1900.

8. Major W G Hurdman (left), officer commanding D Battery, Royal Canadian Field Artillery, and Lieutenant Edward Morrison (right) at Green Point, Cape Town, February 1900.

9. John McCrae in the mess dress of an officer of the Canadian Artillery, 7 March 1901.

10. Sherbrooke Street, Montreal, where it adjoins Metcalfe Street, winter 1896. John McCrae lived not far from this corner in the house of Dr Edward Archibald at 160 Metcalfe Street from October 1910 until the Great War.

11. John McCrae (centre) with Beatriz d'Arneiro (left)
and Elizabeth Morrison (right), Paris, November 1906.

12. Sir William Osler (centre front) and Lady Osler (far right) with a group of
friends at 13 Norham Gardens, Oxford, 1907. Seated behind Lady Osler is Sir
William's niece Amy Gwyn, who later married Tom McCrae.

13. Members of Earl Grey's 1910 expedition outside the Wawaskkeski Clubhouse. John McCrae is seated left with Earl Grey standing behind him. Leo Amery is seated centre.

14. John McCrae circa 1908 with the daughter of a friend, possibly Dr Edward Archibald's daughter, Margaret.

15. Dr Tom McCrae with his sister Geills Kilgour and her children Margaret (standing left), Katherine (standing right), David (seated left) and Jack (seated centre). The photo is likely to have been taken either in the summer of 1914 or spring of 1915.

16. Onlookers watching the arrival of the Canadian Expeditionary Force at Plymouth, 14 October 1914.

17. Top row from left: Lt. Alexis Helmer, Dr Edward Archibald, Dr Lawrence Rhea, Capt. Lawrence Cosgrave
Bottom row from left: Dr Herbert Birkett, Dr W. G. Turner, Professor J. G. Adami, Dr Francis Scrimger.

18. John McCrae seated on "Bonfire", his faithful companion throughout the war, Boulogne 1916.

19. Her Majesty Queen Mary visits No. 3 Canadian General Hospital (McGill), 3 July 1917. Accompanying the Queen are Matron MacLatchy (on her right), Colonel Birkett (turning to her left) and John McCrae (walking directly behind Matron MacLatchy).

man who had made all this possible, could be proud of the fact that the McGill Medical School was now one of the foremost in North America.

Visiting students and graduates of Oxford or Cambridge could not help comparing McGill's impressive surroundings with those of their own universities. One admirer of Montreal that summer was Robert Vernède, an Oxford graduate and school friend of the writer, G.K. Chesterton. He had arrived on the Allan Line ship, *Empress of Britain* with a crowd of emigrants and found Canada a 'highly exciting country'.[5] Marvelling over the fact that he had been told Montreal had 'sixty-four millionaires; self-made not descended',[6] Vernède climbed the wooded Mount Royal on a sunny day and discovered 'the most beautiful view of a city that can be seen'.[7] The memory of Canada's 'illimitable space' and 'irrepressible men'[8] was to inspire him to immortalise her in both prose and poetry a few years later. A young Fellow of Kings College, Cambridge, also passed through Montreal that summer, noting the 'Scotch spirit sensible in the whole place' and the 'air of dour prosperity'.[9] Rupert Brooke's travels were to lead to beautiful descriptions of the west, but it was in eastern Canada that he noted approvingly, 'the sight of kindly, English-looking faces, and the rather lovely sound of the soft Canadian accent in the streets'.[10]

On both sides of the Atlantic, the summer of 1911 was destined to be long, hot and golden. As Coronation Day approached and royalty, nobility, ambassadors and envoys converged on London, an envelope from 10 Downing Street had already been delivered to 13 Norham Gardens, Oxford. The customary Coronation Honours List would shortly be published to mark the great occasion and the letter had enquired whether Professor Osler would accept a knighthood. The great doctor received the news 'much to the embarrassment of his democratic simplicity' and remarked modestly to his wife that 'I think I'll have to accept – Canada will be so pleased – there's only one Canadian baronet.'[11] Osler was an excellent correspondent but so vast was the flood of telegrams, letters and good wishes that it took him many weeks to answer them all.

Huge crowds gathered in Britain's capital on 22 June, filling the route to Westminster Abbey, marvelling at the magnificence of the great procession and hoping to catch a glimpse of their new monarch. Londoners rejoiced in the streets and parks, enjoying the weather and the general mood of exultation. In comparison with his urbane father, King George V was a man of simple tastes with a sense of orderliness, organisation, self-discipline and consistency instilled into him by a youth spent in the Royal Navy. After the gaiety and fashionable society of Edward VII's court, the King and his wife, Queen Mary, appeared somewhat reserved. Nevertheless, they maintained from the beginning a standard of unostentatious, regal splendour at their Court. It was an exciting time to be alive, and as the festivities reached a peak, a stunning new arrival became the crowning glory of the London scene. The Russian impresario Sergei

Diaghilev[12] brought his Ballets Russes to Covent Garden and Britain's capital was treated to the spectacle of 'Schéhèrazade' starring the great dancer, Nijinsky.[13] The combination of choreography, music, costumes and sets brought people flocking night after night to the performances. As the season progressed, however, there was one young man who sensed something sinister behind the wonderful sunny days. To Osbert Sitwell, everything, 'seemed to possess a strange fullness and richness typical of the epoch' but 'during this whole time, the shadow that moved with us, was growing and darkening . . . Something was going wrong in the world, and could surely be felt by the sensitive, through the intense sweetness of being alive at that time.'[14]

Before his return to Germany, Kaiser Wilhelm who had been thoroughly enjoying the military pageantry, ceremonial and grandeur of it all, approached his cousin, King George, at the behest of the German Chancellor, Theobald von Bethmann-Hollweg. The main topic for discussion was the problem of Morocco, over which friction between Germany and France had continued since 1905. That spring, the government in Paris, complaining that the Sultan of Morocco was no longer able to maintain order in the interior of his country, had despatched an expeditionary force. The German Foreign Ministry claimed that, since France was clearly about to establish a protectorate over Morocco, Germany had commercial interests and treaty rights that entitled it to compensation. Kiderlen-Waechter, the German State Secretary for Foreign Affairs, argued that if the French were anxious for the safety of their own nationals in Morocco, Germany, too, had a right to protect hers. Although there were no German soldiers in the country, the despatch of one or more warships to safeguard the property and lives of any German nationals in southern Morocco could achieve the same effect.[15]

The Kaiser was concerned over British reaction to such a move and had made up his mind to measure the pulse before sanctioning the plan. Having listened to what King George had to say and promising that Germany would never go to war or interfere over Morocco, Wilhelm returned home concluding that if his country intended to oppose the French intervention in Morocco, she would have to do so alone. Nearly a fortnight later, the despatch of the German cruiser *Panther* to anchor off the Moroccan coast at Agadir, created a storm of international suspicion. Britain asked for more information on German intentions. She was concerned not only about Germany's sudden action but about France, the Entente and the possible establishment of a German naval station close to existing British sea routes to South Africa. By 21 July no reply to the British enquiry had been received and in a speech that evening to city bankers at their annual dinner at the Mansion House, the Chancellor of the Exchequer, David Lloyd George, gave a strong warning. Although he did not mention Germany or her cruiser, he made it very clear that

Britain would not be treated 'as if she were of no account' on a continent 'where her interests were vitally affected'.[16] From a man who was known to be strongly in favour of an Anglo-German understanding, this warning that Britain would fight to maintain her influence and authority came as a shock to many in Britain and Germany.

The existing atmosphere of tension prevailed for several weeks and the crisis was serious enough for many to view war as a real possibility. From his home in Sussex, Rudyard Kipling must have watched events with great concern as Kaiser Wilhelm spoke in Hamburg of his wish to see the German navy further strengthened so 'no one can dispute with us the place in the sun that is our due'.[17] After the Anglo-German aspect of the crisis was over in late July, negotiations between Germany and France dragged on until their eventual resolution in mid-October. What emerged from the crisis, apart from German anger and resentment at the final settlement, was that almost any confrontation between the major European powers was now capable of bringing them to the brink of war. Britain's First Sea Lord, Admiral Sir Jacky Fisher, had by this point decided that it would be 'October 21, 1914 when the Battle of Armageddon comes along'[18], for this was the date that corresponded with the likely completion of improvements to the Kiel Canal – the canal that would allow the passage of large German battleships from the Baltic to the North Sea.

At a time when the two European power blocs were becoming more rigid, a new wave of revolutions had been adding more flammable material to 'a world already preparing to go up in flames'. Russia had narrowly survived a revolution in 1905 that had temporarily destabilised the Czar and encouraged Germany to assert her claims in Morocco. A revolution in Turkey two years later had destroyed carefully constructed provisions for maintaining the international equilibrium in the Near East. The dispute with Russia that had followed Austria-Hungary's annexation of Bosnia and Herzegovina had been settled only by the threat of German military support. This latest international crisis was further evidence that clear signs of strain were beginning to show in the political structures designed to provide secure management of regimes. The situation in the international arena was becoming more dangerous.[19]

Although the world was drifting into conflict, it was at the same time bound more tightly by modern communications. Luxurious sea and rail travel and the lure of new destinations were temptations to anyone with the time and means at their disposal. For John McCrae, one of the advantages of university teaching and a bachelor's life, was that he could indulge his fondness for travel. As he began to think about his next European holiday, others were on the move too. After a long period as Assistant Professor of Medicine at Johns Hopkins University, 1911 was the year in which Tom McCrae decided to accept an appointment as Professor of Medicine at Jefferson Medical College in Philadelphia. He and his wife

Amy would shortly be leaving the familiar surroundings of Baltimore for the city that was to be their home for many years to come. Although John was one of McGill's more senior and respected teachers and could also consider a career move, he was loath to do so, confessing in a letter to Oskar Klotz that 'the idea of "up and out" rather daunts me'.[20]

With more engagements and weddings among his friends, John told Oskar that among 'all these marryings and givings in marriage, you will wonder that 160 [Metcalfe Street] has nothing doing'.[21] Over the period of the previous twelve months he had written Oskar several letters bemoaning the pressures of work and mentioning a romance. As ever, he referred to the lady in question, who appeared to travel frequently, in very discreet terms, admitting to Oskar that he missed her 'sadly', and that during one of her absences, he had decided to 'cut girling out of my time-table.'[22] Work seemed to offer little solace and a few weeks later John complained:

> What a – of a stale thing is life! . . . I have so damned many things on my soul at present that I can't sit down and be ordinarily gay without my conscience saying 'my dear fellow, art is long and time is fleeting, and you ought to be doing this or that!' Isn't that a pitiful state . . . to be in . . . My humble respects to your esteemed lady. My est[eemed]. lady seems to be liking N[ew]. Y[ork]. fairly well, and declares she is <u>never</u> coming back.[23]

When nothing came of the liaison, John decided that the 'girl market' was 'much depressed, even if one had time to cultivate it'.[24] Despite periodic rumours that 'this or that young lady would be married to John McCrae',[25] the handsome, personable and charming doctor was still single. In many ways this was understandable. He had been working hard to establish himself professionally at a period when it was usual for a man to wait until he had done so before seriously considering marriage. University salaries were not large and John had not been making much from his private practice. A friend later remembered that 'his patients were his friends. His kindly presence and his sturdy strength in a sick room were better than any tonic'.[26] Medical treatment had to be paid for in those days, and John McCrae often treated his poorer patients for little or no money. This fact, coupled with his liking for travel, had made it difficult for him to amass the means to support a family. Although John was certainly a man's man, he was also delightful company from a woman's point of view, as Beatriz d'Arneiro had observed in Paris. The social life of the 'Square Mile' brought him into contact with many women, who, while finding him charming and courteous, were used to a much more ostentatious lifestyle than John could provide. Even if he could have afforded to wed, this man, who set conscience and duty before success and all its trappings, knew that his career and aspirations belonged elsewhere. John McCrae was no Dr Tertius Lydgate.

Little correspondence survives to tell much of John's activities in the latter part of 1911 and the first half of 1912, but he would assuredly have been pleased at the success of Stephen Leacock's book, *Sunshine Sketches of a Little Town*, and interested in the outcome of Canada's general election of 1911. Leacock, known affectionately to his students as 'Leaky Steamcock',[27] had written a humorous account of town life in English-speaking Canada. Its winning portrayal of a community in the era of golden calm before the coming storm, was to make it a national favourite. The country's election results brought about political change as Wilfrid Laurier's Liberal government was finally ousted from office in 1911 by a Conservative victory. The man who forced the election and led his party to the winning post was Nova Scotian lawyer, Robert Borden. As Canada's new Prime Minister, he was to prove a remarkable leader in the dark years that lay ahead.

John continued to write regularly to his mother and enjoyed hearing news of his sister's growing family. He now had two nieces, Margaret, aged four, and Katherine, two years her junior, with whom he had been able to spend time during his visit to Geills and her husband the previous year. Katherine was the recipient of a rhyme John wrote and illustrated especially for her, about a 'Goop'.[28]

> The place for jam is on the plate,
> And here it gives me pain to state
> That I have known a certain place
> Where children have it on the face:
> That is what Goops are apt to do.
> I hope it's not at all like you!
> DON'T BE A GOOP!!!

World events in the spring of 1912 spotlighted the tragic sinking on her maiden voyage of the *Titanic*, pride of the White Star Line; and the launch by Kaiser Wilhelm of the world's biggest luxury liner, the Hamburg-Amerika Line's *Imperator*, with its tennis and squash courts, elevators and Ritz-Carlton restaurant. Nijinsky starred in another of Diaghilev's ballets, this time the erotic 'Afternoon of a Faun' with music by the French composer, Claude Debussy. That autumn, war broke out in the Balkans and troops of the Balkan alliance threw the once invincible Turkish army into disarray.

John McCrae's letters indicate that he spent part of the summer of 1912 with friends at a pleasant retreat in Quebec province, and shared an early autumn fishing trip with his brother, Tom, during which they sighted moose, partridge and a skunk, discovered one night 'calmly sitting up

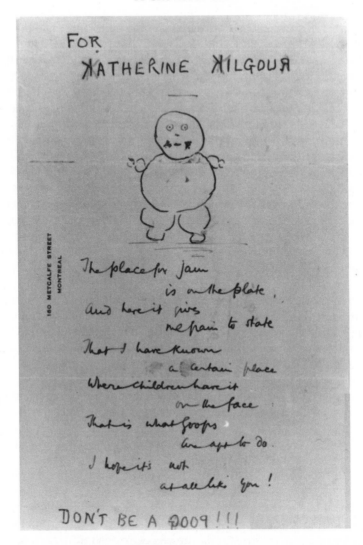

Drawing and rhyme in John McCrae's handwriting
to his niece Katherine Kilgour.
Courtesy of Guelph Museums, Guelph, Canada
It reads as overleaf:

on a grub box eating our butter'.[29] By the end of the year, he was feeling somewhat tired and stale. There were 'hosts of invitations'[30] to be accepted or rejected, the marriage of Earl Grey's daughter, Lady Evelyn, to attend and the usual professional tasks that filled his day. Continuing to work on George Adami's Pathology textbook, he had also promised Oskar Klotz that he would produce medical abstracts for the *American Journal of Medical Science*, of which Oskar was now the editor. It was a daunting schedule and Andrew Macphail later wrote that John's heavy workload hinged on his own admission that 'I have never refused any work that was given me to do'.[31] But even John's seemingly unending capacity for labour was beginning to wane, prompting him to admit by the end of January 1913 that the 'only thing I look forward to is getting to bed, and it is very hard to leave it in the morning'.[32] Nevertheless, he kept up with social commitments, enjoying a meeting the following month with the Norwegian explorer, Roald Amundsen who, at the end of 1911, had been the first to reach the South Pole ahead of the ill-fated Captain Scott and his expedition. John liked the Norwegian and discovered they had much in common: 'I heard Capt[ain]. Amundsen lecture, and afterwards met him at supper at Leacock's. I was greatly taken with him: clean cut, capable looking, modest, speaks English very well and talks most interestingly. Evidently he is very fond of dogs.'[33]

The fine new Strathcona Medical Building at McGill had now been in use for over six months and the spring of 1913 began on a positive note when Sir William Osler came to visit it as part of the extended inaugural festivities. Speaking of McGill's transformation, Osler was reminded of what he had recently told the students at Johns Hopkins, Baltimore: 'To have lived through a revolution, to have seen a new birth of science, a new dispensation of health, reorganized medical schools, remodelled hospitals, a new outlook for humanity, is not given to every generation.'[34]

As that delightful spring progressed, attention turned to Germany and what was to be the last of the kind of great royal family gathering that had been such a feature of the European scene. Kaiser Wilhelm's only daughter Princess Victoria Louise married the Duke of Brunswick-Lüneburg and among the family members present were his cousins George V and Nicholas II, who bore a striking resemblance to each other and shared the same well-intentioned demeanour. In contrast to his father, who had visited Europe frequently, this was King George's first continental visit. Berlin spared no expense, with huge banquets, military parades, a gala performance at the opera and the wedding itself with its traditional Fackeltanz or Torch Dance in the magnificent White Hall of the Old Palace. Although the Kaiser spent part of the time imagining that plots were being hatched behind his back by his British and Russian cousins, he did not show it, still hoping Britain might be lured out of her Entente with Russia and France. For his part, King George left Berlin with the feeling that his visit had been very successful and the Kaiser very hospitable. He hoped it would improve relations between the two countries.

All this while, the lot of Dr John McCrae continued, not surprisingly, to be a hectic one. As work on the new book progressed, his private practice chose to increase and he declared to his mother that, 'I have been at it ding-dong all day and every day.'[35] Although tired, he was brightened by the idea of a possible visit to southern France or Spain, to be fitted around the XVII International Medical Congress which he planned to attend in London that August. As Europe braced itself for another brilliant summer, Montreal experienced an early heatwave from which John was happy to escape. A short visit to Boston in June 1913 made a welcome and pleasant interlude for he enjoyed the city's Colonial charm and the opportunity to visit the battlefield of Lexington. Friends like Dr Harvey Cushing, who now held the senior Chair of Surgery at Harvard University, welcomed him, and everyone enjoyed dining 'al fresco' in the warmth of the New England evenings.

Although John had not been active in the militia for some years, he had retained a strong interest and kept in touch with his friend from South Africa, Edward Morrison, who was now both editor of the *Ottawa Citizen* newspaper and director of militia artillery. Since South Africa there had been a period of marked development and progress for both the permanent and non-permanent artillery in Canada. The gunners had learned the need for greater centralisation of control over batteries and for heavier field ordnance. The Boers had also taught them the value of concealment in action. Organisational changes in 1905 had grouped the twenty-four separate militia field batteries into ten larger brigades. Annual training had been moved to the spacious facilities of Camp Petawawa beside the Ottawa River using the new 18-pdr field gun, which had become the standard weapon of Canada's field artillery.

The election that had swept Robert Borden's Conservatives into power had also brought Colonel Sam Hughes into office as Canada's Minister of Militia. The controversial figure, whom John McCrae remembered from South Africa, had also foreseen the German military threat and had never tired of warning the Canadian parliament and people of the imminence of war with Germany. In his first full fiscal year in office, Hughes increased militia expenditure by a million and a half dollars and insisted on realistic training for the militia.

In Britain that summer, Rudyard Kipling was invited to watch the British army conduct field exercises around Frensham Ponds at Aldershot. The troops in action were those that would form the future 8th Division and many of the officers had seen service in the South African War. Under the vivid blue sky and in the heat haze that surrounded them, the sound of rifle fire reminded Kipling of the Karoo. He could visualise that 'anything might be afoot in such weather, pom-poms for instance, half heard on a flank, or the glint of a helio through a cloud-drift'. He found himself imagining the dead of the South African War 'flickering and re-forming as the horizon flickered in the heat'[36] as if it were some kind of premonition.

By early July John McCrae, his brother Tom and some of the other doctors from Montreal were on their way to England aboard the Allan Line ship, *Victorian*. After a delightful visit to the Oslers in Oxford, where he found 'a perfect eruption of Canadians at afternoon tea',[37] John and a colleague, Dr Hamilton White, set off for a holiday in France. They arrived via the Newhaven-Dieppe ferry on 14 July, Bastille Day, to fireworks and huge crowds, and early next morning, began the journey that was to take them to Dijon, Lyons, Avignon, Nîmes, Toulouse, Bordeaux and the château country. John sent his mother letters and postcards along the way that enthused about 'the cookery of France in good moderation';[38] Arles with its pink and white oleanders in bloom; the magnificent Roman temples at Nîmes; and the medieval fortress city of Carcassonne. On their return to Paris, the two doctors visited the Institut Pasteur and found themselves a hotel close to the Rue de Rivoli which advertised the latest amenities of 'lumière éléctrique' and 'salle de bain'.

As the cream of the medical profession gathered for the XVII International Medical Congress, they found London in the grip not only of hot weather and fancy dress balls, but also ragtime and the latest dance craze, the tango. Adding to the city's joie de vivre had been a spectacular new Diaghilev ballet, 'Sacré du Printemps'. With music by Igor Stravinsky and brilliant sets by the designer, Leon Bakst, it had taken the imperial capital by storm and performed to packed houses night after night. The atmosphere that year in 'the gayest, richest and largest capital in the world'[39] seemed positively vibrant and the London season glittered and glowed with so much vitality that the rich, the powerful and the adventurous found themselves irresistibly drawn to it.[40]

John McCrae received a warm welcome from Sir William and Lady Osler, who were installed in a large suite at Brown's Hotel where they hosted friends and colleagues on a daily basis. Sir William's niece, Nona Gwyn, was with them and John was one of a dozen or so guests invited to lunch and to a private dinner given by Sir William in the very dignified surroundings of Pall Mall's Automobile Club. The opening session of the Congress on 6 August 1913 was a memorable occasion, with almost seven thousand delegates packing the Royal Albert Hall from ceiling to floor. Canada's newest Governor General Prince Arthur, Duke of Connaught, formally opened the proceedings and Britain's Foreign Secretary, Sir Edward Grey, spoke on behalf of the government. A number of John McCrae's friends presented papers including Edward Archibald, whose offering was well received by the 'surgical greats' of the day. Nothing short of a crystal ball could have told any of the doctors at that august gathering that, a little over a year later, many of them would be in uniform and preparing to go off to war. One such man was Nobel Prize winner and German Rhodes scholar, Professor Paul Ehrlich, the bacteriologist who had discovered salvarsan.[41] Ehrlich, a friend of Osler and others present, gave a memorable address to the Conference on chemotherapy. His brilliant career had not long to run for it was to end in 1915 with his death on the battlefield.

During its six-day duration the Congress moved along successfully, punctuated at intervals by interruptions from suffragette hecklers, for these were the years of militancy in which that movement sought to obtain votes for women. To the visiting doctors, London hospitality was bountiful to say the least. Magnificent dinners were held – one for five hundred guests at the Hotel Cecil given by the British government, and another at the Savoy. There were invitations to the theatre; receptions at Windsor Castle, Lambeth Palace, and all the London hospitals; a lavish soirée at the Victoria & Albert Museum; weekend visits to Oxford and Cambridge; river trips on the Thames; and special services at St Paul's and Westminster Abbey. The Oslers were most kind to John throughout and took him with them to lunch at 'Cliveden', the home of the American millionaire, Waldorf Astor, and his beautiful wife Nancy. The influential people that made up the Astors' salon were known as the 'Cliveden Set' and their splendid residence struck John as 'a perfectly regal place'.[42] Perhaps most picturesque of all the social events was an evening fête in the Botanical Gardens of Regents Park hosted by Lord Strathcona, McGill's great benefactor and Canada's High Commissioner. Guests arrived to the sound of the pipers of the Scots Guards and found the whole place strikingly lit by colourful Japanese lanterns hanging from long bamboo poles. That memorable night, the ninety-three-year old Lord Strathcona insisted on shaking hands with as many of his thirteen hundred guests as possible.[43]

London was not the only capital city enjoying a memorable summer. The story was similar in Paris, Vienna and Berlin, the latter celebrating twenty-five years of Kaiser Wilhelm's reign. Messages of goodwill came from far and wide and among those bringing greetings to Berlin in person was the Canon of Westminster, Dr William Boyd Carpenter, a great favourite of the Kaiser's mother before she died. Both he and the Bishop of London, Dr Arthur Winnington Ingram, knew Germany well and it was not Dr Boyd Carpenter's first visit. After his audience with the Kaiser to offer congratulations on behalf of the British Council of Churches, he came away disquieted, for although he had found the German Emperor, 'quite cordial', he had also detected:

> a note which was new to me; it was no longer the note of hope and joyous anticipation; he seemed to me to be apprehensive; he spoke of the dangerous position in which Germany was placed, between two powers which understood one another and might prove hostile. When I left him, I felt the Emperor was under the influence of a great fear. 'He is changed', I said to myself. I was afraid, for I knew that there was no passion so cruel as fear.[44]

Within Germany itself, the few warning notes about the dangers of impending conflict being sounded by Germans to their own countrymen passed unnoticed in a nation whose overriding mood was one of ebullience and pride. The Crown Prince summed up the prevailing German senti-ment in the introduction he wrote to a book celebrating the hundredth anniversary of the 1813 defeat of Napoleon at Leipzig: 'the sword will remain the decisive factor till the end of the world.'[45]

After a quiet week in Scotland with the Oslers, the Cushings and Nona Gwyn, John returned to London having found the Highlands beautiful, but for some reason 'inexpressibly sad'.[46] He sailed for Canada on 27 August 1913 and, on his return to Montreal, was soon caught up in his usual maelstrom of duties and diversions. He was reminded of the Highlands a few weeks later when his friends Hamilton and Marguerite Gault invited him to dinner to meet Lochiel, Chief of the Clan Cameron. That autumn, manoeuvres of the British and French armies were held in East Anglia and Touraine respectively. Representatives from around the Empire were invited to attend and Edward Morrison, on behalf of the Canadian artillery, was among the Canadian officers who accompanied Sam Hughes. On their return to Canada, the report of the visit, prepared under Hughes' direction, stated that the 'employment of mobile artillery as demonstrated at the manoeuvres left little to be suggested in the way of improvement of training in Canada'.[47]

In Germany, meanwhile, the country's military leaders were now in a state of high activity. With the Schlieffen Plan ready for execution, its success depended on the attitude of Belgium, the country through which German troops would be required to pass, although Prussia had been one of the guarantors of Belgian neutrality in perpetuity. Kaiser Wilhelm decided to invite King Albert of the Belgians to Potsdam that November in order to judge his reaction. Having listened to a discourse on the invincibility of the German army, King Albert quietly but emphatically assured his hosts that his country would remain neutral unless attacked, but that if she were attacked, she would fight back. On his return to Brussels, the King reinforced his words with a statement to the effect that Belgium would declare war on any power that violated her territory.

With Christmas approaching, the great houses of Montreal were lav-ishly decorated for the festivities and there was an atmosphere of gaiety about the cold winter evenings. Stephen Leacock invited John to dinner and presented him, as his personal physician, with an inscribed copy of his latest book *Behind the Beyond*. John himself was again in print with what was to be the last of his poems to appear in *The University Magazine*. As he spent a memorable pre-Christmas evening at Lady Allan's ball held at her splendid home, 'Ravenscrag', John could not have known how different his next Christmas would be – the stark contrast between the warmth, elegance and richesse of 'Ravenscrag', and the cold, damp and misery of life in a military tent. There had been little time for poetry in the past three years but now, whether consciously or unconsciously, he captured in another poem, 'The Night Cometh', the sense that a shadow was about to be cast over countless lives. The metre of this latest composition was one that Andrew Macphail would later recognise again in the poem that was to bring John McCrae lasting fame.

The Night Cometh

Cometh the night. The wind falls low,
The trees swing slowly to and fro:
Around the church the headstones grey
Cluster, like children strayed away
But found again, and folded so.

No chiding look doth she bestow:
If she is glad, they cannot know;
If ill or well they spend their day,
Cometh the night.

Singing or sad, intent they go;
They do not see the shadows grow;
'There yet is time,' they lightly say,
'Before our work aside we lay';
Their task is but half-done, and lo!
Cometh the night.[48]

In later years, Winston Churchill described the last few years before the war as 'the old world, in its sunset'.[49] Now the sun had all but disappeared below the horizon and the darkness was fast approaching.

NOTES

1. From 'The Night Cometh' by John McCrae, *The University Magazine* (Volume 12, No. 3, April 1913), p. 145. Micro mfm/AP/U577, UTL.
2. JM to Janet McCrae, 9 November 1910, GM Papers.
3. Cushing, *Sir William Osler*, Volume II, p. 264.
4. Cushing, *Sir William Osler*, Volume II, p. 273.
5. R.E. Vernède, *The Fair Dominion* (London 1911), Preface, p. vi.
6. Vernède, *The Fair Dominion*, p. 69.
7. Vernède, *The Fair Dominion*, p. 77.
8. Vernède, *The Fair Dominion*, Preface, p. vi.
9. Sandra Martin and Roger Hall, *Rupert Brooke in Canada* (Toronto, 1978), pp. 24–25.
10. Martin and Hall, *Rupert Brooke in Canada*, p. 28.
11. Cushing, *Sir William Osler*, Volume II, p. 275.
12. Sergei Pavlovich Diaghilev (1872–1929) was the founder of the celebrated Ballets Russes and worked at the forefront of promoting Russian arts in the West – especially in Paris – in the first decade of this century. After graduating from St Petersburg University, his career as an editor, art critic,

curator and impresario led to his eventual exile from Russia in 1914. The Ballets Russes dispersed around Europe and America and from 1915, a caucus of the company, including Diaghilev, remained in Lausanne to lay the foundation of its final phase, which embraced international Avant-Garde.

13. The Russian-born ballet dancer Vaslav Nijinsky (1890–1950) achieved almost legendary fame for his spectacular leaps and sensitive interpretations.

14. Osbert Sitwell, *Great Morning* (London, 1948), p. 41.

15. Massie, *Dreadnought*, p. 722.

16. Palmer, *The Kaiser*, p. 145.

17. Morton, *Pageant of the Century*, p. 203.

18. Massie, *Dreadnought*, p. 407.

19. E.J. Hobsbawm, *The Age of Empire* (London, 1987), p. 321.

20. JM to Oskar Klotz 13 June 1911, MG 30, B61, Klotz Papers, NAC.

21. JM to Oskar Klotz, 20 December 1911, MG 30, B61, Klotz Papers, NAC.

22. JM to Oskar Klotz, 26 January 1911, MG 30, B61, Klotz Papers, NAC.

23. JM to Oskar Klotz, 13 March 1910, MG 30, B61, Klotz Papers, NAC.

24. JM to Oscar Klotz, 7 December 1910, MG 30, B61, Klotz Papers, NAC.

25. Howitt, 'John McCrae', p. 15.

26. Professor John Macnaughton, 'In Memoriam – Lieut.-Col. John McCrae', *The University Magazine* (Volume 17, No. 3, April 1918), p. 242. Micro mfm AP/U577, UTL.

27. Legate, *Stephen Leacock*, p. 37.

28. Meaning a 'spill' or, in this case, someone who makes a mess.

29. JM to Janet McCrae, 20 September 1912, GM Papers.

30. JM to Janet McCrae, 28 November 1912, GM Papers.

31. Macphail, *In Flanders Fields*, p. 125.

32. JM to Janet McCrae, 17 March 1913, GM Papers.

33. JM to Janet McCrae, 25 February 1913, GM Papers.

34. Cushing, *Sir William Osler*, Volume II, p. 350.

35. JM to Janet McCrae, 3 May 1913, GM Papers.

36. Rudyard Kipling, *Something of Myself* (London, 1937), p. 214.

37. JM to Janet McCrae, 13 July 1913, GM Papers.

38. JM to Janet McCrae, 17 July 1913, GM Papers.

39. Fleur Cowles, *1913: The Defiant Swansong* (London, 1967) p. 1.

40. Cowles, *1913*, p.31.

41. Salvarsan was the trade name for arsphenamine, the compound discovered by Paul Ehrlich as a treatment for syphilis. It was replaced in the 1940s by antibiotics.

42. JM to Janet McCrae, 15 August 1913, GM Papers. Waldorf, 2nd Viscount Astor (1879–1952), was an agricultural expert and a Member of Parliament from 1910–1919. His wife Nancy, Viscountess Astor, (1879–1964) became the first woman to sit in the House of Commons.

43. Prescott, *In Flanders Fields*, p. 72.

44. Wilson, *The Great War*, Volume 10 (London, 1917), p. 558.

45. Barbara Tuchman, *The Proud Tower: A Portrait of the World before the War 1890–1914* (London, 1966), p. 344.

46. JM to Janet McCrae, 15 August 1913, GM Papers.

47. Colonel G.W.L. Nicholson, *The Gunners of Canada* (Toronto/Montreal: 1967), Volume I, p. 188.

48. *The University Magazine* (Volume 12, No. 3, April 1913), p. 145. Micro mfm AP/U577, UTL.

49. Aronson, *Crowns in Conflict*, p. 24.

CHAPTER TEN

' . . . and lo! Cometh the Night'[1]

January–October 1914

The year 1914 began quietly enough for John McCrae in Montreal, but on the evening of 10 January, a pain in his abdomen was quickly diagnosed as appendicitis. On hand to handle the emergency was his landlord and, by 'day light,' John wrote to Oskar Klotz, 'Archibald had my appendix out: it was going fast towards a perforation.'[2] While he was convalescing in Philadelphia with Tom and Amy McCrae, Lord Strathcona died on 21 January at his London home in Grosvenor Square. The man whose remarkable career had begun in the fur trade and carried him to fame and fortune as 'one of the bulwarks of the British Empire'[3], was buried in Highgate Cemetery. Among the ten pall bearers at the funeral service in Westminster Abbey was Sir William Osler.

Work continued unabated on John's return to Montreal, and his spare time was well occupied by a flurry of invitations. He attended 'a house dance at Herbert Molson's',[4] an artillery officers' dance at the Ritz Hotel, a hockey match, a card party and a performance of 'Tannhäuser' at the opera. At home in Metcalfe Street, Edward Archibald's second daughter, Nancy, was now a source of great enjoyment. John, who was fond of the Archibald children and enjoyed devising nicknames for them like 'Slip McGloober', 'Peglegs' and 'Hunkamunk', wrote frequently about her to his mother, relating on 19 March that, 'Nancy has just gone up stairs calling "Allo, doc A'Kay"'.[5]

On the evening St George's Day, John made his way to the University Club in evening dress. Now housed in a splendid new building,[6] the Club was entertaining Canada's Governor General, His Royal Highness The Duke of Connaught. John reported on Prince Arthur's visit in his next letter home: 'Last ev[enin]'g the Univ[ersity] Club gave a dinner to H.R.H.(Connaught) which went off extremely well: the speeches were good; Leacock's very funny.'[7] The new Club premises provided comfortable, elegant surroundings that lent themselves to a formal dinner, a quiet meal with an associate, a pleasant hour behind a newspaper or a game of bridge. Its atmosphere of conviviality and intellectual stimulation was enjoyed by all its active members and for Stephen Leacock, it was to become a favourite daily destination for years to come.

As May heralded warmer, sunny days and the sight of spring flowers, John's former teacher, George Adami, sailed from Montreal with his daughter, Isabel, for an extended visit to Europe. John now became the custodian and supervisor of the galleys, manuscripts, illustrations and necessary but routine work that had to be completed for the second edition of their joint book, *A Textbook of Pathology for Students of Medicine*. He consoled himself with some good meals at the University Club and, by 21 June, had completed his own part of the project. While awaiting the proof of the book from the publisher, John learned that he had been elected a Member of the Association of American Physicians, making him one of only a handful of Canadian doctors to be awarded the distinction. It was difficult to make any holiday plans while there was still work to be done on the book, and to make his proof-reading as enjoyable as possible, John decided to take himself to the east coast resort of Atlantic City, New Jersey. There he could swim, walk and do his work in weather that was 'hot but bright and lots of oxygen.'[8] Whilst enjoying the benefits of sun and sea, he wrote as a final comment in one of his letters to his mother: 'What an awful thing in Austria!'[9]

The 'awful thing' to which he referred, was a double assassination in the Bosnian capital of Sarajevo on 28 June 1914. Austria had become very concerned at the growth of revolutionary feeling in Bosnia-Herzegovina and three months earlier, Kaiser Wilhelm had visited Vienna to reassure his aged ally, Emperor Franz Joseph. The improvements to the Kiel Canal were nearing completion and while the German emperor was playing host to a squadron of British warships moored at Kiel for the Elbe Regatta, Franz Joseph's nephew and heir, Archduke Franz Ferdinand, paid a visit to Bosnia. As a field marshal and inspector general of the Austro-Hungarian army, Franz Ferdinand had decided to ride through Sarajevo with his wife in an open car.

Many of the Serbs, Croats and southern Slav inhabitants of Bosnia and Herzegovina were resentful at having been brought under Habsburg rule in 1908 and as the procession neared the City Hall, a bomb was thrown from the crowd. By accelerating, the Archduke's chauffeur managed to avoid it and it exploded beneath the wheels of the car behind. It was decided to leave the city by a different route from the one planned but a young Slav nationalist, Gavrilo Princip, seized his opportunity and, stepping forward, shot dead both the Archduke and his wife. The news came as a great shock to Kaiser Wilhelm at the Elbe Regatta, for he had seen Franz Ferdinand only two weeks earlier and the dead Archduke had been a guest at Kiel the previous year. Four days of garden parties, dances and yacht races came to an abrupt end and with them, the British naval courtesy visit.

News of events in Sarajevo temporarily distracted attention in Britain from scenes of domestic unrest. Throughout the beautiful spring of 1914, the focus had been on strikes, the suffragettes and Ulster, where long-standing discontent had gradually developed into outright nationalism. As Sarajevo passed out of the headlines, British newspapers turned their attention to the traditional outdoor sporting pursuits and reported on the Americas Cup yachting trials, the British open golf championship, Henley, Wimbledon and cricket at Lords.

As far as the two European power blocs were concerned, tension was no greater than in previous years: indeed, Britain and Germany were now on more friendly terms. Admiral von Tirpitz's date – the date he had set as the earliest point at which the German navy would be too strong for England to attack – had not yet arrived,[10] but there was no escaping the fact that Germany's power on land was unquestionable. The German army was ready for a lightning campaign and better so than her potential adversaries. Kaiser Wilhelm, ever alert to the possibility of German encirclement, kept a close watch on events to the east, and Russia's military preparations that spring prompted a review of Germany's military plans against both Russia and France.

The seeds of a terrible conflict had been sown but, across the North Sea in Britain, the summer of 1914, like its predecessors, seemed on course to produce cloudless skies and soft breezes. In the light of what followed, it was a summer that came to be viewed as a sunny idyll and, together with the belle époque to which it belonged, it was to pass into a vanished world whose innocence and substance could never be recaptured. The myth that would later grow up around it seemed to contain 'a sense of timelessness, a feeling of certainty, a sunlit pastoralism . . . held fast by the sticky bonds of nostalgia' and an appeal enhanced by the 'haunting realisation' that the door of time had closed upon it for ever.[11]

Osbert Sitwell, the young man who had sensed the presence of a dark shadow behind those seemingly happy years, was now an officer in the Grenadier Guards. To him, there was 'no ruffle of wind across the century-old calm'[12] of that glorious summer. Never had Europe seemed so carefree and full of gaiety, but somehow he knew he belonged to a doomed generation. Just ten days after Sarajevo, as he lunched in London with an acquaintance, his attention was drawn to a well-known arms dealer sitting at a nearby table. Sitwell's lunch companion informed him that there 'must be something up, or he wouldn't be here! His arrival is always a sign of trouble, and every European Chancellery makes a point of knowing where he is.' As Sitwell wrote, 'already in every capital, the birds of prey were assembling, hovering, watching: the politicians would supply the carrion.'[13]

In both town and country, the season offered its usual heady round of social events. Nancy Astor hosted her annual house party at Cliveden, and London society talked of the grandeur of the last Court Ball before the war, at which some two thousand guests waltzed beneath Buckingham Palace's magnificent chandeliers to the music of Strauss. Raymond Asquith, son of the British Prime Minister, was at the centre of a young society group known as the 'Coterie'. Late the previous summer, its members had enjoyed the carefree delights of Venice – gondola races on the canals, games of charade, a wonderful fancy dress ball given by an Italian Marchesa and the romance of the city by moonlight.[14] They and their generation had been raised to young adulthood in the years that marked the twilight of a long and relatively untroubled period of British security and prosperity since 1815. Thoughts of that British victory of long ago were in the mind of Rupert Brooke, who had returned from his travels and was also enjoying London to the full. Writing to his friend Edward Marsh on 26 July 1914, he queried: 'Do you have a Brussels-before-Waterloo feeling that we'll all – or some – meet with other eyes in 1915?'[15]

As John McCrae worked in the sun and walked at intervals along the famous boardwalk of Atlantic City, New Jersey, he was contemplating another European holiday and the possibility of meeting up with George Adami and his daughter. The Adamis had been enjoying a delightful few weeks meandering through the French château country to Provence and were captivated by the town of Avignon, where the professor spent hours sketching its fortress, ruins and river. For him 'the breath of the coming storm was abroad, but it was not yet enough to alter the plans of ordinary people'.[16] Kaiser Wilhelm, too, was about to set off for his annual summer cruise aboard his yacht, *Hohenzollern*. The next twenty days would find him in Norwegian coastal waters but never out of touch. Important messages could be telegraphed to him and the wires were certainly busy in the crucial days ahead.

John McCrae returned to Montreal on 8 July to embark upon the exacting task of preparing the index of his book. He could now plan a holiday and decided to book his passage on the Allan line ship, *Scotian*, due to sail for England on 29 July. Preparing to sail in the opposite direction were Lady Osler and her son, Revere, soon to leave Oxford to visit family and friends in America. Sir William was remaining behind to attend the British Medical Association annual conference in Aberdeen and to spend a few days with the family of Lord Strathcona on the Scottish island of Colonsay. He had promised Tom McCrae that he would be in Philadelphia in time to give the introductory lecture to the students at Jefferson Medical College at the start of the new school year in September. As people in Britain enjoyed picnics, rambles, garden parties, village cricket and the pleasures of seaside resorts, little did they know that they were enjoying the last days of peace. On 23 July, as the time of departure for both John McCrae and the Oslers approached, Austria-Hungary issued an ultimatum to Serbia.

Following the Sarajevo assassinations, Vienna had sought Germany's safeguard against Russia before deciding to issue the ultimatum, intended to humiliate Serbia. In the city of operetta and the waltz, the mood was very serious. Without waiting to read the Serbian reply agreeing to all Austrian demands except two, the Austro-Hungarian ambassador broke off diplomatic relations and, on 28 July 1914, Austria-Hungary declared war on Serbia. This was primarily a diplomatic manoeuvre for the Austro-Hungarian army would not, in fact, be ready for war for many weeks.[17] Russia, seeing herself as protector of the Balkan Slav states, sensed the possible threat of Austro-German domination of the region to her vital trade route through the Dardanelles Straits. She therefore mobilised, not seeking war, but to make the point that one threat could be countered by another.

As had been evident for some time, any confrontation between the two blocs in which one side or the other was expected to back down, would bring them to the verge of war. The two European systems were 'fitted and fastened' into 'an immense cantilever'[18] and beyond a certain point the mobilisation of military forces – without which such a confrontation would not have been 'credible' – could not be reversed. The plans for mobilisation of the large conscript armies of all the European powers were dependent upon movement of troops by rail. The age that had created luxury trains like the Orient Express and the famous Blue Train from Paris to the South of France – an art déco masterpiece – now dictated the movement of the armies and their equipment. Once in motion, it was very difficult to reverse orders for 'the wagons and carriages must roll remorselessly and inevitably forward to their predestined goal'.[19] A deadly chain of events was in motion, a chain that had to involve Britain, if only to make her decide to remain non-aligned. It was already enough to spur a gifted British journalist named Philip Gibbs into catching a train to the Continent. The *Daily Chronicle's* special correspondent had an instinct for a potential story.

On 31 July 1914, Germany sent an ultimatum to Russia demanding that she should cease mobilisation within twelve hours. When the Russians refused, Germany declared war on Russia on 1 August and her Triple Entente partner, France, ordered general mobilisation of her troops. By this time, John McCrae's ship, the *Scotian*, had left the coast of Canada. John discovered to his delight that her captain had been the First Officer of the *Laurentian*, the ship that had taken him to South Africa. The two men enjoyed a pleasant chat over old times but their reminiscences were overtaken by news of the international situation. John wrote to his mother: 'With the world so disturbed I would gladly have stayed more in touch with events, but I dare say one is just as happy away from the hundred conflicting reports.'[20]

The British government had been making every effort to avert war.

Britain's Foreign Secretary, Sir Edward Grey, hoped to avoid hostilities but, at the same time, he knew his duty was not only to seek peace but to prepare for war and told his colleagues, 'we cannot stand aside with our arms folded'.[21] When the time came, Britain, France and Russia stood together. On Sunday 2 August, Germany issued an ultimatum to Belgium. On Monday 3 August, a cloudless Bank Holiday, Members of Parliament converged on the House of Commons while excited crowds milled around outside waiting for news. Among those present in the packed House that day was John McCrae's erstwhile travelling companion, Leo Amery. Throughout the past ten years, Amery had 'dreaded a major European War which would find us once more unprepared'.[22] Like most other people, he had been little aware of the impending catastrophe, the situation in Ulster having absorbed the House for most of July. It was apparent that:

> Even those in the inner circles of Whitehall did not foresee that, within six weeks of the Archduke's murder, the grim and apparently inevitable processes of threat and counter-threat, mobilisation and counter-mobilisation, would lead to the launching of the greatest war in human history.[23]

The German High Command was now prepared and ready to execute the Schlieffen Plan, which required passage through Belgium for her troops. King Albert of the Belgians had appealed to King George V for Britain's intervention to safeguard Belgian neutrality guaranteed by the Treaty of London, to which both Britain and Prussia had been signatories in 1831. Having won the support of the House both on the issue of defending the independence of Belgium and a Cabinet decision to bar the German Fleet from the English Channel, Sir Edward Grey pondered events. As he watched the street lamps being lit and uttered his famous words,[24] Germany declared war on France.

Next morning, as news was received that German troops had crossed the Belgian frontier, Britain sent Germany an ultimatum to stop the invasion. It was due to expire late that day at 11.00 p.m. British time. The warm evening of 4 August 1914 brought crowds of people to London's West End, Trafalgar Square, Whitehall and Downing Street as the final hours ticked away. As they heard Big Ben strike eleven times and knew their country was at war with Germany, a great cheer went up and the crowds sang 'God Save the King'. At his home in Sussex, Rudyard Kipling, the man who had predicted it all, wrote to a friend that he felt 'like Jonah, or whoever it was who went about saying "I told you so." '[25] He added a simple postscript to his wife's diary entry for 4 August 1914: 'Incidentally, Armageddon begins.'[26]

Across the North Sea the man who, in the words of one historian, 'when not blowing his own trumpet' was 'sounding the war bugle and seeking to saturate his people with the war spirit'[27] had continued to cherish the naive hope that Britain would remain neutral and that the war could be contained on the Eastern front. As exultant crowds in Berlin threw flowers to the German troops on their way toward Paris, Kaiser Wilhelm knew he was powerless to stop the tide of events and that he had finally come face to face with what his first Chancellor, Bismarck, had 'always done his utmost to avoid: a nightmare of coalitions'.[28] Wilhelm had convinced himself that Britain would remain neutral, and could only write 'in a passion of grief and fear' that the 'famous circumscription of Germany has finally become a complete fact.'[29] As he berated the English as 'that mean crew of shopkeepers',[30] he urged his people to begin 'the final fight which shall settle for ever our great position in the world'.[31] To the Prussian Guards Regiment at Potsdam he brandished his own sword above his head saying 'I have drawn the sword, which without victory and without honour I cannot sheathe again.'[32]

The *Scotian* was eight days out of Montreal when it received news of the outbreak of war. John wrote to his mother that,

> All is excitement over the war; and the ship runs without lights at night, altho' we had light indoors last ev[enin]'g. Surely good old Emperor Billy has got his head in the noose at last; it is now he or us, good and well . . . my services are at the disposal of the country if she needs them. I am afraid my holiday trip is knocked 'galley west'. However, we shall see.[33]

The ship was diverted via the south coast of Ireland and made its way cautiously up the English Channel to Portland. Any hope of John meeting up with George Adami and his daughter had gone. The Adamis had now reached Venice and were among the few tourists left in a city that, in contrast to the gaiety of the previous autumn, was now sombre and empty. The customary bustle of its streets and canals had been replaced by an unnatural silence and, as the professor and his daughter waited for passage on a ship from Genoa, they had the place almost to themselves.

A young American woman named Moina Michael was also stranded in Italy during that August of international tension. Moina was a teacher from Georgia who had been travelling and studying in Europe. After a glimpse of the beautiful English spring, she had passed through Holland, Belgium, France, Switzerland and into Germany. Some of the cream of the Kaiser's troops were at Cologne while she was there, a few actually staying at her hotel close to the city's lovely cathedral. The sight of their helmets, heavy boots and spurs stayed with her that last week of July although she too admitted that 'on the brink of the cataclysm we were unconscious of the impending danger'.[34] As war became imminent, she and her tour group were among thousands of Americans heading for Rome and every Mediterranean coastal port with access to routes that would not cross the war front. While passage to the United States was being arranged, Moina volunteered to help a new American Committee set up to assist United States citizens. At her desk in the lobby of Rome's Hotel Royal, she spent long hours helping with the completion of necessary forms and paperwork, and providing information to her anxious countrymen and women.

In Canada, the outbreak of war followed a holiday weekend of sports and entertainment. The summer meeting of the Hamilton Jockey Club was under way; St Catharines in the Niagara peninsula was hosting the Canadian equivalent of Henley; the Canadian tennis championships were about to begin. Many Canadians were sailing, swimming or picnicking on their traditional summer cottage holiday at one of the country's innumerable lakes. Stephen Leacock wrote that in Canada the news seemed so unbelievable, coming as it did

out of a clear sky – the clear sky of vacation time, of the glory of Canadian midsummer, of summer cottages, of bush camps, and for the city population the soft evening sky, the canopy of stars over the merry-go-round resorts in the cool of the summer evening.[35]

Huge crowds in a mood of patriotic fervour gathered outside newspaper offices in cities and towns to hear the latest bulletin. In western Canada, people sat at stations along the railway line so that the telegrapher could read off the wire what was happening. One man who later recalled those few days, wrote that it 'is difficult to think in terms of the emotion generated by the events in that last week in July 1914', for, 'if ever a country wanted war it was Canada'.[36]

As supportive outbursts of patriotism could be heard throughout the Empire, the response to Canada's declaration of war was immediate. In Toronto, a gigantic parade carrying banners of the Empire made its way through the streets and 'hats shot aloft, ten thousand throats boomed out a concentrated roar – a warning to the enemy, an inspiration to every soul in the British Empire, Canadians still belong to the breed.'[37] In Montreal, crowds sang 'Rule Britannia' and 'La Marseillaise'. The Duke of Connaught opened Parliament wearing the uniform of a field marshal and the Canadian Prime Minister, Robert Borden, spoke of standing shoulder to shoulder with Britain. In every western city from Winnipeg to Victoria there were impromptu parades, flag waving, street processions of decorated vehicles and speeches. None of this would have come as any surprise to Sir Arthur Conan Doyle, who had returned from a triumphant Canadian speaking tour a few weeks earlier and been impressed by 'a very real and widespread element of loyalty and imperialism'.[38] Within two days, this 'unmilitary nation'[39] was mobilising under the direction of Canada's ebullient Minister of Militia, Sam Hughes, who channelled his amazing energy into taking personal charge of Canada's war preparations. German troops, meanwhile, were marching through Belgium towards France as the Schlieffen Plan unfolded and, as John McCrae made his way to London, the British Expeditionary Force began crossing to France.

Britain had a very small but very professional army. Lord Roberts, whose hand John McCrae had shaken in South Africa, had continued to campaign unsuccessfully for national conscription, which would have provided the basis on which to build a large conscript army in an emergency. In the absence of conscription, the most practical way of expanding Britain's army lay in building onto the existing territorial organisation and enlisting all those with experience and enthusiasm. On 5 August, the press learned that Lord Kitchener had accepted the appointment of Secretary of State for War, making him the first soldier on active duty to join the Cabinet since the time of Charles I. His face was soon to become very familiar on recruiting posters displayed in towns and cities all over the country. Leo Amery immediately volunteered his services, and his knowledge, interest and ideas were quickly put to good use with his appointment as Director of Civilian Recruiting for the Southern Command.

The first British soldiers to disembark at the quays of Boulogne met with a joyful reception. As infantry and artillery marched through the city, the soldiers were showered with flowers, women rushed up to bestow kisses and men cheered until their throats were hoarse. For two days the khaki columns wound their way through the town's narrow cobbled streets to the sounds of bands, bagpipes, whole companies whistling 'La Marseillaise', and one particular song that everyone seemed to be singing. Introduced by music hall star Florrie Forde, 'A Long Way to Tipperary' was a simple ballad about an Irish boy in London who found himself far from home and his favourite girl.

John McCrae, now also in London, decided to make his base the Kenilworth Hotel in Great Russell Street. He wrote to his brother, Tom, that the 'town is quiet; the theatres are almost empty'. He was forty-one years of age and knew what lay ahead: 'It will be a terrible war, and somebody's finish when all is said & done . . . I can scarcely believe that the awful bogie of years, has materialized.'[40] Yet, in spite of an understandable reluctance to take part and a wish that he could 'go home with a clear conscience'[41], he admitted to his mother that 'I like still less to stay away . . . although I know that any one man is merely bagatelle in a big game.'[42] John was now established at the forefront of his profession through his expertise, teaching, publications and reputation. Once again, it was all to be set aside. He knew the war could destroy his future and possibly his life, but the tremendous sense of duty he felt was one shared by many of his generation. It was not that they felt especially strong anti-German or pro-French sentiments, it was 'more the result of their high sense of purpose and honour', for these men were 'the flower of the Empire at its zenith'.[43] Many were men of talent and some – like John McCrae – of brilliance. For those who had not yet made their mark in the world, it was as if the years that had gone before had been a preparation for this moment; for those who had achieved success in their fields, the fact remained that evil had to be fought, if need be, by self sacrifice. Implicit in John McCrae's strong instinct against injustice and inequality, were truth, honesty and an integrity that demanded that a personal effort be made. Perhaps he remembered one of the verses he had pasted in his scrapbook as a young man:

> So nigh is grandeur to our dust
> So near is God to man,
> When Duty whispers low 'thou must'
> The youth replies 'I can'.[44]

Knowing fully what lay ahead, John cabled Edward Morrison in Ottawa to offer his services in either a combatant or medical capacity.

Since Canada's permanent force was tiny, the militia would provide the basis for the wartime expansion of the Canadian army. As Director of Artillery, Morrison was responsible for all his country's artillery units and knew the capabilities of every single militia battery. That summer of 1914 there had been more than ten thousand officers and men concentrated at Petawawa for combined manoeuvres that came closer to achieving active service conditions than in any previous year in Canada. As far as the artillery was concerned, 'Thanks to the excellent facilities at Petawawa it was to be expected that Canadian batteries should be "fairly well trained in manoeuvre, long and medium range fire and the selection of positions."'[45] In later years, a veteran Canadian gunner of the Great War paid tribute to what was accomplished by Morrison and his small staff: 'I can only say that the Canadian Artillery could never have done the job it did without the wonderful pre-war training we had under the officers and gunnery instructors of the R.C.H.A. at Petawawa . . . To them Canada's debt is very great.'[46]

While awaiting Morrison's reply, John McCrae made no plans. Sir William Osler contacted him and after a visit to Oxford, he motored down to Eastbourne with a married couple that he knew, visiting their country home on the way back – a beautiful ancient manor house surrounded by a moat. The English countryside seemed especially captivating, its beauty made more intense by the prospect of leaving it.

Recruiting in Canada, meanwhile, had exceeded all expectations. In the three weeks since it began on 8 August, 45,000 volunteers had come forward. Sam Hughes had arbitrarily scrapped the pre-determined mobilisation plans and made each of Canada's 226 militia units responsible for raising the necessary manpower. In his mind was a vision of what he was later to describe as 'a call to arms like the fiery cross passing through the Highlands of Scotland or the mountains of Ireland in former days'.[47] Volunteers came from the rural settlements, small towns and busy cities of Ontario, Quebec and the Maritime Provinces; from the homesteads and farms of the Prairies; from the forests and mines of British Columbia, and from as far as the Yukon. Men often walked to the nearest recruitment office, sometimes involving distances of more than a hundred miles from isolated settlements. The chosen recruits were sufficient to provide sixteen provisional infantry battalions in four provisional brigades. Not for nothing was Hughes hailed as the 'Kitchener of Canada' as he continued his efforts by encouraging prominent citizens to raise troops in each community. David McCrae was one such helper. Although now sixty-nine years of age, he was keen to do what he could and, after Hughes told him to raise an artillery battery, he promptly set about the task.

From Montreal's fabulous 'Square Mile' came generous contributions to the war effort. Among John McCrae's friends and acquaintances, the millionaire James Ross donated a steam yacht and a hundred thousand pounds to the fund that would pay for the transportation of a Montreal unit to England. Hamilton Gault persuaded Sam Hughes to allow him to raise an entirely new regiment. It was to be called Princess Patricia's Canadian Light Infantry, after the Duke of Connaught's daughter. The crest chosen for the cap and collar badges was a single white daisy, in honour of Hamilton Gault's beautiful wife Marguerite, who had been hostess to John McCrae on a number of occasions. This was no ordinary body of men – nearly all those enlisted had spent some time with the British regulars and their number included recruits from backgrounds as varied and individual as cow-punchers and prize-fighters. Less than three weeks after the first call for recruits, the 'Patricias' held their first church parade.

As the mobilisation of artillery units proceeded, Edward Morrison cabled his old friend in London. Morrison himself was taking command of lst Brigade, Canadian Field Artillery.[48] He had wanted to give John command of his own brigade but John's ten-year absence from the militia had ruled out this possibility. Instead, Morrison offered John a dual appointment in the brigade as second-in-command and brigade surgeon. The newly-minted Major John McCrae was to report as soon as possible and he obtained a passage back to Canada on the *Calgarian*, scheduled to leave on 28 August. Of those stranded in Italy, George Adami and his daughter had finally managed to secure places on a ship from Genoa to London. The American teacher, Moina Michael, still working in Rome, had learned that she could proceed to Naples to board the *Carpathia*, the ship that had rescued the survivors of the *Titanic*. In the scramble to get back to Canada, John found himself on the same sailing as his old doctor from Guelph, Dr Henry Howitt senior, who was travelling home with his two daughters. He told the Howitts that, 'from South Africa he knew all that war meant,' and

> had no illusions about it. Now, at his age, he would prefer to be out of it. He was in practice in Montreal, doing well and had a splendid future ahead of him. The war would ruin it all; but he felt it was his duty and he was on his way back to enlist with the Canadian forces.[49]

As the *Calgarian* began its crossing of the Atlantic, alert for mines and submarines, the *Carpathia*, with Moina Michael on board, was also being guided through the thickly-mined area protecting the Straits of Gibraltar. During her sixteen-day voyage to New York, Moina caught up with the latest news in the English papers. She returned to the University of Georgia knowing that she would find it very hard to settle into normal life whilst others were fighting, suffering and dying.

As soon as he reached Montreal, John put his personal possessions into storage as he had done when he had set out for South Africa fourteen years previously, and bade farewell to the Archibald family. He decided not to go to Guelph but spent his last evening in Montreal dining with Andrew Macphail at the University Club. Although he had missed seeing the departure of the Montreal regiments, he heard how, in his absence, the city had turned out in full to give them a great send-off as they marched from their armouries to the station. In a letter to his sister Geills, he wrote: 'Out on the awful old trail again! And with very mixed feelings, but some determination. I am off to Valcartier to-night . . . I was really afraid to go home for . . . it would only be harrowing for mater, and I think she agrees. We can hope for happier times.'[50] Equipped with a new uniform cap and a pocket case of medical instruments – a present from some of his medical colleagues – John made his way to Camp Valcartier. All over Canada there were emotional scenes as men boarded trains heading for the same destination.

Valcartier was located on a plateau some fifteen miles from the historic city of Quebec, 'where a little river winds over a sandy, slightly hilly plain, dotted with woods and lonely farms, among [the] lovely Laurentian mountains'[51]. Built from scratch within a very few weeks, it was equipped with permanent buildings, showers, electric light, a good water supply and a huge firing range. To the 33,000 men of the First Canadian Contingent it quickly became home. Among them was a high proportion of Britons who had gone out to Canada before the war and a large number of outdoorsmen, who were tough and fit. Memories of Valcartier brought to mind hot days and beautiful scenery; pipers practising in the nearby woods; cold tents and hard ground at night; splendid comradeship; and Sam Hughes, Minister of Militia, 'the dominating spirit of the camp.'[52] Canon Frederick Scott, a militia chaplain before the war and now Senior Chaplain to lst Canadian Division forming at Valcartier, remembered Hughes' briefing to the army chaplains. When one of them asked if he would be permitted to carry a revolver, the minister's reply was firmly negative and the others found it hard to keep a straight face when Hughes urged the man in question to instead 'take a bottle of castor oil'.[53]

When Canon Scott and John McCrae met at Valcartier it was not their first meeting. Scott was rector of St Matthew's Anglican Church in Quebec City and the two men had been introduced there a few years earlier when John had attended a meeting to discuss a possible new sanatorium. At Valcartier, every man had to pass a medical and John McCrae examined a good many. Among the men of lst Brigade CFA that he passed fit for duty was Cyril Allinson, a 21-year old from Forest Hill in south east London. Allinson had already served almost three years with the Royal Canadian Engineers doing fortress and field training and, for the past two years, had been employed making military maps in Nova Scotia during winter and in Quebec province during the summer. His fortress duties had been under the command of Captain 'Tommy' Morrison, Edward's nephew. Allinson's request to transfer to the artillery had been granted and, as a permanent force soldier, he was a welcome addition to the ranks of 1st Brigade CFA.

John McCrae's rank entitled him to a horse. It was while he was at Valcartier that his friend, Dr John Todd, made him a present of 'Bonfire', an Irish hunter that was to be his unfailing companion in the coming years. John wrote to his mother that he was getting used to being back in the saddle. He described the living as 'rough: we are going practically on rations, and the cookery is not very grand; but we manage well enough. The Staff Mess is Col[onel]. Morrison, Col[onel]. Dodds, 'Jim' Mills, L[ieutenan]t. Cosgrave, L[ieutenan]t. Dixon an Imp[erial] army man and myself.'[54] John was to become close friends with both William Dodds and Lawrence Cosgrave. Dodds, from Nova Scotia, was nearer John's age and had been active in the militia for twenty-five years while Cosgrave, a subaltern, was a recent graduate of both McGill and the Royal Military College, Kingston.

During periods of leave, officers and men often took the train to Quebec. Although hundreds of miles from the open Atlantic, it was a busy port. Now its docks were crowded with ships and men and its accommodation with wives, mothers, fiancées, sisters and friends of the men at Valcartier. Above the St Lawrence river at Sir William Van Horne's famous and imposing hotel, the Château Frontenac, traditional English afternoon tea on the terrace was a 'most popular rendezvous; at every table, drab khaki alternates with pretty, summery, floor-length dresses surmounted by wide-brimmed, soft straw hats adorned with gay ribbons or artificial flowers'. Soldiers and officers enjoyed both the company and the setting, with not 'the vaguest thought that one of them will not come back to Canada'.[55] Shortly before the contingent, now designated 1st Canadian Division, was due to leave for Britain, a great church parade was held at the camp in the presence of massed bands, the Governor General, the Prime Minister and other notables. On that sunny day, with autumn tints colouring the maple trees on the sides of the surrounding mountains, Canon Scott preached to a vast congregation of no fewer than fifteen thousand men.

With the Canadians making ready for their departure, events in Europe were progressing along their grim course. At his headquarters in Koblenz, the Kaiser learned of the progress of his armies in Germany's plan to crush France. The Schlieffen Plan involved a rapid attack through Belgium and northern France in an arc that was intended to see victorious German troops marching into Paris thirty days after war was declared. At first all had gone well but the German war machine had been derailed by stubborn French resistance at the First Battle of the Marne. French, British and Belgian troops had then continued to give ground in the face of the German onslaught but, in early September, after the Germans themselves had altered their original plan, the French and British armies held their ground in the bloody four-day Second Battle of the Marne. Of their own accord, the various German army commanders had begun to make local withdrawals and by mid-September, the first offensive was over. Germany would shortly be switching her main attack towards the Channel Ports.

By the third week in September, the First Canadian Contingent was preparing to leave Valcartier for embarkation to England. Although there had not been time for much formal training, it had begun to develop the cohesion and discipline needed to change a group of people into an effective military formation. The men had mastered enough drill to move together and had some target practice with their Ross rifles. Units prepared for embarkation over the three days from 22 to 24 September. The 23 officers, 772 other ranks and 748 horses of lst Brigade CFA marched out of camp at sunset on 24 September 1914. Lieutenant-Colonel Edward Morrison handed young Cyril Allinson a map and said, 'You've been making these maps, now let us see if you can read them – guide us to the docks at Quebec.'[56] As they reached the St Lawrence, they saw some of the thirty-three ships that had been requisitioned to transport the contingent to Britain.

John McCrae travelled with part of lst Brigade CFA on the Cunard ship, *Saxonia*. The great flotilla began its five-hundred-mile journey down river to the mouth of the St Lawrence, where it was due to gather in the shelter of the Gaspé basin to await its escort of British warships. As the last ships left Quebec, onlookers sang 'It's A Long Way to Tipperary' and the men on deck looked back at the deep crimson of the sunset sky until Quebec and its lights were obscured in the purple mists of evening. During the three-day journey to the rendezvous point, Francis Scrimger, who was going as a medical officer with the 2nd Field Ambulance, saw the familiar coves and capes where he had spent happy holidays as a child and which were home to colonies of puffins and terns. The lower St Lawrence offered good cod, shrimps and crabs and in summer, the patient observer might well spot blue, finback or minke whales along the north shore. George Nasmith, an analytical chemist from Toronto, whom Scrimger would meet with again under fateful circumstances, recalled waking on the third day of the voyage to the sight of the quiet, peaceful haven of the Gaspé basin with its waterworn cliffs, grey beaches and scattered fishermen's houses. For John McCrae, the journey was a reminder of his expedition with Earl Grey four years earlier under very different circumstances.

On 2 October 1914, Sam Hughes passed through the line of transports in a noisy tugboat distributing copies of his rousing valedictory, 'Where Duty Leads'. At 3.00 p.m. the following day, Saturday, the convoy sailed. It was a typical bright, sunny autumn day in Canada and, as the transports formed in line about a thousand yards from one another and the whole force moved towards the Atlantic, the soldiers looked across to 'the shores of Gaspé, dotted with white cottages; yellow stubble fields; hills red and purple with autumnal foliage – these were our last pictures of Canada – truly the last that many of us were ever to see, and we looked upon them, our hearts filled with emotions.'[57]

The convoy made its way through the Gulf of St Lawrence and the Cabot Strait that separated Cape Breton Island from the independent colony of Newfoundland, the oldest member of the British Empire. Waiting to join the convoy off Cape Race on the Avalon Peninsula – Newfoundland's most south-eastern point – was a small passenger steamer, the S.S. *Florizel*, proudly bearing the steady, courageous men of the Newfoundland Regiment, known as the 'Blue Puttees' because of their distinctive dress. There had been no difficulty in raising recruits among the island's small community of barely two hundred and fifty thousand people. They now stood on deck taking a last look at their home as the little ship took its place among the rest.

Conditions during the Atlantic crossing were cramped for many of the troops. With hammocks so close they touched each other, poor ventilation and the inevitable seasickness, the journey was not always pleasant. The men played cards, sang to the piano and complained about the food, of which porridge and tripe were staple items. No smoking was allowed and the convoy travelled at a speed of about 18–19 knots without lights. Thirty-three ships carrying thousands of fully armed and equipped troops would have been wonderful prey for German submarines, but they were never attacked. An escort of destroyers came to strengthen the convoy's protection and John McCrae later wrote to his brother, Tom, that 'our escort is now up to 7, – all battleships . . . so we feel secure enough'.[58] He listed among them HMS *Queen Mary,* a massive battle cruiser, which presented an impressive sight to the Canadians as she steamed through the convoy columns at dusk one evening.[59]

In the wake of rumours of a German submarine in the Channel, the contingent's destination was changed from Southampton to Plymouth. Early on 14 October, the first Canadian transports entered Plymouth Harbour, their arrival a complete surprise to the local people. Little steamboats, sirens and hooters added to the din of the welcome, made more noisy by the skirl of the bagpipes being played on the Canadian ships as they passed up Plymouth Sound. All that day and the following day, ship after ship moved slowly by. A British journalist, Herbert Russell, who chanced to be at Plymouth on 15 October, watched with fascination, as,

A big steamship was coming directly shorewards, like a vast phantom emerging from the mist . . . a great white patch on her bow gave me to believe that she was a transport . . . And then suddenly, it seemed to me like a cinema transformation, her contour seemed to be traced in khaki . . . then I caught the wavering sounds of a band playing somewhere on board and gave a start as the revelation came upon me for the first time that it was 'The Maple Leaf For Ever' . . . A naval petty officer paused at my side and exchanged looks, 'The Canadians' he said in a voice tense with pent-up enthusiasm, 'Thirty-one transports full of them! That's the tenth which has gone up harbour so far.'[60]

The Times of 15 October 1914 reported that the long line of ships,

presented a magnificent spectacle . . . Crowds of people lined the Hoe and piers, while others went out in boats and heartily cheered the ships as they passed . . . As the ships lay in the stream at night they were ablaze with lights, and the sounds of music and merriment came across the waters to the crowds.

It was a sight, recorded one witness, 'hardly to be paralleled since the Crusades'.[61]

NOTES

1. From 'The Night Cometh' by John McCrae, *The University Magazine* (Volume 12, No. 3, April 1913), p.145. Micro mfm/AP/U577, UTL.
2. JM to Oskar Klotz, 10 February 1914, MG 30, B61, NAC.
3. Edith Gittings Reid, *The Great Physician* (Toronto, 1931), p. 240.
4. JM to Janet McCrae, 18 February 1914, GM Papers.
5. JM to Janet McCrae, 18 February 1914, GM Papers.
6. The design of the building, which still stands in Mansfield Street, Montreal, was the work of Percy Nobbs, Professor of Design at McGill University's School of Architecture. Nobbs, a Scot, was a member of the Pen and Pencil Club and an important force in early Canadian architectural education.
7. JM to Janet McCrae, 24 April 1914, GM Papers.
8. JM to Janet McCrae, 25 June 1914, GM Papers.
9. JM to Janet McCrae, 1 July 1914, GM Papers.
10. Massie, *Dreadnought*, p. 182.
11. Kirsty McLeod, *The Last Summer: May to September 1914* (London, 1983), p. 13.
12. Sitwell, *Great Morning*, p. 264.
13. Sitwell, *Great Morning*, pp. 267–268.
14. McLeod, *The Last Summer*, pp. 70–71.
15. McLeod, *The Last Summer*, p. 105.
16. Adami, *J. George Adami*, p. 59.
17. A.J.P. Taylor, *The First World War: An Illustrated History* (London, 1963), p. 14.
18. Aronson, *Crowns in Conflict*, p. 24.
19. Taylor, *The First World War*, p. 14.
20. JM to Janet McCrae, 29 July 1914, GM Papers.
21. Clifton Daniel, *Chronicle of the 20th Century* (New York: 1987), p. 187.
22. Rt Hon. L.S. Amery, *My Political Life* (London, 1953), Volume II, War and Peace, 1914–1929, p. 9.
23. Harold Macmillan, *The Winds of Change, 1914–39* (London, 1966), p. 59.
24. His words were: 'The lamps are going out all over Europe: we shall not see them lit again in our life-time'. Grey of Falloden, *Twenty-Five Years, 1892–1916*. (New York: 1969) Volume II, p. 20.
25. Rudyard Kipling to Colonel Fielden on 4 August 1914, as quoted in Birkenhead, *Kipling*, p. 258.
26. Birkenhead, *Kipling*, p. 258.
27. Wilson, *The Great War*, Vol. 10, p. 560.
28. Aronson, *Crowns in Conflict*, p. 24.
29. Winston Churchill, *Great Contemporaries*, p. 26.
30. Palmer, *The Kaiser*, p. 172.
31. 'A Vision of the Future', *The Times*, 5 August 1914.
32. Wilson, *The Great War*, Vol. 10, p. 562.
33. JM to Janet McCrae, 5 August 1914, GM Papers.
34. Moina Michael, *The Miracle Flower: The Story of the Flanders Fields Memorial Poppy* (Philadelphia, 1941), p. 27.
35. Leacock, *Canada*, p. 222.

36. G.R. Stevens as quoted in W.D. Mathieson, *My Grandfather's War. Canadians Remember the First World War 1914–1918* (Toronto, 1981), p. 4.
37. Article, *The Globe and Mail*, 4 August 1914
38. Sandra Gwyn, *Tapestry of War* (Toronto, 1992), p. 16.
39. Colonel G.W.L. Nicholson, *Canadian Expeditionary Force 1914–1919. Official History of the Canadian Army in the First World War* (Ottawa, 1964), p. 6.
40. JM to Tom McCrae, 5 August 1914, GM Papers.
41. JM to Janet McCrae, 13 August 1914, GM Papers.
42. JM to Janet McCrae, 18 August 1914, GM Papers.
43. Margaret Fitzherbert, as quoted in John Buchan, *These For Remembrance* (London, 1987), Introduction p. 24.
44. John McCrae's Scrapbook, MH.
45. Colonel G.W.L. Nicholson, *The Gunners of Canada. The History of the Royal Regiment of Canadian Artillery*. Volume 1, 1534–1919 (Toronto, 1967), p. 188.
46. Dr James C. Ross to Lt. Col. B. Tedman dated 28 March 1965. Nicholson, *Gunners of Canada*, p. 174. In 1914, the regular field artillery component of the Canadian army was designated the Royal Canadian Horse Artillery while the militia (or territorial) component, was designated the Canadian Field Artillery. There was also a corresponding regular Royal Canadian Garrison Artillery and militia Canadian Garrison Artillery.
47. A.M.J. Hyatt, *General Sir Arthur Currie: A Military Biography* (Toronto, 1987), p. 15.
48. 1st Brigade, CFA, consisted of three batteries, numbered 1 through 3, each with six 18-pdr. quick-firing field guns. The brigade was formed from prewar militia field batteries stationed in Ottawa, Belleville, Ganonoque and Kingston, all towns in eastern Ontario. In November 1914, the brigade was re-organized on the basis of four-gun batteries, numbered 1 through 4. See Nicholson, *Gunners of Canada*, p. 197n, 204–205n.
49. Howitt, 'John McCrae', p. 15.
50. JM to Geills Kilgour, 4 September 1914, GM Papers.
51. Mary Plummer, *With the First Canadian Contingent* (Toronto, 1915), p. 17.
52. Frederick G. Scott, *The Great War as I Saw It* (Toronto, 1922), p. 17.
53. Scott, *The Great War as I Saw It*, p. 22.
54. JM to Janet McCrae, 12 September 1914, GM Papers.
55. Allinson, 'John McCrae,' p. 88.
56. Allinson, 'John McCrae,' p. 88.
57. George G. Nasmith, *On The Fringe of the Great Fight* (Toronto, 1917), p. 5.
58. JM to Tom McCrae, 11 October 1914, GM Papers.
59. Unfortunately, HMS *Queen Mary* was sunk at Jutland in 1916.
60. Canadian War Records Office, *Canada in Khaki 1918* (London, 1918), pp. 17–18.
61. Suzanne Kingsmill, *Francis Scrimger: Beyond The Call of Duty* (Toronto, 1991), p. 46.

CHAPTER ELEVEN

'Tell them, O Guns, that we have heard their call'[1]

October 1914–March 1915

After sixteen days at sea, the Canadians were pleased to find themselves at the end of another stage of their journey to the front. Many on board the convoy were returning to the land of their birth and were keen to go ashore, but had to wait their turn to disembark. By now the ships were running short of decent food, prompting some of the men on board to cut out large sheets of cardboard asking for help. After they threw them in the water, small boats soon began to arrive bringing Cornish pasties and all kinds of other good things to eat.[2]

The Canadians were formally greeted at Plymouth by Lieutenant-General Edwin Alderson, a British regular officer with active service in Egypt and South Africa who had recently been appointed to command 1st Canadian Division.

When the troops finally went ashore, the welcome was warm and they were greeted with cheers, handshakes, kisses, cigarettes and drinks.[3] To the locals, these men from Canada who had come so far to assist Britain in her hour of need were a source of endless fascination. Canada conjured up images of a country of trackless forests, everlasting snow, camp fires, bears and wolves, and they were impressed by the tough, calm Canadian troops with their easy manner and quick wit. The new arrivals looked fine men physically and seemed to possess the 'independence of attitude of the New World and a fresh light from their eyes'[4] that reflected a fearlessness, resourcefulness, initiative and capacity for endurance. One enthusiastic account of their arrival concluded that, 'in England's hour of danger the old gods came back to her,' and Britons 'will never forget the coming of the men of Canada'.[5]

Having completed their lengthy disembarkation, the troops proceeded by train to Salisbury Plain and into tented encampments which were at least ten years old. They had been used by British Territorials for summer training and British engineers had erected thousands of bell tents, marquees and kitchen shelters. 1st Brigade CFA arrived at their destination on 18 October and took over quarters with the rest of the artillery at West Down North Camp, west of the Salisbury-Devizes Road and about three miles from 'Ye Olde Bustard', the isolated inn where Lieutenant-General Alderson had his Divisional Headquarters. The lovely river Avon traversed the Plain, the villages in its valley forming 'civilian islands in the military area',[6] and the historic cathedral town of Salisbury, 'threw the glamour of romance and chivalry over the new soldiers in the new crusade'.[7] The Canadians' immediate surroundings, however, were exposed and isolated, and the roads had not been constructed to stand the strain of such large numbers of troop movements.

The training begun at Valcartier was resumed in the first week of November 1914 and continued throughout the winter. The Duke of Connaught had expected that considerable preparation would be needed before the Canadian troops would be ready for war. Canada's Prime Minister, Sir Robert Borden, also realised its necessity and importance for one 'might as well send untrained men off the streets to contend with an expert hockey, lacrosse or football team as to send untrained and unprepared men to meet the most highly trained military organisation in the world'.[8] Despite a shortage of instructors the Canadians persevered with drills, endless route marches and musketry practice as they worked to attain the British army standard of fifteen aimed shots per minute. Many of the newcomers were superb marksmen, a skill that they were to put to full use in the months and years ahead. The artillery, however, found the existing ranges inadequate and with six British divisions competing with the Canadians for their use, the Canadian batteries were only able to complete one week of range practice.

For the first few days on the Plain the weather was delightfully autumnal, but it soon began to rain and continued to do so for 89 of the next 123 days. Just beneath the surface of the ground was a solid layer of chalk and the ground quickly became waterlogged. Life grew very trying in camp grounds that were 'just one sea of mud'[9] and the road from Salisbury to Bustard Camp deteriorated into a stagnant knee-deep muddy rivulet. With no means of drying their clothing, men often had to let their wet uniforms dry on their backs. Their Canadian-made boots simply disintegrated on long sodden marches and had to be replaced by the heavy, hobnailed British variety. Tea, porridge and stew appeared day after day in the mess halls and one soldier, who was jailed for causing trouble, likened imprisonment to a hotel compared with life on the Plain. No liquor was allowed in camp – a rule of the Canadian militia dating from 1893 – and the soldiers would inevitably head for local towns. Disturbances soon followed but the situation improved rapidly after the sale of beer was authorised in the camp canteens. While a building programme got under way to replace the tents with huts, the Canadian troops maintained a good standard of morale despite the deplorable conditions. On 4 November they were reviewed by King

George and Queen Mary, accompanied by Lords Kitchener and Roberts, and later in the day by Lieutenant-General Alderson.

The general health of the troops had remained good and it was only when they moved into more crowded huts that John McCrae and the other Medical Officers had to deal with an outbreak of respiratory and intestinal complaints, and a number of cases of meningitis. John organised lectures for his brigade and Lieutenant-Colonel George Nasmith spoke to the men on the dangers of impure water and the value of anti-typhoid vaccination. Apart from general medical work and his responsibilities as second-in-command of the brigade, John had time on Salisbury Plain to train stretcher bearers, whose dangerous job it would be to collect the wounded and bring them back to their own trenches whilst dodging snipers' bullets and mud holes.

For medicine, the challenges were enormous and from the outset, the medical profession had been deeply concerned with its own aspect of the war. The *Canadian Medical Association Journal* offered the opinion that the,

> vast number of opposing armies and the deadly efficiency of the modern engines of destruction make it certain that the sacrifice of life and limb will be appalling . . . There has been no difficulty in recruiting the field ambulances up to war strength, and in filling the ranks with a fine class of men. . . . Our present duty is plain; and so long as the Empire has need of our aid, we in Canada will continue to give willingly of our best.[10]

Sir William Osler had been at the forefront of activities ever since finding himself temporarily stranded on the island of Colonsay on 4 August. A few days before Britain's entry into the war, a War Emergency Committee had been formed by the British Medical Association and Osler's name headed the list of Committee men whose objective was to facilitate the government's best use of all available medical expertise. As soon as Lady Osler and their son, Revere, returned from America in September, husband and wife flung themselves into efforts to help wherever possible. Revere Osler, a student at Christ Church, Oxford, joined the University Officers' Training Corps and the 'Open Arms' became busier than ever with visitors, including some Belgian refugee families from the University of Louvain. When the Canadians arrived in England the Oslers were ready to help them and nobody ever returned to Salisbury Plain empty-handed. Sir William, who was already a territorial officer, was appointed Physician-in-Chief to the Queen's Canadian Military Hospital at Shorncliffe in Kent, and visiting Physician to the Duchess of Connaught's Canadian Red Cross Hospital, established on the estate of Waldorf and Nancy Astor. Lady Osler became

President of the Soldiers' Guild and ran a workroom that made clothes and other items.

Deeply concerned about the health of the troops, Osler conducted a campaign for typhoid inoculation and took a keen interest in wounds and the results of wounds. He wrote to his German friend, Paul Ehrlich, in the hope that they could get salvarsan manufactured in America and available to help both sides in the war. From now on, a great deal of his time would be spent visiting camps and hospitals, attending meetings on medical affairs and giving lectures. He also received a letter from George Adami, safely back in Montreal, pointing out that Great Britain had not worked thoroughly on its medical history of previous wars. Adami suggested a way by which each base hospital could take charge of all case sheets, preserve materials for museums and obtain full records for a medical and surgical history of the war. Sir William passed the letter on to the Director General of the Army Medical Service, Surgeon General Sir Alfred Keogh, who in turn appointed a retired RAMC officer to undertake the necessary preparatory work for such a project.

Although he was now fifty-two years of age, George Adami was determined to do his bit. By October 1914 he had signed on as a private soldier in the McGill University Battalion and had to sit the examination for entry into the Canadian Army Medical Corps. For the professor, who for twenty years had been writing and marking examination papers, it was a novel experience.

On Salisbury Plain, meanwhile, the officers and men of 1st Brigade CFA continued their training in the rain, mud and autumn gales that blew down their tents and made life wretched. A welcome retreat was, however, situated not far away in the attractive Wiltshire market town of Devizes, whose famous old coaching hostelry, the 'Bear Inn', served as the Brigade officers' mess. First licensed in 1599, the inn fronted the Market Square and had boasted many famous visitors over the years including George III and Queen Charlotte. With its beams, log fires, comfortable lounges and bars serving local ales, it was understandably popular with the officers. John McCrae and his colleagues also attended church parades and services at the town's St John's Church conducted by Canon John Almond, a chaplain friend of John's from Montreal.

The Canadians enjoyed the solace of 'The Bear Inn' but John soon found himself in rather more luxurious surroundings. Together with Lawrence Cosgrave and Edward Morrison, he took a few days' leave in London and, deciding to indulge themselves, the three booked rooms at the Savoy. After the miseries of the Plain, the famous hotel seemed the next best thing to paradise. He informed his mother unashamedly that, 'I am in the lap of luxury for a couple of days.'[11] London was quiet with 'perhaps one tenth of the street lamps being lighted. From the parks they have great searchlights playing up into the sky to search for aeroplanes'.[12]

By what appeared to be a complete coincidence, John chanced to meet someone he had not seen for several years: 'Yesterday I saw my friend L.S. Amery (of Hudson Bay days) he was at the station (9 a.m.) and had been under fire at 1 p.m. the previous day.'[13] Leo Amery had, in fact, returned in haste from the Belgian town of Ypres. Having finished his recruitment work at the War Office, he had asked his friend, Lieutenant-General Sir Henry Rawlinson, if he could join his staff and had set off for Flanders early in October. The city of Antwerp having fallen to the Germans, Rawlinson's army was commanded to fall back on Ypres in mid-October. Amery and his colleagues were welcomed by the Burgomaster in his beautiful offices at the eastern end of the Cloth Hall, regarded by many as the 'noblest monument of the wealth and proud splendour of medieval Flanders'.[14]

As the First Battle of Ypres began, Amery was sent out most days to report on operations. He later recalled scenes typical of that autumn in the Salient, with 'church and village a blaze of fire against an inky sky; our men advancing by rushes under heavy rain; the continuous flash and vicious crack of shrapnel overhead, followed by the swish of the shrapnel bullets'.[15] Tasked with writing a report, Amery had returned to Ypres to complete it, working on it all day and most of the night by candlelight. With Rawlinson on a brief visit to Lord Roberts in England, Amery was required to deliver his report in person. As he prepared to leave Ypres, the first enemy shells hit the Cloth Hall. It was on the following day, as he arrived in London on his way to Rawlinson, that he happened to meet John McCrae.

After his brief glimpse of luxury, John returned to Salisbury Plain. A further period of leave before Christmas enabled him to visit Earl Grey in London and the Oslers in Oxford, where Lady Osler plied him with supplies of socks for the men. As that first Christmas of the war approached, Canon Scott was granted permission by the Rector of Amesbury to use the parish church for midnight Eucharist on Christmas Eve. For some of the men who were thousands of miles from their home, that Christmas service in Wiltshire had a special significance. On Christmas Day, two gunners from the brigade who were in the guard tent for causing a disturbance in the town of Bath, received a special treat from their Medical Officer. Knowing they would get little in the way of Christmas cheer, John sent each of them a small bottle containing a dark liquid and labelled: 'To be taken before meals'. It was a ration of service rum.[16] The officers of 1st Brigade CFA also managed to introduce some merriment into their festivities. When invited to have a glass of wine with Colonel Morrison, one came dressed in the white jacket and apron of a waiter, prompting John to write to his mother that 'I wish Kipling could have seen that afternoon, for I am sure he would have found it funny.'[17]

Although the Princess Patricia's Light Infantry had crossed to France with the British 27th Division and had thus become the first Canadians to reach the front line in the war, for most of the Canadians the real nightmare was yet to begin. Like the other troops, they had been trained for the wrong kind of war. The cavalry practised their traditional charges; the horse-drawn artillery moved about open countryside and the infantry rehearsed charging shoulder to shoulder with fixed bayonets. It would all be of little use. The war had already demonstrated with chilling reality how right Kipling had been, for in the words of one commentator: 'Attack is now possible by earth, water & air, & the destruction attainable by modern war machines . . . is unthinkable & past imagination.'[18]

Defensive positions were absolutely essential for survival against modern weaponry, particularly the machine gun. The field-grey German legions had begun to dig theirs north of the Aisne River and the Allies countered with trenches of their own. Both sides then extended these positions, which had at first been only temporary and, by early 1915, two defensive parallel lines stretched from the English Channel to Switzerland. Trench warfare had arrived and for a long time to come, the Western Front would not deviate more than ten miles in either direction.[19]

As a result of heavy rain and damaged drainage systems, the ground became a sea of mud interspersed with the wreckage of what had once been thriving communities. The soldiers shared their miserable existence in the trenches with rats in a degree of squalor unknown since the Middle Ages. They came to know fatigue that was at times so acute that men actually fell asleep as they marched. They also experienced the crippling cold, the shock, the terror, the filth and the horror of life in a hell of mud, terrible injuries and appalling loss of life. It was a world in which it felt at times like being 'on the edge of a precipice with nothing beyond but a great void',[20] a world where chance was often the only arbiter between life and death. The dream of the summer of 1914 and the expectation of a great adventure had turned into the nightmare of the first winter of a war in which, 'One came to manhood through a terrible gate, and suddenly, without the preparation that had been expected. Boyhood, in those days, did not pass quietly into manhood but was rent away in a gun-flash and departed for ever in a single night of violence.'[21]

On 2 February 1915, when orders were received announcing that lst Canadian Division would be inspected by His Majesty King George two mornings later, everyone knew that embarkation for France would soon follow. 4 February was cold and dry as the King and his Secretary of State for War, Lord Kitchener, duly arrived for the review. After the King's visit, the units were grateful to be able to break up their wretched cantonments on Salisbury Plain and put a miserable experience behind them. A few days later on Sunday 7 February, the first units began to board trains for the port of Avonmouth on the Bristol Channel. It was still raining even as they departed.

An efficient four-day schedule enabled the division to join their ships in an orderly manner. Morrison and 1st Brigade CFA were given sole use of a ship called the *African Prince*. The bad weather persisted and the ships were caught in a very severe storm in the Bay of Biscay. What should have been a 36-hour journey ended up in some cases as a five-day ordeal and a number of the horses were so exhausted and badly injured that they had to be shot and put overboard. By 16 February the last Canadian unit had landed at St Nazaire to a warm welcome from the local people who threw apples and oranges to the newcomers. Only six months had gone by since 1st Canadian Division had assembled at Valcartier and it now became the first non-regular British division to land in France.[22]

The troops marched from the docks to the railway station and climbed into the small French box cars with their chalked descriptions, 'Hommes 40, Chevaux 8'[23] which would become depressingly familiar in the months and years ahead. Their train journey of two days and nights took them through the fertile Normandy countryside and into the Pas de Calais. For men from a country which was normally snow-covered until almost April, the primrose-covered banks and budding greenery of the early European spring were a fascinating sight in February. As they approached their final destination of Hazebrouck, a town fifteen miles behind the sector of the front line held by the British Second Army, the Canadians could already hear the sound of the guns.

Late in February 1915, 1st Canadian Division was introduced to the new warfare when each of its three brigades did a brief tour in the lines with experienced British divisions. On 20 February, the Commander-in-Chief of the British Expeditionary Force, Field Marshal Sir John French, inspected the Canadians and pronounced them 'well-trained, and quite able to take their places in the line of battle'.[24] On 3 March, Lieutenant-General Edwin Alderson assumed responsibility for the stretch of line in front of Fleurbaix and 1st Canadian Division replaced 7th British Division to form the left wing of the British 4th Corps under Lieutenant-General Sir Henry Rawlinson. John McCrae and 1 CFA marched twenty miles to Armentières and were attached to the Royal Artillery. It was a miserable sector since in this area, the water level was close to the surface; trenches were shallow and flooded, and built up with earthworks and sandbags. Small woods nearby provided good firing positions for numerous German snipers,[25] though in this respect the Canadians were to prove more than a match for their enemy. They were also hardened to living in wretched, muddy conditions after their winter in England.

For their first week in the line, things were quiet but on 10 March 1915, the war heated up for the Canadians when they were ordered to hold the enemy opposite them in position as their part in the first British-initiated attack against the village of Neuve Chapelle.

Beginning at 7.30 a.m. on 10 March 1915, the divisional artillery opened fire and some 300 guns of all calibres poured destruction onto the German lines. Infantry and machine-gunners opened bursts of fire which continued throughout the day and, according to one Canadian officer, sounded at times 'something like the distant sound of Niagara Falls'.[26] At Canadian divisional headquarters in a town three miles away, the streets were full of ammunition wagons, limbers, motor ambulances, staff officers in cars, orderlies on motor bikes and wounded men covered in mud and swathed in bloody bandages. The British attack, which took place to the left of the Canadian Division, was successful. Neuve Chapelle was taken without difficulty but the assaulting troops then halted along a pre-arranged line waiting for further orders. When, after five confused hours, they were finally told to resume the advance, it was nearly dusk. By the time the British attacked again the following day, the element of surprise had been lost. The delay had enabled the Germans to reinforce their positions and machine-gun and artillery fire cut down the assaulting British troops as they crossed the flat fields. After a determined German counter-attack was beaten off on 12 March, Sir John French notified his superiors on 13 March that it was necessary to halt the offensive because of a shortage of ammunition and because his troops were tired. Both sides settled down to consolidate the positions they held. The battle of Neuve Chapelle ended at a cost of nearly 13,000 Allied casualties.[27] The War Diary of lst Brigade CFA recorded their part in the battle:

10th March. Opened fire 7.30. Observation good. Salvos fired at 5-minute intervals at Germans. Infantry reported it very effective. More howitzer shelling of Fl[eurbaix]. but no casualties. In evening, learned that the Indian Division, 5 miles S[outh].W[est]. of us had captured Neuve Chapelle and portion of ridge along front of this Division up to Armentières. Casualties 1700.

11th March. Brigade opened fire at 7.20 am in misty weather difficult to see even from trenches. Fired 10 rounds per gun. Located one enemy trench from where a spring mortar was throwing bombs into our trenches. Germans shelled Brigade during day chiefly with 6" Howitzer. L[ieutenant]t. Gen[eral]. Lord Dundonald visited Brigade.

12th March. Continuing foggy weather made observation hard. Opened again at 7.30 firing 10 rounds per gun. Afternoon shelled snipers house left of Inf[antry]. trenches and had 3 direct hits. Considerable trouble rear of our own lines with snipers and cutting of wires apparently by civilians remaining in houses along Cron Ballot road.[28]

John summed up the brigade's role in the action in a letter to his mother saying that 'our part was merely to keep busy our front so that no reinforcements would be detached to send a mile down the line'.[29] At one point, 'Bonfire', John's horse, had narrowly missed injury, causing John to note in his diary that he was thinking 'of calling him Gunfire'.[30] According to Sergeant-Major Cyril Allinson, the shortage of artillery ammunition had meant that the field artillery had been limited to fifteen rounds per gun per day. For the medical officers encountering the war for the first time, it was a sobering experience. They found themselves faced with pools of blood, severed limbs with no owners, shattered corpses and groaning wounded. By the time some of them could be treated, their wounds were already two days old and in a very serious condition. John McCrae had been fulfilling his dual role of brigade medical officer and second-in-command to Morrison, helping to direct the fire of the brigade's sixteen 18-pdr guns. He had also done splendid work among the wounded, not just his own men but those of neighbouring units. On several occasions he had had narrow escapes from shells while running to give help and he highlighted the problems of bringing the wounded back safely:

> I attend the gun lines; any casualty is reported by telephone and I go to it . . . It is not nice to come upon a pool of blood, because one speculates just what kind of a knock the chap got, and so on. The wounded and sick stay where they are till dark, when the field ambulances go over certain ground and collect. A good deal of suffering is perhaps entailed by the delays till night; but it is dangerous for wheeled vehicles to go on the roads within 1500 yards of the trenches. They are willing enough to go. Most of the trench injuries are of the head, and therefore there is a high proportion of killed in the daily warfare as opposed to an attack. Our Canadian plots fill up rapidly.[31]

Quite apart from caring for the wounded and visiting outposts when needed, John was also responsible for maintaining the brigade's health. In essence, his medical work could be likened to that of a general practitioner to the soldiers. Not only was it important to combat infection but also to try to lessen the effect of strain and exposure by insisting as far as possible on adequate meals, dry bedding and cleanliness. He also had to continue the training of stretcher bearers, issue rum when required and deal with daily sick parades and malingerers.

John's eminence as a physician and experience as a soldier made him a first-class medical officer whose military training and instincts would not allow him to wear the Red Cross armband of a non-combatant. He was a strict disciplinarian who was respected by the men, but he was also fair and at times his eyes sparkled with the humour for which he was renowned. As he had done on Salisbury Plain, he continued to emphasise the importance of hygiene and sanitation, remembering only too well the unnecessary sickness and death he had seen in South Africa. When lecturing the gunners, John left them in no doubt as to what he would do if he found any of them were not paying proper attention to the removal of lice.[32] He did his work well and at Neuve Chapelle the men were very fit. After the battle, John McCrae wrote to Dr Charles Martin, head of Medicine at the Royal Vic. in Montreal, describing how terrible the noise of the artillery fire had been. He also reported one close call that had occurred when was observing trench positions in a house behind the front line. The Germans began to shell it and John had to dive rapidly for shelter in the cellar.

The performance of the Canadians at Neuve Chapelle convinced the British High Command that the Canadian gunners knew their business as well as the Royal Artillery and that their engineers were first-class. 1st Brigade moved to Fleurbaix, less than four miles away, where they continued to hold the line for twenty-four days. By the time they were stood down on 25 March, Sir Henry Rawlinson had gained a very favourable impression of his Canadian troops, who had been quick to pick up new conditions and familiarise themselves with trench warfare.

On 27 March 1915, after their first taste of fighting on the Western Front, lst Canadian Division went into reserve at Estaires. During a week of intensive activity, the division was fully occupied with working parties and training schemes. For John, it was a time to enjoy welcome letters from Lady Osler and Earl Grey, a chocolate and coconut cake from an acquaintance in Paris, and a ramble up a hill three miles away, whence he could make out 'the sea at one spot on the horizon'.[33] By 2 April the bitter March winds had given way to sunny, balmy days, and John spotted cherry blossom and some early pansies in a ruined garden. On Easter Sunday 1915, Canon Almond preached at Church Parade with the sounds of artillery in the background. Later that day in a letter to Geills, John wrote that,

The war here seems to be at a momentary halt, but it will not likely be for long. Indeed today there is heavy firing a few miles to the North East of where we are. As I write, I can hear the guns roaring every couple of minutes, or oftener . . . Nearer the lines (we are about 4 miles back), everything is in ruins, and the country is scarred with reserve trenches, gunpits and graves.

It was, he concluded, a 'fine ground for Easter lilies'.[34]

NOTES

1. From 'The Anxious Dead' by John McCrae, *The Spectator*, 30 September 1917.
2. Mathieson, *My Grandfather's War*, pp. 31–32.
3. Nicholson, *Canadian Expeditionary Force*, p. 32.
4. Austin Harrison, 'The Coming of the Canadians', *Canada in Khaki 1917* (London, 1917), p. 38.
5. Harrison, 'The Coming of the Canadians,' p. 38.
6. Nicholson, *Canadian Expeditionary Force*, p. 34.
7. Scott, *The Great War as I Saw It*, p. 30.
8. Allinson, 'John McCrae', p. 90.
9. Nicholson, *Canadian Expeditionary Force*, p. 37.
10. Editorial, *Canadian Medical Association Journal* (Volume 4, 1914), p. 803.
11. JM to Janet McCrae, 1 November 1914, GM Papers.
12. JM to Janet McCrae, 1 November 1914, GM Papers.
13. JM to Janet McCrae, 1 November 1914, GM Papers.
14. Amery, *My Political Life*, Volume II, p. 38.
15. Amery, *My Political Life*, Volume II, p. 42.
16. Prescott, *In Flanders Fields*, p. 80.
17. JM to Janet McCrae, 28 December 1914, GM Papers.
18. Vera Brittain, *Chronicle of Youth: Vera Brittain's War Diary, 1913–1917* (London, 1981), p. 85.
19. Nicholson, *Canadian Expeditionary Force*, pp. 40–45.
20. John Buchan, *Memory Hold The Door* (London, 1940), p. 279.
21. Sir Charles Petrie, *The Edwardians* (New York, 1965), p. 12.
22. Nicholson, *Canadian Expeditionary Force*, pp. 39–40.
23. The translation reads 'Men 40, Horses 8'.
24. Nicholson, *Canadian Expeditionary Force*, p. 49.
25. Nicholson, *Canadian Expeditionary Force*, pp. 49–50.
26. J.A. Currie, *The Red Watch: With the lst Canadian Division in Flanders* (Toronto, 1916), p. 168.
27. Nicholson, *Canadian Expeditionary Force*, pp. 50–53.
28. War Diary, lst Brigade CFA, October 1914–July 1915, MG 30, III, D3, Vol. 4964. NAC.
29. JM to Janet McCrae, 8 April 1915, GM Papers.
30. JM Diary, 28 March 1915, GM Papers.
31. JM to Tom McCrae, 30 March 1915, GM Papers.
32. Prescott, *In Flanders Fields*, p. 83.
33. JM to Janet McCrae, 17 April 1915, GM Papers.
34. JM to Geills Kilgour, 3 April 1915, GM Papers.

CHAPTER TWELVE

'Some yielded, No, not we!'[1]
April–May 1915

John's prediction proved correct. Lieutenant-General Alderson was soon informed that 1st Canadian Division had been assigned to General Sir Horace Smith-Dorrien's V Corps in the Ypres Salient and, later that week, they began marching across the flat Flanders countryside to take up new positions west of the town of Ypres. The Canadians were now part of Second British Army which had the task of relieving the French troops defending the Salient, a semi-circular bulge in the front line around Ypres that had resulted from the fighting of the previous autumn. The Salient was overlooked on three sides by high ground from which the Germans could pour enfilade fire onto Allied positions and bring down artillery on Ypres itself. This fine old moated town, which had grown to prominence in the Middle Ages as a weaving centre, possessed beautiful houses, the magnificent Cloth Hall to which Leo Amery had referred, a Cathedral and a large square where a market was regularly held.

It was both a jewel of the medieval age and a strategic fortress town dominating the routes that converged on the Channel Ports. Although it had suffered damage during the autumn fighting, the population had largely returned and, when the lst Canadian Division arrived, its market was in full swing and its shops were doing a lively trade.

From the centre of Ypres a network of roads spread out across the Flanders plain to villages and hamlets. Countless ditches criss-crossed the flat clay countryside and the roads were elevated above the fields. The two main occupations of the area were weaving and farming, but it was also 'full of breweries, broken down wind-mills and hop yards'.[2] Although it had been a relatively quiet sector throughout the winter, the Ypres Salient was always a potential danger spot for exposed Allied units positioned there.

Despite the war, the local people had largely managed to continue their everyday life to within a relatively few miles of the front line.[3] Along the route of their march, the Canadians saw magnificent, docile Flemish horses pulling carts and ploughs, healthy brown cows that turned out to be prolific milkers, large pigs and excellent poultry. They quickly found that the Belgian farmers used manure in large quantities and the soil was thus rich in nitrates, potash and bacteria. If wounds were not sterilised immediately, infection would follow rapidly. As the Canadians approached the front line, all was deserted. Not a human being nor an animal was to be seen as they passed empty farms, cottages with doors and shutters closed, and thatched roofs torn off by shells. During lulls in the steady rumble of artillery fire, the only sounds the men could hear were birds singing and the crunching of their own boots on the road.

For their first few days in the new sector, lst Canadian Infantry Brigade and its attendant artillery, including John McCrae's unit, were in reserve near Vlamertinghe. John wrote to his mother telling her that friends had been keeping him informed of events and sending him newspapers from Canada. George Adami had also written, asking him to undertake another book on pathology after the war. John's comment was 'Sufficient unto the day – I cannot recall that there ever was a time when I knew any pathology.'[4] He already felt the war deeply but he was resolute:

> We all said that if this war ever happened it would be a terrible one. Have you seen the statement that the battle around Ypres which ended in the early part of Nov[embe]r (which lasted a couple of weeks) was responsible for as many casualties as <u>the entire civil war</u>. Nothing has impressed me so much as that statement.[5]
>
> We would be terrible traitors to the world & the future if we stopped any time before the snake is scotched . . . Germany has got to get a lot of lessons yet.[6]

Brigadier-General Arthur Currie's 2nd Brigade and Richard Turner's 3rd Brigade had been allocated a sector of the front line to the north east of Ypres. Some four thousand yards long, it was flanked on the left by the 45th and 87th French divisions (Algerian and Territorial respectively) and on the right by V British Corps. As they moved into their new positions over the period 14–17 April 1915, the Canadians discovered that the French troops whom they had relieved had quite different ideas about fortification and sanitation. The trenches they took over were in a shocking condition, not much better than a series of unconnected and shallow 'scrapes' in the ground. An engineer officer with 2nd Canadian Brigade described them as 'being in a deplorable state and in a very filthy condition, all the little broken down side trenches and shell holes apparently being used as latrines and burial places for bodies.'[7] Five days of unceasing work followed as the division tried to put their sector in order, a task made more difficult by the fact that the water table in this low-lying area was so high that any hole dug to a depth of more than two feet soon became water-logged.[8]

Brigadier-General Malcolm Mercer's 1st Brigade, still in reserve, moved to the village of Proven for employment, if needed, in an operation by II

British Corps against Hill 60 on the crest of the Messines-Passchendaele ridge. Although the assault subsequently took place and resulted in bitter fighting, 1st Brigade did not become involved. It was soon to be needed elsewhere when, on 22 April 1915, the Germans launched a major attack against the Ypres Salient.[9] The existence of the Salient, which cut into the German front line, had for some time been regarded as an irritation by the German Fourth Army. No attack had so far been made because of a decision by the German High Command to remain on the defensive in the west while committing all possible troops against Russia. In April 1915, however, orders were issued to commanders on the Western Front to engage in 'lively activity' to conceal these troop movements.

General Duke Albrecht of Württemberg, commander of the Fourth German Army, was therefore ordered to attack the Ypres Salient with a new secret weapon – gas – whose use directly contravened the Hague Conventions of 1899 and 1906. As early as January 1915, Albrecht began positioning gas cylinders along his front and, by 11 April, more than five thousand containers of the deadly substance were ready. His attack was to have limited objectives; the intention was not to push the British and Canadian troops out of the Ypres Salient but to use the new weapon to seize objectives that would force them to abandon it. For ten days, meteorological conditions were not favourable but on 21 April 1915, the wind began to shift and the attack was ordered for the following day.[10]

Allied intelligence officers had been aware of the Germans' intention to use gas for some weeks. However, senior commanders simply refused to believe that the enemy would resort to such a dreadful weapon despite the fact that German deserters provided accurate information on both the new weapon and where it would be utilised. After he had issued orders for measures to be taken to repel a gas attack, the commander of the French 11th Division was told by his superiors, that 'all this gas business need not be taken seriously'.[11] A few days later, his formation was relieved by 1st Canadian Division.

During this period, John McCrae and 1st Brigade CFA were stationed at Oudezeele. On 18 April they marched to Poperinge to continue their programme of exercises, gun drill and route marching. As they and the 1st Canadian Infantry Brigade were in reserve, they were able to enjoy brief periods of relaxation in Poperinghe. Like Ypres, this town had found prosperity through cloth and the inability of English traders to pronounce its name had led to the term 'poplin' for the type of cloth it produced. The Stadhuis or Town Hall served as headquarters for the forces in the front line around Ypres and Talbot House, which the soldiers abbreviated according to the alphabetical short form of the time to 'Toc H', run by the Reverend 'Tubby' Clayton, was a rest house for all ranks. Throughout the war, thousands of officers and soldiers received the Sacrament in its chapel. Despite long-range shelling, the narrow streets of 'Pops', as it was known to the British, bustled with life and the 'Tommies' also gave nicknames to some of its establishments. The 'Café de Ranke' which catered only to officers, became known as 'Ginger's' on account of the owner's three red-headed daughters. It was said that 'more champagne corks popped here during the war than anywhere else in France or Belgium'.[12] The 'Café de la Commerce des Houblons' or 'Hop Market Café' reminded one young officer of the famous Skindles Hotel at Maidenhead and in time the proprietress, Madame Beutin, adopted the name.[13] At a variety of other well-run places, the soldiers could get simple, wholesome meals served with wine and the shops did a lively trade in souvenirs, cigarettes, cigars, postcards, watches and the like. Local barbers continued to cut hair 'but not while the Germans are shelling'.[14]

The night of 21 April 1915 was clear and calm as the Canadians manned their newly-cleaned and rebuilt trenches. The previous day, the Germans had been taking observations from three huge balloons and now, from where his 2nd Brigade held the line, Arthur Currie could hear the continuous sound of wagons and limbers along the German front opposite and sensed that something was about to happen. Although German aircraft bombed Poperinghe on the morning of 22 April and German artillery had been shelling Ypres for several days, elsewhere the day started routinely for the Canadians. The weather was warm and sunny and under the cloudless sky, the spring countryside was at its best. Wooded areas were carpeted with celandines, violets and wild strawberry, and hedgerows were white with hawthorn blossom. The work of Captain William Boyd, in command of a hospital for infectious diseases at Bailleul, took him to see a medical officer friend with a British artillery unit in the village of Kemmel. Behind him rose Kemmel Hill, one of the great artillery observation points in the Allied line, and Boyd was invited up to one of its well-hidden observation stations. Through a telescope, he found he had almost as good a view of the Flanders plain as the German aircraft flying overhead. On 'this glorious afternoon,' Boyd saw,

a wonderful panorama . . . Immediately opposite at a distance of a couple of miles were the German trenches, and over those lines the shrapnel was bursting in little fleecy clouds. Away to the left lay Ypres, like some dream city in the warm light of the sinking sun, with delicate wisps of mist eddying around its shattered spires. In between was Hill 60, where a furious bombardment was in progress. And yet with it all not a living creature nor moving thing could be seen for miles.[15]

In Ypres, Canon Frederick Scott, the much-loved Senior Chaplain to the 1st Canadian Division, was billeted in a house on the northern edge of the town. That beautiful spring afternoon he had just returned from conducting a burial service to write some letters. Madame, his landlady, who played hymns from the Canadian hymn book on her harmonium, had recently buried twelve valuable family clocks in the garden in case of a German advance. From where he now sat, Madame's grandfather had watched the British marching to the Battle of Waterloo. Canon Scott had become fond of the stout-hearted local people who revered their warrior-King Albert, and was distressed that German shelling had once again forced them to abandon their homes and flee into the countryside. Just a few days earlier he had sensed 'that we were resting on the top of a volcano'[16] and now, as the bombardment intensified, large-calibre shells rained down on the lovely old buildings.

At four o'clock that afternoon, the Germans stepped up the tempo and began a tremendous bombardment of the Allied positions. An hour later, as a steady late-afternoon breeze began to blow, German pioneer units opened the valves of their containers and released 160 tons of chlorine gas. The gas has been pumped in under pressure and when it was released it spurted out with great force and did not float on the breeze until it was about one hundred yards from the German trenches. It was the beginning of the first gas attack in the history of warfare.

The 'devilish incense'[17] wafted like a deadly fog bank in the direction of the French trenches to the left of the Canadians. Depending on the position of the observer, it appeared to be different colours. From their positions, the Canadians reported 'a cloud of greenish vapour several hundred yards in length' drifting toward the French lines.[18] To allied aircraft who observed the scene, it appeared as a bluish-white mist – such as is seen over water meadows on a frosty night. Other onlookers thought the French trenches were aflame and giving off white smoke. Close up, the chlorine was a greenish-yellow colour but, by that time, its awful smell had created a dreadful 'burning sensation in the eyes, nose and throat' followed quickly by loss of breath as lungs, seared by the irritant gas, became waterlogged and began to strain for air.[19] As it drifted over the French lines there was panic both at the gas and the sight of the oncoming Germans, some of whom wore gas masks,[20] and bore more than a passing resemblance to outlandish monsters. Choking, coughing and vomiting, men either died or turned and fell back towards the Yser Canal, half blind and suffering greatly. Captain Guy Drummond, son of Sir George and Lady Drummond of Montreal, tried to rally the fleeing French soldiers but was killed by a bullet in the neck and became one of the early Canadian casualties in the Second Battle of Ypres.

As the first soldiers of the Empire to face a new weapon against which they had no defence, the Canadians peered out from their positions at the approaching gas. Behind it advanced the German infantry and, within minutes, the entire left flank of the Salient had collapsed.[21] The situation of the 3rd Canadian Brigade on the left of the British line was very serious;

it had no support on one flank and the Germans were moving behind its lines. It therefore readjusted its position to form an acute angle facing the enemy on either side.

Two Canadian officers were among the first to identify the terrible new weapon. Lieutenant-Colonel George Nasmith, the analytical chemist from Toronto who was now attached to No. 5 Canadian Mobile Laboratory, had driven over to the 2nd Field Ambulance Advanced Dressing Station at Wieltje, north east of Ypres. Here he found a medical officer who happened to be John McCrae's former student, Captain Francis Scrimger. Scrimger had arrived late in France after contracting pneumonia on Salisbury Plain and was now with 14th Battalion Royal Montreal Regiment. The two men went for a stroll in the direction of St Julien but as they looked towards the French line they spotted a 'yellowish-green cloud rising on a front of at least three miles and drifting at a height of perhaps a hundred feet towards us'. Nasmith remarked that it must be 'the poison gas that we have heard vague rumours about' and added, 'It looks like chlorine and I bet it is'. Francis Scrimger 'agreed that it probably was'.[22] Nasmith recorded that they diagnosed the gas as 'chiefly chlorine, with perhaps an admixture of bromine'.[23] He was one of the first to advise G.H.Q. as to the nature of the gas and suggested that a solution of hyposulphite of soda should be used with a protective mask to cover the nose and mouth. Scrimger, meanwhile, devised a more immediate solution. He instructed the men of his battalion to 'urinate on your pocket handkerchief [and] tie it over your mouth'.[24] The Canadians had no immediate protection against the poison gas other than hasty improvisation, but the quick thinking of Scrimger in creating this less than pleasant emergency measure, which caused the chlorine to crystallise, saved many lives over the next few days.

Canon Scott in Ypres had no idea of the terrible drama that was unfolding just a few miles away until a battery of artillery galloped into the town around 7.00 p.m. One of the drivers told him that the Germans were in pursuit and Scott knew he must find his way to the Canadian lines. He left with one of the ammunition columns, only to find it was being moved well out of range of the oncoming Germans. Returning in the hope of finding another Canadian regiment going to the front, he passed the unfortunate citizens of Ypres pouring in the opposite direction to escape the Germans. Having hastily collected a few possessions from his billet, Scott heard the welcome sound of the bagpipes of 16th Battalion Canadian Scottish who were on their way to close the gap where the Germans had broken through. By now it was dark and the sky was lit not only by the moon but by flares. As Scott and the 16th Battalion reached Wieltje, the dressing station was already full of casualties. At the front, the roar of artillery, the rattle of the machine guns and the crack of thousands of rifles told them a great battle was taking place.

At the observation station on Kemmel Hill, Captain William Boyd continued to watch as great incendiary shells fell on Ypres and every gun for miles around appeared to go into action. He could see 'nothing . . . but wicked red tongues of fire, which seemed to stab into the blackness of the night', while the 'noise was just like hell let loose' for 'over the trenches there was a storm of bursting shrapnel and high explosive in which it seemed that no man could live'.[25]

In fact, the British and Canadian reaction to the crisis had been swift and was assisted by the fact that the German infantry themselves were fearful of the ghastly new weapon and moved forward with caution. By 8.00 p.m. the German advance had halted and Allied commanders prepared to counter attack while desperately trying to patch together a defence line to prop up the left flank of the Salient. It was to be a grim night. The 3rd Canadian Brigade was ordered to put in an attack on Kitchener's Wood. As the 10th Infantry Battalion and the 16th Battalion Canadian Scottish fixed bayonets in the darkness, they had no clear idea of the enemy's strength and position. Canon Scott stayed with them through the hours of waiting, in the front line and among the men he cared for. He recalled that a 'great storm of emotion swept through me and I prayed for our men in their awful charge, for I knew that the Angel of Death was passing down our lines that night'.[26]

Advancing in the misty moonlight with only limited artillery support, the two Canadian battalions met a hail of intense machine gun and rifle fire. Although outnumbered, they managed to create the impression that they had very considerable support and this enabled them to drive the Germans back out of the wood and recapture a British howitzer battery. Next morning, however, only 5 officers and 188 men of the 10th Battalion were on parade for roll call, and only 5 officers and 260 men of the 16th Battalion. Sadly, the Canadians were forced to abandon the wood when promised French help did not arrive. The cost had been terrible, but it was this kind of counter-attack that was effective in preventing the Germans from exploiting their early successes.

Canon Scott helped to take some of the wounded to the dressing station at Wieltje and as he watched the doctors at work, he witnessed the effects of what the men of the Canadian Scottish had endured. Many of the wounded were men he knew personally, and he stayed with them throughout that night of suffering. Finally, when dawn came, Canon Scott accepted a ride back towards Ypres and felt compassion for the tired, hungry young British battalions he passed on their way to the line as 'they had had a long march, and, as it turned out, were going up, most of them, to their death.' He tried to cheer them by hailing them and telling them that 'it was all right, as the Canadians had held the line, and that the Germans were not going to get through'.[27]

Among the British troops arriving that day were the men of the Royal

189

Warwickshire Regiment. They encountered vicious machine gun and artillery fire and suffered heavy casualties, particularly around Wieltje. One of the Warwickshire's officers wounded in this action was Lieutenant Bruce Bairnsfather, creator of the famous cartoon character 'Old Bill' who would bring so much cheer to soldiers and civilians alike throughout the war years. Another British officer with a special affection for Canada was Lieutenant Robert Vernède of the Rifle Brigade, who, on hearing about the battle, remembered well the 'irrepressible men' he had met in Canada a few years earlier. As black-bordered letters and telegrams arrived across the Atlantic notifying families of those killed, wounded and missing, his poem, 'To Canada', paid tribute in the last verse to the bravery of her troops:

> So where the bugles call, there where the thin lines reel,
> Far from the land where their homes and hearts be,
> Stalwart and terrible, into the hail of steel,
> Canada, lo, they are marching for thee![28]

In a poignant twist of fate, Vernède was killed leading his platoon in an attack on Havrincourt Wood on 9 April 1917, the day of Canada's great victory at Vimy Ridge.

General Sir Horace Smith-Dorrien, commander of V British Corps, concluded that the Canadian brigades in the front line must have been shattered by the nature of the German attack and would retreat across the few bridges that led out of the Salient. At first he refused to believe the Canadians were actually holding – it did not seem possible that humans could stand such strain, but Currie, Turner, Mercer and their men rose to the occasion. Their commanding officer, Lieutenant-General Alderson had urged them to follow the example of his old regiment, the Royal West Kents and had told them, 'The Army says "The West Kents never budge". I am proud of the great record of my old regiment . . . and before long the Army will say "The Canadians never budge". Lads, it can be left there . . . The Germans will never turn you out.'[29] As the Germans poured everything they had against the Canadians, Lieutenant-Colonel John Currie, in command of a battalion of the 48th Highlanders of Canada, witnessed the heartbreaking sight of his men fighting against odds of at least ten to one, many so badly wounded and gassed that they could not even crawl, let alone stand. They hung on like demons, but in retrospect he wondered how they had managed to do it. 'How anything could live in that seething vortex, created by the bursting high explosive shells, is a mystery,' he later wrote, having known full well that many 'a brave Highlander would see the lone shielings and the misty mountains of Canada no more'.[30]

The events of the coming days were to produce countless acts of bravery as British and Canadian troops strove to hold the Salient. In the fierce battle of St Julien, 3rd Canadian Brigade holding the left flank of the new Salient north of the village had to withdraw on account of a gas attack, but returned through terrible artillery fire to recover their trenches. A company of Royal Highlanders of Montreal held their trench despite being attacked from the rear. When finally ordered to retreat by their wounded captain, he remained with three loaded revolvers to aim at the first line of oncoming Germans and thus win more time for his men to get clear. At his Advanced Dressing Station a surgeon-major of the 48th Highlanders stayed heroically for twelve days and nights to save the lives of his wounded. The medical system had been completely disorganised before the gas attack by the very heavy bombardment that had destroyed or caused the evacuation of many posts and dressing stations. This, plus the hurried arrangements to deal with the mass wounded and the problems of treating the new gas casualties, placed a very great strain on medical personnel. In terms of battle decorations, the greatest went to none other than the quiet, dedicated Captain Francis Scrimger. His valour and devotion to duty in caring for the wounded when the 3rd Brigade's headquarters at Mouse Trap Farm was shelled and set on fire, made him the first Canadian officer to win the Victoria Cross in this war.

Back at Poperinghe, 1st Brigade CFA was hastily ordered up to the front line during the early evening of 22 April. Throughout the following two and a half weeks, John McCrae kept daily notes on his unit's activities which he later wrote up as a diary, written from the point of view of a field officer rather than a military doctor. He began with the brigade receiving orders to move up on 22 April:

> As we moved up last ev[enin]g, there was heavy firing about 4.30 on our left, the hour at which the Ger[man]. attack with gas was made when the Fr[ench]. line broke. We could see the shells bursting over the town ahead (Yp[res].) and in a small village to our left.[31]

He recorded how the batteries of the two other artillery brigades in forward positions had,

> had a terribly tough time but got away safely and did wonderful service. One battery fired in 2 opposite directions at once and both batteries fired at point blank, open sights, at Germans in the open; they were at times quite without infantry on their front, for their position was behind the Fr[ench]., to the left of the British line.[32]

Continuing his account, John described the scene as the 1st Brigade approached the front:

As we sat on the road, we began to see the French stragglers: men without arms, wounded men, teams, wagons, civilians, refugees – some by the roads, some across country, all talking, shouting – the very picture of a debacle. I must say they were the 'tag enders' of a fighting line rather than the line itself. And they streamed on and shouted us scraps of not too inspiriting information – while we stood and took our medicine, and picked out gun positions in the fields in case we had to go right in there and then. The men were splendid: not a word: not a shake. And it was a terrific test. Traffic whizzed by: ambulances, transport, ammunition, supplies, despatch riders – and the shells thundered into the town or burst high in the air nearer us, and the refugees streamed. Women, old men, little children, hopeless, tearful, quiet or excited, tired, dodging the traffic – and the wounded in singles or in groups: here & there I could give a momentary help, and the ambulances picked them up as they could. So the cold, moonlight night wore on – no change save that the towers of Ypres showed up against the glare of the city burning – and the shells still sailed in.[33]

John's feelings that night went out to the poor, gassed French soldiers, gasping for air through tortured lungs. They were a terrible sight – another witness remembered them being 'blinded, coughing, chests heaving, face an ugly purple' and 'lips speechless with agony'.[34] John also admired the cheery steady British reinforcements moving up quietly past the Canadians. Finally at 4.30 a.m., 1st Brigade CFA was ordered to go in and support a French counter-attack. They covered the remaining three miles as quickly as they could, but the pre-selected gun positions had been overrun and they had to find new locations in the darkness with no accurate information on German positions. The German advance had stopped about a mile and a half north and three and a half miles east of Ypres. Here a canal ran between Ypres and Nieuwpoort on the Belgian coast. The Brielen Bridge or Bridge No. 4, was close to the boundary between the French and British sectors and the only bridge capable of carrying heavy traffic. John's friend and commanding officer, Lieutenant-Colonel Edward Morrison, set up his headquarters nearby.

Hardly had Morrison got the first of his guns into position than the brigade was called to support a Canadian counter-attack along the Canal. Later they found out that two Canadian regiments and one artillery battery were all that filled the one and a half mile gap that the French troops had left in the line. Soon, the remaining guns of the brigade had dug themselves into position with Morrison controlling their fire from a forward observation post. For the next seventeen days, his gunners were to remain there providing artillery cover for troop movements deeper in the Salient.

John McCrae's diary provided a description of his surroundings:

Behold us now anything less than 2 miles N[orth] of Y[pres]. on the west side of the Canal: this runs north, each bank planted with high tall elms, with bare trunks of the familiar Netherlands type. A few yards to the west a main road runs, likewise bordered: the Censor will allow me to say that on the high bank between these we had our headquarters: the ridge is perhaps 15–20 feet high, and slopes forward 50 yards to the water, the back is more steep and slopes quickly to a little subsidiary waterway – deep but dirty. Where the guns were I shall not say, but they were not far away and the Ger[man]. aeroplanes that viewed us daily with all but impunity knew very well . . . Looking to the S[outh]. between the trees, we could see the ruins of the city: to the front on the sky line, with rolling ground in the front, pitted by French trenches, the German lines; to the left front, several farms and a windmill, and the farther left, again near the canal, thicker trees & more farms. The farms & windmill were soon burnt. Several farms we used for observing posts, were also quickly burnt, during the next three or four days. All along behind us at varying distances, Fr[ench]. and Brit[ish]. guns: the flashes at night lit up the sky.[35]

Facsimile of a sketch by John McCrae on the back of a card looking south towards Ypres from his position by the Yser Canal during the Second Battle of Ypres.
From 'In Flanders Fields and other Poems' by Lieut.-Col. John McCrae, M.D. with An Essay in Character by Sir Andrew Macphail. Toronto: William Briggs, 1919

The Canadian gunners had with them a very capable British artillery officer who was not only their link with the French but was a great comfort to them, since,

> the entire battle was largely fought on our own, following the requests of the infantry, on our front, and scarcely guided by our own staffs at all. We at once set out to register our targets – and almost at once had to get into steady firing on quite a large sector of front. We dug in the guns as quickly as we could, and took as H.Q. some infantry trenches already dug on a ridge near the canal.[36]

The dug-out that was to be John's dressing station for the coming days was a basic hole in the rear side of the twenty-foot high canal bank. Measuring eight feet square, it was roughly roofed to keep out the rain, and sandbagged at the entrance to prevent pieces of shrapnel from coming in – John described it as a 'square hole'.[37] Sometimes men were shot on the top of the bank and rolled down in front of the dressing station, causing him to comment that even the hospitals in Montreal did not have such an efficient delivery service. Despite the dangers, John did sterling work among his own wounded and those of neighbouring units. His time was split fairly evenly between combatant and medical work and he was under constant pressure.

From his post, the road was clearly visible. It was an extremely dangerous place that came to be known by the Canadians as the 'Devil's Corner':

> Along the road, which was constantly shelled 'on spec' by the G[ermans]. one saw all the sights of war. Wounded men, limping or carried, ambulances, trains of supply, troops, army mules, – and tragedies. I saw one bicycle orderly, a shell exploded and he seemed to pedal on for eight or ten revolutions & then collapse in a heap – dead. Straggling soldiers would be killed or wounded, horses ditto – until it got to be a nightmare. I used to shudder every time I saw wagons or troops on that road. My dug-out looked out on it.[38]

As 23 April wore on, a major counter-attack by British troops against the German gains was halted by heavy enemy fire and a shortage of artillery ammunition. By dusk, the British and Canadians were again on the defensive, setting up positions that were thinly-held because of a shortage of troops.[39]

Encouraged by his early successes, Albrecht ordered a new gas attack for the early hours of 24 April 1915. At four in the morning, the containers were opened again and their awful contents launched against the positions of 2nd Canadian Brigade, holding the apex of the Salient. The brigade resisted desperately but the deadly vapour was too powerful. Although the brigade did not break, by 6.30 a.m., the Germans had driven a wedge deep into their positions. At mid-morning came the turn of the 3rd Brigade to the left when a reinforced German division, following a heavy artillery bombardment but no gas, put in a massive attack directly on their positions. Crippled by the heavy losses it had suffered the previous night, the 3rd Brigade was forced back but withdrew in good order to new positions to the rear. As night fell on this day of bloody fighting, 1st Canadian Division was barely hanging on – but it was hanging on.

Casualty clearing stations were full of wounded and gassed men gasping for air and in terrible distress. In a schoolhouse at Vlamertinghe, the 3rd Canadian Field Ambulance[40] had established its main dressing station but was desperately short of stretchers and blankets as most of its equipment had been lost at Ypres. Ambulances came and went hour after hour with hardly a pause and by midnight the schoolhouse was full to overflowing. The wounded started to fill the village church, where Canon Scott was on hand to give Communion to the dying and comfort and cigarettes to the less seriously wounded. He felt powerless at the sight of so many young lives ebbing away and full of admiration for the heroic work of the doctors. As he did his best to uphold morale, all who could prayed with him. Lieutenant-Colonel W. Watt, the medical officer in command, described the appalling ordeal he and his staff experienced through that first awful week as they treated,

> One never-ending stream which lasted day and night for seven days without cessation: in all some five thousand two hundred cases passed through our hands. Wounds here, wounds there, wounds everywhere. Legs, feet, hands missing; bleeding stumps controlled by rough field tourniquets; large portions of the abdominal walls shot away; faces horribly mutilated; bones shattered to pieces; holes that you could put your clenched fist into, filled with dirt, mud, bits of equipment and clothing, until it all became like a hideous nightmare, as if we were living in the seventh hell of the damned.[41]

By the Yser Canal, John and his unit also felt the effects of the day's gas attack as the 'fumes came very heavily: some blew down from the infantry trenches – some came from the shells: one's eyes smarted, and breathing was very labored. Up to noon today we fired 2500 rounds'.[42] He had not slept well the previous night, for although he and Edward Morrison had been given accommodation at a nearby French colonel's headquarters, their room had filled up with wounded and John awoke to share his bed with 'a chap next to me with a wounded leg and a chill.'[43]

By 25 April, enough British reinforcements had arrived for the Canadians to give up some of their widely-extended positions. The Second Battle of Ypres would continue for another week but 1st Canadian Division, worn out from combatting the menace of the terrible new weapon, remained on the defensive or in support. When the infantry of the division were withdrawn from the Salient on 2 May 1915, it had lost more than half its strength. The divisional artillery remained in the Salient – 1st Brigade, CFA, which had been continuously engaged since the first gas attack of 22 April, would remain there until 9 May 1915.

It was a terrible ordeal for the gunners as John recorded. On 25 April 1915,

> The weather brightened up, and we got at it again. This day we had several heavy attacks, prefaced by heavy artillery fire: these bursts of fire would result in our getting 100 to 150 rounds right on us or nearby: the heavier our fire (which was on the trenches entirely) the heavier theirs.[44]

He described his feelings of anger and impotence at seeing German aeroplanes over their position, and conversely, his pleasure at seeing the hard-working horses pulling the ammunition wagons:

> The good old horses would swing around at the gallop & then pull up in an instant, and stand puffing & blowing, but with their heads up, as if to say 'wasn't that well done!' It makes you want to kiss their dear old noses & assure them of a peaceful pasture once more. To-day we got our dressing station dug-out complete: & slept there at night.[45]

John shared his dug-out with Captain Lawrence Cosgrave. That same day he treated a number of French among the wounded, but there was little sleep to be had when night fell because,

> after dark, we got a terrible shelling, which kept up till 2 or 3 a.m. Finally I got to sleep, though it was still going on. We must have got a couple of hundred rounds – in singles or pairs. Every burst over us would light up the dugout – and every hit in front would shake the ground and bring down small bits of earth on us, or else the earth thrown into the air by the explosion would come spattering down on our roof, and into the front of the dugout. Col[onel]. Morrison tried the Mess house, but the shelling was too heavy & he & the Adjutant joined Cosgrave & me, and we 4 spent an anxious night there in the dark.[46]

The following day, 26 April, he recorded yet more 'heavy actions, but last night much Fr[ench]. & Brit[ish]. artillery has come in and the place is thick with guns – there are many hundreds now in these 2 miles of front.'[47]

From his position he could see the dead lying unburied in the area between the German and Allied positions. The road continued to be a dangerous spot and at times the gas fumes were heavy. Despite the noise of shell and gunfire, on 26 April, John noted blackbirds singing overhead in the surrounding trees. But the war continued:

> Yesterday up to noon, we fired 3000 r[oun]ds. for the 24 hours – but to-day we have fired much less, but we have registered fresh fronts and burned some farms behind the Ger[man]. trenches . . . To all this, put in a background of anxiety lest the (Fr[ench].) line break, for we are just where it broke before. (We wish we had our own troops to support.)[48]

On 27 April, the brigade was busy,

> registering batteries on new points . . . At 1.30 a heavy attack was prepared by the French and ourselves: the fire was very heavy for half an hour and the enemy got very busy too. I had to cross over to the batteries during it – an unpleasant journey. More gas attacks in the afternoon . . . At night usually the 'heavies' farther back take up the story, and there is a duel – the Ger[mans]. fire on our roads after dark to catch reliefs and transport – I suppose ours do the same.[49]

That night, however, he got some rest and wrote next day:

> I have to confess to an excellent sleep last night: at times anxiety says 'I don't want a meal' but experience says 'you need your food' so I attend regularly to that. . . . Much Ger[man]. air reconnaissance over us, and heavy firing both sides during the day . . . At 6.45 we again prepared a heavy artillery attack, but the infantry made little attempt to go on. . . . This 6-mile front is constantly heavily engaged. At intervals, too, they bombard Ypres. Our back lines have to be constantly shifted on acc[oun]t. of shellfire . . . In the evening rifle fire gets more frequent, and bullets are continually singing over us.[50]

As the fighting continued, John recorded that he had made a new friend:

> This morning our billet was hit and put somewhat 'on the blink' . . . We fire less these days – 2 days – 2000 r[oun]ds. – but still a good deal . . . The 'gas' attacks can be seen from here – the yellow cloud rising up is

for us a signal to open – and we do . . . Several days ago during the firing a big Oxford-grey dog, with beautiful brown eyes came to us in a panic: he ran to me and pressed his head <u>hard</u> against my leg. So I got him a safe place and he sticks by us. We call him Fleabag – for he looks like it. This night they shelled us again heavily for some hours . . . One gets dreadfully irritated by the constant din – a mixture of anger & apprehension.[51]

Lieutenant-Colonel John Currie and his battalion of 48th Highlanders were now helping to guard the bridge and saw at first-hand the work of 1st Brigade CFA:

Our batteries were in action along the banks and they were very skilfully hidden. I looked them up and found some old friends from Ottawa, Lieut[enant].-Colonel Morrison, the commandant, amongst them . . . Our guns were in action one evening when the major of one of the Indian batteries came along inspecting his observation wires.[52]

As the two officers watched some of Morrison's men taking ammunition caissons to the guns through 'a perfect hailstorm of shells,' the Indian Army major,

remarked to me that the Canadian gunners were magnificent, and that they did not have six drivers in the Indian Army that were as well trained and as good at their work as the Canadian boys who were driving the limbers we were looking at. That was a high compliment from a regular officer as the Indian Army knows its trade.[53]

On 30 April, John's account recorded a,

Thick mist this morning, and relative quietness, but before it cleared the Ger[mans]. started again to shell us: At 10 it cleared and from 10 to 2 we fired very constantly (probably 650 rounds). The French advanced and took some ground on our left front and a batch of prisoners . . . This ev[enin]g from 8 to 10 we had a heavy shelling again, 80 to 100 shells coming just over the crest of our ridge. Some better activity in the afternoon by the Allies' aeroplanes: the Ger[man]. planes have had it too much their own way lately.[54]

At the beginning of May, when it became clear that there was little hope of recapturing the ground they had lost, the Allies made a further strategic withdrawal to shorten their defensive line and make easier their main task of holding the town of Ypres.

By now, the weather was exceptionally warm. Captain William Boyd,

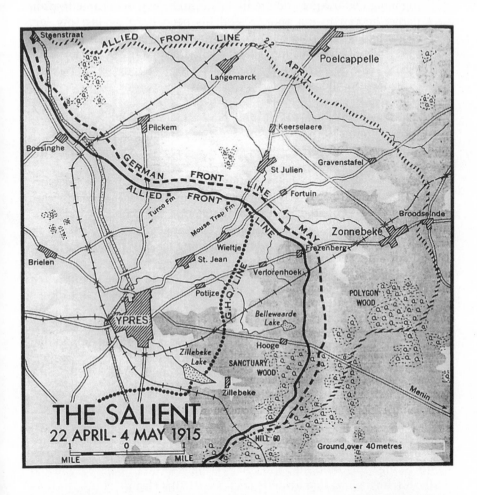

THE SALIENT
22 APRIL- 4 MAY 1915

the Canadian medical officer serving with 3rd British Field Ambulance at Bailleul remembered May Day as 'hot enough for summer, but with all the freshness of spring.' In this landscape of beauty and terror, he was struck by the abundance of wild flowers – especially the carpets of bluebells on Kemmel Hill – and reflected that 'we might have been wandering through English meadows'.[55] For John McCrae, 1 May 1915 was marked by a 'heavy bombardment at intervals thro[ugh]' the day' and in the evening and night, there was 'heavy firing at intervals'.[56] The following day was to be a bad one for 1st Brigade CFA.

Alexis Helmer, the young man who had enrolled at Lisgar Collegiate, Ottawa, in 1905, was now a thoroughly pleasant young man of twenty-two and one of the young officers of lst Brigade CFA. Having secured a place at the Royal Military College, Kingston, and encouraged by his father, Director of Musketry of the Canadian Department of Militia and Defence, Alexis had been commissioned as a lieutenant in the Canadian field artillery. At that time, the R.M.C. did not have the status of a university, so he had entered McGill to study for a degree in Civil Engineering and graduated shortly before the outbreak of the war. During his time at McGill, Alexis had been an active member of the university unit of the Canadian Officers Training Corps and had joined the militia artillery. Cyril Allinson described the fair-haired, blue-eyed young man as a born leader with many characteristics similar to John McCrae and it was perhaps not surprising, therefore, that John and Alexis had become good friends.

Sadly, it was not a friendship destined to last long, for on 2 May 1915, John recorded:

> Heavy gunfire again this morning. Lieut[enant]. Helmer was killed (and L[ieutenan]t. Hague severely wounded) at the guns. He was our Mess Sec[retar]y and a very nice boy – grad[uate]. of R.M.C. & McGill. His diary's last words were – 'It has quieted a little and I shall try to get a good sleep!' His girl's picture had a hole right through it – and we buried it with him. I said the Committal service over him, as well as I could from memory. A soldier's death! . . . The French lines are very uneasy, and we are correspondingly anxious. Infantry fire very heavy and we fired incessantly, keeping on into the night. Despite the heavy fire I got asleep at 12 till daylight.[57]

Captain Lawrence Cosgrave remembered Helmer's death:

> Shortly after eight o'clock on the morning of May 2 Lieut[enant]. Helmer was killed. We had just met, the first time in ten days of the battle. A shell fell in front of him and he was instantly killed. I was knocked down. Lieut[enant]. Owen Hague had his leg badly torn and died that night.[58]

Both Alexis Helmer and Owen Hague – another McGill graduate – had been popular in the brigade. When the shelling stopped, two gunners went to dig a grave in the nearby burial ground while others were deputed to collect Helmer's scattered remains. These were placed in sandbags which, in turn, were placed inside an army blanket that was secured with safety pins to resemble a human shape. When the time came for the burial, the chaplains were a mile away ministering to the infantry, so John McCrae performed the service. Among those present at the simple ceremony were Lawrence Cosgrave and a couple of young lieutenants not on duty.

Since the awful afternoon of the first gas attack, John McCrae's calm devotion to duty and presence in the forward area a good deal of the time had been a source of inspiration and reassurance to the officers and men of his unit. As he fought, he felt both pride and grief. His experiences in South Africa fifteen years earlier had in no way prepared him for the ordeal through which the Canadians were now passing in this, their great test. As his mind went back and forth over the terrible sights and tragedies of the past ten days that he had described in his diary, Canada must have seemed as remote as a dream. Here his world consisted of the canal bank with its warren of dug-outs and stunted remains of the once graceful elm trees; the near-suicidal road and its daily tragedies; the sights and sounds of the wounded he cared for at his dressing station; the cheerful, plucky, resilient men at the gun positions; and the small burial ground with its sad crosses where the hot weather had brought into bloom some early poppies. During those awful days of late April and early May 1915, the sights and sounds of spring were a poignant antithesis to the decay, death and destruction that enveloped them. In the midst of a nightmare, this brilliant, charming, steadfast yet whimsical man who had once delighted in the 'light and shadows of a summer sunset, the soft whisper of a breeze through the trees, the gentle waving of the tall river flags, the far-off creak of the lock-gate, the dreamy cawing of a distant rookery'[59] could find a measure of consolation in the reminders of new life, renewal and continuity.

The inevitable and growing conflict between John's instincts as a soldier and his compassion as a doctor must have given him cause to wonder if the loss of young men like Alexis Helmer was a price worth paying. Whatever he felt, it was certain that he believed their deaths must not be in vain.

Opinions differ as to the circumstances of John's composition of his best-known poem during the Second Battle of Ypres. Lawrence Cosgrave had spent much time with him and his account points to the likelihood that Helmer's death acted as a catalyst for John to take up his pen. Cosgrave, a young Toronto businessman, had also been a close friend of Helmer for they had been through the R.M.C. and McGill together. Cosgrave maintained that the burial took place at 11.00 on the morning of Sunday, 2 May 1915,

about 100 yards from the Ypres bridges. Helmer was a very close friend of Col[onel]. McCrae's and the colonel buried him himself, reading aloud the Anglican service from memory; myself and other officers were present. It was during the battle and there was no padre at hand to conduct the service. Col[onel]. McCrae was deeply affected by Lieut[enant]. Helmer's death . . . While watching the grave from the dugout where he sat Col[onel]. McCrae admired the vivid red poppies that were beginning to bloom among the graves, larks were flying over the field singing as they circled about, the wind was blowing quietly and the poppies were blowing in the breeze. It was a sad – but magnificent sight. Col[onel]. McCrae commented on the surroundings out in the battlefield and then went out and wrote 'In Flanders Fields'. He wrote the poem sitting on the back of an ambulance, and he did it to relieve his feelings as he was deeply depressed over Helmer's death. He composed the poem in twenty minutes. He did not decide what he would do with the poem at the time but kept it.[60]

Sergeant-Major Cyril Allinson, on the other hand, indicated that Helmer's funeral took place after sunset and that John, knowing Helmer had been a Methodist and with no padre available, was able to recite, thanks to his phenomenal memory, extracts from the Church of England 'Order of Burial of the Dead', the closest thing he could manage to the Methodist service.

Both John and Lawrence Cosgrave were on duty that night and, after spending the hours of darkness directing the fire of one of the batteries from a nearby command post, John came off duty early next morning. Allinson recorded the events of that early morning of 3 May 1915:

I took the mail first to the fire command post that was dug into the bank near McCrae's, then crossed past the little cemetery to a razed farmhouse where the mess was located.

I saw him sitting on the ambulance step, a pad on his knee. He looked up when I approached, but continued to write. He was my senior officer, second in command of the brigade, and I did not interrupt him. He wrote on for five minutes more, than as I handed him his mail, he handed me his pad.

His face was very tired but calm as he wrote. He looked around from time to time, his eyes straying to Helmer's grave. The poem was almost an exact description of the scene in front of us both.[61]

Allinson liked the poem and tried to memorise it so that he could later write it down. Edward Morrison, John's commanding officer and friend, had no doubts about the circumstances that gave rise to the poem's conception. According to Morrison, it was, 'born out of the fire and blood of the most bitter phase of the Second Battle of Ypres.' Morrison remembered that:

A couple of hundred yards away, there was the headquarters of an infantry regiment and on numerous occasions during the sixteen day battle, we saw how they crept out to bury their dead during lulls in the fighting. So the rows of crosses increased day after day, until in no time at all it had become quite a sizeable cemetery. Just as John described it, it was not uncommon early in the morning to hear the larks singing in the brief silences between the bursts of the shells and the returning salvos of our own nearby guns. I still have a letter from him in which he claimed that he had written the poem 'partly to pass the time between the arrival of two groups of wounded and partly to experiment with different variations of the metre.'[62]

Given the existence of several draft versions of other poems by John, notably his last poem, 'The Anxious Dead', it is possible that he produced a first draft which he then re-wrote. The first draft may have been completed on 2 May and re-worked the following morning, John fashioning a version more to his liking which he showed to Allinson. This poem, written during one of the most bitter early battles of the war, enabled John McCrae to express his sorrow, anguish and desperate concern that the loss of so much life should not be in vain. It spoke not only for Alexis Helmer, Owen Hague and all those of the 1st Brigade Canadian Field Artillery who had already died but, tragically, for the millions who would fall in the following months and years. Its three brief verses captured the mood of the time and gave it a universal appeal that was to make it one of the best known poems of the Great War.

Whatever the circumstances of its creation, John put the poem aside as German aerial reconnaissance continued and attacks steadily built up over the next few days. By 8 May 1915, things were getting critical, as the lst Brigade's CFA's War Diary illustrates:

Firing all day. Several enemy attacks on 12th Bde front. Enemy massing for attack and 1 Battery heavily shelled with several casualties. Heavy shelling all day and ammunition expended last 30 hours 3500 rounds. lst Battery so heavily shelled it is imperative to use it only when intense fire required. Firing so heavy oil in buffers boiling. Springs broken or tired. Packing burnt out. Only 7 guns available.[63]

John's diary entry for that day also emphasised the seriousness of the situation:

The whole front is constantly watered by big gunfire – its racket never ceases. At 7 this morning we were heavily shelled: on our right a half hour's very heavy bombardment, we firing only intermittently. We have now to do most of the work for our left, as the line (ours) appears to be much thinner than it was. Ger[man]. attack followed the shelling at 7, and we were fighting hard till 12, and less regularly all the afternoon. We suffered much, and at one time were down to 7 guns, & of those two were smoking at every joint, and the levers were so hot that the gunners had sacking for their hands. The pace has got much hotter, and the needs of the infantry for fire more insistent. The guns are in bad shape, by reason of dirt, injuries, heat etc . . . E'[venin]g brought a little quiet, but very disquieting news (which afterwards proved untrue), and we had to face a possible retirement. You may imagine our state of mind, unable to get anything sure in the uncertainty except that we would stick out as long as the guns would fire and we could fire them. That sort of night brings a man 'down to his bare skin', I promise you.[64]

Firing continued all the following day, 9 May, along a line from Steenstraat to Hill 60. Five German attacks were repulsed and nearly all phone lines were cut. During the heavy bombardment, John gave shelter to a canine 'refugee':

As I sat in my dug-out a little white & black dog, with some tan spots, during heavy firing bolted in over the parapet & going to the farthest corner began to dig furiously. Having scraped out a pathetic little hole 2" deep, it sat down and shook, looking most plaintively at me. A few minutes later, her owner came along, a Fr[ench]. soldier. 'Bissac' was her name, but she would not leave me at the time. When I sat down a little later, she stole out and shyly crawled in between me and the wall. She stayed by me all day, and I hope got later on to safe quarters.[65]

That evening 1st Brigade CFA was withdrawn from the line. With the exception of one French battery, it had been the most advanced of all the Allied artillery units in the Ypres Salient and had been positioned farther ahead than the French unit for a couple of days during the battle. The continuously changing position of the enemy forces on the left flank had made the task of directing fire very difficult but, in all respects, the Canadian gunners had given their best. Now, however, both men and equipment were exhausted.

John described their withdrawal to Steenwerck on 9 May 1915:

At dusk we got the guns out by hand, and all batteries rendezvoused at a given spot in comparative safety. We were much afraid they w[oul]d. open on us, for at 12 o'clock on they gave us 100 or 150 rounds of field gunfire, hitting the trench parapets again & again. However, we were up the road, the last wagon half a mile away before they opened. One burst near me, and splattered some pieces around, and they got a horse on the last wagon, but we got clear, and by 10 were out of the usual fire zone. Marched all night, tired as could be, but happy to be clear. I was glad to get on dear old Bonfire again, I assure you. We made about 16 miles, and got to our billets at dawn.[66]

The next day, John summarised his overall impressions of the battle in a letter to his mother:

At 8 we got started at clearing out of the 'hell-hole' that we have been in. I have no proper diary of the time, only notes; but I hope to write it day by day. But the general impression in my mind is of a nightmare, and you can gather up the impressions and piece them together. We have been in the most bitter of fights – for 17 days and 17 nights none of us have had our clothes off, nor our boots, even, except occasionally for a change of sox [sic] in a quiet hour of the day. In all that time, while I was awake, gunfire and riflefire never ceased for sixty seconds, and it has been sticking by a weak line all but ready to break, to our utmost, knowing nothing of what was going on, depressed by reports of anxious infantry and in 17 days visited <u>twice</u> by one staff officer, once by another . . . if Col Morrison had not been capable self reliant and a fighter, God knows what would have happened to us. The men & the Division are worthy of all praise that could be given. It has been magnificent.

Our casualties were half the number of men in our firing lines . . . I have done what fell to hand: my clothes, my boots, my kit & my dugout have at various times been sadly bloody; . . . we have had constant heavy accurate shell fire but we have given back no less. And behind it all, the constant background of the sights of the dead, the wounded, the maimed – and a terrible anxiety that the line should not give way . . . But how tired we are! Weary in body & wearier in mind.[67]

For the next few days Morrison's men took a well-earned rest. Ironically, news of the gunners' participation in the battle did not reach the people of Canada, who were told that the Canadian artillery was in reserve throughout the battle. In fact, the men of 1st Brigade CFA had, as John put it, seen 'the show from the soup to the coffee'.[68] Their commanding officer had nothing but praise for his men who had been,

as cool as veterans – a great deal cooler than many veterans I have seen . . . We have been firing about one hundred and fifty rounds per gun per day, supporting French attacks on the ridge, subjected day and night to a gruelling bombardment from 17-inch, 12-inch and 6-inch shells. Of the men actually engaged with the guns, I have lost over fifty killed and wounded . . . My men are standing the gaff splendidly. Whatever may happen I think Canada can depend we will finish in style.[69]

On 13 May 1915, Lieutenant-General Alderson visited the brigade, complimented them on their part in the battle and read out messages of congratulations from King George V, the Governor General of Canada, Canadian Prime Minister Robert Borden and Generals Sir John French and Sir Horace Smith-Dorrien.

As Canon Scott watched the great pall of smoke hanging over Ypres burning furiously in its death throes, he looked back on the battle that had been fought to hold the ancient town. Until that battle, the Canadians had seen themselves merely as troops expected to hold the line and do useful spade work. Nobody had ever questioned their bravery, willingness or ingenuity, but they had not been put to the test. Now, after 'Second Wipers', they knew they could meet any task put to them.

To their eternal glory, the Canadians had shown extraordinary courage in the face of an enemy not only immensely superior in infantry and artillery but willing to use the appalling weapon of poison gas. For the Canadian soldier, Ypres had been a fearful baptism of fire. For the Canadian public, it was an immense shock to realise that, of a division of twenty thousand men, more than six thousand had been killed, wounded or posted missing. In the weeks that followed, as flags were flown at half-mast and memorial services held throughout Canada, the young Dominion understood for the first time the true nature of this awful new war. Like all first experiences, it left an indelible impression. Along with mixed feelings of pride and sorrow came a determination to carry on to the end. The losses had been great, but in the words of Canada's official historian,

> Against these losses must be set the immense gain in stature which their achievement had brought the Canadians. Henceforth their morale would be high, for they had proved themselves more than a match for the enemy and not less than the equal of their Allied comrades in arms. In their first major operation of the war Canadian soldiers had acquired an indomitable confidence which was to carry them irresistibly forward to the battles which lay ahead.[70]

At a memorial service held for the Canadians at St Paul's Cathedral on 2 May 1915, the Bishop of London, Dr Arthur Winnington Ingram, gave an address. The Bishop had visited Canada twice and during a recent visit to the Western Front shortly before the Second Battle of Ypres, had praised a gathering of ten thousand Canadian troops for their loyalty, enthusiasm and self-sacrifice. Now he made a moving tribute to the fallen of the lst Canadian Division:

> It was on that tremendous day when French and British had been overpowered by poison gas that the manhood of Canada shone out like pure gold. The example of these men will never die, but will remain as a perpetual inspiration to their successors.[71]

From the battle had also come a poem that was to have an effect its writer could not possibly have dreamed of in those grim days of early May 1915. John McCrae decided to call it 'In Flanders Fields'.

In Flanders Fields

In Flanders fields the poppies blow
Between the crosses, row on row,
That mark our place; and in the sky
The larks, still bravely singing, fly
Scarce heard amid the guns below.

We are the Dead. Short days ago
We lived, felt dawn, saw sunset glow,
Loved and were loved, and now we lie,
In Flanders fields.

Take up our quarrel with the foe:
To you from failing hands we throw
The torch; be yours to hold it high.
If ye break faith with us who die
We shall not sleep, though poppies grow
In Flanders fields.[72]

NOTES

1. 'The Unconquered Dead' by John McCrae, *The McGill University Magazine*, (Volume 5, No. 1, December 1905), p. 97. Micro mfm/AP/U577, UTL.
2. Currie, *The Red Watch*, p. 119.
3. Nicholson, *Canadian Expeditionary Force*, pp. 55–56.
4. JM to Janet McCrae, 8 April 1915, GM Papers.
5. JM to Janet McCrae, 13 April 1915, GM Papers.
6. JM to Janet McCrae, 20 April 1915, GM Papers.
7. 'Report on Condition of Trenches' by Officer Commanding, 2nd Field Company, Canadian Engineers, 21 April 1915, quoted in Nicholson, *Canadian Expeditionary Force*, p. 57.
8. Nicholson, *Canadian Expeditionary Force*, pp. 56–57.
9. Nicholson, *Canadian Expeditionary Force*, p. 58.
10. Nicholson, *Canadian Expeditionary Force*, pp. 59–62.
11. Account of divisional commander reproduced in British Official History, Vol. I, pp. 188–190, quoted in Nicholson, *Canadian Expeditionary Force*, p. 61.
12. Tonie and Valmai Holt, *Major & Mrs Holt's Battlefield Guide to the Ypres Salient* (London, 1995), p. 29.
13. Rose Coombs, *Before Endeavours Fade* (London, 1994), p. 11.
14. Holt, *Battlefield Guide to the Ypres Salient*, p. 28.
15. William Boyd, *With a Field Ambulance at Ypres* (Toronto, 1916), p. 55.
16. Scott, *The Great War as I Saw It*, p. 55.

17. Basil Liddell Hart, *History of the First World War* (London, 1977), p. 243.
18. 3rd Canadian Infantry Brigade Message 739, 22 April 1915, quoted in Nicholson, *Canadian Expeditionary Force*, p. 62.
19. *Personal Protection Against Gas* (London, 1938), p. 9.
20. William Moore, 'Falkenhayn's Green Genie', *Military History*, June 1984, p. 274.
21. Nicholson, *Canadian Expeditionary Force*, pp. 63–64.
22. Nasmith, *On the Fringe of the Great Fight*, p. 93.
23. Nasmith, *On the Fringe of the Great Fight*, p. 95.
24. Daniel J. Dancocks, *Welcome to Flanders Fields. The First Canadian Battle of the Great War: Ypres, 1915* (Toronto, 1988), p. 115.
25. Boyd, *With a Field Ambulance*, pp. 57–58.
26. Scott, *The Great War as I Saw It*, p. 62.
27. Scott, *The Great War as I Saw It*, p. 67.
28. From 'To Canada' by R.E. Vernède, *War Poems and other Verses* (London, 1917), pp. 49–50.
29. Lyn Macdonald, *1915: The Death of Innocence* (London, 1993), p. 201.
30. Currie, *The Red Watch*, p. 237.
31. JM Diary of the Second Battle of Ypres, Friday 23 April 1915, GM Papers.
32. JM Diary of the Second Battle of Ypres, Friday 23 April 1915, GM Papers.
33. JM Diary of the Second Battle of Ypres, Friday 23 April 1915, GM Papers.
34. Moore, 'Falkenhayn's Green Genie', p. 274.
35. JM Diary of the Second Battle of Ypres, Saturday 24 April 1915, GM Papers.
36. JM Diary of the Second Battle of Ypres, Friday 23 April 1915, GM Papers.
37. JM Diary of the Second Battle of Ypres, Saturday 24 April 1915, GM Papers.
38. JM Diary of the Second Battle of Ypres, Saturday 24 April 1915, GM Papers.
39. Nicholson, *Canadian Expeditionary Force*, pp. 67–70.
40. A Field Ambulance was a medical unit with 241 all ranks. Three were allotted to each British or Canadian infantry division and each was made up of three sections, capable of acting independently when required. A section contained medical officers, stretcher bearers, nursing orderlies, clerks, cook etc. with separate equipment, horse and motor transport. Each Field Ambulance generally marched with its own brigade, whose sick and wounded it was responsible for collecting and treating.
41. J.G. Adami, *The War Story of the C.A.M.C.*, pp. 118–119.
42. JM Diary of the Second Battle of Ypres, Saturday 24 April 1915, GM Papers.
43. JM Diary of the Second Battle of Ypres, Saturday 24 April 1915, GM Papers.
44. JM Diary of the Second Battle of Ypres, Sunday 25 April 1915, GM Papers.
45. JM Diary of the Second Battle of Ypres, Sunday 25 April 1915, GM Papers.
46. JM Diary of the Second Battle of Ypres, Sunday 25 April 1915, GM Papers.
47. JM Diary of the Second Battle of Ypres, Monday 26 April 1915, GM Papers.
48. JM Diary of the Second Battle of Ypres, Monday 26 April 1915, GM Papers.

49. JM Diary of the Second Battle of Ypres, Tuesday 27 April 1915, GM Papers.
50. JM Diary of the Second Battle of Ypres, Wednesday 28 April 1915, GM Papers.
51. JM Diary of the Second Battle of Ypres, Thursday 29 April 1915, GM Papers.
52. Currie, *The Red Watch*, p. 279.
53. Currie, *The Red Watch*, p. 279.
54. JM Diary of the Second Battle of Ypres, Friday 30 April 1915, GM Papers.
55. Boyd, *With a Field Ambulance*, pp. 69–70.
56. JM Diary of the Second Battle of Ypres, Saturday 1 May 1915, GM Papers.
57. JM Diary of the Second Battle of Ypres, Sunday 2 May 1915, GM Papers.
58. Lawrence Cosgrave, 'M'Crae Wrote Classic In Twenty Minutes', *Toronto Star*, 14 May 1919.
59. John McCrae, 'My Day Dreams', *Saturday Night* (Volume 6, No. 16, 11 March 1893), p. 9. Micro mfm AP/588, UTL.
60. Cosgrave, 'M'Crae Wrote Classic in Twenty Minutes'.
61. Cyril Allinson, as quoted in Mathieson, *My Grandfather's War*, p. 264.
62. Note on the writing of 'In Flanders Fields' by E.W.B. Morrison. Papers of Edward W. B. Morrison, MG 30, E81, Vol. 10, NAC.
63. War Diary, 1st Brigade, CFA, 8 May 1915, RG 9, III, D-3, vol. 4964, NAC.
64. JM Diary of the Second Battle of Ypres, Saturday 8 May 1915, GM Papers.
65. JM Diary of the Second Battle of Ypres, Sunday 9 May 1915, GM Papers.
66. JM Diary of the Second Battle of Ypres, Sunday 9 May 1915, GM Papers.
67. JM to Janet McCrae, 10 May 1915, GM Papers.
68. JM to Janet McCrae, 12 May 1915, GM Papers.
69. Report by Edward Morrison, *Hamilton Herald*, 20 May 1915. Papers of E.W.B. Morrison, MG 30, E81, NAC.
70. Nicholson, *Canadian Expeditionary Force*, p. 92.
71. Dr Arthur Winnington Ingram, as quoted in Nasmith, *On the Fringe of the Great Fight*, p. 190.
72. First published in *Punch* magazine, 8 December 1915.

CHAPTER THIRTEEN

'The hand we gave the weary and the weak'[1]
June 1915–December 1916

The day before 1st Brigade CFA was withdrawn from the front line, the world learned of the sinking of the liner *Lusitania*, pride of the Cunard Line, off the Irish coast. American newspapers had carried a black-bordered warning from the Imperial German Embassy in Washington that the war zone included waters adjacent to the British Isles where vessels flying the British flag would be liable to destruction. The *Lusitania*, bound for Liverpool with its name covered over and its funnels painted black, was flying no flag and nearly twelve hundred civilian lives were lost. The shocking news led to a wave of anti-German sentiment throughout the world, particularly in the United States.

On 14 May 1915, John's brigade, strengthened with reinforcements and equipped with new guns, moved south to Festubert. Here they joined what was left of 1st Canadian Division to participate in an Allied offensive already under way. The fighting followed the pattern of frontal assaults against the enemy's powerful defences and, with inadequate artillery support, the attacking French and British troops were decimated by machine gun fire. The Canadians achieved their objectives but again the cost in human terms was extremely high and many of them would never again see the lilac and early roses blooming here and there in the ruined gardens behind the lines. The intensity of the shelling was very apparent from John McCrae's last letter to his mother from Festubert: 'They shelled us for 1hr 50 minutes, and we estimate that they put in 230 rounds within 200 yards of us – all 4 or 5 inch shells.'[2] The battlefield was,

> strewn with bits of clothing, pouches, equipment, broken rifles – and here and there an unburied body with black swollen face, and the flies buzzing around. The whole ground is seamed in all directions by trenches and scattered defences, wire, sandbags & dugouts in bewildering disorder.[3]

When men were wounded, they moved along a chain of treatment and clearing stations to a base hospital. During Second Ypres and Festubert, the personnel of the Canadian Army Medical Corps had shown the highest degree of courage and devotion to duty. The official record of the CAMC emphasised that its system was one which had previously been untried in actual warfare. Ypres had demonstrated that the medical service had been developed along the right lines and that the system evolved over the previous decade in peace time could and did take the strain of wartime conditions.

The previous autumn, Dr Herbert Birkett, Dean of the Faculty of Medicine at McGill, had put forward the idea of a hospital to be staffed by doctors and medical students from the university. Birkett had served for many years in militia units of the CAMC and been appointed Assistant Director of Medical Services at Valcartier, where he had discussed his idea for a McGill unit with John McCrae.[4] With Sir William Osler's help, the proposal was forwarded to London and accepted. Like the British Army General Hospitals, the McGill unit was to consist of 1040 beds and its personnel to be drawn from the McGill medical teaching staff and students, with nurses from the Royal Victoria and Montreal General hospitals. Many Canadian nurses came from moderately wealthy families and tended to be very independent, resourceful and versatile but used to strict discipline. These young women were eager to do their bit in the war and had before them the example of one of their profession whose experience in South Africa had carried her a long way in the intervening years. Nursing Sister Margaret Macdonald, who had sent John McCrae books and other comforts on his long vigil guarding the railway lines in 1900, was now Matron-in-Chief of the Canadian Nursing Service.

The new medical unit, officially designated No. 3 Canadian General Hospital (McGill), was mobilised on 4 March 1915 with Birkett as commanding officer and Lieutenant-Colonel John M. Elder, whom John McCrae had known since his first days in Montreal, as Officer in Charge of Surgery. There was also a slot for Major, soon to be Lieutenant-Colonel, John McCrae as Officer in Charge of Medicine. The hospital staff sailed from Montreal on the S.S. *Metagama* on 6 May 1915, and while at sea learned of the terrible news of the *Lusitania* disaster. It transpired that Lady Allan of Montreal and her three daughters had been among the passengers and two of the girls were missing. The atmosphere aboard the *Metagama* was therefore somewhat tense as the ship drew nearer to the British Isles. One of the doctors with the unit was John's friend, Edward Archibald, who recorded that about three hundred miles from Ireland, the ship was instructed to go south and meet up with an escort off the coast of France 'about the level of Brest.'[5] On a dark night with no moon, and guarded by a destroyer on either side, it moved quietly in a north easterly direction to its final destination of Plymouth.

On 29 May 1915 John McCrae received preliminary orders directing him to leave 1st Brigade CFA and report to London prior to joining the McGill unit on its arrival in England. With the new post came his promotion, backdated to 4 April 1915. His expertise as a doctor was so highly valued that the McGill unit would not have been complete without him. John was only too well aware of the gravity of the military situation and, although orders had to be obeyed, he did not want to leave the comrades with whom he had shared the ordeal of Second Ypres – men like Lawrence Cosgrave, who had been blown into the air by a shell and escaped with only a sprained wrist; William Dodds, who had shown his customary cool-headedness throughout; and his old friend Edward Morrison, who had proved such a first-rate commanding officer. He also thought of the courageous and devoted Francis Scrimger, whom he had seen at Festubert. John spent his last night with the brigade sleeping in a covered wagon, his replacement having already commandeered his quarters. When he departed on 2 June 1915 he was, according to Cyril Allinson, both sorry and angry. 'He was all man,' Allinson later wrote, 'and a man who could curse when he was angry. He told me "all the goddam doctors in the world will not win this bloody war; what we need is more and more fighting men."'6

Leaving 'Bonfire' in the care of his groom, John proceeded to London. To him it was a familiar and well-loved city, but for some of the recently-arrived McGill unit, London, albeit wartime London, was a new and thrilling experience. Sister Sophie Hoerner, the former matron of a hospital at Saranac Lake in New York State, was delighted to be able to lunch 'at Lyons'7, to marvel at the National Gallery, to attend a service in St Paul's Cathedral and to sample the West End theatre. The unit had been split while awaiting orders to depart for France and some of the nurses, Hoerner included, were being sent ahead to work temporarily with other medical units. As she spent her last hours in Britain's capital, she knew that all too soon she would be entering the darker reality of the war.

Among the unit's officers posted temporarily to the Queen's Canadian Military Hospital at Shorncliffe, Kent, was Edward Archibald. He had time to explore the area and the nearby coastal towns from where, on a clear day, he could see the French coast. At Folkestone, a road led down a harbour that was constantly busy. In the peaceful pre-war days civilians had strolled up this road to reach 'The Leas', a pleasant clifftop walk adjacent to some of the town's fashionable hotels. Now it echoed to the sound of boots. In later years, that short stretch of road would be re-named 'The Road of Remembrance' in honour of the hundreds of thousands of men who passed along it on a one-way journey to the Western Front. A few miles farther along the coast was the town of Dover and it, too, handled a lot of marine traffic. Here, Archibald saw 'hydroplanes, and destroyers, and minesweepers'8 and three hospital ships that were transferring wounded to a London-bound hospital train. The joy on the faces of the wounded was evident, and Archibald was comforted 'to find them so well looked after'.9

Not unnaturally John McCrae felt relieved to be away from the horror of the front but, at the same time, he felt ashamed to admit that relief, confessing to his mother that 'it doesn't seem fair to the rest'.[10] The Oslers had invited him to Oxford, and here he found the customary atmosphere of warmth that never once diminished throughout those difficult years. Sir William had also invited Edward Archibald, who was greatly pleased to see John looking fit and seemingly, 'just as jolly as ever'.[11] Lady Osler, however, saw the signs of strain beneath the bright exterior:

> Sunday afternoon Jack McCrae came – I am *glad* and *sorry* you did not hear him. He looked thin and worn, but was intensely interesting; 31 days in the trenches with eight days' rest . . . His clothes were awful. I have sent everything to the cleaner's. He says the British hatred for the Germans increases daily since the *Lusitania* . . . He feels that the Allies will win but nothing can be ended except by absolute exhaustion. The nerve strain he says is beyond any sensation possible to describe . . . they were at it day and night, saving the situation as we know. Really I felt sick when he left Monday night.[12]

Finally able to relax after the nightmare of the front, the effects of John's ordeal had begun to catch up with him. After Sir William had left for his customary Monday visit to the Duchess of Connaught's Canadian Red Cross Hospital at Taplow, John spent a welcome day soaking up the peace of the Oslers' lovely garden. There was still much to do before joining the McGill unit: clothes to order from his tailor; friends like Earl Grey and George Adami to see; and social engagements that included a day in the Surrey countryside and a visit to Brighton. Here, John found that 'a good hotel served to help the undeniable monotony of a coast town. The beach is utterly stony and the bathing far behind Atlantic City'. He also observed that the 'people seem to spend their time mainly in being afraid of Zeppelins'.[13]

The majority of the McGill unit sailed from Southampton for France on 17 June. Their ship left by night without lights, steered carefully through a minefield by an Admiralty pilot. There was no smoking allowed on deck and not a voice was raised above a subdued normal level. With everyone together for the first time since Montreal, John saw old friends and colleagues like Campbell Howard, Lawrence Rhea, Bill Francis and Bill Turner. Among the party was Sir William Osler's son, Revere, who was to be the unit's assistant quartermaster. On arrival at Boulogne, everyone proceeded to their new location at Dannes-Camiers on the north French coast. It was a peaceful area of pine forests, small villages and deserted dunes covered in marram grass and sea rocket. The hospital, according to Edward Archibald, was 'situated on a plain which runs down into the sand dunes lining the shore, about 1 to 2 miles away . . . On the other side are low hills, perhaps 400 feet high, on the slopes of which is pasture land & some ploughed fields . . . there is usually a decent breeze which helps to keep flies away.'[14]

The main accommodation took the form of large, colourful tents: marquees for the patients and bell tents for the medical personnel of all ranks that had been given to the War Office by an Indian prince. While these and telephone lines were being erected, drainage laid and roads dug and levelled, the doctors were able to enjoy the chance to walk, swim and play tennis on the court of a deserted beachside hotel two miles away. John was delighted to be reunited with 'Bonfire' who had been transported from Festubert to his new quarters and could now enjoy fields of clover and lanes fragrant with wild honeysuckle. For Sister Sophie Hoerner, the countryside already offered a much-needed escape; it was so peaceful that she could hear 'no noise but the birds and rabbits running every which way'.[15] On her solitary evening walks over the dunes, the moods of the sea and ever-changing sky were a balm to her troubled mind as she tried to come to terms with the suffering she had begun to see, and the wounds 'so dreadful that one's most vivid imagination couldn't even faintly picture them'.[16]

In the last week of July 1915, John, Edward Archibald and another colleague, Dr Donald Hingsten, took the train to Paris from the nearby fishing village of Etaples. They were intending to visit several hospitals, not only to see the medical and surgical work being undertaken, but to find out how practical problems such as the establishment of a water purification plant, pits for sewage, electric light generators and heating could best be handled. Paris, although lovely as ever, was quiet. All the art galleries were closed and the boulevards, squares and embankments of the city's famous river seemed strangely subdued after the vibrant pre-war atmosphere.

The three doctors walked along a deserted Avenue des Champs Elysées, and in deference to Hingsten who was a Roman Catholic, attended Mass at the Madeleine. At the American Ambulance, a hospital at Neuilly, they heard first-hand reports about the great surgical work being done by their friend Dr Harvey Cushing, who had spent five weeks working there in the spring. One of the nursing sisters who met John at Neuilly apparently did not recognise him at first. Although she had known him for a number of years he seemed to have aged considerably, and looked worn and tired.[17] A visit to another French military hospital and a car ride through the Bois de Boulogne was followed by tea at Rumpelmayer's, the great 'confiserie'[18] on the Rue de Rivoli. Edward Archibald described this as being 'full of ladies and pseudo-ladies' and reported to his wife that he had tasted 'the most exquisite chocolate I ever drank, and simply wonderful cakes, of new and strange species'.[19]

By the time they returned, the hospital was just a week away from opening. The staff carried out final rehearsals in preparation for handling incoming convoys of sick and wounded and, on 8 August 1915, No. 3 Canadian General Hospital (McGill) opened its doors. One man in the first convoy who never forgot his reception was a certain Private MacMutchkin. He later recorded that, as he 'was helped out of the ambulance, the Colonel took my hand, then three lieutenant-colonels took my pulse, four majors hurried to take my temperature, and some blighter took my watch'.[20] The unit was required to keep and treat any patient who could be cured in a period of three weeks; to guard against complications and do everything possible to save the lives of the wounded or seriously ill; and to send to England all who could not get well in three weeks but were fit to travel on stretchers. Those who recovered within the given period convalesced as helpers in local camps.

As fighting continued in the Ypres Salient, the hospital witnessed the effects of a terrible new weapon – the flamethrower. Not only was 1915 producing numbers of casualties beyond anything previous envisaged, but it also seemed to mark the end of the last vestiges of any kind of chivalry. Distinguished visitors began to arrive at No. 3. Sam Hughes toured it accompanied by Sir Max Aitken, later to become Lord Beaverbrook, and on 4 September, Lieutenant-Colonel George Adami came from London where he was working on the staff of the Director of Medical Services, Canadians. His vivid impressions of the base hospitals, casualty clearing stations and field ambulances he visited were to be incorporated into a book, *The War Story of the C.A.M.C.* At No. 3's Pathology laboratory, Adami was especially interested in the work of Major Lawrence Rhea, whose compassion and dedication were unceasing. No sooner had George Adami left than Sir William Osler arrived, happy beyond words to see his son and so many old friends and former students. Having been shown all aspects of the hospital's work, Osler was impressed with what he found. A problem that continued to tax all the great medical minds of the day was the effective treatment of wounds. Unfortunately salvarsan was proving disappointing against the wounded soldier's greatest enemy, streptococcus, and its discoverer, Paul Ehrlich, had been killed in that summer's fighting. The search for an answer would continue throughout the war.

Before Sir William returned to England, John McCrae accompanied him on a tour of some front-line areas. They went north east to Merville, then to Armentières and the Canadian headquarters at Nieppe. A visit to a dressing station and mobile laboratory gave Osler his first taste of life in a war zone and he was struck by what Lord Northcliffe, who visited the front the following year, described as 'the immensity of it all'.[21] Before him were stationary balloons, aeroplanes, camps, artillery on the march, mile after mile of motor lorries and a countryside alive with troops. Preparations were under way for another British offensive, this time at Loos. It was a battle in which the British first used gas against the Germans, much of which blew back over their own lines, and casualties soon began arriving at No. 3. Rudyard Kipling received news that his only son, John, was missing, reported wounded in the fighting. Kipling had visited the front earlier that year and recognised among the Canadian troops some of the soldiers he had last seen as students at McGill in 1907. Now his only thought was of his son, whom he had last seen little over a month earlier.

With the onset of the autumn of 1915 came equinoctial gales so violent that the rain burst through No. 3's canvas tents and soaked the beds. On several occasions, the marquees and tents were flattened and had to be re-erected in high winds. On-duty nurses dressed against the elements, as Sophie Hoerner described: 'I have on my rubberboots, my skirts pinned up to my knees, three sweaters on and rain-coat and hat'[22] For her, however, any personal discomfort paled into insignificance compared with her patients. She admitted to a friend that, 'I'll never forget them as long as I live . . . I can never see anything worse and hope I'll never have to.'[23] Edward Archibald, through whose skill many of them were saved or helped, shared her admiration for their bravery: 'When I see these men, cheerful still, or at least uncomplaining, and never a word of fear or of bitterness, or of cant, out of them, facing death and enduring death bravely, and above all quietly, I come near to tears, and count myself as nought.'[24]

Archibald cared not only for his patients but also for his dedicated surgical colleagues who operated long hours in difficult conditions and the hard-working Lawrence Rhea who was much loved and respected by everyone. Then there was his old friend, John McCrae, who was showing definite after-effects from the Second Battle of Ypres and whom he described as 'far from being his old self yet'. Archibald noticed that John was finding it difficult to concentrate, had no energy and was often irritable and argumentative.[25] His former easy manner and joviality had given way to a grim, strict military bearing and he had little time for anyone who did not feel his intense commitment to the war.

Although officers were housed in wooden huts, John felt very strongly that sacrifices must be made and insisted on sleeping in a tent like the men nearer the front. He had confessed in a letter to his friend Oskar Klotz in Pittsburgh that Second Ypres had been 'a corker',[26] a masterpiece of understatement, and that 'I saw enough fighting to do me for my natural life.'[27] John's heart was clearly still with his gunner comrades and his sense of duty was too strong for him to allow himself even a little time for the lighter side of life. With some encouragement, however, he could be persuaded to sample the occasional luxury of a meal expertly cooked by a local chef, or a trip by electric tram to a small, pleasant resort just along the coast. Edward Archibald described it in a letter to his eldest daughter, Margaret, as a place, 'for us all to come for the summer some year . . . There is a lovely beach of hard sand – beautiful to make forts and castles with; and there is a nice golf-course near; and there are lovely drives in the country round about. It is called Wimereux.'[28]

As John tended the sick and injured, the war lay heavily upon him. All around him he saw the sad sight of wounded young men who had done their duty with stoicism, courage and even heroism. When he felt grief over friends and colleagues like young Alexis Helmer, dead before their time, he may well also have felt the sense of guilt experienced by many a survivor of combat. But John McCrae's attitude to their passing was much more than that of a trained doctor. In his characteristic search for perfection, he had continued to work on his poem, 'In Flanders Fields', since the first drafts hastily scribbled the previous May under German shellfire. With encouragement from his commanding officer, Colonel Herbert Birkett, who was familiar with John's poems published in *The University Magazine*, the poem had been sent to *The Spectator* magazine for possible publication but had been rejected, causing John to comment that 'the babe hath returned unto its mother's arms'.[29] Francis Scrimger had apparently urged him to submit it to *Punch* magazine and being a man of 'unflinching honesty and modesty', it was thought unlikely that Scrimger would have let such a story stand unless it were true.[30] Lieutenant-Colonel John Elder remembered sitting beside John while he re-worked the poem in the autumn of 1915.[31] 'In Flanders Fields' eventually found its way to the editor of *Punch* magazine in the briefcase of a prominent journalist returning to London after a visit to the hospital.

As the autumn storms continued, life under canvas at No. 3 became very unpleasant. Mud oozed through the floors of the draughty tents and rain seeped inside, reducing the warmth provided by smoking, stinking braziers. Such were conditions in general at the time, however, that there were few complaints from anyone. John had foreseen the problem for, as he explained in his letter to Oskar Klotz, 'the coast is very open to wind and rain storms with fogs in the interval. Apart from these facts, it will be like the Riviera'.[32] When it became clear that the hospital could no longer operate effectively, a decision was made to close it and seek new and more substantial premises. The senior officers set about locating alternative accommodation and before long a suitable site had been identified. It was an old Jesuit college damaged by fire in 1907 and never rebuilt, located north of Boulogne on the coast road to Calais. To the two remaining wings had been added some wooden huts, for it had been occupied for short periods since the start of the war by a British hospital and the Indian 'Meerut' hospital. It was now vacant and the Canadians decided that with improvements, it could be made to function without too much difficulty.

During the last weeks of 1915 work on the site proceeded and the layout of the new hospital gradually took shape. Christmas was approaching and in the continuing bad weather, John sent seasonal greetings to his sister, Geills, in Manitoba: 'Here we say "a muddy Christmas and a Sloppy New Year" but it may not be so bad as all that.'[33] Four days later, the 8 December 1915 issue of *Punch* printed 'In Flanders Fields' anonymously.

According to Cyril Allinson, *Punch*'s editor, Bernard Partridge, had been delighted with the poem, asking only that he be allowed to make one small amendment. Allinson conjectured whether this might have been in the first line of the third stanza, substituting 'Take up' for the words 'Yours now', which he says were in the original version.[34] A postwar newspaper article claims the change Partridge wanted to make was the substitution of the word 'blow' for 'grow' in the poem's opening line.[35] This was indeed the version Partridge decided to print but it was not the only version in existence. A few months later, John sent a handwritten copy of the poem to American friends in which the word 'grow' appears. The existence of the two variants was to cause considerable speculation as to which version was the original. Later again, John seemed to return to the use of the word 'blow' when he sent a manuscript of the poem to Edward Morrison and it is this version of the text that has been most commonly cited.

The 2nd Canadian Division had by now crossed to France and with it had come John's McCrae's good friend, Major Andrew Macphail. Macphail was second-in-command of 6th Field Ambulance, and his brother James happened to be in command of 6th Field Company, Canadian Engineers. The division had been posted to the notorious Ypres Salient with 6th Field Ambulance occupying a convent at the foot of Kemmel Hill. One day James Macphail came over from his billet to visit his brother with a copy of *Punch* he had picked up on leave in London. Andrew Macphail read the anonymous poem and, as the man who had published so much of John McCrae's work, immediately recognised the style. 'The piece bore no signature,' he later recalled, 'but it was unmistakably from the hand of John McCrae' as 'it was a form' John had 'made his own' and was identical to that used in John's last pre-war poem, 'The Night Cometh.'[36]

The poem gained immediate popularity. In the Salient that December 1915, a company of Canadian infantry marching to the front one night met an oncoming vehicle. From it stepped Canon Scott, who gathered the men around him and read them 'In Flanders Fields'. Although nobody knew who had written the poem, one soldier who remembered the incident said that none of them ever forgot it. In just fifteen lines, John McCrae had captured the prevailing mood at the front which, as Andrew Macphail wrote, 'at the time was universal, and will remain as a permanent record when the mood is passed away'.[37] Before long, 'In Flanders Fields' would become one of the war's best-known poems, 'its images becoming an eternal motif, part of the collective memory of the war'.[38]

After a Christmas dinner with turkey, ham, champagne, crackers, and 'a gorgeous plum pudding, flaming high',[39] work on the new hospital premises was completed. As the move began, Sister Sophie Hoerner took a last look at the dunes of Dannes-Camiers and 'walked for miles along the beach in the pouring rain . . . It was really beautiful, the high sea and the wind . . . I didn't meet a soul but saw sentries on the sand dunes looking very picturesque in their lovely blues.'[40]

No. 3 Canadian General Hospital resumed operation on 28 January 1916, watched over by the figure of Napoleon Bonaparte astride La Colonne de la Grande Armée, a local monument to his legions of the previous century. A main road led incoming ambulances to the unloading point and from there, the wounded were taken to the wards, mostly housed in wooden huts. The Canadian Red Cross Society had erected a recreation hut that made such a good ward that it was later taken over by the Surgical Department. The spacious Operating Theatre had been converted from a former cowshed and other buildings now served as offices and a Pathology Laboratory. Across a field that proved to be an excellent site for growing potatoes, cabbages, peas and beans, was 'The Doll's House,' a small house that served as the Officers' Mess and contained comfortable armchairs, books and a billiard table. The nurses had their own Sitting Room and in time a hospital tennis court was constructed. Paths led through the surrounding woods and provided pleasant walks for staff and patients alike.

In terms of expertise, the hospital medical and surgical teams bristled with men who were experts in their fields. Their ability was tested to the full in coping with wounds, complications from exposure to chlorine and mustard gas and conditions resulting from exposure and the squalid living conditions of the average soldier – bronchitis, rheumatic fever, pneumonia, trench foot, nephritis, infections, fevers and enteric diseases. Many patients arriving from the front were also suffering from symptoms of nervous disorder.

The need to find solutions to the many problems confronting military doctors was leading to advances in all areas of the profession. In the field of bacteriology, one of the great experts was working in nearby Boulogne. Sir Almroth Wright's distinguished career had led him to the position he had held before the war, that of Professor of Bacteriology at St Mary's Hospital, Paddington. A friend of Sir William Osler, he had spent much of his time searching for a means of immunising against typhoid. The doctors in Wright's team at St Mary's were men of superlative quality and under his influence, the hospital had become well known for its work on vaccine therapy. The famous tea parties held in St Mary's library had been attended not only by eminent researchers like Robert Koch[41] and Wright's great friend, Paul Ehrlich, but also by politicians and playwrights such as George Bernard Shaw, who used Wright for the model of Sir Colenso Ridgeon in his play, 'The Doctor's Dilemma'.

At the beginning of the war, Wright had been commissioned in the Royal Army Medical Corps and sent to France to research wound infections at a laboratory set up in Boulogne's elegant Casino building. It was clear that antiseptics were having no beneficial effect and some were actually making infections worse. Wright brought with him his team from St Mary's. One of his assistants was a certain 'short, pale officer who never said more than he had to but always carried on calmly and efficiently with his work'.[42] This was Lieutenant Alexander Fleming, who, without knowing it at the time, was destined to be instrumental in saving human lives and preventing suffering on a massive scale, but not in this war. Fleming had begun working for Wright in 1906 while studying for his medical degree and, from the outset, he had shared his professor's passionate faith in medicine.

John McCrae and his colleagues soon got to know the team at the Boulogne laboratory, which was attached to No. 13 British General Hospital. Not only did the researchers see the lines of ambulances arriving at the nearby Princess Hotel – disembarkation point for the hospital ships – but they had to make their way daily through the wards of No. 13 to get to their laboratory. What they saw affected them deeply. The terrible wound infections, in Wright's words, 'could – if we had the knowledge – be cured'.[43] Medical science had established bacteria as the prime source of human infection and research laboratories were searching for the substance that would destroy bacteria without harming body cells. Fleming wrote, 'Surrounded by all those infected wounds, by men who were suffering and dying without our being able to do anything to help them, I was consumed by a desire to discover . . . something which would kill those germs, something like salvarsan.'[44]

Another eminent doctor working in the vicinity was Sir Bertrand Dawson, physician to Edward VII and now to George V. Sir Bertrand was based at No. 14 General Hospital for Officers, housed in the building of the Hotel Splendide on Wimereux's seafront. With his affinity for animals, John McCrae had already become fond of Sir Bertrand's spaniel,'Sue', and seemed to have found favour with her. He wrote to Geills that 'Yesterday, Sir B[ertrand]. said to me "She has brought you a present" and here she was waiting earnestly for me to remove from her mouth a small stone.'[45] John had also acquired a canine friend of his own called 'Bonneau', 'un épagneul Breton'[46] as he was known in French, belonging to the hospital caretakers, Monsieur and Madame Debacker, and their ten-year old daughter, Yvonne. The gentle-natured 'Bonneau' seems to have adopted both John McCrae and 'Bonfire' as his trusted friends. John told his mother that 'Bonneau sticks these days like a burr: he sits with his muzzle on my knees: his eyes are the most beautiful brown and a trifle sad.'[47]

Although warmer weather in March 1916 encouraged the appearance of crocuses in the hospital flowerbeds, the warmth was short lived. A return to snow and cold weather led to discomfort and chilblains for those, like John, who were still sleeping under canvas. The early months of the year had brought visits from old friends and the opportunity to hear a talk given by the missionary, Wilfred Grenfell, who was visiting the base hospitals. Some of the staff of No. 3 were transferred to new postings including young Revere Osler who, keen to see action, crossed the Channel to join the Royal Artillery. By now, Britain had become an island arsenal whose factories were churning out the munitions of war that would be needed for a planned offensive in the summer involving thousands of young British volunteers. Meanwhile, the Canadians had been in a major action again at the battle of the St Eloi craters. As casualties continued to arrive at the hospital, Lawrence Rhea's post-mortem work at this time revealed the effectiveness of a steel helmet in preventing serious head wounds and saving lives. No. 3 Canadian General Hospital was acquiring a very good reputation among the medical units in France. It was very active research, pathological work and in pioneering the training of nurses to administer anaesthetics. Its findings and those of other hospitals resulted in the issue of the steel helmet as standard equipment for the British and Imperial soldiers in the field.

Elsewhere, the Germans had begun to besiege the French fortress town of Verdun. A garrison since Roman times, Verdun symbolised French resistance to German and foreign aggression and the German commander, General Erich von Falkenhayn, believed that its loss would severely affect French morale and possibly affect the outcome of the war. On a dark morning in February 1916 a German shell landed in the courtyard of the Bishop of Verdun's Palace to begin the terrible battle of attrition that was to last ten months and result in approximately a million casualties.

As the weeks passed, it was clear that 'In Flanders Fields' was a major success beyond anything John McCrae could have imagined when he wrote it. The poem had already begun to appear in magazines, newspapers and soldiers' letters to their loved ones. Its poignant images and its underlying message of respect for the fallen had touched the hearts of millions. In simple style and language it voiced the thoughts of the many thousands of troops at the front and it was no surprise that it was to become the poem of the army. Andrew Macphail later wrote that the 'soldiers have learned it with their hearts, which is quite a different thing from committing it to memory . . . That is the true test of poetry, – its insistence on making itself learnt by heart.'[48] Not everyone who had known John before the war had been aware that he wrote poetry, and some knew him only as the jocund man whose stories had brought laughter to the dinner table or the office. One colleague at the Mutual Life Insurance Company of New York, for whom John had acted as a medical examiner since 1906, read of his success and exclaimed 'Think of it – good old Johnny McCrae!'[49] Those close to him knew that John only wrote about events that had touched him deeply. His experience in the Second Battle of Ypres, which he had referred to as 'seventeen days of Hades' had been unlike anything he had ever experienced before.

The staff of No. 3 were understandably proud of their senior medical officer but, in his typically modest way, John remained unaffected by his rise to fame. In fact, after his morning's work and hospital rounds were complete, he now preferred to spend most afternoons alone. Young Yvonne Debacker was particularly attached to this kindly Canadian officer whom she called 'the Colonel':

> I remember the Colonel very well. He was a very straightforward, very gentle man who you could not help liking. Everything about his face indicated someone very special . . . As my parents' house was next to the camp stables, I had the privilege of seeing the Colonel almost every day. In the afternoon, he used to come to the stables. He very often had sugar in his pocket for his black horse 'Bonfire', and for my parents' dog 'Bonneau'. This was no ordinary dog. He had a very soft bark that he could prolong by way of greeting. It's the reason the Colonel remarked on it. Bonneau always ran up to him . . . His horse was really his confidant. Almost every afternoon, he went off on long solitary rides. Bonneau liked to go with him.[50]

Early in April, John was granted a few days' leave. He made for London where his cousin, Lieutenant-Colonel Walter Gow, was stationed and soon to become Deputy Minister, Overseas Forces of Canada. The break was a tonic in itself and John thoroughly enjoyed himself, admitting it had been 'a real treat to do nothing'.[51] He had a standing invitation to Oxford which he gladly discharged. Sir William Osler was, as ever, tremendously busy with his lecturing work and in his role as Consultant to the Canadian military hospitals. John could see that the knowledge that Revere would soon be in action weighed heavily on his parents' minds. Like so many families, they would become all too familiar with the pattern of short periods of leave followed by long periods of tension and dread, knowing their son was at the front.

Spring was late that year. By mid-April 1916 John could only report that 'the sun struggles through and mid-day is fairly warm. The blossom and the leaves are still very backward, but the birds are trying to persuade themselves that spring is here.'[52] In general, life had become rather quiet, 'perhaps even dull, but cheerfulness is a duty and we try to perform it'.[53] His religious faith and its tenets were as important as ever to him, so much so that John's 'constant attendance at church service made him the source of a good deal of wonder'.[54] As he had done throughout his life, John paid particular attention to each sermon and told his mother that, one evening, the 'Padre nearly got on ticklish ground when he was getting near the statement that we may not hate the Germans.'[55] The choral element of the service also came under scrutiny and John declared that 'much as I like the C[hurch] of England, I don't care if I never hear a canticle again – for the padre makes us sing them, and they are usually rather sorry performances. They take such a lot of bellows, and if not properly phrased, sound like a free for all scurry.'[56] The services appeared to improve markedly when the piano was played by Colonel Elder, a one-time choirmaster.

A month later, David McCrae arrived in England having complied with Sam Hughes' request and raised the 43rd Battery of Artillery. His young recruits were primarily students of the Ontario Agricultural College at Guelph, and the University of Toronto's Knox College. John was granted three days' leave to meet his father in London and found him in good spirits. Enjoying their first meeting for nearly two years, they caught up on news and entertained friends to lunch at Simpson's restaurant in the Strand. Although too old to fight at seventy-one, David was very keen to go to France and see for himself what was going on. John wrote to the military authorities on his father's behalf and sought the assistance of Sir Max Aitken, the charismatic Canadian millionaire with immense energy, drive and personal power. Aitken had seen the war coming much earlier than most people and, through his connections in London, had managed to secure an appointment as an eyewitness to the troops in the field and head of Canadian War Records. When David McCrae received orders to report to Shorncliffe, father and son caught the coast train and lunched in Folkestone's Metropole Hotel. John left him waiting to see whether permission for his visit would be granted. It was not, and David returned to Canada bitterly disappointed.

Away from the front, the summer of 1916 was quite lovely. The journalist, Philip Gibbs, remembered that it came 'with a wealth of beauty in the fields of France . . . The grass was a tapestry of flowers, and tits and warblers and golden oriole were making music in the woods.'[57] While the battle continued to rage at Verdun and the British Grand Fleet scored a strategic victory over the German High Seas Fleet at Jutland, the great offensive that would use the young men of Kitchener's 'new army' was soon to begin. It had originally been planned as a joint British-French attack, but with every able-bodied French soldier drawn into the cauldron at Verdun, the task now fell to the British. The area chosen for the attack was the Somme, an attractive area of gentle, rolling downs with clumps of woodland on the rises, sunken roads and villages nestling in the dips.

The British Commander-in-Chief, now Field-Marshal Sir Douglas Haig, decided to mount a massive preliminary bombardment with over 1400 guns, aimed at destroying the enemy's barbed wire defences and gun positions. The concentration of artillery was so great that, 'it darkened the days with smoke and lit the nights with flashes' and the dust from blown mud and brick 'covered the summer landscape with a kind of haze of hell'.[58] Haig was confident of success and imparted to his troops the importance of his belief in 'a sincere desire to engage the enemy'.[59] The attack was timed to begin at 7.30 a.m. on 1 July 1916. As the sun rose in a clear summer sky, officers counted the minutes. The ending of the bombardment and the detonation of several huge mines had signalled to the enemy that they could expect an attack. Never before in history had there been such vast forces massed on both sides, but, on that fine summer's day, the stage was set for a great tragedy.

For all the might of the Allied bombardment, it had failed both to dislodge the Germans and cut the barbed wire. At the appointed time, wave after wave of British infantry rose from their trenches and started to walk towards the German front line. The soldiers thought they were going across 'no man's land' merely to winkle out any remaining German survivors before the cavalry charged in to open up the war again. Instead they met vicious machine gun fire and fell like cornstalks before a scythe. By the evening of that terrible July day, losses numbered 57,470[60] – the worst single day's casualties in British military history. The men of the 1st Newfoundland Regiment tried to secure a German position near the hamlet of Beaumont Hamel. They were mown down by machine gun fire and of 801 men, just 68 survived. The Newfoundlanders died obeying their orders with courage, steadfastness and pride of purpose – in proportion to numbers, no single unit on the Somme suffered more heavily.

The Somme offensive continued on into the autumn of 1916. Before long there were whole areas without a single house, tree or even a blade of grass remaining, and where not a patch of ground was without a shell hole. The Canadians had been involved in the June Battle of Mount Sorrel but, fortunately for them, had not been part of the tragic 1 July 1916 attack. However, as the offensive continued, they were thrown in at the end of August. They now numbered four divisions and, as the Canadian Corps, marched from the Ypres Salient to their new area of operation. Andrew Macphail and his field ambulance went with them. He described that memorable march, during which

> we had brilliant August weather, with the light in a strong blaze travelling from field to field. France disclosed to us all its dignity, beauty, and richness in dainty chateaux half hidden in wooded parks, in massive buildings set in large undulating and hedged fields. It was for this treasure-house France fought.[61]

Passing hidden lanes, overgrown watercourses, undulating cornfields and dense woodland, he and his comrades entered the zone of desolation to take over a tented hospital about ten miles from Albert.

The Canadians assumed a section of the front line in front of the village of Courcelette. Here they ran into heavy fighting and sustained more than 2500 casualties. At dawn on September 15, an attack began in which the Canadian Corps moved forward behind a creeping barrage – a new artillery tactic. The attack went well and with the main objective taken, the Canadians pushed on to Courcelette and consolidated their position. But the Germans brought up reinforcements and the fighting intensified as the autumn rains began. Edward Morrison, writing to John McCrae to describe the battle, headed his letter 'In a Dugout in a Rainstorm, in Rubber Boots, in France'.[62] Revere Osler also arrived on the Somme in October with the Royal Artillery and soon discovered the realities of life at the front as the heavy fighting continued.

In the following weeks the Canadians repeatedly attacked a series of German entrenchments. The final objective, 'Regina Trench', defied capture and was still not taken by mid-October. The troops fought on knee-deep in mud against determined enemy resistance and it was not until 11 November 1916 that the infamous 'Regina Trench' was finally secured by the courageous and hard-hitting Canadians. Now, however, with the terrain reduced to a huge bog and the conditions so disgusting that according to Edward Morrison, 'they would have revolted the stomach of a decent woodchuck,'[63] the offensive ground to a halt. The entire area had become a ghastly 'Sea of misery'[64] and by the time they ended, the Somme battles had claimed more than four hundred thousand lives.

Throughout the summer and autumn of 1916, No. 3 Canadian General Hospital worked day and night coping with the great numbers of casualties. Whether medical or surgical treatment was required, the staff spared no effort and, in the first week after 1 July, the hospital was stretched to its limit. John McCrae told his father that 'we are fearfully busy, as our people are coming in every hour of the 24.'[65] In the role of Consultant, he was seeing a large number of selected cases every day and, to the delight of the soldiers, 'Bonneau' insisted on accompanying him on his rounds. The weather was gloriously hot and John wrote that 'the bronze colored grain is shot with poppies and blue chicory and yellow daisies, and the fields are very beautiful'.[66] In the warm conditions, patients could be moved outside under the shelter of a canopy or under the trees so that they could enjoy the benefits of sun and air.

The beauty of that summer stood in contrast to the terrible suffering of the wounded. Those who worked in the operating room as assistants to surgeons like Edward Archibald, faced the daily sight of mutilated and mangled bodies and the awful effects of gas gangrene – an appalling infection whereby bacteria flourished in dirty wounds of men, some of whom had laid untended in 'no man's land' for several days. Such wounds became a mass of putrid, rotting flesh or muscle and with no antibiotics, as much diseased tissue as possible had to be cut away. Edward Archibald held his young patients in high regard, describing them as 'such nice lads' who never complained and would tell him that despite awful injuries they were 'feeling champion, doctor!'.[67] The devoted nurses remained after their shifts had ended and gave up their off-duty time to write letters for the soldiers, who were 'so grateful for any attention.'[68] Sophie Hoerner admitted that what she saw that summer made her cry many times for, as she wrote to another friend, 'No one could imagine the horrors of a war like this, unless they are here and could see for themselves'. Her earlier comment that 'what they must suffer, no words can describe,'[69] continued to be agonisingly true.

A seemingly endless round of official visitors also had to be fitted into the busy schedule, sometimes very distinguished visitors such as the Secretary of State for War, David Lloyd George. The hectic pace continued and on 1 October when John wrote to his sister, Geills, describing some of the problems with fever cases, he also pointed out that 'work goes on unceasingly seven days a week, and we rarely have fewer than 500 or 600 medical beds full . . . the laboratory can't keep up'.[70]For all this, he and 'Bonfire' were enjoying the autumn. Their rides took them along country roads edged with 'masses of brambleberries: the chestnut gentleman can tell you all about them, as he eats them by what I judge to be the pint'.[71]

As well as his medical work, John was at this point also responsible for disciplinary and other administrative matters. With everyone working long hours under constant pressure, he dealt with many complaints. The nurses found it hard to dissociate themselves from their civilian experience for, as John wrote to his mother, they wanted 'neatness & a nice-looking ward . . . we stand only for cleanliness and patients who are getting well as rapidly as possible . . . Their training leads them to want to do less in a perfect way, and we want more in a less perfect way, because it is war'.[72]

In their scant free time, the young nurses and doctors working in the Base area were thrown together in a nightmare world in which nobody knew what the future held. Some liaisons resulted in marriage, but for John McCrae there was no romantic attachment during those awful years. With his determination to put the war ahead of any personal consideration, he declared to his mother that he was 'sot agin' lovemaking in wartime'[73] and had 'a deeply rooted objection to paying too much attention to leave while the job lasts'.[74] As always, he was unsparing with himself and took little time off from his official duties. When he did, he enjoyed an occasional game of tennis or a swim at one of the beaches not far away. Boulogne offered a number of excellent restaurants such as 'Mony', known to every English and Canadian officer in France. In this cosy establishment with its sawdust-covered floor and glass partitioned stalls, the patron beamed at his clientele and delicious, substantial meals appeared from the cellar's depths to everyone's great satisfaction. It was a treat that even the self-disciplined John found hard to decline.

Whatever the demands on his time, the dedicated officer never neglected correspondence with his family, especially with his mother. His very regular letters contained an account of his life in general but he spared her the detail of the suffering he witnessed on a daily basis. Instead, he preferred to write about international news, events in Canada, books he had read and his friends, both human and animal. His sister Geills now had four children, the younger two being her sons, Jack and David. The Kilgour children became well acquainted with tales of 'Bonfire', a popular personality at the hospital and a great favourite with the nurses, prompting John to remark jokingly that they loved his horse more than they did him.[75] He told his mother that he wished little Jack could see 'Bonfire' 'getting his face brushed; he shuts his eyes tight, like a small boy, and when he gets his nose washed there is much puffing and blowing as two small boys would make.'[76] John composed a series of letters for Geills' children as if written by 'Bonfire' himself and 'signed' with a horseshoe as his mark. The boys he addressed as soldiers whose behaviour might entitle them periodically to a good conduct stripe or even a promotion. As examples:

Dear Soldiers

As my master is writing to his mother, I send this to tell you I am well. I have been out of straw for my bed but to-day I have got a lot, and I shall have a good bed to-night. A friend of mine gave me some strawberries and sugar to-day, and last week a nursing sister sent me a bag of young carrots, with the leaves on. Do you boys like carrots with the leaves on?

Yours truly
BONFIRE[77]

Dear Margaret:

This is Guy Fox Day! I spell it that way because fox-hunting was my occupation a long time ago before the war. How are Serg[ean]t.-Major Jack and Corporal David? Ask Jack if he ever bites through his rope at night, and gets into the oat-box. And as for the Corporal, 'I bet you' I can jump as far as he can. I hear David has lost his red coat. I still have my gray one, but it is pretty dirty now, for I have not had a new one for a long time. I got my hair cut a few weeks ago and am to have new boots next week. Bonneau and Follette[78] send their love.

Yours truly
        BONFIRE[79]

In October 1916, Edward Archibald wrote to his wife that 'our Jack is his old self now . . . I think he had shell shock last year'.[80] It was now nearly eighteen months since the Second Battle of Ypres and although John had recovered from the after-effects of the battle, he had still not regained his former cheerful demeanour. There were residual effects from the strain he had undergone and George Adami later wrote that the war he felt so intensely 'had changed him'. Whilst John remained 'kindly and devoted to those under him', he neverthless expected from them 'the same military spirit and sense of high responsibility' that he himself felt. When he found either lacking, he tended to be impatient. As Adami explained, 'Not all at first understood the change or could rise to his level of service.'[81]

Although there was consolation in the fact that 'In Flanders Fields' had had a tremendous influence on recruiting in Britain and the Dominions, Andrew Macphail believed that deep down John McCrae felt that he and the rest of the Empire had failed. It was as if, to his 'sensitive and foreboding mind there were sounds and signs that it would be given to this generation to hear the pillars and fabric of Empire come crashing into the abysm of chaos'.[82] John's friend from Guelph, Henry Howitt, attested to the fact that those who had known him in earlier days 'spoke of this change of temperament with subdued voices, as if they were mourners, – as if an Icon had been broken.'[83]

As the war ground on, John treasured more and more his afternoon rides with his animal companions. When time was short, he would ride past the 'Moka', a popular cafe close to the hospital, and into the park of the Colonne de la Grande Armée. But he had also discovered a longer and far more attractive ride. A narrow, wooded lane at the back of the hospital area led down into a beautiful secluded valley surrounded by gentle, rolling hills. It was called the Vallée du Dénacre and as John rode along its narrow track, he passed farms and an old manor house hiding behind high, rose-covered walls. Before long, the track descended to a stream with a water mill where stood the 'Estaminet du 2e Moulin'.[84]

John liked to tether 'Bonfire' here and stand on the bridge while he watched the stream cascading down to the waterwheel. Beyond this point, the lane became a path just wide enough for a horse. Here, between undulating meadows and overhung by alders and other trees, the stream wound its way through the tranquil heart of the valley. In spring the meadows and pathways were edged with wild primroses and violets; in summer dog roses, forget-me-not, wild irises and the lovely pink Indian Balsam caught John's eye; in autumn, red bryony was plentiful, as were the blackberries that 'Bonfire' so liked to eat. Here John could find the peace to be alone with his thoughts and indulge his love of nature, whose gentle permanence was a consolation in an area where it was nothing to hear 'Last Post' played fifteen times a day at military funerals. 'Bonneau' came along on these rambles if he could. Yvonne Debacker remembered that on one occasion:

> the Colonel told Bonneau to stay. He had hardly reached the 'Moka' when Bonneau caught up with him and he hadn't the heart to send him back. When out riding, the Colonel enjoyed jumping ditches. But once, Bonneau stopped in front of one. The Colonel made a half-turn, picked up Bonneau, put him on his saddle and made the jump with him.[85]

Back at the hospital, Edward Archibald's tour of duty was almost at an end and he was preparing to leave for Canada. For John, however, there could be no return as yet for he knew the need for doctors was too important and he would not have agreed to go. For him 'the war had to be won; he could not break faith with the dead of Flanders.'[86] He continued to live quietly, passing many a free evening reading and playing chess or bridge. Despite his waning strength and his feelings about the war, he had not lost his sense of humour. He sent his mother a word sketch that amused him and seemed to have 'a kind of Bairnsfather touch to it!'[87] By now Bruce Bairnsfather's wonderful morale-boosting cartoons had made him famous and would earn him the post-war description as 'the man who made the Empire laugh in its darkest hour'.[88] John's sketch read as follows:

> Scene at the front. The padre has organized a concert and has got a man to play the pipes. The candidate 'skirls' in dismal fashion for 2 minutes. Voice from the back: 'Take that —— off the stage!'
> Irate Padre, advancing to the footlights. 'Who called the piper a —— ?' No answer.
> Irate Padre: 'I insist on knowing <u>who</u> called the piper a —— !!'
> Irate Padre: 'The concert will not proceed until I know who called the piper a —— !!'
> Voice: 'Wot I wants to know is, 'oo called the —— a piper!!!'
> Curtain.[89]

The autumn storms arrived once more and in the lulls between the gales, thick drifting sea fogs blotted out the landscape. John caught a cold and became asthmatic. The 'old enemy' that had left him alone for the past few years had unfortunately returned. Dr Bill Francis wrote in later years that 'three bitter North French winters were too much for his asthma. He tried to live like a real soldier in an unheated tent until our C[ommanding]. O[fficer]. ordered him into a hut'.[90] John agreed to move indoors to warmer quarters, but only 'till it gets better'.[91] Despite an improvement, he remained tired and admitted to his mother that he still had 'the usual awful bark that is as bad as the whooping cough while it lasts'.[92] With a large number of fever cases the pressure of work was heavy, but John was heartened by the Allied effort in the latter days of the Somme battles, for as he had told his mother: 'It is wonderful to think of the punishment we have taken.'[93] Despite his fatigue, the need to exercise 'Bonfire' encouraged him to continue their afternoon rides and on one occasion, 'he and I had a chance of inspecting a dirigible that had to land: he did not like it very much.'[94] Ten days later, with a pain under his shoulder and a temperature, John was taken to No. 14 British General Hospital, Wimereux, and placed under the care of Sir Bertrand Dawson. He had developed bronchitis and required at least two weeks' rest in the solitary grandeur of a room of his own.

Wimereux at that time consisted of a main street and a cluster of hotels, pensions and villas that looked to the summer for their main business. In November 1916 it was decidedly sleepy. No. 14's section for officers, formerly the Hotel Splendide, stood at the end of the promenade and, from his window, John could watch the constant procession of minesweepers and hospital ships against the background of the waves 'roaring away below my windows'.[95] Some of the nurses sent him flowers and he wrote to his mother that he had been presented with '4 big vases of beautiful dark red roses'.[96] John passed his days reading and seeing visitors from No. 3. like Colonel Birkett and Lawrence Rhea. Another surprise visitor had a good deal to say to him, and his next letter to Guelph reported that, 'to-day I saw Bonneau, who put up his nose in the air and whimpered and sighed and told me a number of stories – all very sad and pathetic evidently, by way of intimating that he was glad to see me.'[97] Under Dawson's care, the patient recovered but was told that he would have to convalesce on the Mediterranean. While the prospect of the sun and warmth was no doubt alluring, he typically told his mother that 'I do not need such pampering.'[98]

His personal feelings having been overruled, John arrived on 1 December 1916 at the Cap Martin Hotel, a first class hotel being used as a convalescent home for officers. Located in pinewoods between Menton and Monte Carlo, it was, to John, 'very gorgeous and very dull'.[99] He had nothing to do but take morning and afternoon walks and in the evenings after dinner, play bridge or chess. After three days, he was totally bored. When he felt stronger, he ambled through the woods to Monte Carlo and then along a cliff road with a view over terraced vineyards and a valley of palms, pines, orange and lemon trees. His climb ended at Roquebrune, a little village perched high on a cliff just three miles from the Italian frontier. The convalescent doctor had to admit it was pleasant to be able to enjoy his tranquil surroundings in a temperature of 75 degrees with the Maritime Alps behind him and a profusion of geraniums and other colourful flowers around him. From that day onwards, he went out at every opportunity and told his mother that he liked to 'take a book and toddle up the nearby hills, until I find a quiet spot with a fine view of the Alps, the sea and the olive tree valleys; one could hardly ask more of natural beauty. The mountain tops are all covered with snow from a storm a few days ago.'[100]

It was the first time in more than two years that John really felt distanced from the war, but he knew No. 3 was short-staffed and as soon as he could, he took a train to Paris in the company of another Canadian officer, a Colonel Andras. A warm welcome awaited his return to Boulogne. 'Bonfire' was so pleased to see him that 'he tried to bite off my pocket flaps' while 'Bonneau', who was limping with a bandaged leg, 'put his nose up in the air & told me all about it several times.' As John told his mother, 'it is very satisfactory to be so important to one's family.'[101]

The hospital had well over a thousand patients during the Christmas of 1916, most of them medical cases. The nurses decorated the wards and the parcels that arrived from kind friends and benefactors helped to make it a cheerful time. John was busy working on the problem of fevers of unknown origin until Christmas Eve, when the sound of carols made him realise that it *was* Christmas. After a busy morning and an afternoon ride cut short by freezing fog, he looked forward to the traditional Christmas Day officers' dinner. It was a time for reflection and, as snow started to fall a few days later, Sophie Hoerner – now the hospital's Assistant Matron – could well have pondered her thoughts of the previous Christmas: 'How changed all the world seems, I wonder what it all means and how it will all end and what will become of us all.'[102] She might have found part of her answer in what Edward Archibald had written to his wife shortly before he left the hospital to return to Canada: 'It's a terrible business, but it's the only way. They [the Germans] have to be taught their lesson now and for good; and some of us must die to do it. It's the old story of the sacrifice of the generation, not only for its own liberty, but for that of the next generation; the sacrifice of parents for children.'[103]

NOTES

1. From 'The Pilgrims' by John McCrae, *The McGill University Magazine* (Volume 4, No. 1, January 1905), p. 82. Micro mfm/AP/U577, UTL.
2. JM to Janet McCrae, 28 May 1915, GM Papers.
3. JM to Janet McCrae, 29 May 1915, GM Papers.

4. Allinson, 'John McCrae', p. 134.
5. Edward Archibald to his parents, 14 May 1915, MS 545/1, OL.
6. Allinson, 'John McCrae', p. 130.
7. Sophie Hoerner to her mother, 16 May 1915, MG 30 E290, NAC.
8. Edward Archibald to his mother, 23 May 1915, MS 545/1, OL.
9. Edward Archibald to his mother, 23 May 1915, MS 545/1, OL.
10. JM to Janet McCrae, 5 June 1915, GM Papers.
11. Edward Archibald to his mother, 7 June 1915, MS 545/1, OL.
12. Lady Osler to her sister as quoted in Cushing, *Life of Sir William Osler*, Volume II, p. 480.
13. JM to Janet McCrae, 14 June 1915, GM Papers.
14. Edward Archibald to his mother, 22 June 1915, MS 545/1, OL.
15. Sophie Hoerner to 'Mollie' (surname not given), 8 June 1915, MG 30, E290, NAC.
16. Sophie Hoerner to 'Mollie', 7 June 1915, MG 30, E290, NAC.
17. Prescott, *In Flanders Fields*, p. 101.
18. 'Confiserie' can mean both confectionery and a confectioner's shop. Rumpelmayer's was a famous establishment of the period that served its products on the premises to its clientele.
19. Edward Archibald to his wife, 2 August 1915, MS 545/4, OL.
20. R.C. Fetherstonhaugh, *No. 3 Canadian General Hospital (McGill) 1914–1919* (Montreal, 1928), p. 22
21. Lord Northcliffe, *At the War* (London, 1916), p. 36.
22. Sophie Hoerner to 'Mollie', 25 October 1915, MG 30, E290, NAC.
23. Sophie Hoerner to 'Madeline' (no surname given), 12 September 1915, MG 30, E290, NAC.
24. Edward Archibald to Mrs Agnes Archibald, 3 February 1916, MS 545/4, 1916 (3), OL.
25. Edward Archibald to Mrs Agnes Archibald, 8 October 1915, Acc. 545/4, 1915 (3), Osler Library.
26. JM to Oskar Klotz, 29 October 1915, MG 30, B61, Klotz Papers, NAC.
27. JM to Oskar Klotz, 29 October 1915, MG 30, B61, Klotz Papers, NAC.
28. Edward Archibald to Margaret Archibald, 10 October 1915, MS 545/4, Addenda 1915, (4), OL.
29. Allinson, 'John McCrae', p. 139.
30. Kingsmill, *Beyond the Call of Duty*, p. 52.
31. John Elder, 'In Flanders Fields', *Canadian Daily Record*, 5 March 1919.
32. JM to Oskar Klotz, 29 October 1915, MG 30, B61, Klotz Papers, NAC.
33. JM to Geills Kilgour, 4 December 1915, GM Papers.
34. Allinson, 'John McCrae', p. 139.
35. 'War Poem has Two Versions', *Montreal Star*, 2 November 1968.
36. Macphail, *In Flanders Fields*, pp. 49–50.
37. Macphail, *In Flanders Fields*, p. 53.
38. Giddings, *The War Poets*, p. 55.
39. Edward Archibald to his wife, 28 December 1915, MS 545/5, Addenda 1915, OL.
40. Sophie Hoerner to 'Mollie', 8 January 1916, MG 30, E290, NAC.
41. Dr Robert Koch was awarded the 1905 Nobel Prize for Medicine for his discovery of the tuberculosis bacillus.
42. Paul Hastings, *War and Medicine, 1914–1925* (Harlow, 1988), p. 20.
43. Leonard Colebrook, *Almroth Wright – Provocative Doctor and Thinker*, (London, 1954), p. 70.

44. Hastings, *War and Medicine*, p. 23.
45. JM to Geills Kilgour, 4 December 1915, GM Papers.
46. The literal English translation is 'Breton spaniel'.
47. JM to Janet McCrae, 6 January 1916, MG 30, D209, Micro A-1103, NAC.
48. Macphail, *In Flanders Fields*, p. 57.
49. Edgar Andrew Collard, 'McCrae of Flanders Fields', *Montreal Star*, 4 November 1978.
50. Interview given at her home in Boulogne by Madame Yvonne Deligny (formerly Mademoiselle Yvonne Debacker) to Monsieur Guy Bataille, former editor of *La Voix du Nord*, 12 February 1958. The author is indebted to M. Bataille for bringing this interview to her attention.
51. JM to Janet McCrae, 7 April 1916, MG 30, D209, Micro A-1103, NAC.
52. JM to Janet McCrae, 16 April 1916, MG 30, D209, Micro A-1103, NAC.
53. JM to Janet McCrae, 7 March 1916, MG 30, D209, Micro A-1103, NAC.
54. Clendenan, *The M'Craes of Cairsphairn*, p. 10.
55. JM to Janet McCrae, 9 April 1916, MG 30, D209, Micro A-1103, NAC.
56. JM to Janet McCrae, 9 April 1916, MG 30, D209, Micro A-1103, NAC.
57. Philip Gibbs, *Now It Can Be Told* (New York, 1920), p. 278.
58. John Masefield, as quoted in Henry Williamson, *An Anthology of Modern Nature Writing* (London, 1936), p. 158.
59. Churchill, *Great Contemporaries*, p. 174.
60. British Official History, as quoted in Nicholson, *Canadian Expeditionary Force*, p.163.
61. Macphail, *In Flanders Fields*, pp. 75–76.
62. Edward Morrison to John McCrae, 25 September 1916, GM Papers.
63. Edward Morrison to John McCrae, 3 December 1916, GM Papers. For 'woodchuck', see Chapter 1, endnote 19.
64. Letter from unnamed friend to Maude Abbott dated 16 October 1916, MS 438/68, Misc. 1, OL.
65. JM to David McCrae, 4 July 1916, MG 30, D209, Micro A-1103, NAC.
66. JM to Janet McCrae, 30 July 1916, MG 30, D209, Micro A-1103, NAC.
67. Edward Archibald to his wife, 21 July 1916, MS 545/4, 1916 (1), OL.
68. Sophie Hoerner to 'Mollie', 11 November 1915, MG 30, D209, NAC.
69. Sophie Hoerner to 'Carrie' (no surname given), 10 June 1915, MG30, E290, NAC.
70. JM to Geills Kilgour, 1 October 1916, MG 30, D209, Micro A-1103, NAC.
71. JM to Geills Kilgour, 1 October 1916, MG 30, D209, Micro A-1103, NAC.
72. JM to Janet McCrae, 20 February 1916, MG 30, D209, Micro A-1103, NAC.
73. JM to Janet McCrae, 27 August 1916, MG 30, D209, Micro A-1103, NAC. 'Sot agin' (Scottish dialect) meant 'opposed to'.
74. JM to Janet McCrae, 13 August 1916, MG 30, D209, Micro A-1103, NAC.
75. Archdeacon H.G. Hepburn, as quoted in R.O. Speckley, 'John McCrae of Flanders Fields', *The Legionary* (November 1948), p.13.
76. JM to Janet McCrae, 6 February 1916, MG 30, D 209, Micro A-1103, NAC.
77. Undated letter from 'Bonfire' to Jack and David Kilgour, MH.
78. Follette was Bonneau's mother and spent much time in and around the stable of 'Bonfire', John McCrae's horse.
79. Undated, but presumed to have been written on 5 November 1916, Macphail, *In Flanders Fields*, pp. 108–109.
80. Edward Archibald to his wife, 8 October 1916, MS 545/4, OL.
81. J.G. Adami, 'Lt. Col. John McCrae', *British Medical Journal,,* 9 February 1918, p. 4 .

82. Macphail, *In Flanders Fields*, p. 86.
83. Howitt, 'John McCrae', p. 17.
84. Translation: 'Estaminet of the second mill' (there were two operating mills in the valley at the time). Estaminet meant literally a canteen, and it would serve basic meals as well as wine.
85. Interview with Madame Yvonne Deligny, *La Voix du Nord*, 4 February 1958.
86. Prescott, *In Flanders Fields*, p. 110.
87. JM to Janet McCrae, 22 October 1916, MG 30, D209, Micro A-1103, NAC.
88. Tonie and Valmai Holt, *In Search of the Better 'Ole* (Portsmouth, 1985), p. 78.
89. JM to Janet McCrae, 22 October 1916, MG 30, D209, Micro A-1103, NAC.
90. David P. Boyd, 'Doctors Afield', *New England Journal of Medicine* (Volume 260, No. 23, 4 June 1959), p. 1178.
91. JM to Janet McCrae, 22 October 1916, MG 30, D209, Micro A-1103, NAC.
92. JM to Janet McCrae, 29 October 1916, MG 30, D209, Micro A-1103, NAC.
93. JM to Janet McCrae, 1 October 1916, MG 30, D209, Micro A-1103, NAC.
94. JM to Janet McCrae, 5 November 1916, MG 30, D209, Micro A-1103, NAC.
95. JM to Janet McCrae, 20 November 1916, MG 30, D209, Micro A-1103, NAC.
96. JM to Janet McCrae, 16 November 1916, MG 30, D209, Micro A-1103, NAC.
97. JM to Janet McCrae, 26 November 1916, MG 30, D209, Micro A-1108, NAC.
98. JM to Janet McCrae, 20 November 1916, MG 30, D209, Micro A-1103, NAC.
99. JM to Janet McCrae, 1 December 1916, MG 30, D209, Micro A-1103, NAC.
100. JM to Janet McCrae, 10 December 1916, MG 30, D209, Micro A-1103, NAC.
101. JM to Janet McCrae, 17 December 1916, MG 30, D209, Micro A-1103, NAC.
102 Sophie Hoerner to 'Janet' (no surname given), 13 December 1915, MG 30, E290, NAC.
103. Edward Archibald to his wife, 23 September 1916, MS 545/4, 1916(1), OL.

CHAPTER FOURTEEN

'To you from failing hands we throw the torch'[1]
January 1917–January 1918

In northern France, the year 1917 announced its arrival with bitter weather. At No. 3 Canadian General Hospital, tent flaps froze solid and water pails were covered with ice. John McCrae found that sleeping was difficult, for despite wearing layers of clothing, thick socks and a heavy cap, 'as one turns one's chin, a face comes into a semifrozen blanket where one's breath has congealed'.[2] He had 'never suffered so from cold in my life . . . going to bed & getting up are nightmares'.[3]

The weather exacerbatèd the many cases of pneumonia in the wards of No. 3 but it also brought compensations. Morning after morning of heavy hoar frost silvered the countryside and John, always one to appreciate the seasons, commented that the 'valleys here are beautifully wooded, and many of the tree trunks are entirely hidden by ivy: there are great quantities of yellow gorse in bloom, and much holly in the hedgerows'.[4] When he was unable to ride he went walking, spotting hares, an occasional partridge and other birds. The cold did not appear to put 'Bonfire' off his daily treats and he was happy to accept a piece of sugar and a frozen apple with 'a great snorting and foraging until I produce them'.[5] By early February, however, the combination of cold and the constant rush of work had begun to tell. John wrote that 'our tempers are a frazzle, and we all actually suffer somewhat by the intensity of the weather'.[6] He finished his letter of 11 February to his mother 'From your partly thawed and always affect[ionate]. son.'[7] In these miserable conditions, it was cheering to hear from family and friends such as Oskar Klotz, Nona Gwyn and Lady Osler. Earl Grey sent him a book, and he was delighted to receive a note from his small nephew, David, saying simply: 'Uncle Jack. I like you. I wish you were here.'[8]

John had been been working since the previous autumn on another poem. Calling it firstly 'The Message of the Guns 1916–14'[sic], then 'The Living to the Dead 1916–14', he finally opted for a different title. At the end of January, he was able to tell his mother that he had received 'a letter of acceptance of a piece of verse, from the Spectator – a long cherished ambition . . . It is entitled "The Anxious Dead"'.[9] The poem would be published seven months later.

After almost another month the cold abated, making life easier though no less exhausting for everyone. The arrival of nightly convoys meant broken sleep and tiring days. Although the hospital continued to receive distinguished visitors, including the Canadian Prime Minister, Sir Robert Borden, the tenor of life in general seemed to John 'very quiet, even dull'.[10] As ever, it was his bird and animal friends that brightened his waking hours. He recorded one comical occasion when the hospital hen 'invaded a ward . . . hopped on the beds, and was very popular, finally laying an egg by way of thanks'.[11]

Early in April, John was granted Easter leave. He made for London and one of his favoured hotels, the Bedford in Southampton Row. The benefits of a rest and change of scenery were immediately felt and he found both his cousin, Walter Gow, and George Adami – with whom he lunched at the Savile Club – in good spirits. John took a train to Oxford and stayed a night with the Oslers, who were keen to hear the news from No.3. There was also much discussion of the recent announcement of America's entry into the war on 6 April 1917 following Germany's proclamation of her intention to indulge in unrestricted submarine warfare in the Atlantic. By now, 'In Flanders Fields' was known throughout the English-speaking world. Its message and rallying call had been used extensively to further the war effort and John was receiving many letters requesting permission to use it for raising money. As American mobilisation began, it was quoted widely and John McCrae became a household name in the United States. The poem had already evoked a number of 'replies' in answer to its message. One – perhaps the most quoted of them – had been written the previous year by an American, R.V. Lillard, and published in the *New York Evening Post*. Its first three lines seemed to speak for his countrymen as they now prepared to take up John's torch and go to war:

> Rest ye in peace, ye Flanders dead.
> The fight that ye so bravely led
> We've taken up.[12]

On John's return to Boulogne, everything was soon 'at concert pitch'.[13] During his absence, the Canadian Corps had brought off a spectacular success at Vimy Ridge on Easter Monday, 9 April 1917. This attack had been part of a much larger offensive by the British Third and First Armies. The Germans were in no doubt about the importance of the ridge and had tried to render it impregnable with three defensive lines strung with miles of barbed wire. However, the Canadians had tackled their task with immense energy, building tunnels to the ridge and roads and railways to move supplies and wounded quickly. As always, the Canadian artillery was professional and the counter battery staff officer of the Canadian Corps, Major Andrew McNaughton, pinpointed German gun positions with great precision. As the hours ticked by towards daylight that cold April morning, the men waited in their tunnels and rehearsed yet again what they had to do. The artillery had been busy all night at a deliberately decreasing rate to lull the enemy into thinking that an attack was not imminent. Canon Scott, who was with the men as they waited for zero hour, sensed that 'all along that front the eager heart of Canada waited impatiently for the dawn'. For him 'it was a thrilling moment. Human lives were at stake. The honour of our country was at stake'.[14]

At 5.30 a.m. on 9 April, every Canadian gun went into action and the whole weight of the artillery swept the German line as all four Canadian divisions walked out behind it 'amid the chilling sleet of that deafening Easter dawn'.[15] Above the noise of the big guns could be heard the sound of the enemy machine guns as they tried to stop the approaching Canadians. This time, however, they did not succeed and one officer remembered that when 'we reached the German lines we hardly recognized them. What had once been trenches were only mere sunken lines.'[16] By mid-morning, as the sun broke through, Canadian troops were on the crest of the ridge overlooking the Douai plain.

The combination of leadership, courage, planning and co-operation between artillery and infantry had produced an outstanding Canadian tactical victory but the victory resulted largely from the contribution of Canada's gunners. Edward Morrison wrote to John McCrae after the battle that it 'certainly was the greatest day in the history of the gunners . . . All Arms are unanimous that the Artillery preparation and support on this front was as near perfection on a gigantic scale as the science of the arm has ever been brought . . . If you were only here I think my enjoyment would be complete.'[17] Morrison added an anecdote about the British commander of the Canadian Corps, Lieutenant-General Sir Julian Byng:

> You know General Byng delights in Canadian slang. He repeats it over and chuckles to himself when it is expressive. He likes my expression 'go to it.' At the height of the battle when I got the report we had taken the Ridge, I went to him and said: 'General, everything is jake! We are shelling the retiring Bosches'. He sprung his jolly smile and gave the historic order: 'Morrison, go to it'! (This is history 'as she is made', not as she is writ!)[18]

Edward Morrison is reputed to have kept an original copy of 'In Flanders Fields' in his despatch book throughout the war. Perhaps he had showed it to the corps commander, for the postscript to his letter describing Vimy reads: 'Please send me a copy of "In Flanders Fields" for General Byng.'

Vimy Ridge demonstrated that the Canadian Corps was now one of the élite fighting formations of the allied armies but as always, there was a stiff price to be paid for victory. Although the soldiers in the first waves of the assault had suffered greatly, the planning of Byng and his right-hand man, Major-General Arthur Currie, who 'by following his dictum of paying for victory in shells rather than in lives',[19] had kept Canadian casualties lower than the terrible norm of many previous major assaults. Andrew Macphail, who was at Vimy with 6th Canadian Field Ambulance, later paid tribute to the efficiency of the Canadian Army Medical Corps in handling the wounded. Convoys began arriving at No. 3 the day after the battle and John McCrae and his medical team handled large numbers of chest wounds. Yet despite their pain and distress, the survivors of Vimy Ridge were positively aglow with pride at Canada's victory.

After the bitter winter, the spring of 1917 was slow in making an appearance. Riding along his favourite route, John enjoyed the birds 'keeping the world as merry as they can',[20] and the sight of apple and pear trees in blossom. In his first letter to his mother that May, he enclosed a photograph that was to remain a great favourite. It showed John seated next to 'Bonneau' and holding his paw, a pose he had managed to achieve with patience. The ever modest John added the comment: 'I know you will admit it is one of the best dog pictures you ever saw. I am only an accident in the picture.'[21] 'Bonneau' now had another dog companion, 'Mike', an Irish terrier pup who had lost an eye chasing a cat. John told Janet McCrae that 'Bonneau & the new pup are great pals' and 'the little fellow is as merry as can be.'[22] He quickly became fond of 'Mike' who was only '14 inches long, and has such a whiskery nose that he is very ugly but a beautiful little chap all the same'.[23] Both dogs were very vocal and 'Mike' soon learned to copy 'Bonneau' and offer his paw. The pair reminded their friend of 'a perfect dignity and impudence'.[24]

At times, John could not help grumbling to his mother about items in the news: 'Do you see that Britain is paying the Duchess of Saxe Coburg Gotha £6000 a year? She lives in Ger[many]. and has a son in the Ger[man]. army. Something more to thank our dear old Queen V[ictoria]. for, besides the Albert Mem[orial]. and the Lake Poets. Verily we are a d[amned]. f[ool]. nation in some ways.'[25] The Sunday he wrote this was one of the rare occasions that he had not been to church, giving as his excuse that it was not 'that I was afraid of the chorus hymns but they lessen the regret.'[26] A letter dated some three weeks later found him in a more cheery frame of mind. He had been to an open-air concert to hear Harry Lauder, whom he had met in Montreal before the war, and had thoroughly approved of Lauder's 'first rate war sermon to the soldiers to hold on and finish the job'.[27] Also, *The Spectator* had just sent him a cheque for his poem 'The Anxious Dead', leading him to speculate that 'probably the verse is imminent. It would fit very well the Messines-Ypres advance.'[28]

After the late cold spring, summer chose to arrive early, and by 17 June the weather was blazing hot. Things at No. 3 were quieter than at any time since Vimy Ridge and there was a chance to enjoy the long, twilight evenings. The hospital vegetable garden promised to produce a good crop of lettuce and beans, and the wheat in the fields was ripening. John wrote his letters on the shaded verandah of the officers' mess anteroom to the sound of larks and thrushes while 'Bonfire' – of whom John had commented that 'there never was a more industrious grazer'[29] – steadily demolished a nearby patch of clover. It appeared that his companion had also developed 'a great weakness for blooms of all sorts – flowers he gobbles at all opportunities'.[30]

On 3 July 1917, the hospital wards and facilities were made to look their best in readiness for a very important visitor. Her Majesty Queen Mary was touring the Base hospitals, and at No. 3 the senior staff accompanied her as she made her way round in bright sunshine. Another visitor was Lieutenant-Colonel Harvey Cushing, who had been posted to the American Base Hospital No. 5 at Camiers and was living temporarily at Sir Almroth Wright's house in Boulogne. Tom McCrae had also come over to Europe, and was now head of medicine at The Ontario Military Hospital at Orpington, Kent. Situated close to the town with easy access to the railway line, it had been built and paid for by the Province of Ontario in the autumn of 1915 and was one of the largest and most up-to-date military hospitals of the time. One of its most interesting departments was that of plastic surgery, where important pioneering work was being done to construct prostheses for disguising facial and other disfigurements.

During the weeks that followed, John's letters talked of Tom's enjoyment of his work at Orpington; of the arrival of a new clutch of officers who all required induction and familiarisation; and of the fact that life seemed quiet and 'monotonous, for all that it is wartime'.[31] He was nearing the completion of three years of active service and recalled the fact to his mother: 'To think of the days when I wanted to be a soldier: little did I think I would get it in such over-measure.'[32] Like so many others, he was burdened by the weight of the seemingly unending struggle and the sense that, despite the great effort being made, he was not doing enough to keep faith with those who had fallen in action. The arduous work of commanding the hospital had by now taken its toll on the health of Colonel Birkett, who was preparing to leave. His successor in command of No. 3 was to be Colonel John Elder, the officer in charge of Surgery. Although John McCrae had more seniority and was disappointed in some ways not to be given a promotion, he accepted the decision in a soldierly manner. A welcome visit from Edward Morrison brought him up to date with events at the front, where a major new offensive was about to commence.

By the spring of 1917, the British Army had begun to bear the main burden of fighting on the Western Front as the French armies, after sustaining huge losses at Verdun, were no longer capable of a major offensive until they had re-organised. New offensives and wholly new tactics were tried during the fourth summer of the war. After Canada's success at Vimy Ridge, the Royal Engineers tunnelled nineteen huge mines beneath the massive German fortifications south of the Messines Ridge. Packed with over one million pounds of high explosive, the explosions were detonated on 7 June to coincide with a rolling barrage and the advance of General Plumer's Second British Army which, by evening, had attained all its objectives.

Late in July, the British commander, Sir Douglas Haig, launched a drive in Flanders aimed at breaking through the front and capturing the German submarine bases on the Belgian coast from which U-boats were threatening Britain's maritime communications. Messines, in John McCrae's mind after he wrote his poem 'The Anxious Dead', had indeed provided a successful prelude, but this success was followed by weeks of delay. The main phase of the new offensive began with a tremendous artillery barrage as Haig still placed great store by this tactic which, unfortunately, both forewarned the Germans and destroyed the carefully prepared drainage systems of that part of Flanders. As the offensive began, heavy summer rains began to fall and the area quickly became a quagmire.

While the fighting continued through late August, back in Boulogne John's Irish terrier pup 'Mike' died and he was once again beset by his 'old enemy', asthma. He wrote to Janet McCrae that 'I am ashamed to say that I have been tied by the heels for the last couple of days . . . a real snorter of an attack, beginning for no reason at all that I could see.'[33] By early September he pronounced himself fit again 'except for occasional bursts of coughing. I sleep well & greedily'.[34] He seemed in an optimistic frame of mind about the outcome of the war, but his mood and that of his comrades at No. 3 was dashed by news that reached them from the Ypres Salient. On 29 August 1917 Lieutenant Revere Osler and eighteen men were bridging a shell hole in preparation for moving the guns in their battery when a German shell exploded in their midst. The wounded were brought back first to John McCrae's old dressing station at Essex Farm and from there to No. 47 Casualty Clearing Station.

Harvey Cushing, who had been asked to help during the British offensive, happened to be nearby at No. 46 Casualty Clearing Station, about nine miles from the front near Proven. Hearing the news after an eighteen-hour stretch in the operating theatre, Cushing rushed over to No. 47 to do whatever he could to help Revere, whose injuries were very serious. Despite his best efforts and those of his colleagues, the young man died next day and was buried in the windy, overcast early morning.

That same day in Oxford, the Oslers received a telegram at teatime informing them that Revere was dangerously wounded. When Sir William Osler read it, the great doctor, who had had a premonition from the outset that the war 'was somehow to bring home to him a great sorrow'[35], knew it was the end. Like his friend, Rudyard Kipling, who continued to mourn his son after two years, Osler now faced the terrible pain of losing his beloved 'Ike'. He wrote in his diary that: 'A sweeter laddie never lived . . . We are thankful to have the precious memory of his loving life.'[36] John McCrae wrote to his mother that 'We are all sorry to hear of Revere Osler's death: a bitter blow to his parents, poor people.'[37] Although Sir William put on a brave face in the months ahead, those who knew him well saw that beneath it, his heart was truly broken.

In the continuing autumn rain, the troops fighting in Haig's offensive in Belgium, known as the Third Battle of Ypres, were enduring appalling conditions and, in the base hospital area, enemy air raids became an additional hazard. One German airman who had been shot down told his rescuers that if they persisted in placing hospitals beside railway lines, they would continue to be bombed. John McCrae tried to be philosophical and yet again, took comfort and relief in the antics of the animals. 'Bonfire', who traditionally disliked pigs, was 'in lack of better friends . . . trying to "take up" with the house pig' while 'Bonneau', John's constant companion on ward rounds, one day decided to 'go around the hospital, carrying a large bone'.[38]

A short visit from Lawrence Cosgrave and a letter from a Toronto publisher expressing interest in publishing John's poems made him restless for a glimpse of the world away from the hospital. He was much in credit with leave and managed to secure a few days' entitlement without difficulty. Once again he headed for London and took a train to Orpington for a happy reunion with Tom McCrae. The brothers, making the most of John's short leave, spent an evening together in London. It was the last time they would see each other.

As the Third Battle of Ypres ground on, the capture of the village of Passchendaele, situated on one of the Salient's low ridges, was proving almost impossible. The Germans had built a defensive system that used barbed wire and concrete pillboxes with interlocking fields of fire. By early October, British troops had advanced only six miles at the cost of 200,000 casualties. On 13 October, Haig asked Lieutenant-General Sir Arthur Currie, recently knighted and now commanding the Canadian Corps, to put forward a plan. With his usual attention to detail, Currie worked to coordinate the infantry and artillery by sharing all available information. Lieutenant-Colonel Andrew McNaughton proceeded with counter-battery work; the Canadians constructed 'corduroy' roads with logs to cross the sea of mud that was the battlefield, an idea borrowed from the pioneer days in their native country. They also built a sawmill and made duckboards to move troops and supplies. Passable routes were marked with white tape, which proved to be a lifeline, for in that desolate and terrible place, injured men were doomed. Many soldiers, wounded and able-bodied, fell into shell holes full of water and drowned. Those who managed to struggle out were like wasps writhing out of syrup.

On 26 October 1917, the Canadian artillery opened fire and the infantry began their advance, among them the Princess Pats. It was hopeless. Within an hour every officer in the PPCLI had been killed or wounded. Over the next few days of attack and counter-attack the fighting was desperate and the ordeals dreadful in a hell of rain, mud and incessant shell and machine-gun fire.

The journalist, Philip Gibbs, watched through the smoke and mist as 'men held on quite grimly in their isolated bog'[39]. The 3rd and 4th Canadian Divisions finally took the dead husk of the village of Passchendaele on 6 November and Gibbs paid tribute in print to the unbroken spirit of the Canadians. Canon Scott, just back from leave, looked across the wasteland at the ruins of Passchendaele after the battle. The scene before him was a bleak and desolate sea of mud in which the dead lay where they had fallen and huge water-filled shell holes – often reddened with blood – remained deathtraps for the men who had survived the fighting and now walked in single file silhouetted against the grey sky, their gas capes blowing in the wind and rain. The autumn 1917 battles, which had cost almost half a million casualties, would remain forever a testament to the useless sacrifice of brave soldiers. John McCrae's poem 'The Anxious Dead', published on 30 September 1917, could also be considered a fitting tribute to the men who fought and died in the Third Battle of Ypres.

The Anxious Dead

O Guns, fall silent till the dead men hear
Above their heads the legions pressing on:
(These fought their fight in time of bitter fear,
And died not knowing how the day had gone.)

O flashing muzzles, pause, and let them see
The coming dawn that streaks the sky afar;
Then let your mighty chorus witness be
To them, and Caesar, that we still make war.

Tell them, O guns, that we have heard their call,
That we have sworn, and will not turn aside,
That we will onward till we win or fall,
That we will keep the faith for which they died.

Bid them be patient, and some day, anon,
They shall feel earth enwrapt in silence deep;
Shall greet, in wonderment, the quiet dawn,
And in content may turn them to their sleep.

When the lengthy convoys of muddy wounded from Passchendaele reached the hospitals, the staff of No. 3 saw the results of the heart-breaking struggle that had taken place. During October 1917, it handled more than six and a half thousand admissions, and on one occasion as many as eight hundred wounded were received in a twenty-four hour period. Working under constant pressure and the threat of air raids, the staff gave their all throughout that autumn. John McCrae managed to snatch a further six days' leave in November. He decided to go to Paris, and walked its quiet streets alone with his thoughts, for it was hard to tear his mind away from the war. In that same month, the British 3rd Army mounted one of the great surprise attacks of the war at Cambrai. This was the first effective tank attack in history and, with its initial success, the hoped-for breakthrough seemed to have come at last. Church bells were rung in Britain, but the British lacked armoured reserves and a German counter-attack recaptured much of what had been gained. In recognition of its role in the battle, the Newfoundland Regiment was granted the title 'Royal' – a regimental honour unique in the Great War.

It was almost the end of a year that was, in many ways, the nadir of the war for the Allies and Germans alike. Talks of peace had been shelved and on both sides there was a widespread feeling of war-weariness. The Allied 1917 offensives had achieved little result in real terms and the bleak and terrible months of the Third Battle of Ypres had seen unparalleled misery and suffering. Philip Gibbs, who continued to witness the cumulative effect of the conflict upon those whose fate it was to be caught up in it, felt that, in late 1917, the British army, for the first time, lost its spirit of optimism. Among many officers and men he found a great sense of depression: 'They saw no ending of the war, and nothing except continuous slaughter . . . They hated this war . . . Death had no allurement for them, except now and then as an escape from intolerable life under fire.'[40]

At No. 3 Canadian General Hospital, the weather and the pressure of dealing with the great numbers of wounded from the autumn battles continued to have an impact. On clear nights, the risk of German air raids increased and John McCrae wondered if he would ever enjoy moonlight again. Evacuation of patients from the hospital to England was held up by storm conditions in the Channel and the seemingly endless convoys of wounded from the last stages of the battle of Cambrai kept the unit very busy. On 9 December, however, spirits at No. 3 were lifted by the news from another war front, for it was learned that the Turks had surrendered Jerusalem to General Allenby's imperial forces. A few days later, a group of officers attended a Te Deum service in Boulogne Cathedral where, beneath its great dome, the Bishop of Arras gave a powerful address referring not only to the skill and bravery of Allenby's army and its leaders, but to the certainty that victory had been made possible by divine assistance.

On 13 December, Major-General G.L. Foster, Director of Medical Services for the Canadian contingents, sent Colonel Elder a telegram informing him that there would shortly be a vacancy for command of No. 1 Canadian General Hospital. He asked Elder to confirm whether Lieutenant-Colonel McCrae would be available and willing to take the position, since it was proposed to offer it to him. This was welcome news for John. A promotion at last, albeit to another hospital, was proof that he had not been forgotten. A reply to the telegram was to be sent after Christmas and meanwhile, thoughts at No. 3 turned to the festive season. The night of 22 December was cold, clear and moonlit – the sort of night, as the Boulogne base now knew, when enemy air activity could be anticipated. At 9.00 p.m. the siren sounded and the hospital stood on alert. It did not receive any direct hits but four bombs crashed into huts occupied by troops stationed near the town and forty men were killed. Surrounded by tragedy, it was hard to feel much Christmas cheer and John could only hope that 'it will be together that we shall spend the next one'.[41]

The staff of No. 3 tried to make that fourth wartime Christmas as happy as they could. At 11.00 a.m. on Christmas Day, dinner was served to the 1300 patients in the wards. Each man was given turkey, plum pudding or mince pies, nuts, raisins, oranges and tobacco or cigarettes, thanks once again to generous donations from Canada. Colonel Elder, Lieutenant-Colonel Alfred Bazin, who was now No. 3's Officer in Charge of Surgery, the Matron, Katherine MacLatchy and John, toured the hospital during the day to wish the soldiers a merry Christmas. As daylight faded, preparations were made for the evening, when the officers and nursing sisters were to dine together in the Recreation Hut.

When they arrived, they found the hut looking very festive. Not only had it been scrupulously cleaned, polished and decorated for the occasion with holly, mistletoe, evergreens and ivy, but someone had even managed to find some roses for the dinner table. After an excellent meal serenaded by the hospital orchestra, resounding cheers broke out when Colonel Elder read a telegram of good wishes from Colonel Birkett, the former commander of No. 3. Later, after the tables had been cleared, music and dancing continued until nearly midnight and all present could enjoy a brief respite from their duties.

On 28 December, Colonel Elder sent a reply to the telegram from Major-General Foster confirming that, while Lieutenant-Colonel McCrae naturally looked forward to succeeding to the command of his present unit, he was quite willing to take command of No. 1 General Hospital at any time.

A cold New Year 1918 was warmed by the news that Alfred Bazin had been awarded the DSO and two of the nursing sisters had been mentioned in Sir Douglas Haig's despatches. On 5 January, an additional and unexpected honour for John came in the form of another telegram from Major-General Foster:

> Since receiving your letter I have information from G.H.Q. that they will appoint a Consultant Physician to the British Armies in the Field, and have indicated their desire for Lieut.-Colonel McCrae for this duty. This is a much higher honour than commanding a General Hospital, and I hope he will take the post, as this is a position I have long wished should be filled by a C[anadian]. A[rmy]. M[edical]. C[orps]. officer.[42]

John happened to be away that day giving a lecture on fevers to the personnel of field ambulances of the Canadian Corps near Lens. On his return, he found Harvey Cushing taking tea with Colonel Elder and Lawrence Rhea. To Cushing, John did not seem 'at all like the "In Flanders Fields" person of former days' but was 'silent, asthmatic, moody'.[43] Elder gave John the news of his prestigious appointment which carried with it the temporary rank of colonel. It would make him the first Canadian to be appointed to such a senior position and reflected the very high regard in which he was held.

While the paperwork for his new appointment was making its way through official channels during January, John was concerned not only with his patients but, typically, with another of his animal friends. He wrote in a letter dated 9 January 1918 to Dr Maude Abbott in Montreal:

> To-day I am sorry to say that I lost a 'special' patient. A couple of months ago 'Windy', lst Batt[alio]n Lincoln reg[imen]t., a nice big old dog came off the hospital train with his labels tied on his collar and his second wound – a broken leg. He had been through Gallipoli. The leg recovered, but two days ago he took suddenly ill, and in 48 hours, in spite of all we could do, he went the way of a lot of other good soldiers. He will have [a] decent burial, and a headboard in our woods. How one hates to lose the faithful beasts! . . . All good wishes for the Year . . . I claim a regretful thought for poor old Windy, rest him![44]

It appears that 'Windy' arrived at No. 3 with his master and, while the latter went on to England for further treatment, the dog, with one leg in a plaster cast, consoled himself by spending time with John. When his leg was healed, 'Windy' enjoyed himself by joining John and 'Bonfire' on their afternoon rides. A true soldier's dog, 'Windy' had unfortunately decided that anyone who did not wear a khaki uniform was either a 'slacker' or an enemy. The fact that he had taken to chasing and biting any civilian who came along made him understandably rather unpopular in certain quarters and on 7 January, John found him lying on the mat beside his stove. Poor 'Windy' could keep no food down and hardly had the strength left to lick John's hand. All 'sorrowing Jack'[45] could do was to ease his pain with some morphia and Lawrence Rhea later pinpointed the likely cause of death as poison.

On the afternoon of 23 January, two days after The Duke of Connaught had visited No. 3, Colonel Elder was surprised to find John asleep in his chair in the officers' mess. He complained of a slight headache and was sent off duty to bed. That evening the confirmation of John's new appointment arrived and Elder hurried to congratulate him before making an official announcement to the other officers at dinner. Although very pleased, John's temperature was up and he remained in bed. Next morning, Elder found him sleeping soundly and when he awoke later with no pain, cough or fever, he felt considerably better. In the afternoon, however, he asked his superior to look in again. John was convinced that he was developing pneumonia and knowing he was not someone to express such an opinion without good reason, Elder arranged for a chest examination and specimens to be taken. No sign of pneumonia was found, although there was evidence of infection in John's sputum.

Despite the absence of physical symptoms, Colonel Elder telephoned Sir Bertrand Dawson who came that evening from No. 14 British General Hospital in nearby Wimereux. Sir Bertrand could also find no physical signs of pneumonia, but had to agree there was probably an undiscoverable patch of the disease. After a disturbed night with a headache and a temperature of 101 degrees, John fell into a peaceful sleep towards dawn and later that morning, was moved to No. 14 where he could be given the very best treatment. Two of the nurses from No. 3 volunteered to give him 24-hour care and by the end of that day there appeared to be quite an improvement. Yvonne Debacker later heard that John had spent time sitting by the window of his room contemplating with sadness the distant white cliffs of the English coast.[46]

The improvement did not last. During the following afternoon, John's condition deteriorated and symptoms of cerebral irritation began to appear. The next morning his temperature suddenly dropped and his pulse grew alarmingly weak.

He had become very sleepy and early that day, he gradually lapsed into a coma. At Sir Bertrand Dawson's invitation, Colonel Elder and Lawrence Rhea came to take a blood culture and perform a lumbar puncture. John's friends and colleagues had been able to offer him the best medical care available, but he did not have the strength left to fight. At 1.30 a.m. on the morning of 28 January 1918, John McCrae died. Over a quarter of a century earlier, he had written that "'tis but one step from the midst of stormy life to the precincts of everlasting rest.'[47] Now, he had taken that step.

Colonel Elder and Private Dodge, John's groom, went to the phone together in the early hours to find out about John's condition. Dodge remembered that, after Elder replaced the receiver and told him the sad news with a broken voice, 'we both went away blubbering like two schoolchildren'.[48] Even 'Bonfire' seemed to know what had happened. John had visited the stable every morning to bring him a couple of sugar lumps and the morning after John's death, 'the old horse suddenly turned to the stable door, about the usual time, and stared, as if he could see him, and whinnied'.[49]

The self-diagnosis proved correct. A post-mortem revealed that John had not only developed pneumonia in both lungs, but also meningitis. True to himself, he had given everything he could but the lingering effects of Second Ypres, the arduous years of work at No. 3, the effect of the cold, damp climate on his asthma and his susceptibility to chest infections had proved a fatal combination. Harvey Cushing, who had visited him the night before he died, described John in his last hours as 'a bright flame rapidly burning out'.[50] He also knew that as a soldier through and through, John would have detested the idea of dying in bed. Cushing later recalled that some of the more senior members of the hospital staff who had served with John almost from the beginning, went out scouring the fields in the hope of finding some chance winter poppies to put on his grave. The flowers were, according to Cushing 'to remind him of Flanders where he would have preferred to lie' and he summed up the friend he had just lost: 'Was anyone ever more respected and loved than he?'[51]

News of John's death spread quickly throughout the Boulogne Base to the troops in the trenches and out into the wider world. It had been so quick and sudden that there was shock, disbelief and great grief. Messages of regret began to pour in from his friends, former colleagues and countless others with whom he had unknowingly communicated through his poem.

Arrangements were made to hold the funeral on 29 January 1918 at the cemetery on the hillside above Wimereux. The afternoon was unusually warm and springlike, and overcoats were not necessary. Colonel Elder described John's funeral as 'the largest and most impressive I have seen here; indeed it was the most impressive military funeral I have ever seen anywhere.'[52] At about the same time David McCrae received the news of his son's death by telegram, the funeral procession left No. 14 and made its way along the main street of Wimereux, across the river and up the hill to the cemetery. The coffin was draped with a Union Jack as opposed to the Canadian Red Ensign because John had died in a British hospital. Behind it, John's faithful groom, Dodge, led 'Bonfire' with John's boots reversed in the stirrups. The horse's head drooped as if he knew he would not see his master again.

Since Tom McCrae had finished his war service and returned to Philadelphia, John's cousin, Walter Gow, came from London to represent the family. Another old friend who set out for France as soon as he heard the news was John Almond, now Director of Chaplain Services Europe at Canadian Military Headquarters in London. He helped to conduct the service that, with so many friends and colleagues present, was held in an atmosphere of unrestrained grief. In a letter to a friend written later that same day one of No. 3's nurses, Sister Isobel Davies, left a detailed description of the funeral which is worth quoting in full:

Tuesday January 29th 1918
My dear Miss Leaford
Long before this reaches you, you will know about Col. McCrae's death, at present we simply cannot believe it . . . Sir Bertrand Dawson sent him to No. 14 – no particular anxiety was felt till Saturday p.m. He had had a very restless day – pulse and temp[erature]. almost normal. But Sunday about 2–3 a.m. he became unconscious and so remained till his death, Monday at 1.30 a.m.

It was all so sudden that it leaves one stunned. We have just come back from the funeral, and a wonderful and impressive ceremony it was. The service was delayed till this afternoon to allow his cousin (Gough, I think was the name) to come from England and Gen[eral]. Morrison, his friend and late O[fficer]. C[ommanding]. to come from the front. – I have never seen such a gathering of military notabilities before in France. It was a great and well deserved tribute to the honour and esteem in which Col[onel]. McCrae was held. Gen[eral]. Currie and his staff. Sir Arthur Sloggett D[eputy] D[irector] M[edical] S[ervices] France and Staff. Gen[eral]. Morrison. Two Generals whom I did not know; all the consultants in the area, and from Camiers representatives from each Hosp[ital]. English, Canadian, Portuguese and American; all our medical officers; 50 of our men, and all the original sisters now with the unit – about 40 – Col[onel]. Elder had to get special permission from the Base Commandant for us to be present. We wore long blue coats and white veils.

The funeral procession started from No. 14 Gen. The coffin on a wheeled stretcher pulled by R[oyal]. A[rmy]. M[edical]. C[orps]. men. The coffin covered with the Union Jack, and heaped high with flowers (we sent a pillow of violets), his belt and cap, of course immediately following the coffin came his horse 'Bonfire', his bridle all laced in white ribbon – no mourning is allowed, and the long boots reversed in the stirrups. Poor Bonfire! – he was a pathetic sight – and seeing him riderless brought home to us more forcibly than anything else could that Col[onel]. McCrae had left us.- Immediately behind Bonfire came the chief mourners including his cousin, Gen[eral]. Morrison, Gen[eral].

Dodds, Col[onel]. Elder – then the firing party – North Staffords, about 50 strong, then the officers – lastly the men.

The cemetery is a mile distant from the Hospital so we took the cars which brought us over to the Cemetery where we found several staff officers waiting – I wish I could describe the burial. It is an old cemetery on the side of a hill. As you stood on the top looking towards his grave, more hills rose up to the left with the straight French roads crossing them, while on the right lay the Channel, blue and sparkling in the sunshine. It was a glorious day – clear over the sea – a misty purple haze over the hills. At the cemetery gates, the coffin was lifted from the carrier to the shoulders of 6 of our tallest sergeants, and by the side walked the pall bearers, four L[ieutenan]t. Col[onel]s. All the A[rmy]. M[edical]. C[orps]. officers. (I enclose a diagram, roughly made, of how they were standing during the service). There were 3 padres – the Presbyterian Service, a prayer, a short reading from the Bible – then another prayer – the burial prayer bringing in 'Dust to dust.' There was hardly a dry eye. Poor Col[onel]. Elder just put his cap over his face. The firing party went through the form but did not fire – the bugles blew the 'Last Post'. One hears it every night – but – it was very different this afternoon.

It seemed so unkind to come away and leave him there, but it is a beautiful peaceful hillside, facing the sea. Do you remember his poem 'We are the dead' – he little thought at the time of writing 'In Flanders Fields' how soon he would be numbered with them – Col[onel]. Elder is broken hearted. He looks absolutely crushed – On Wed[nesday]. last Col[onel]. McCrae's orders came through to go to the First Army as a Consultant. It was a great honour to a Canadian, but not more than he deserved. I believe that at dinner in the Mess that evening, Col[onel]. McCrae was not present, had gone to bed, not feeling too well – In a little speech, Col[onel]. Elder told the officers about Col[onel]. McCrae's orders and said such nice things, a warm tribute and an appreciation of him, as a man, a soldier and a physician. So many things have happened in the last four weeks which at the time seemed everyday happenings, but now have a great significance. The official photographer was there, both when the Cortege left No. 14 and at the Cemetery so you will doubtless see the photographs . . . I don't think I will ever forget today – We can think of nothing else tonight. I thought you would like to hear a few particulars. – The first time I ever met Dr. McCrae I was at a lecture with you.

Good night – much love

Isobel Davies'[53]

Her colleague, Sister Margaret Woods, one of the nurses who had come from the Royal Vic., also wrote to a nursing friend to tell her about the funeral. The following extract reveals much about the effect of John's death on his friends at No. 3:

> of course you remember him as a fine, strong, healthy man, young, I can see him yet as he lectured to us, also the quiet sadness of his 'good-bye' when he came over here. He joined our Hospital in the summer of 1915, a changed man, yes older in appearance, his heart seemed to be with his friends of his who 'paid the big price' in the Battle of Ypres . . . We only wish we could have done something to show our appreciation, but man like, he did not want to be thought sick, and he has gone never knowing how much we cared.
>
> We miss his familiar face and his cheery stories always something to make us laugh. – Poor Miss MacIntosh misses him sadly, she has been in Pneumonia Hut latest, and Col[onel]. McCrae spent a good deal of his time on patients there. With his going the last home tie seems gone.
>
> Col[onel]. Elder is feeling very sadly, for nights he could not sleep, he feels too, that he is strangely alone, no one to talk things over with. Col[onel]. Elder thought of everything that Col[onel]. McCrae loved. His horse 'Bonfire' was at the burial, all his special friends too, they were broken hearted because he became unconscious so quickly that they could not see him . . . All came as we did, because we loved him and wanted to show him this last mark of respect.[54]

Harvey Cushing remembered that, as John 'was being lowered into his grave there was a distant sound of guns – as though called into voice by the occasion'.[55] Cyril Allinson, who was also present, recalled that on top of the many, many floral tributes was a wreath of artificial poppies that the officers of No. 3 had managed to obtain from Paris. It was a gesture that John McCrae would surely have appreciated. Walter Gow took with him John's personal effects to return to Janet and David McCrae.

Yvonne Debacker had her own treasured memories of 'the Colonel', particularly the time he had wanted to attend her first Communion but was prevented by his work, but had nevertheless asked for a photograph of her as a memento of the occasion. Then there was the time when he had contributed to Christmas presents for her and her family in a quiet and modest way. She tried to comfort 'Bonneau' but he remained inconsolable and, for a month after John's death, she heard him howling daily as he mourned the man who had been such a friend to him and all other animals.[56]

At the McGill Medical Museum, Dr Maude Abbott received John's letter of 9 January on the same day that she learned of his death. She wrote straightaway to Oskar Klotz in Pittsburgh:

Jan 30. '18

Dear Dr. Klotz

I know you will be distressed beyond measure to hear the sad news of our dear Col[onel]. John McCrae – our hero of heroes – our man of men. Report has it he died of pneumonia and this is confirmed to Dr. Archibald by a wire from his people in Guelph. The news was cabled from France yesterday.

This morning's post brought me a letter from him which, under the circumstances, is the most pathetic I ever read. I enclose a copy of it for you. I think he had seen my Irish terrier dogs and knew how fond I was of them . . . Mrs. Birkett tells me this was to have been his last winter there.

His friend – and yours -

Maude Abbott[57]

All John's friends were effusive in their tributes to him as messages poured into the hospital and his parents' home from far and wide, bearing witness to his impact upon the lives of all who had known him. Two of the most eloquent came from his old teacher, George Adami, and from his friend and colleague at McGill, Professor William Caldwell. Adami's long tribute opened with the words, 'There have been few finer characters, or men of richer and more varied endowment in the Imperial Medical Service than John McCrae.'[58] Caldwell eulogised John as,

> one of the finest men I have ever met in any University. I had remarked to one or two colleagues recently, 'Think of it, a poet and a scientist and a soldier – a scholar, a gentleman, a Christian, a fine fellow, generous, unselfish, a tireless, aggressive worker.' And over all this there was the charm, the esprit, the freshness of the bubbling personality of Jack McCrae . . . He was indeed a rare humanist, and the University can ill afford to lose him and his influence as a man and as a teacher.[59]

John's parents took comfort over their loss from the very faith they had instilled into their children. Janet McCrae, who had always been so close to her younger son, bore her sorrow privately. Despite their grief, she and her husband could take pride in John's achievements and David McCrae began to paste tribute after tribute into his scrapbook. Janet had kept the letter John had sent to her just before his ship had sailed for South Africa in 1900. Now that 'something untoward'[60] had happened, she opened it and later told Andrew Macphail that 'It lay in my Bible, unopened, for 19 years, but – worth waiting for.'[61]

At a Memorial Service held at McGill University on 4 February 1918,

251

the black-robed professors gathered with the McCrae family and friends to hear John Macnaughton gave an address that spoke of John's life, character and personality, his friendship, his interests, his many talents and the unshakeable belief that had underpinned his entire life:

> He never lost the simple faith of his childhood . . . He was so sure about the main things, the vast things, the entirely and obviously indispensable things, of which all formulated faiths are but a more or less stammering expression . . . His instinctive faith sufficed him.[62]

Walter Gow sent John McCrae's personal effects home to Canada but his most precious legacy remained in France and Belgium, its universal truth enshrined in the hearts of the soldiers. For them, John's poem expressed their deepest thoughts and was passed by word of mouth from one soldier to another – those who survived would pass it on to their children.

NOTES

1. From 'In Flanders Fields' by John McCrae, *Punch*, 8 December 1915.
2. JM to Janet McCrae, 21 January 1917, MG 30 D209, Micro A-1103, NAC.
3. JM to Janet McCrae, 28 January 1917, MG 30, D209, Micro A-1103, NAC.
4. JM to Janet McCrae, 3 February 1917, MG 30, D209, Micro A-1103, NAC.
5. JM to Janet McCrae, 11 February 1917, MG 30, D209, Micro A-1103, NAC.
6. JM to Geills Kilgour, 4 February 1917, MG 30, D209, Micro A-1103, NAC.
7. JM to Janet McCrae, 11 February 1917, MG 30 D209, Micro A-1103, NAC.
8. JM to Janet McCrae, 25 February 1917, MG 30, D209, Micro A-1103, NAC.
9. JM to Janet McCrae, 28 January 1917, MG 30, D209, Micro A-1103, NAC.
10. JM to Janet McCrae, 22 March 1917, MG 30, D209, Micro A-1103, NAC.
11. JM to Janet McCrae, 22 March 1917, MG30, D209, Micro A-1103, NAC.
12. Macphail, *In Flanders Fields*, p. 58.
13. JM to Janet McCrae, 29 April 1917, MG 30, D209, Micro A-1103, NAC.
14. Scott, *The Great War as I Saw It*, pp. 166–167.
15. Hon. Ian Mackenzie, as quoted in *The Epic of Vimy* (Ottawa, 1936), p. 95.
16. Lieutenant Gordon Chisholm, as quoted in Brereton Greenhous & Stephen Harris, *Canada and the Battle of Vimy Ridge* (Ottawa, 1992), p. 90.
17. Edward Morrison to JM, 11 April 1917, GM Papers.
18. Edward Morrison to JM, 11 April 1917, GM Papers. 'Jake' was an expression of the time meaning 'O.K.'
19. Jim Lotz, *Canadians at War* (London, 1990), p. 42.
20. JM to Janet McCrae, 14 May 1917, MG 30, D209, Micro A-1103, NAC.
21. JM to Janet McCrae, 7 May 1917, MG 30, D209, Micro A-1103, NAC. Detail from the photograph John refers to is shown on the front cover of the book.
22. JM to Janet McCrae, 3 June 1917, MG 30, D209, Micro A-1103, NAC.
23. JM to Janet McCrae, 1 July 1917, MG 30, D209, Micro A-1103, NAC.
24. JM to Janet McCrae, 14 July 1917, MG 30, D209, Micro A-1103, NAC.
25. JM to Janet McCrae, 20 May 1917, MG 30, D209, Micro A-1103, NAC.
26. JM to Janet McCrae, 20 May 1917, MG 30, D209, Micro A-1103, NAC.

27. JM to Janet McCrae, 10 June 1917, MG 30, D209, Micro A-1103, NAC.
28. JM to Janet McCrae, 10 June 1917, MG 30, D209, Micro A-1103, NAC.
29. JM to Janet McCrae, 17 June 1917, MG 30, D209, Micro A-1103, NAC.
30. JM to Janet McCrae, 10 June 1917, MG 30, D209, Micro A-1103, NAC.
31. JM to Janet McCrae, 14 July 1917, MG 30, D209, Micro A-1103, NAC.
32. JM to Janet McCrae, 2 September 1917, MG 30, D209, Micro A-1103, NAC.
33. JM to Janet McCrae, 26 August 1917, MG 30, D209, Micro A-1103, NAC.
34. JM to Janet McCrae, 2 September 1917, MG 30, D209, Micro A-1103, NAC.
35. Cushing, *Sir William Osler*, Volume II, p. 423.
36. Cushing, *Sir William Osler*, Volume II, p. 578.
37. JM to Janet McCrae, 2 September 1917, MG 30, D209, Micro A-1103, NAC.
38. JM to Janet McCrae, 9 September 1917, MG 30 D209, Micro A-1103, NAC.
39. Sir Philip Gibbs, 'I Saw Passchendaele Taken', *The Great War – I Was There*. Part 35 (London, 1938), p. 1402.
40. Gibbs, *Now It Can Be Told*, p. 485.
41. JM to Janet McCrae, 2 December 1917, MG 30, D209, Micro A-1103, NAC.
42. Macphail, *In Flanders Fields*, p. 133.
43. Harvey Cushing, *From a Surgeon's Journal* (London, 1936), 6 January 1918.
44. JM to Dr Maude Abbott, 9 January 1918, MH.
45. Cushing, *From a Surgeon's Journal*, 29 January 1918, p. 283.
46. Interview with Madame Yvonne Deligny, *La Voix du Nord* (February 1958).
47. John McCrae, 'Reflections', *The Varsity*, Volume 11, No. 13, 9 February 1892, p. 178, Micro mfm/LH/V377, UTL.
48. Undated letter (circa February 1918) from W. Dodge to Mrs. J. Matthews, MH.
49. Undated letter (circa February 1918) from W. Dodge to Mrs. J. Matthews, MH.
50. Cushing, *From a Surgeon's Journal*, 28 January 1918, p. 280.
51. Cushing, *From a Surgeon's Journal*, 28 January 1918, p. 280.
52. G.M. Elder, Obituary of Lieutenant-Colonel John McCrae, *British Medical Journal*, 9 February 1918, p. 191.
53. Isobel Davies to Miss Leaford, 29 January 1918, MH.
54. Margaret Woods to Miss Hall, 5 February 1918, MG30 B61, Klotz Papers, NAC.
55. Cushing, *From a Surgeon's Journal*, 29 January 1918, p. 281.
56. When she saw the anguish of the faithful 'Bonneau', Yvonne Debacker could not bear to be parted from him and the dog remained with her and her family until 1921 or 1922 when he was stolen by a group of travelling gypsies. Yvonne never saw him again. Interview with Madame Yvonne Deligny, *La Voix du Nord*, 12 February 1958.
57. Dr Maude Abbott to Oskar Klotz, 30 January 1918, MG 30, B61, Klotz Papers, NAC.
58. J.G. Adami, 'Obituary of John McCrae', *British Medical Journal* (9 February 1918), pp. 190–191.
59. Professor William Caldwell, 'Honored Memory of Late Lt.-Col. McCrae', *Montreal Gazette*, 5 February 1918.
60. JM to Janet McCrae, 21 January 1900, MG 30, D209, Micro A-1102, NAC.
61. Undated letter from Janet McCrae to Sir Andrew Macphail, Macphail Papers, MG 30, D150, NAC.
62. John Macnaughton, 'In Memoriam, Lt.-Col. John McCrae', pp. 236-237.

CHAPTER FIFTEEN

'. . .we will onward till we win or fall'[1]
January 1918–May 1919

The war continued for nine months after John McCrae's death – nine months of drama and desperation before the curtain finally fell on Kipling's 'Armageddon'. After a period of relative quiet during the first quarter of the year, the storm broke out with renewed fury in March 1918. Desperate to land a decisive blow that would bring the Allies to the peace table before American manpower tipped the balance, the German army launched a massive offensive, the 'Kaiserschlacht' or 'Kaiser's Battle' in March. Over the next few months there followed a series of major attacks against the Allied armies in the areas of Ypres, Reims and Soissons. Each achieved considerable success and, by early June, the Germans were within sixty miles of Paris. Unified under the French Marshal Foch's direction and, with the steady build-up of new American troops to provide much-needed reserves, Allied troops reeled and retreated at the onslaught but the front did not collapse. When American troops entered the line at Veuilly-la-Poterie, they decorated their steel helmets with poppies.[2]

The German gamble had failed. Philip Gibbs later recalled the masterly skill, strength and speed of the German offensive; the quiet, grim courage of the Allied soldiers; the dreadful prospect of losing all the old Somme battlefield areas that had been won from the Germans at such fearful human cost. Yet throughout he had marvelled at the 'absence of panic, the fatalistic acceptance of turn of fortune's wheel . . . and the refusal . . . to give way to despair in those days of tragedy and crisis'.[3]

Early in July 1918 a model Allied attack was launched at Hamel. Masterminded by the Australian Lieutenant-General Sir John Monash, it was an outstanding success and pointed the way to the future with its use of tanks and the dropping of ammunition by parachute to machine gunners in forward positions. The German commander, General Erich Ludendorff, struck one further blow either side of Reims on 15 July but, under the command of Foch and with two American divisions as their spearhead, the Allies launched a huge and successful counter-attack on 18 July between the Marne and Aisne. It was to prove the turning point of the war. The German army had shown itself capable of superhuman effort but, unable to achieve total victory, a gradual erosion of its spirit and motivation began slowly but surely to take place. In contrast, the British Expeditionary Force, after all its trials, had become better balanced and more flexible as a fighting force.

Throughout this period, the hospitals worked at full stretch to cope with the wounded. British casualties at the front averaged about ten thousand a week and a major influenza epidemic was beginning to sweep Europe. At No. 3 Canadian General Hospital, Colonel Elder received news of his promotion to the position of Consultant Surgeon to the British Army, Rouen area. The arrival on 31 July of Colonel Elder's replacement, Colonel Lorne Drum, coincided with the start of a visit to the hospital by Sir William Peterson, Principal and Vice-Chancellor of McGill University. He was delighted to see that McGill's traditions were continuing to be so well upheld by the unit.

After the first major American participation at Château Thierry, their presence began to have a considerable effect on Allied strength. By 6 August the Germans had withdrawn behind the Aisne. Finally, after four terrible years, there was a realisation that the key to breaking the deadlock of trench warfare lay in planned, precise co-ordination of all arms and the use of the element of surprise that had somehow been lost in the desperate search for more and greater firepower. For the Allies the crisis was over but for the Germans, it was about to begin. On 8 August and turning the weather to their advantage as the Germans had done five months earlier, the British Fourth and French First Armies struck east of Amiens in conditions of thick mist. The Australian and Canadian Corps, two of the finest fighting formations in the BEF, played a crucial part. The reputation of the Canadians by now was such that their presence would have alerted the Germans to an offensive, so two battalions were purposely left in Flanders as a deception. Starting with a ferocious surprise bombardment, the Allies advanced up to eight miles on the first day and the German commander, Ludendorff, later called it 'the black day of the German army in the history of this war'.[4] Just as he now foresaw the destruction of the German war-machine and its spirit, Sir Douglas Haig saw opportunities for an outright victory before the winter.

For Canada, the period from 4 August to 11 November 1918 became known as 'the Hundred Days'. News of the Allied success spread quickly and, at No. 3 Canadian General Hospital, its impact helped to cheer the patients and speed their rate of recovery. Spirits were also high when George Adami hosted a lunch for Sir William Peterson on his arrival in London. Some thirteen members of the McGill Medical Faculty were present, among them Andrew Macphail and Charles Martin, another friend and former colleague of John McCrae's, who was on his way to No. 3 to fill the senior medical post vacant since John's death.

Ludendorff's offer of resignation was rejected by Kaiser Wilhelm but there was agreement in Berlin that the war must be brought to an end. Germany had lost half a million troops in five months and on 14 August, the German Foreign Secretary was instructed to make peace overtures via the Queen of the Netherlands. The Allied advance continued and the Germans retreated from most of the ground they had won in April. Daring attacks by the Australians and the Canadian Corps compelled Ludendorff to order a retirement to the major German defensive line, the so-called Hindenburg Line. The Allied advance of some 25 miles along a 40-mile front meant they were now approaching that line. Further progress involved crossing the heavily fortified Canal du Nord but, assisted by tanks, the Canadians successfully negotiated this formidable barrier and achieved the long-sought goal – a complete breakthrough of the German defences.

It was an immense psychological blow for Germany and German leaders realised that the war was lost. By the end of September Ludendorff was urging peace and, on 3 October, Prince Max of Baden, a known advocate of peace, agreed to take over as Imperial Chancellor. Peace notes were sent the following day by both Germany and Austria-Hungary to the American President Woodrow Wilson, whose Fourteen Points – a series of conditions for peace which had been set before the U.S. Congress in January 1918 – would serve as a basis for negotiations. German morale may have been low, but the continuing Allied advance met with stiff and tenacious resistance from the German artillery. The faithful Canon Scott, still with the Canadian troops in the front line near Cambrai, suffered serious wounds in both legs which caused him to call for his first and last tot of rum during the war. He was distraught at having to leave the men who for four years 'had been my beloved companions and my constant care'[5] and whose courage had been an inspiration to him.

Despite heavy losses, British and Canadian troops entered Cambrai by 9 October. Elsewhere there was jubilation as French and Belgian cities were liberated. On 8 October, President Wilson replied to the German peace note, insisting that the U-boat campaign must be stopped and confirming that the Allies would only negotiate with a democratic German government. Prince Max signalled Germany's willingness to meet these conditions and a further American note demanded what amounted to an unconditional surrender. For Ludendorff, this was more than his pride could stand. He again offered his resignation and this time it was accepted. As the progress of the Allied armies continued, the Canadian artillery continued their great contribution and John McCrae's old friend, Edward Morrison, now in overall command of the Canadian Corps Artillery, wrote on 13 October that:

We have been fighting steadily for nearly three months, but we are not tired . . . This open fighting suits the Canadians down to the ground. When the Boche sent over word what he was going to do to the Canadians in open fighting, his appreciation of the situation was entirely wrong. He must since have been very sorry that our people ever came out of the trenches.[6]

The beginning of November marked the final collapse of the Central Powers. Turkey had already signed an armistice and Austria-Hungary followed suit on 3 November. A revolt by German sailors at Kiel meant that by 4 November, the major German naval base was in the hands of the mutineers and anarchy was starting to spread across the country. President Wilson presented the agreed Allied terms on 6 November and gave Germany seventy-two hours to accept or reject them. On 9 November, the Kaiser's abdication was announced and with it, the renunciation by the German Crown Prince of his claim to the throne. As Wilhelm II slipped away to exile in Holland a German republic was proclaimed. On his arrival at the isolated estate of a Dutch nobleman who had agreed to give him sanctuary, the former Kaiser's first request was for 'a cup of really good English tea'.[7] At approximately 5.00 a.m. on the morning of 11 November 1918, the final armistice agreement was signed in Marshal Foch's special train in the Compiègne Forest.

The coming of dawn that day brought with it a strange symmetry. As Canadian troops, now in Mons, cleared the town of the German rearguard, the Allies were back where they had begun over four years earlier. The last British troops to leave Mons on 23 August 1914 had been the 42nd Highlanders, the Black Watch. The first troops to enter the city at the close of the war were their imperial counterparts, the Black Watch of Canada, together with the Princess Patricia's Canadian Light Infantry, the first Canadian unit to see combat in the war. The ceasefire was set at the eleventh hour of the eleventh day of the eleventh month. All eyes were on watches for the precise moment and, as the gunfire was halted, the eerie silence that descended marked the end of what had been the most terrible war in human history. Those in Mons that morning remembered the mist and the sunlight glinting on the copper of the autumn leaves; the intermittent sullen bark of a gun; a distant bugle call of 'Cease Fire'; and, faintly from across the fields, the sound of a cheer.

Many soldiers simply could not believe that it was over. The end was something of an anticlimax and, above all, the most remarkable feature of that day and night was the uncanny silence. Philip Gibbs, who had witnessed events throughout those tragic years, realised that he had written his last account as a war correspondent. That evening in Mons was one to remember as the soldiers were mobbed by friendly local people and offered beer and wine that had been hidden from the Germans. It was a toast to life and the beginning of freedom.

At the Base hospitals, struggling with the influenza epidemic and the many resulting cases of pneumonia and chest infections, the significance of the approaching Armistice was all but lost. One of the nurses at No. 26 General Hospital, Camiers, recollected that when the news was received, 'there wasn't one man in the ward who knew. They were all . . . too ill. There wasn't one man who understood. Not one man.'[8] While the influenza epidemic was taking its toll the surgery team at No. 3 Canadian General Hospital continued to operate day and night on seriously wounded patients. On 10 November, however, there was a realisation that the conflict was almost over and, early the next afternoon after cheers for the King and Canada, the hospital bugle formally sounded the ceasefire.

In London the news was received with a mixture of jubilation and relief. Leo Amery, now assistant secretary to the Secretary of State for War, was on his way to Whitehall on the morning of 11 November. Since leaving the Western Front early in 1915 he had served as a Balkans specialist in the Intelligence Department and been posted to the staff of the Salonika Army before taking up the work that had led him to his present post. During the past few months, Amery had watched the events leading up the Armistice at close range. As he walked towards Downing Street he found a large crowd ahead of him and the Prime Minister, David Lloyd George, standing on the doorstep of Number 10 telling them that within a few minutes the war would be over. 'In a moment,' Amery remembered, 'Whitehall was singing with joyous crowds and with taxis, each loaded with the best part of a dozen cheering passengers.'[9]

The city became jubilant from that moment. Office workers filled the streets waving flags and the sound of wartime songs brought a lump to many throats. Traffic in Whitehall was at a standstill and crowds swept down the Mall to Buckingham Palace. After the years of blackout, the lights in the Houses of Parliament were switched on again that first evening of peace. From his room on the seventh floor of the Endsleigh Palace Hospital near Euston Station, Canon Scott, still recovering from his wounds, glimpsed the wild rejoicing. Celebrations continued after dark as bonfires were lit in Trafalgar Square and other open spaces. At the Piccadilly Hotel, which was full to bursting, people danced on the tables as the champagne flowed.

In Canada, the news was received around 3.00 a.m. local time in Toronto. The city was awoken by the siren of one of the main department stores and women munitions workers left the night shift and paraded up Yonge Street beating tin pans and blowing whistles. There were scenes of joy and relief everywhere with civil holidays announced, parades, torchlight processions and bonfires on which effigies of the Kaiser were burnt. In countless churches across the young nation, prayers of thanksgiving and remembrance were said.

After the years of anguish and strain, people understandably felt a spontaneous outburst of joy. Yet beneath the outer demonstrations, there was a palpable bleakness in this victory that dawned 'upon a world too weary for jubilation, too weary even for comprehension'.[10] So many families had lost loved ones that for them it was also a time of great sorrow. The Armistice and the feelings of those who had survived the war were evoked in the bitter words of another war poet, Siegfried Sassoon, while Thomas Hardy wrote of the misery and pity in the new silence, now that much of the 'young life and laughter of old days'[11] had gone. Kipling, who had predicted it all, wrote a poem laying the blame at the feet of statesmen who had failed to heed the warnings.

The transition from war to peace began straightaway. Recruiting ceased and call-up notices were cancelled. Canadian troops remained in Europe to share in the Allied occupation of Germany. As they crossed the Rhine bridge and entered Bonn, Lieutenant-General Sir Arthur Currie took the salute on 13 December 1918. At the outbreak of war, he had predicted that his men in the Second Infantry Brigade would 'fight like Billy be damned'[12] and, in the light of the past four years, the same could be said of the entire Canadian Corps. With Sir Arthur that day was Edward Morrison who later wrote to Geills Kilgour that, as,

> I rode . . . across the great bridge on the Rhine with the Corps Commander and his staff and then watched our magnificent Canadian divisions tramping across with bands playing and colours flying you can imagine how I wished that Jack and 'Bonfire' were with us. We felt sure he was with us in spirit and were glad that we were able to have kept faith with those who died.[13]

In January 1919 the peace conference was formally opened at Versailles, near Paris, and the Allies agreed to adopt the Covenant of President Wilson's proposed League of Nations, a vision of a new world order where countries would be united by a common pledge to preserve peace and submit their differences to a supreme court of arbitration. A Victory Parade of overseas Dominion troops took place in London on 3 May 1919 with the Canadians leading the way, Sir Arthur Currie proudly before them as the procession marched across Hyde Park, down Constitution Hill and past King George V on a dais outside Buckingham Palace. The Allied peace terms were handed to Germany and on 28 June 1919, five years to the day after gunshots in Sarajevo sparked a worldwide war, the final peace treaty was ratified in the Versailles Hall of Mirrors. That day, Canada came of age as a nation for her gallant and superbly capable citizen-soldiers had earned her the right to be a separate signatory.

The units in which John McCrae had served sailed for home with distinguished war records. The Canadian artillery had rendered sterling service under the command of Major-General Edward Morrison. Of

Morrison's original 1st Brigade CFA, two colonels – one of whom was William Dodds – had gone on to become brigadier-generals commanding divisional artillery. Two majors and a captain had become brigade commanders, Lawrence Cosgrave being the captain in question. Now Lieutenant-Colonel Cosgrave, DSO and Bar, Croix de Guerre, he it was who finished the war as commanding officer of lst Brigade CFA.

The Empire's first university hospital unit closed its doors on 29 May 1919. Heading No.3's surgical team during the final months was Lieutenant-Colonel Francis Scrimger VC, who, when not operating, helped throughout the worst of the influenza epidemic until he fell ill himself. Like its sister Canadian hospitals, No. 3 Canadian General Hospital (McGill) had achieved great success in the face of tremendous workloads. During its four years of operation, it handled 143,762 admissions and registered 986 deaths – less than one per cent of the total. These figures represented thousands of hours of highly skilled and faithful work by all who served there. Apart from those like John McCrae who had died in its service, there were others like Herbert Birkett, Lawrence Rhea and Francis Scrimger who had put their own health in jeopardy for the sake of the patients in their care. Sir William Osler could be proud of the doctors and nurses from Canada, many of whom had, either directly or indirectly, followed his precepts and example.

That same month Canon Frederick Scott arrived at his home city of Quebec with some of the returning Canadian troops. As Scott watched the bright faces of his men, a lump came to his throat when he thought of what they had endured. Parting company with them for the last time, he visualised the thousands like John McCrae who had left Valcartier that September four years and seven months earlier, and who would never see their homeland again. It brought to mind a verse he himself had written, that was now recorded on the city's memorial to the men of Quebec who had given their lives in the South African War:

> Not by the power of commerce, art or pen,
> Shall our great Empire stand; nor has it stood;
> But by the noble deeds of noble men,
> Heroic lives and heroes' outpoured blood.

NOTES

1. From 'The Anxious Dead' by John McCrae, *The Spectator*, 30 September 1917.
2. Report dated 6 June 1918 by Associated Press, MH.
3. Gibbs, *Now It Can Be Told*, p. 498.
4. Gibbs, *Now It Can Be Told*, p. 501.
5. Scott, *The Great War as I Saw It*, p. 317.

6. Edward Morrison to H.P. Hill, 13 October 1918, MG 30, E81, Vol. 10, Morrison papers, NAC.

7. Palmer, *The Kaiser*, p. 213.

8. Lyn MacDonald, *The Roses of No Man's Land* (London, 1993), p. 293.

9. Amery, *My Political Life* Vol. II. p. 173.

10. Buchan, *The King's Grace*, p. 235.

11. From 'Looking Forward' by Geoffrey Winthrop Young, as quoted in Coombs, *Before Endeavours Fade*, p. 4.

12. Dancocks, *Sir Arthur Currie* (Toronto, 1985), p. 31.

13. Edward Morrison to Geills Kilgour, 31 January 1919, GM Papers.

CHAPTER SIXTEEN

'. . . we will keep the faith for which they died'[1]
1919–1997

A generation had marched away from 'the unclouded blue of that summer'[2] of 1914 to a world of unimaginable horror. With the first months of peace came a time of reckoning and of mourning for much of the civilized world. Quite apart from the enormous war casualties, the influenza epidemic had assumed global proportions and would ultimately claim over twenty million lives. So many deaths left a 'great emptiness'[3] behind them and the 'pensive and melancholy face'[4] of history that Andrew Macphail later described, would always apply to the immediate post-war years.

The emotional impact of the Great War upon the people of the participating nations was enormous. The bereaved faced the trauma of coming to terms with their losses and the survivors, many of whom bore physical or mental scars, would never be the same again. Few returning veterans would ever shake off the memories that were to haunt them. What lay before them all was a changed world in which they felt strangely at sea, and most were at a loss to know how to take up where they had left off in peacetime. In the wake of the conflict, the twentieth century seemed to be starting anew and those alive to remember 'absent friends' on New Year's Eve 1918 felt an obligation to their dead comrades to make decent use of the post-war life that they had been granted. With that sense of obligation came a recognition of the importance of honouring their dead.

For Britain, the war had proved a terrible awakening after long years of basking in the glory and security of her Empire. It had destroyed the continuity of life and impacted dramatically on the century that lay ahead. The generation that had thought itself 'modern' had been savaged by weapons derived from its own inventiveness and that of its forefathers. As one contemporary historian expressed it, the British people 'felt that the First World War was a national trauma, for it violated their sense of history as well as their human feelings'.[5] By British standards, her casualties had been unprecedented. So much young life had been expended on the battlefields, its intelligence, enterprise, vision and potential lost for ever. The dead were part of what would later become known as the 'lost generation', the 'innocent flower of the nation crystallized in perpetual youth.'[6] Although the British monarchy stood firm as ever while other crowns had fallen, the country had 'lost the panache of Empire'[7] and the ebullience of her past triumphs. She was a changed nation.

For Canada in her evolution from a rural, agricultural nation to an urban, industrialised one, the war had also proved a great divide. It had cost her her innocence and a death toll of more than sixty thousand. Having been forced to examine carefully both the strengths and limitations of the modern state, she could no longer share a faith in the moral wisdom of Britain and her Allies or a belief in the old order of things. Canada's participation in the war marked her transition in status to a junior, but sovereign, ally of Britain.[8]

The signing of the Treaty of Versailles was followed by peace celebrations and a great parade in London on 19 July 1919 at which representative units from each of the Allied forces commemorated their victory by parading before King George V. Yet everywhere around the Empire, families continued to mourn their dead and cope as best they could with their private grief. Along with countless others, Rudyard Kipling, Sir Harry Lauder, Sir Arthur Conan Doyle and Sir William Osler had each lost their only son. Their lives continued but they could not escape their feelings. Kipling spent much of his time searching for his son's last resting place while Osler found solace in his devotion to others and kept constantly busy. He worked tirelessly throughout the influenza epidemic of 1918–19 and, on one visit to a little girl he knew he could not save, he brought from his garden the last remaining rose of that summer for 'his little lassie'.[9] Yet beneath his wonderfully kind and thoughtful exterior, he was aching with grief and his health began to fail.

When the staff of No. 3 Canadian General Hospital returned to Montreal, they found a city still coming to terms with its losses. McGill University had sustained its share of tragedy and misfortune, as had the community of the 'Square Mile'. Captain Guy Drummond, son and heir of Sir George and Lady Drummond, had been one of the first killed in the Second Battle of Ypres. Sir Montagu and Lady Allan, whose parties and dances John McCrae had attended, had lost two of their three daughters in the *Lusitania* disaster and their only son, Flight Lieutenant Hugh Allan. Five members of the Molson family had been killed and John McCrae's friend, Brigadier Hamilton Gault, had lost a leg.

In Guelph, Janet McCrae was one of many Canadian mothers mourning their sons. John McCrae's celebrity, the tributes paid to him and the family's strong religious faith were a source of strength to both her and her husband. There was so much to be proud of, yet nothing could ease the sense of loss of the very close lifelong relationship between Janet and her 'Jack'. As James Kilgour, her son-in-law, wrote, it was 'hard to conceive of a more complete intimacy & comradeship & two-sided devotion than existed between Jack & his mother'.[10]

By the end of 1919 both Sir William Osler and Janet McCrae were dead. Janet, quiet and serene of spirit, died peacefully and suddenly after complaining of feeling unwell. Sir William, after a bout of influenza and months of insomnia, caught a cold. When bronchopneumonia developed he, like John, had neither the heart nor the strength to combat it. The man who had 'taught the humanity of medicine and practised it supremely'[11] died on 29 December 1919, six months after his seventieth birthday. On New Year's Day 1920, the cathedral of Christ Church, Oxford, was the scene of a very moving funeral service for 'one of the most greatly beloved physicians of all time'.[12] Sir William Osler had always been the first to admit that his life had been blessed in so many ways but the loss of Revere was a tragedy from which he never recovered.

Rudyard Kipling continued to search the graveyards of the Western Front as he contemplated a 'world to be remade without a son'[13] and thought of the uniformed figure he had last seen in August 1915. It has been suggested that, in the process of coming to terms with bereavement, 'it is necessary to construct a story which makes sense of the death and finds some good in the event'[14] and Kipling volunteered to write a history of the Irish Guards, the regiment in which John Kipling had been commissioned.[15]

On the former battlefields, the huge task of identifying bodies and permanently marking and caring for the graves of those who had died, had already begun to be undertaken by the Imperial War Graves Commission. With a membership representative of each Dominion, India and the Colonies, it had commissioned a report on the construction of military cemeteries in the battlefield areas two years earlier. In imperial tradition, the war dead were to remain where they had fallen and the three-man delegation that had visited the Western Front in 1917 had included the prominent British architect, Edwin Lutyens. From their base at a quiet château behind the lines, Lutyens and his two colleagues travelled to view the temporary graveyards. 'What humanity can endure and suffer is beyond belief,'[16] wrote Lutyens, who was deeply affected by what he had seen. As he sat alone a month or so later in his London club, the normally jovial, optimistic man was filled with dejection at 'the beastly waste of war, the loss of life and happiness'.[17] He threw himself into the debate about the form war monuments should take and put forward his proposal of a simple, non-denominational 'Stone of Remembrance'. As one of the three principal architects appointed by the Imperial War Graves Commission in February 1918 to work on its cemeteries in Belgium and France, Lutyens' idea was accepted. His 'Stone of Remembrance' and a 'Cross of Sacrifice' designed by another architect, Reginald Blomfield, were to be central to every cemetery.

As the months passed, physical memorials began to be erected and Books of Remembrance placed in churches, cathedrals and chapels in Britain and elsewhere. As the date for the 1919 London Victory Parade approached, Lutyens was summoned to 10 Downing Street for an audience with the Prime Minister, David Lloyd George. Another design was needed very quickly, this time for a temporary memorial in Whitehall as a saluting point for the planned march past of Allied troops. With the idea of a non-denominational stone still in his mind, Lutyens' design took the form of a cenotaph, or empty tomb. It was intended to be entirely symbolic, neither glorifying war nor applauding victory. The temporary memorial was greeted with such enthusiasm and praise for its simplicity and suitability – evocative of the mood of collective bereavement of the time – that it was rapidly adopted as a national monument. It was here on the first anniversary of the Armistice, that many came to pay their respects.

At eleven o'clock on 11 November 1919, a silence fell across Britain. People and traffic stood still; railway trains were halted; factories, dock-yards, offices and telephone exchanges ceased to function. Special school assemblies and church services were held as the nation paused to remember. The man who had proposed the idea of two minutes' silence was Sir Percy Fitzpatrick, a former High Commissioner to South Africa. Deeply affected by the loss of his son on the Western Front, Fitzpatrick realised that in 'the hearts of our people there is a real desire to find some lasting expression of their feeling for those who gave their lives in the war'.[18] Although initially rejected as impracticable, the British government accepted the idea and the request for the silence was carried by all newspapers a few days earlier as a personal message from King George V. Its impact, both as a public and a private commemoration, was enormous.

On that first Armistice anniversary, Prime Minister Lloyd George was among those who, after his sovereign, placed a wreath of 'orchids and roses with a background of laurels'[19] at Lutyens' Cenotaph. Across the Atlantic, however, another flower was much on the mind of the young American woman who had been trapped in Italy when the storm broke in 1914. Moina Michael had spent most of the war years working at the University of Georgia and, after America's declaration of war in 1917, had volunteered her services. Assigned to the training establishment for overseas YMCA war workers at Columbia University, her post on the staff of the President of the Overseas YMCA had given her a wide overview of events and brought her into contact with many prominent people.

On the morning of 9 November 1918, Moina was attending the 25th Conference of the Overseas YMCA War Secretaries. A young soldier happened to leave a copy of the American magazine, *Ladies Home Journal*, on her desk. Reading through it in a quiet moment, Moina's eye alighted upon John McCrae's poem 'In Flanders Fields'. She had read it many times before but in this magazine it was printed beside a striking picture of ghostly soldiers rising over ground covered with poppies and crosses. As she studied it, it was as if,

the silent voices again were vocal, whispering, in sighs of anxiety unto anguish, 'To you from failing hands we throw the Torch; be yours to hold it high. If ye break faith with us who die we shall not sleep, though poppies grow in Flanders Fields.'[20]

Moina knew what had to be done. In 'a high moment of white resolve I pledged to KEEP THE FAITH and always to wear a red poppy of Flanders Fields as a sign of remembrance and the emblem of "keeping the faith with all who died." '[21] She immediately wrote her own reply to 'Flanders Fields', which she entitled 'We Shall Keep the Faith':

> Oh! You who sleep in 'Flanders Fields,'
> Sleep sweet – to rise anew!
> We caught the torch you threw
> And, holding high, we keep the Faith
> With all who died.
>
> We cherish, too, the poppy red
> That grows on fields where valor led;
> It seems to signal to the skies
> That blood of heroes never dies,
> But lends a lustre to the red
> Of the flower that blooms above the dead
> In Flanders Fields.
>
> And now the Torch and Poppy red
> We wear in honor of our dead.
> Fear not that ye have died for naught;
> We'll teach the lesson that ye wrought
> In Flanders Fields.[22]

As she completed this poem, three Conference delegates appeared at her desk with a cheque for ten dollars in appreciation of her having organised their accommodation. She told them that she would use the money to buy twenty-five red poppies and explained why. The men took the poem into the Conference and returned later asking for poppies to wear. Finding poppies in New York City on a November afternoon did not prove an easy task but Moina was finally rewarded at Wanamaker's Department

Store where she purchased some small silk poppies. She later pinpointed the occasion as,

> the first group ever to ask for poppies to wear in memory of our soldier dead, and since this group gave me the money with which to buy them, I have always considered that I, then and there, consummated the first sale of the Flanders Fields Memorial Poppy.[23]

Having met with an enthusiastic reaction from her colleagues, Moina began to seek approval from individuals, groups and organisations for a 'Flanders Fields Memorial Poppy' and devoted all her spare time to her campaign to make what she called her 'miracle flower'[24] the accepted symbol of remembrance.

By the end of March 1919 and with the entire American press carrying publicity, she had launched her chosen design of a poppy and the torch of Liberty. Thousands of letters were sent out to civil clubs, women's clubs, patriotic organisations, college presidents, university chancellors, national leaders and other prominent citizens. Her efforts began to bring results when, on 21 August 1920, the Georgia convention of the State Department American Legion passed a resolution to endorse the movement to have the poppy 'adopted as the Memorial Flower of the American Legion'.[25] Little over a month later, Moina was overjoyed to read in the press that, at its National Convention on 29 September 1920, 'the American Legion had made the Flanders Fields Memorial Poppy its national emblem of remembrance'.[26]

She later discovered that attending the Convention was a woman who had travelled to Cleveland, Ohio from her home in Paris. Madame Anne Guerin had brought artificial poppies to sell, made by the widows and orphans of the American and French Childrens' League, the organisation she had founded in the autumn of 1919. Her presence, energy and powers of persuasion impressed her American hosts, especially when they learned that sale proceeds would help to raise money for the rehabilitation of some of France's devastated areas. There was interest and sympathy, too, with the League's other aim of teaching the children of both nations to remember and foster the joint friendship created on the battlefield. Anne Guerin had read 'In Flanders Fields' and the many 'replies' that had been written and published. As she explained in her first annual report, John McCrae's poem and Moina Michael's 'reply' had together moved her to act:

> Those two poems were my inspiration for the 'Poppy Days'. Yes, the red Poppy of France would finish the work – it would be the national emblem, the international one that would allow the American and French Children's League to carry on the work of Justice, Humanity,

and Remembrance ... When the resolution was adopted by the American Legion, my joy was so deep that tears filled my eyes and I could hardly contain my emotion when they asked me for a speech in their Convention Hall. They called me 'The Poppy Lady from France'! – I do not wish a more glorious title than this one.[27]

As the second anniversary of Armistice Day approached in 1920, one American newspaper article reported that 'every patriotic man, woman and child over here will wear a poppy to show that the "brave dead have not died in vain." '[28] In France, the American and French Childrens' League covered the graves of American soldiers with poppies and crowds in Paris witnessed the burial of an unknown French soldier of the Great War in honour of all the nation's unnamed war dead. In London, Lutyens' temporary Cenotaph had been rebuilt in Portland stone and was unveiled by King George V. The bugles that blew in Whitehall marked an occasion made all the more poignant by the fact that the British had also chosen this day for the burial of an unknown British soldier in Westminster Abbey. As the sun struggled through the mist of that November morning, the gun carriage bearing the coffin paused at the Cenotaph before proceeding to the Abbey for the funeral service and its final resting place. During the next four days, it was estimated that over one million people came to Whitehall to pay their personal tribute and leave their own floral offerings. A year later, Canada unveiled a cenotaph in Ottawa's Dominion Square and among those present at the ceremony were members of John McCrae's family.

For many in the crowd at Whitehall that day, times were hard. After their terrible ordeal, British ex-soldiers had come home having fought for what they had regarded as a just cause and in the belief that their country would reward them in a just manner. Yet their return had brought further adversity. With widespread unemployment in the post-war period, both ex-soldiers and ex-officers stood in line for any job they could get. It was far removed from the expectations they had cherished and there was both poverty and disillusionment. A number of ex-servicemen's organisations sprang up to promote the interests of the returned servicemen. Field Marshal Douglas Haig, who had been Commander-in-Chief Home Forces until January 1920, was deeply concerned about their problems and saw it as his duty to establish the basic rights of his former soldiers. He refused to accept any honour until 'he was satisfied that adequate provision had been made for the men and officers who had served under him'.[29] Haig worked consistently towards the goal of unity between the disparate groups. In August 1920 a Joint Conference on Unity took place at the Royal United Services Institution in Whitehall and in June 1921, the British Legion was created.

Two months later, the enterprising Madame Anne Guerin arrived at its offices, asking if the Legion would be interested in buying her money-raising poppies. Although most of the staff knew John McCrae's poem, the idea of a poppy as a symbol of remembrance was totally new in Britain. It was soon accepted and the Legion's *Journal* suggested that people should wear a small red poppy as a token of remembrance. On the first Poppy Day, held on 11 November 1921, the sum of £106,000 was raised.

Madame Guerin had by now also visited Canada and her poppies were sold there for the first time on the same day. In the city that had been John McCrae's home for some fourteen years, almost everyone seemed to be wearing one:

> Montreal presented the appearance of a gorgeous fête today, when every citizen, big and little, wore a red poppy in his button-hole in memory of the men who lie asleep in 'Flanders Fields.' Not only were the windows of practically every store artistically decorated with the bright-colored emblem, the painstaking work of French war orphans and widows, but many private houses had clusters of the flowers in their windows. 'Honour the dead, by helping the living' was the Governor General's message, and every Montrealer . . . did his best to help the cause of the veterans today by the purchase of the silken poppies.[30]

'The French Visitor',[31] as Moina Michael called her, was now selling millions of French-made artificial poppies in the United States and by 1922, the two women were in correspondence. Soon after the first British Poppy Day the notion arose in Britain, as it had in America, that if poppies were selling, why should they not be manufactured within the country? The man who approached Earl Haig and the British Legion with the idea of making poppies was Major George Howson MC, a talented engineer who had served in the war and subsequently founded the Disabled Society. Like many others, Howson, whose principal interest was the improvement of the quality and supply of artificial limbs for ex-servicemen, found himself up against the difficult economic conditions of the immediate post-war years. A grant from the Unitary Relief Fund enabled him to see if his poppy idea would work and he was realistic about his prospects, as he explained in a letter to his parents:

> I have been given a cheque for £2,000. 0. 0. to make poppies with, it is a large responsibility and will be very difficult. If the experiment is successful it will be the start of an industry to employ 150 disabled men. I do not think it can be a great success but it is worth trying. I consider the attempt ought to be made if only to give the disabled their chance.
>
> I have to find a factory to-morrow and interview men and choose a man to be in charge of it.[32]

The site selected by Howson was the former Mitchell's Collar Factory, off London's Old Kent Road. In June 1922 he and five employees began poppy production and a month later, the factory was employing forty-one men. As Armistice Day approached, posters promoting poppy sales began to appear. They showed a host of poppies beneath a single cross, urged the public to 'Wear a Flanders Poppy' and included the last two lines of John McCrae's poem.[33] Progress was also continuing in other parts of the world. Earl Haig had visited South Africa the previous year, where unification of the existing ex-servicemen's organisations had been achieved. In Canada the first poppies were now being made by disabled veterans under the sponsorship of the Department of Soldiers' Civil Re-establishment. In Australia, the *Melbourne Argus* newspaper announced that silk poppies would be sold throughout the country in an effort to help restore the devastated homes of Flanders.

Throughout the Allied nations, each successive year saw the erection of more war memorials. Whether on a village green in England, at a dusty settlement in the Australian interior or in one of Stephen Leacock's small Canadian towns, these poignant tributes to the lost of the Great War would form an integral part of the ritual of remembrance. In the Imperial War Graves Commission's permanent cemeteries, simple headstones replaced wooden crosses and Lutyens' Stone of Remembrance carried the words 'Their Name Liveth For Evermore', the choice of Rudyard Kipling. As a newly-appointed IWGC Commissioner, Kipling accompanied King George and Queen Mary when they visited the war cemeteries of the Boulogne area in May 1922. At the cemetery above Wimereux, the Royal party paused at John McCrae's grave.

Many permanent graves already existed but there still remained thousands of soldiers whose last resting place was known only to God. To commemorate these men, great memorials were built like the Menin Gate in the ruined town of Ypres and Lutyens' Memorial to the 73,357 Missing of the Somme at Thiepval. Among the 55,000 names listed on the Menin Gate was that of Lieutenant Alexis Helmer of Ottawa. The grave in which John McCrae had buried him had been obliterated after May 1915 and all that could be traced was the cross that had marked it, discovered in 1919 near the site of John McCrae's dressing station. Elsewhere, smaller memorials told their own sad stories. The people of Newfoundland chose a bronze caribou to mark the site at Beaumont Hamel where the flower of the island's youth had been all but massacred, and a mile to the north of St Julien, the Canadians erected a memorial showing a soldier, his head bowed in perpetual homage to his colleagues who had fallen in the Second Battle of Ypres.

The imagery of 'In Flanders Fields' was also portrayed in Canada's major war memorials. The National War Memorial in Ottawa's Confed-eration Square was designed by Vernon March of Farnborough, Kent, and sculpted by him and his six talented brothers. Above its granite arch, a winged figure was portrayed holding up John McCrae's torch. Walter Allward, the Canadian architect responsible for his country's main war memorial in Europe, visualised his design in a dream and saw at its base, the 'Spirit of Sacrifice' throwing the torch to his comrades. Appropriately, Allward's memorial was erected on the highest point of Vimy Ridge, its two towering white pylons visible for miles as a permanent reminder of all Canada's sons who fought and fell in the Great War. Among the thousands of Canadians who attended its unveiling in 1936 was Canon Scott, by then the Venerable Archdeacon Scott. His visits to Beaumont Hamel, St Julien and some of the other cemeteries recalled the men with whom he had walked 'the borderlands of death,'[34] and moved him to pen his own reply to 'In Flanders Fields':

Rememberance

Now roses of rememberance grow,
Where once the poppies used to blow
In Flanders Fields.

The scent of sweet forget-me-not
Now hovers round each sacred plot,
And those who sleep are not forgot
In Flanders Fields.

The price for peace our heroes gave,
Pray God from future wars may save,
Lest other heroes find a grave
Like Flanders Fields.

The torch they threw from stricken hand,
God grant shall light a better land,
And all the world united stand
By Flanders Fields.[35]

Poppy Day rapidly became an accepted part of the fabric of British life and poppy sales were soon well established in Canada too. After Earl Haig's visit of 1925, some fourteen ex-service organisations came together to form the Canadian Legion. Many a Canadian veteran benefited from its help and one later remembered that the new organisation did 'wonderful work' and 'never forgot the comradeship. It made some of them certain that helping others gave life meaning after the war.'[36]

With British poppy sales continuing to rise, Major Howson found he needed new premises for his factory, which in 1925 became known as the British Legion Poppy Factory. The following year he relocated to the site in Richmond which the factory occupies to this day. As a pioneer in the science of ergonomics, Howson's inventiveness earned him the description of the 'Edison of Richmond Hill'.[37] In 1928 Howson and a few disabled ex-servicemen grouped themselves around a battlefield cross in the churchyard of St Margaret's, Westminster, and invited passers-by to take a poppy from their tray. This visible act of remembrance caught the imagination of the general public and soon became an annual event at which individuals and organisations could plant small poppy crosses in the churchyard's 'Field of Remembrance' to commemorate their war dead and contribute towards the Poppy Appeal.

As the years passed and Armistice anniversaries came and went, strong feelings of pacifism gained ground, supported by those who felt that the annual ceremonies had become a prescribed form of remembrance bound implicitly to militarism. In 1933 the Women's Cooperative Guild chose a white poppy as an alternative emblem of remembrance and a 'definite pledge to peace that war must not happen again'. The following year, the Peace Pledge Union was founded with the aim of fostering a deeper understanding of conflict. Among its activities, it set out to promote a white poppy (and continues to do so to this day) as 'a future commitment to resolve conflicts non-violently'.[38] The wearing of white poppies became central to alternative remembrance events that were held regularly from 1935. The British Legion was concerned that the public should continue to recognise the authorised Haig poppy, and they did. Its sales continued to rise, for in the eyes of many ex-servicemen whose feelings of pacifism were based on personal experience, it stood for all that they and their dead comrades had endured. To these men, the white poppy felt 'too close to the white feather for comfort'.[39]

Twenty-one years after the Armistice, the world was at war again and the Allied nations stood together once more in combat and ultimate victory. Throughout the years of conflict and subsequent peace, the British Legion continued its work, and when it celebrated its Golden Jubilee in 1971, it acquired the prefix 'Royal'. Under the patronage of Her Majesty the Queen, the Royal British Legion has now passed its seventy-fifth anniversary and is proud of its story of dedicated and unrivalled social service. John McCrae's heart would have been especially gladdened to know that part of the organisation's work has been concerned with children and young people. In his own country too, the funds of the Royal Canadian Legion are used partly to benefit and support youth initiatives. The Royal British Legion Festival of Remembrance is an important event in the nation's annual calendar. Those who attend it unite by the medium of television and radio with millions around the world in a single committed act of remembrance. Towards its conclusion, many thousands of poppy petals are released from the ceiling of the Royal Albert Hall onto the gathering below.

The poppies that John McCrae saw in the rough graveyard at Essex Farm near Ypres in May 1915 remain inseparable from memories of the 'Armageddon' of 1914–1918. The Royal British Legion Poppy Appeal has developed into a great British institution that, by means of a wide range of advertising and promotional initiatives, successfully reaches the broader public. The Poppy Factory manufactures between 30 and 34 million poppies, 100,000 wreaths and half a million Remembrance crosses each year, and the almost universal support the Poppy Appeal receives bears witness to the fact that 'it is perceived by the public in a different way to all other charities'.[40] In recent years, major 50th Anniversary commemorations have also featured the poppy, as on 19 August 1995, when a great throng of people gathered in the Mall and around Buckingham Palace to remember the ending of the Second World War in Asia. During a service held in the presence of Her Majesty the Queen, a Lancaster bomber flew overhead dropping a great quantity of poppy petals over the crowds around the Victoria Memorial, the memorial that Grace Osler had seen unveiled in 1911.

To this day, the Allied nations continue to honour their war dead and at countless annual remembrance ceremonies around the world, the poppy wreaths laid echo the spirit of John McCrae's poem and remind us that 'sacrifice and honour are no vain things but truths by which the world lives'.[41] In the beautiful Commonwealth War Graves Commission cemeteries, a reply to 'In Flanders Fields' can occasionally be found carved on one of the lovingly tended gravestones. Appropriately perhaps, at Etaples cemetery, close to the place where John McCrae and his colleagues first set up their hospital in France, one Canadian officer's grave bears the words 'I have fought the good fight. I have kept the faith.'[42] The buglers of the Ypres Fire Brigade also keep faith when they sound 'Last Post' every evening at the Menin Gate in memory of the thousands of men, like young Lieutenant Alexis Helmer of Ottawa, whose names are commemorated on its walls. There, as at so many other places, they are not forgotten.

All those who had a part in John McCrae's story and survived the war carried his torch into the future. Moina Michael proudly watched the success in America of what became known as the 'Buddy Poppy'. She was described on a nationwide American broadcast as 'the best friend the war veteran has'.[43] Rudyard Kipling worked as a Commissioner with the Imperial War Graves Commission until his death in 1936. He also travelled more than fifteen hundred miles in a fruitless search for his son's last resting place.[44] Of John McCrae's two closest friends in the artillery, Edward Morrison, who was knighted and died in 1925, had a firm hand in making the Canadian artillery the leading arm of service in the post-war years. Lawrence Cosgrave pursued a distinguished public service career, serving during the Second World War as Canadian Military Attaché in the South West Pacific area. On

4 September 1945, he was on board the U.S.S. *Missouri* to sign, on behalf of Canada, the acceptance of the Japanese surrender.

Stephen Leacock remained at McGill University and by the time he died in 1944, he was perhaps the English-speaking world's best-known humorist. Leo Amery's long and distinguished career in politics lasted into the next war and his famous speech in the House of Commons on 7 May 1940 led to the departure of Neville Chamberlain. Soon afterwards, Winston Churchill became Britain's Prime Minister. The Venerable Archdeacon Scott continued his ministry in Quebec City. Such was the love and esteem in which he was held by his country that when he died in 1943, more than a thousand people took part in his funeral procession and police had to stop the traffic at every intersection along its route.

Dr Tom McCrae remained as Professor of Medicine at Jefferson Medical College and Physician to the Jefferson & Pennsylvania Hospitals until shortly before his death in 1935. He delivered the prestigious Lumleian Lectures[45] at the Royal College of Physicians in London in 1924. Harvey Cushing, Edward Archibald, Francis Scrimger, Lawrence Rhea, Bill Turner and John McCrae's other medical colleagues pursued distinguished medical careers. Andrew Macphail, who was knighted for his services to literature and the 6th Field Ambulance, published John McCrae's collected poems with an essay on character in 1919. Professor George Adami decided to return to Britain after the Great War and accepted the position of Vice Chancellor at Liverpool University, which he held from 1919 until his death in 1926. Sir Alexander Fleming's research was to lead ultimately to the discovery of penicillin in 1928, the saving of thousands of lives during the Second World War, and countless since.

Sir William Osler bequeathed his magnificent medical library to McGill University. He had often discussed this intention with his nephew, Dr Bill Francis, whom he appointed in his will to be Librarian of the collection. Francis spent seven years in Oxford completing a catalogue of the collection before escorting it to McGill in 1929. As the first Osler Librarian, he presided over it until his death in 1959. There is an Osler Banquet every year at McGill at which the great doctor is toasted from a handsome loving cup bequeathed by Lady Osler.

Down through the years, McGill University has maintained its international reputation in the teaching of medicine. It was here, in the building where John McCrae passed the torch of knowledge to the doctors of the future, that in 1922 Sir Arthur Currie unveiled a memorial to the three members of McGill's medical teaching staff who had died on active service. All three men, Lieutenant-Colonel H.B. Yates, Lieutenant-Colonel R.P. Campbell and Lieutenant-Colonel John McCrae, had been friends through peace and war, and are commemorated in a stained glass window designed by their friend, Percy Nobbs. The centre panel, dedicated to John McCrae, shows row upon row of crosses amid blood red poppies. A jewelled plaque bears a book and quill while a radiant sun is rising on the horizon, its rays spreading into the other two lights. The description beneath it reads 'Pathologist, Poet, Soldier, Physician, a Man Among Men'.

This 'man among men' has been commemorated in many ways and many places. In Canada, scholarships were set up in his memory, schools, a road and a medical unit named after him and plaques unveiled at many of the sites associated with his life. The University Club of Montreal has a library dedicated to John McCrae and in the Peace Tower of the Ottawa Parliament buildings, an extract from 'In Flanders Fields' is inscribed in its Memorial Chamber. The Guelph branch of the Royal Canadian Legion became known as the Colonel John McCrae Memorial Branch 257, and made the first contribution towards a preservation fund to save from demolition the cottage where John McCrae was born. A group of public-spirited Guelph citizens formed themselves into the Colonel John McCrae Birthplace Society and succeeded in securing hundreds of donations from organisations and individuals in Canada and overseas. The old McCrae home was designated a National Historic Site by the Canadian government and opened in August 1968 as a museum. 1972, the centenary year of John McCrae's birth, was designated Poppy Year throughout Canada.

With its lattice windows and grape arbour, the McCrae House museum has an atmosphere both mellow and warm, in which history and tradition have been effectively blended together to produce a national treasure. The fine collection of artefacts and exhibits connected with John McCrae's life and times includes items of furniture from 'Janefield', contained in two period display rooms. An adjoining memorial garden, planted with a fine selection of poppies, also contains a shrine. The museum runs a very active programme of events and special group visits.

In Belgium, the people of Flanders have done much to honour John McCrae and his generation. In the years that followed the Great War, the town of Ypres was painstakingly rebuilt and restored to its former glory as a memorial to the sacrifice of the thousands of men who died in its defence. With the passing of time, the town became a city and in the reconstructed Cloth Hall, a museum tells some sixty to seventy thousand visitors annually about the terrible years of 1914–1918. In 1998, it will be upgraded to become the new and innovative 'In Flanders Fields' museum. The past never ceases to touch the present in this corner of Belgium, and Armistice Day is commemorated every year in Ypres, perhaps never more movingly than on the 75th anniversary in 1993. After the traditional service broadcast from the city's St George's Church[46] and a poppy parade, a service of remembrance was held beneath the arches of the Menin Gate. An 18-pdr field gun on loan from Royal Armouries fired a round for each year of the war while a lone British RAF jet flew overhead in tribute. As the sound died away, thousands of poppy petals floated down from the roof of the Menin Gate onto the people below and church bells rang out in bright sunshine over the city that has risen to become a symbol of peace, hope, courage and renewal.

Two years later, 1995 marked the 80th Anniversary of the writing of 'In Flanders Fields' and Ypres remembered John McCrae and his poem with a programme of special events. The 'square hole' where he had had his dressing station at Essex Farm in 1915 had remained in use with the other bunkers dug by the Canadians. In 1917 these shelters had been reinforced with concrete to withstand almost continuous bombardment and after the war, had been used as housing by returning civilian refugees. By 1992, when a commemorative tablet was erected to John McCrae in front of the adjacent Essex Farm cemetery and the bunkers were designated a protected monument, they were in a bad state of repair. The Provincial Government of West Flanders decided that they should be renovated and, through the combined efforts of a local architect, the students of a nearby technical school and private donations, the Essex Farm Bunkers were completely renovated. On the afternoon of 3 May 1995, the site, which also incorporates a permanent medical exhibition, was officially opened by the Canadian Ambassador to Belgium. It will remain a permanent reminder of the distant, terrible days of the spring of 1915.

From Ypres to the coast of northern France is now a reasonably short journey by car. The town of Wimereux retains its charm and among the many modern buildings can still be found houses and villas surviving from John McCrae's time. The road that leads uphill to the Communal Cemetery affords the views of the surrounding countryside that John McCrae loved. Although Wimereux's expansion has all but obscured the sight of the sea visible from the cemetery in 1918, it can just be glimpsed from the highest ground. A calvaire[47] watches over those at rest, and a plaque and a memorial seat to the poet of 'In Flanders Fields' have been erected.[48] These are rare exceptions to the Commonwealth War Graves Commission rule of no special monument of any kind to any individual. Every year on 11 November, poppy petals are scattered on John's grave when the Mayor of Wimereux, a deputation from the town and representatives of the Royal British Legion's Boulogne Branch gather to remember him.

The simplicity of John's resting place reflects the man for, as Cyril Allinson wrote, the 'many physical memorials to John McCrae would be somewhat embarrassing to him: he was, deep-down, very humble and self-effacing; but the marvellous good being done by the Poppy Day sales on Remembrance Day would gladden his heart; it is an embodiment of his own basic ethic – DO GOOD UNTO OTHERS.'[49] It is perhaps in Wimereux Communal Cemetery that one can best pay quiet tribute to the Canadian whose poem has kept alive the memory of a generation and inspired people never to forget 'what riches of heart and mind, what abounding zest for life, what faithfulness and courage, were bartered for six feet of French or Flemish soil.'[50]

NOTES

1. From 'The Anxious Dead' by John McCrae, *The Spectator*, 30 September 1917.
2. J.B. Priestley, as quoted in Buchan, *These For Remembrance*, Introduction, p. 25.
3. Buchan, *These for Remembrance*, Note for Alice, John, William and Alastair Buchan. p. 3.
4. Macphail, *The Medical Services: Official History of the Canadian Forces in the Great War 1914–1919* (Ottawa, 1925), p. 1.
5. John Terraine, quoted in David Harrison, 'Lies, Damned Lies and Statistics', *Western Front Association Bulletin* (No. 39, June 1994), p. 27.
6. McLeod, *The Last Summer*, p. 160.
7. Morris, *Farewell The Trumpets*, p. 209.
8. J.L. Granatstein and Desmond Morton, *Marching to Armageddon: Canadians and the Great War 1914–1919* (Toronto, 1989), p. 1.
9. Reid, *The Great Physician* (Toronto, 1931), p. 280.
10. James Kilgour to his parents, 28 January 1918, GM Papers.
11. Reid, *The Great Physician*, Frontespiece.
12. Cushing, *Sir William Osler*, Volume II, p. 685.
13. Birkenhead, *Rudyard Kipling*, p. 287.
14. Adrian Gregory, *The Silence of Memory: Armistice Day, 1919–1946* (Oxford, 1994), p. 23.
15. It was entitled *The Irish Guards in the Great War* and published in 1923.
16. Clayre Percy and Jane Ridley, *The Letters of Edwin Lutyens* (London 1985), p. 349.
17. Susan Mary Alsop, *Lady Sackville* (London, 1978), p. 255.
18. Gregory, *The Silence of Memory*, p. 9.
19. *Daily Express*, 12 November 1919, p.1
20. Michael, *The Miracle Flower*, p. 47.
21. Michael, *The Miracle Flower*, p. 47.
22. Michael, *The Miracle Flower*, pp. 47–48.
23. Michael, *The Miracle Flower*, p. 49.
24. Michael, *The Miracle Flower*, p. 88.
25. Michael, *The Miracle Flower*, p. 78.
26. Michael, *The Miracle Flower*, p. 80.
27. Report of First Year of American & French Children's League, October 1919 – October 1920. Archives of the Royal British Legion Poppy Factory.
28. Undated newspaper article (circa 1921), "The Poppy Lady" Brings Flowers from Flanders Field for Memorial Day', MH.
29. Duff Cooper, *Sir Douglas Haig 1861–1928* (London, 1935), Vol. II, p. 41.
30. 'Everyone Wore Poppy Today to Honor Those of Flanders Fields', *Montreal Star*, 11 November 1921.
31. Michael, *The Miracle Flower*, p. 81.
32. Major George Howson MC to his parents, 14 May 1922. Archives of the Royal British Legion Poppy Factory.

33. Debbie Eales, *The Royal British Legion Poppy Factory: A Celebration of the First Seventy Years* (London, 1992), p. 3.
34. Scott, *The Great War as I Saw It*, p. 5.
35. Archdeacon Scott deliberately chose to spell the title of the poem as 'Rememberance'.
36. Mathieson, *My Grandfather's War*, p. 329.
37. Eales, *The Royal British Legion Poppy Factory*, p. 4.
38. Peace Pledge Union leaflet entitled 'Remembrance – Another View,' printed November 1994.
39. Gregory, *The Silence of Memory*, p. 157.
40. Ian P. Cannell MBE, as quoted in Eales, *The Royal British Legion Poppy Factory*, p. 18.
41. From the war memorial at Cobourg, Ontario.
42. Inscribed on the grave of Lieutenant J.R. Mitchener, Princess Patricia's Canadian Light Infantry, who died on 27 September 1916 and is buried at Etaples Commonwealth War Graves Commission Cemetery, France.
43. Michael, *The Miracle Flower*, p. 127.
44. In July 1992 the Commonwealth War Graves Commission replaced the headstone of an unknown Irish Guards officer buried in St Mary's Advanced Dressing Station CWGC Cemetery on the Loos battlefield, with another bearing the name of Lieutenant John Kipling. This exceptional action would not have been taken without what was considered to be watertight evidence of identification. The proof that the body was that of John Kipling rested on the premise that he was the only full lieutenant among three subalterns of the 2nd Battalion, Irish Guards, who were posted missing on 27 September 1915. The map reference where the body was found in September 1919 had been incorrectly recorded at that time. The author is grateful to Tonie and Valmai Holt for providing this information.
45. John, Lord Lumley (1534?–1609), was educated at Cambridge University and was one of the lords appointed to attend Queen Elizabeth I on her accession to the throne as she journeyed from Hatfield to London. In 1582–3 Lumley, in conjunction with Richard Caldwell M.D., founded a surgery lecture in the Royal College of Physicians, endowing it with an annual stipend. A member of the Elizabethan Society of Antiquaries, Lumley also formed a collection of portraits and a considerable library which was purchased on his death by James I and became part of the royal library later presented to the British Museum by George III. In recent times, the Lumleian Lectures have been a series of three given on a subject in Clinical Medicine. Sir William Osler gave the Lumleian Lectures in 1910 on the subject of 'Angina Pectoris'. The subject of Tom McCrae's lectures was 'Foreign Bodies in the Bronchi'.
46. In St George's Church, Ypres, can be found a tablet erected by the Royal Canadian Army Medical Corps in memory of John McCrae and all ranks of the Canadian Army who paid the supreme sacrifice in the two world wars.
47. 'Calvaire' (lit. translation: Calvary) is a representation of the Crucifixion, often found in the form of a wayside cross in countries where the Roman Catholic faith predominates.
48. John McCrae's horse 'Bonfire' was sold into honourable retirement. The proceeds of the sale were sent to Janet McCrae, who donated them to the committee responsible for raising the money to pay for the stone seat at Wimereux Communal Cemetery.
49. Allinson, 'John McCrae', p. 210.
50. Buchan, *These for Remembrance*, Note for Alice, John, William and Alistair Buchan, p. 3.

EPILOGUE

'Be thou faithful unto death and I will give thee a crown of life'[1]

In July 1922, Dr Tom McCrae boarded a train bound for Inverness. He had not long arrived in Oxford to stay with Lady Osler, when news reached him of an important event that made him hasten north. Were he to make his journey today he would probably go by car, coming eventually to a road that winds its way from Fort William along the banks of Loch Ness and into the great wilderness of north west Scotland. In earlier times, this road was no better than a muddy track but the visitor today can pass with ease through the Kintail Forest, with its mountains, lochs, glens and rivers. Within reach of the coast, the mountains close in to form the entrance to a rugged, steep-sided glen where the brooding silence is broken only by the cries of birds and the gentle babbling of nearby streams. As the road leaves Glen Shiel – for so it is called – and approaches the first of a trinity of sea lochs, it passes close to an ancient burial ground. It is here that generations of MacRaes have been laid to rest.

Tom McCrae had been to Scotland before, but on this occasion his visit had a more solemn purpose. The car that met him at Inverness station was taking him to the rallying place of the Clan MacRae, a 'lone shieling on an island', albeit somewhat grander than that visualised in John Galt's poem. The island of Eilean Donan lies at a point where Loch Duich adjoins Loch Long and the lovely Loch Alsh, whose shores are clustered with wild daffodils in spring; foxgloves and creamy Burnet roses in summer; and brightened by the yellow of gorse and the russets of changing leaves in autumn. At dawn and sunset, nature's paintbrush adds yet more colour to a landscape swathed in muted mosses and lichens and overlooked from a distance by the Cuillin Hills of Skye.

The MacRaes were the hereditary constables of the stronghold built on that island and MacRae men had held Eilean Donan until its destruction during the troubles of 1719. It lay, ruined, for almost two hundred years but, shortly before the Great War, Lieutenant-Colonel John MacRae-Gilstrap of Ballimore purchased the site and set about restoring Eilean Donan to its former glory. The work of rebuilding the picturesque fortress began while its owner was away commanding the 11th Battalion of the Black Watch on the Western Front and was a lengthy task, but when Tom

279

McCrae arrived in 1922, the new Eilean Donan was already beginning to take shape.

Today, it stands as a proud monument to a turbulent and romantic past and is one of the most photographed and famous castles in the British Isles. Any visitor who cares to walk the walls of Eilean Donan will find an 18-pdr field gun pointing down Loch Alsh towards the open sea. It is placed beside a special commemorative plaque to all the members of Clan MacRae who died in the Great War, at the base of which can be found a replica of the poet's seat at Wimereux and the first few lines from 'In Flanders Fields'.

On the bright, sunny afternoon of 15 July 1922, Tom McCrae was a principal guest and speaker among some five hundred MacRae clansmen and women who gathered at nearby Cnoc-a-Clachan, the Clan burial ground, to unveil a memorial to their dead from 1914-1918. In his address, he recited the first stanza of John Galt's poem about the 'lone shieling' familiar to him from his childhood days in Guelph.

> From the lone shieling on the misty Island
> Mountains divide us and the waste of seas.
> But still the blood is true, the heart is Highland
> And we in dreams behold the Hebrides.
> Fair these broad meads, these hoary woods are grand;
> But we are exiles from our fathers' land.[2]

He then recited 'In Flanders Fields'. 'To one like myself,' he concluded,

> who comes here for the first time, the occasion and surroundings arouse deep feelings – of the many on whose memory this monument is placed. One was my brother and best friend . . . The situation of this monument seems peculiarly appropriate, overlooking the burial ground of the Clan, where for centuries our dead have been laid.[3]

The descendants of the mighty swordsmen who had fought against the English and their German king near this spot in 1719 had acquitted themselves well in the intervening centuries. Speaking on behalf of his Clan, Sir Colin MacRae talked of the stern lessons that had come with the loss of life in the recent war – lessons of self-sacrifice, duty and devoted service. He concluded that, 'in the words of our poet, we have learned the lesson that ye taught in Flanders fields.'[4]

As Andrew Macphail wrote: 'A man neither lives to himself nor in himself. He is indissolubly bound up with his stock . . . The life of a Canadian is bound up with the history of his parish, of his town, of his province, of his country, and even with the history of that country in which his family had its birth. The life of John McCrae takes us back to Scotland'.[5] Thus, after two hundred and three years, the trail that had led the McCraes to Ayrshire, Galloway and Guelph, returned to Kintail. Possessed of the MacRae blood, blessed with their rich array of talents and their traditions, Lieutenant-Colonel John McCrae is remembered in the place of his kinsmen. Close to the glory of the wild sea lochs, the icy streams that tumble through wooded glens, the lapping waves and the ever-changing sky, it is a place he would have loved.

John McCrae was one of more than 120,000 Canadians who have died in two world wars and year after year the poppy recalls to us the losses of all the Allied nations. The exceptional man whose poem inspired this symbol of remembrance wears his crown of life securely, for his story will endure as long as the poppy endures. As we think of him, we think of a generation whose promising world was shattered and irrevocably changed by a horrific war in which they paid a terrible price. The cause they fought for may have receded into history but their suffering and sacrifice have not, for their tragedy is a part of our heritage. At the end of a violent century that began with their young laughter, it is consoling that the fields of Flanders and many other places where they fell, have now known peace for over fifty years. May it forever remain so.

A final tribute to John McCrae is left to a young contemporary who also lies buried far from his homeland. Rupert Brooke, who had seen and appreciated the best of Canada, died on 23 April 1915[6] as John and his fellow Canadians were fighting desperately near Ypres. Lines from Brooke's poem, 'The Dead', pay eloquent homage to Canada's soldier-doctor-poet, and those who marched with him to Armageddon:

> He leaves a white
> Unbroken glory, a gathered radiance,
> A width, a shining peace, under the night.[7]

NOTES

1. Revelation, Chapter 2, verse 10. This verse is quoted on a stained glass window in St Peter's Anglican Church, Cobourg, Ontario. The window commemorates Major Herbert George Bolster, 2nd Battalion Canadian Expeditionary Force, lst Brigade, lst Division, an officer from Cobourg who was reported missing at Langemarck on 24 April 1915 during the Second Battle of Ypres. Of its three panels, the left incorporates the image of the flaming torch from 'In Flanders Fields', surrounded by poppies and maple leaves. There is also an inscription that reads, 'He died that honour and justice might live'. St Peter's is the garrison church of the Royal Marines in Canada.
2. See Chapter One, note 1.
3. Programme of the Unveiling Ceremony of the Clan MacRae Memorial on 15 July 1922, p. 10, MH.

4. Programme of the Unveiling Ceremony of the Clan MacRae Memorial, p. 12. MH.
5. Macphail, *In Flanders Fields*, p. 112.
6. Rupert Brooke died of blood poisoning caused by a gnat bite. He was on his way to Gallipoli and had spent only a few nights on active service.
7. Rupert Brooke, *The Collected Poems* (London, 1918), 'The Dead', p. 301.

BIBLIOGRAPHY

PRIMARY SOURCES

Gardner-Medwin Family Papers
John McCrae, correspondence with family members, 1901–1914
John McCrae, Diary of the battle of Neuve Chapelle, 1915 and Second Battle of Ypres, 1915
Edward Morrison, correspondence with John McCrae and the McCrae family, 1915–1918

McCrae House, Guelph
Cyril L. C. Allinson, Unpublished manuscript: 'John McCrae: Poet, Soldier, Physician,'
David McCrae, scrapbook, M968.453.1
John McCrae,
   Diary of the 1910 Expedition, M988.1.1
   Scrapbook, M968.429.1
   1892 Sketchbook, M996.1.1.28x
   1896 Sketchbook, M996.2.1.12x
Boer War Ledger, M968.451.1x
Correspondence of the McCrae family
Various newspaper articles and memorabilia

National Archives of Canada, Ottawa
Manuscript Group 30
   B61
      Dr. Oskar Klotz, Correspondence and Papers, 1908–1918
   D150
      Sir Andrew Macphail, correspondence with Janet McCrae, 1918–1919
   D209
      Microfilm Reel A–1102
         John McCrae, Correspondence relating to the South African War, 1900
         John McCrae, Diary of the South African War
      Microfilm Reel A–1103
         Journals of David McCrae.
         Family correspondence 1884–1889
         Letters from John McCrae to his family while on active duty in France during the First World War
      Microfilm Reel A–1108

Correspondence, chiefly from John McCrae to his family, 1890–95.
Microfilm Reel A–1109
Correspondence, chiefly from John McCrae to his family, 1896–99.
E81, Volume 10
Edward W.B. Morrison, Correspondence and Papers, 1901- 1925;
Diary, 1899–1901
E290
Sophie Hoerner, Papers and Correspondence, 1915–1916
Record Group 9, Records of the Department of Militia and Defence
II, A3, Vol. 33
War Diary, D Battery, Royal Canadian Field Artillery, 1899–1901
III, D3, Vol. 4964
War Diary, 1st Brigade, CFA, October 1914-July 1915

Osler Library of the History of Medicine, McGill University, Montreal
MS 545/4 and 545/5
Edward Archibald Correspondence
– Letters from Edward Archibald to his wife 1906–1934, 1944.
MS 545/1
Edward Archibald Correspondence
– Letters from Edward Archibald to his parents.
Acc. 326/2, Box 7
Sir William Osler Papers: Miscellaneous.
MS 438/49
Letters of Maude Abbott
E.H. Bensley Files
– John McCrae
MS 264
– Autopsy Book 1902–3

University of Guelph Library, Special Collections
Edward Johnson Collection
Letters from Beatriz d'Arneiro to Edward Johnson, 1906

University of Toronto, John P. Robarts Reference Library
Microfilm mfm/LH/V377
The Varsity magazine 1892, 1893, 1894 containing John McCrae's
three published poems of 1894 and articles by him entitled 'Reflec-
tions' (Volume 11, No. 13, 9 February 1892, p.178) and 'How the
Twenty-Third Paid Forfeit' (Volume 13, No. 20, 22 March 1894,
pp.4–6).
Microfilm mfm/AP/U577
The McGill University Magazine (1901–1907) containing five pub-
lished poems by John McCrae and articles by him entitled 'The

Builders of Empire' (Volume 1, No. 1, December 1901, pp. 66–74) and 'Hasty Notes and Judgements' (Volume 2, No.1, December 1902, pp.108–118).
The University Magazine (1907–1918) containing six published poems by John McCrae.
Microfilm mfm/AP/S388
   Saturday Night magazine, containing the article 'My Day Dreams' by John McCrae (Volume 6, No. 16, 11 March 1893, p.9).
   Massey's Magazine 1896–1897 containing two published poems by John McCrae.

Metropolitan Toronto Reference Library, Baldwin Room
The Canadian Magazine of Politics, Science, Art and Literature 1895–1898 containing six published poems by John McCrae.

The Presbyterian Church of Canada Archives, Toronto
Microfilm mcfm T3W4
   The Westminster Magazine, June 1896 – June 1898 containing three published poems and one article entitled 'The Comedy of a Hospital' by John McCrae (Volume 1, No. 3, 11 September 1897, p.182).

SECONDARY SOURCES

Books
Aberdeen, Jennie. W. *John Galt*. London: Oxford University Press, 1936.
Adami, J.George. *War Story of the C.A.M.C. 1914–1915*. Volume 1. London: Colour Ltd and The Rolls House Publishing Co. Ltd., 1918.
Adami, Marie. *J. George Adami: A Memoir*. London: Constable & Co., 1925.
Alsop, Susan Mary. *Lady Sackville*. London: Weidenfeld & Nicolson, 1978.
Amery, L.S. *Days of Fresh Air: Being Reminiscences of Outdoor Life*. London: Jarrolds, 1939
Amery, The Rt. Hon. L.S. *My Political Life*. 2 Volumes. London: Hutchinson 1953
Aronson, Theo. *Crowns in Conflict: The Triumph and the Tragedy of European Monarchy 1910–1918*. London: John Murray, 1986.
Begbie, Harold. *Albert Fourth Earl Grey: A Last Word*. London: Hodder & Stoughton, 1917.
Bensley, Edward H. *McGill Medical Luminaries*. Montreal: McGill University Press, 1990.
Birkenhead, Lord. *Rudyard Kipling*. New York: Random House, 1978.
Boyd, William. *With a Field Ambulance at Ypres: Being letters written March 7 – August 15 1915*. Toronto: The Musson Book Company, 1916.

Brinnin, John Malcolm. *The Sway of the Grand Saloon: A Social History of the North Atlantic*. New York: Delacorte Press, 1971.

Brittain, Vera. *Chronicle of Youth: Vera Brittain's War Diary 1913–1917*. Edited by Alan Bishop. London: Book Club Associates, 1981.

Brooke, Rupert. *The Collected Poems*. London: Sidgwick & Jackson, 1918.

Broster, D.K. *The Flight of the Heron*. London: William Heinemann Ltd., 1925.

Buchan, John. *These for Remembrance: Six friends killed in the Great War*, with an Introduction by Peter Vansittart. London: Buchan & Enright, 1987.

Buchan, John. *The King's Grace 1910–1935*. London: Hodder & Stoughton, 1935.

Buchan, John. *Memory Hold The Door*. London: Hodder & Stoughton, 1940

Buitenhuis, Peter. *The Great War of Words*. London: B.T. Batsford, 1989.

Byerly, A.E. *The Beginnings of Things*. Guelph: Guelph Publishing Company, 1935.

Canada in Khaki. London: Published for the Canadian War Records Office by The Pictorial Newspaper Co., 1918.

Churchill, Winston S. *Great Contemporaries*. London: Odhams Press, 1937

Clendenan, Mae Stuart. *The M'Craes of Carsphairn*. Reprinted from the Gallovidian Annual 1938. Edinburgh Public Library.

Colebrook, Leonard. *Almroth Wright – Provocative Doctor and Thinker*. London: William Heinemann, 1954.

Collard, Edgar Andrew. *Montreal Yesterdays*. Toronto: Longmans, 1963.

Coombs, Rose. *Before Endeavours Fade*. London: Battle of Britain Prints International, 1994.

Cooper, Duff. *Sir Douglas Haig 1861–1928*. London: Faber and Faber, 1935.

Cowles, Fleur. *1913: The Defiant Swansong*. London: Weidenfeld & Nicolson. 1967.

Craigie, Edward H. *A History of the Department of Zoology up to 1962*. Toronto: University of Toronto Press, 1966.

Currie, J.A. *The Red Watch: With lst Canadian Division in Flanders*. Toronto: McClelland & Stewart, 1916.

Cushing, Harvey. *The Life of Sir William Osler*. 2 Volumes. Oxford: Oxford University Press, 1925.

Cushing, Harvey. *From a Surgeon's Journal 1915–1918*. London: Constable, 1936.

Dancocks, Daniel G. *Sir Arthur Currie*. Toronto: Methuen, 1985.

Dancocks, Daniel G. *Welcome to Flanders Fields. The First Canadian Battle of the Great War: Ypres 1915*. Toronto: McClelland & Stewart, 1988.

Daniel, Clifton: *Chronicle of the 20th Century*. New York: Chronicle Publications, 1987.

Fetherstonhaugh, R.C. *No. 3 Canadian General Hospital (McGill) 1914–1919*.

Montreal: Gazette Publishing Company, 1928.

Fulton, John F. *Harvey Cushing*. Springfield, Illinois: Charles C. Thomas, 1946.

Gibbs, Philip. *Now It Can Be Told*. New York: Garden City Publishing, 1920.

Giddings, Robert. *The War Poets*. London: Bloomsbury Publishing Ltd., 1988.

Gillen, Mollie. *Lucy Maud Montgomery: The Wheel of Things*. Don Mills: Fitzhenry & Whiteside Ltd., 1975.

Gow, J.E. *John Eckford & His Family: Bruce Pioneers*. Quebec, 1911

Greenhous, Brereton & Harris, Stephen. *Canada & The Battle of Vimy Ridge*. Ottawa: Department of National Defence, 1992.

Gregory, Adrian. *The Silence of Memory: Armistice Day 1919–1946*. Oxford: Berg Publishers, 1994.

Gregory, Alexis. *The Gilded Age: The Super-Rich of the Edwardian Era*. London: Cassell, 1993.

Grey of Falloden, Viscount. *Twenty-Five Years, 1892–1916*. 2 Volumes. New York: Frederick A. Stokes, 1925.

Gwyn, Sandra. *Tapestry of War*. Toronto: Harper Collins, 1992.

Hastings, Paul. *War and Medicine 1914–1945*. Harlow: Longman Group, 1988.

Hobsbawm, E.J. *The Age of Empire*. London: Weidenfeld & Nicolson, 1987.

Holmes, Richard. *Edward VII, His Life and Times*. 3 Volumes. London: Amalgamated Press, 1910.

Holt, Tonie and Valmai. *In Search of The Better 'Ole*. Portsmouth: Milestone Publications, 1985.

Hyatt, A.M.J. *General Sir Arthur Currie: A Military Biography*. Toronto: University of Toronto Press, 1978.

Hurford, Elaine. *The Mount Nelson: In Grand Tradition*. Cape Town: The Millenium Group, 1992.

Johnson, Leo A. *History of Guelph 1827–1927*. Guelph Historical Society, 1977.

Kingsmill, Suzanne. *Francis Scrimger: Beyond the Call of Duty*. Toronto & Oxford: Hannah Institute & Dundurn Press, 1991.

Kipling, Rudyard. *Something of Myself*. London: Macmillan & Co., 1937.

Kipling, Rudyard. *Letters of Travel 1892–1913*. London: Macmillan & Co., 1920.

Leacock, Stephen. *Montreal – Seaport and City*. New York: Doubleday, Doran & Co, 1942.

Leacock, Stephen. *Sunshine Sketches of a Little Town*. London: The Bodley Head, 1912.

Leacock, Stephen. *Canada: The Foundations of Its Future*. Montreal: Privately printed (Gazette Printing Co.), 1941.

Legate, David M. *Stephen Leacock: A Biography*. Toronto: Macmillan of Canada, 1970.

Lotz, Jim. *Canadians at War*. London: Bison Books, 1990.

Liddell Hart, B.H. *History of the First World War*. London: Pan Books, 1977.

Mackay, Donald. *The Square Mile: Merchant Princes of Montreal*. Vancouver: Douglas & McIntyre, 1987.

Macdonald, Lyn. *The Roses of No Man's Land*. London: Penguin Books, 1993.

Macdonald, Lyn. *1915: The Death of Innocence*. London: Headline Book Publishing, 1993.

Macmillan, Harold. *The Winds of Change 1914–1939*. London: Macmillan & Co Ltd., 1966.

Macphail, Sir Andrew. *In Flanders Fields and Other Poems by Lieut.-Col John McCrae, M.D. with An Essay in Character*. Toronto: William Briggs, 1919.

Macphail, Sir Andrew. *The Medical Services. Official History of the Canadian Forces in the Great War 1914–1919*. Ottawa: Department of National Defence, 1925.

Magnus, Philip. *Edward VII*. London: John Murray, 1964.

Marquis, Thomas. G. *Canada's Sons on Kopje and Veldt*. Toronto: The Canada's Sons Publishing Co., No date given.

Marshall, Dorothy. *The Life & Times of Queen Victoria*. London: Weidenfeld & Nicolson, 1972.

Martin, Sandra and Hall, Roger. *Rupert Brooke in Canada*. Toronto: PMA Books, 1978.

Massie, Robert K. *Dreadnought: Britain, Germany and the Coming of the Great War*. New York: Random House, 1991.

Mathieson, W.D. *My Grandfather's War: Canadians Remember the First World War 1914–1918*. Toronto: Macmillan, 1981.

McLeod, Kirsty. *The Last Summer: May to September 1914*. London: Collins, 1983.

Michael, Moina. *The Miracle Flower: The Story of the Flanders Fields Memorial Poppy*. Philadelphia: Dorrance & Co., 1941, Re-published by Elliott & Fitzpatrick, Athens, Georgia.

Miller, Carman. *Painting the Map Red: Canada and the South African War 1899–1902*. Montreal: Canadian War Museum and McGill-Queen's University Press, 1993.

Morris, Jan. *Heaven's Command*. London: Penguin Books, 1979.

Morris, Jan. *Farewell The Trumpets*. London: Penguin Books, 1979.

Morrison, Edward.W.B. *With the Guns in South Africa*. Hamilton: Spectator Printing Company, 1901.

Morton, H.V. *The Pageant of the Century*. London: Odhams Press, 1933.

Morton, Desmond and J.L. Granatstein. *Marching to Armageddon: Canadians and The Great War 1914–1919*. Toronto: Lester & Orpen Dennys Ltd., 1989.

Murray, W.W. *The Epic of Vimy*. Ottawa: The Legionary, 1936.

Nasmith, George G. *On The Fringe of The Great Fight*. Toronto: McClelland Goodchild & Stewart, 1917.

Newman, Peter C. *Canada 1892: Portrait of a Promised Land*. Toronto: Penguin Books, 1992.

Nicholson, Colonel G.W.L. *Canadian Expeditionary Force 1914–1919: Official History of the Canadian Army in the First World War*. Ottawa: Department of National Defence, 1964.

Nicholson, Colonel G.W.L. *The Gunners of Canada: The History of the Royal Regiment of Canadian Artillery. Volume I 1534–1919*. Toronto: McClelland and Stewart, 1967.

Northcliffe, Lord. *At the War*. London: Hodder & Stoughton, 1916.

Palmer, Alan. *The Kaiser: Warlord of the Second Reich*. London: Weidenfeld & Nicolson, 1978.

Percy, Clayre and Jane Ridley. *The Letters of Edwin Lutyens*. London: Collins, 1985.

Petrie, Sir Charles. *The Edwardians*. New York: W.W. Norton, 1965.

Plummer, Mary. *With The First Canadian Contingent*. Toronto: Hodder & Stoughton, 1915.

Prescott, John F. *In Flanders Fields: The Story of John McCrae*. Erin, Ontario: Boston Mills Press, 1985.

Reid, Edith Gittings. *The Great Physician*. Toronto: Oxford University Press, 1931.

Ross, A.M. *The College on the Hill: A History of the Ontario Agricultural College 1874–1974*. Toronto: 1974.

Rubio, Mary and Waterston, Elizabeth. *The Selected Journals of L.M. Montgomery, Volume II 1910–1921*. Toronto: Oxford University Press, 1987.

Ruskin, John. *Proserpina. Studies of Wayside Flowers Part I*. Orpington: George Allen, 1875.

Scott, Frederick George. *The Great War as I Saw It*. Toronto: F.D. Goodchild Co., 1922.

Sitwell, Osbert. *Great Morning: Being the Third Volume of Left Hand, Right Hand!*. London: Macmillan & Book Society, 1948.

Smith, William H. *Smith's Canadian Gazetteer*. Toronto: H & W Rowsell, 1846.

Taylor A.J.P. *The First World War: An Illustrated History*. London: Hamish Hamilton, 1963.

Terry, Neville. *The Royal Vic: The Story of Montreal's Royal Victoria Hospital*. Montreal: McGill-Queen's University Press, 1994.

Tuchman, Barbara. *The Proud Tower: A Portrait of the World Before the War 1890–1914*. London: Hamish Hamilton, 1966.

Vernède, R.E. *The Fair Dominion*. London: Kegan Paul Trench Truebner & Co., 1911.

Vernède, R.E. *War Poems and Other Verses*. London: Kegan Paul Trench Truebner & Co., 1917.

Williamson, Henry. *An Anthology of Modern Nature Writing*. London: Thomas Nelson & Sons, 1936.

Wilson, H.W. *The Great War*. 12 Volumes. London: Amalgamated Press, 1917.

The Canadian Encyclopaedia. 3 Volumes. Edmonton: Hurtig Publishers Ltd, 1985.

Publications

Eales, Debbie. *The Royal British Legion Poppy Factory: A Celebration of the First Seventy Years*, Ashford: 1992

Holt, Tonie and Valmai. *Major and Mrs Holt's Battlefield Guide to the Ypres Salient*. London: T. & V. Holt Associates, 1995.

Articles

Adami, J.G. 'Lt. Col. John McCrae, C.A.M.C.', *British Medical Journal*, 9 February 1918. pp.1–6.

Bataille, Guy. 'Mme Deligny-Debacker recalls the memory of Lieutenant-Colonel John McCrae and the last days of the "Soldier Poet"', *La Voix du Nord*, 12 February 1958.

Belanger, Réal. 'Sir Wilfrid's Sunny Ways,' *Horizon Canada*, Volume 7. No. 77, August 1986, pp. 1825–1831.

Boyd, David P. 'Doctors Afield: John McCrae (1872–1918)', *The New England Journal of Medicine*, Volume 260, No. 23, 4 June 1959, pp. 1178–1180.

Collard, Edgar Andrew. 'McCrae of Flanders Fields', *Montreal Star*, 4 November 1978.

Graesser, Mary. 'The Childhood of John McCrae,' *The Ontario Agricultural College Review*, Volume 37, No. 11, July 1925. pp.420–421.

Harrison, David. 'Lies, Damned Lies and Statistics', *Western Front Association Bulletin* No. 39, June 1994

Hinds, Margery. 'A Governor General Goes North,' *The Beaver*, Summer 1971, pp. 14–19.

Howitt, Henry Orton. 'John McCrae,' *The Torch, Yearbook of the Colonel John McCrae Memorial Branch 257*, Volume VIII, 1940. pp. 7–17.

Macnaughton, John. 'In Memoriam. Lieut.-Col. John McCrae,' *The University Magazine*. Volume 17, April 1918, pp.235–245.

Moore, William. 'Falkenhayn's Green Genie', *Military History*, June 1984. pp. 271–279.

Prescott, John F. 'The extensive medical writings of soldier-poet John McCrae,' *Canadian Medical Association Journal*, Volume 122, 12 January 1980, pp.110–114.

Spreckley, R.O. 'John McCrae of Flanders Fields', *The Legionary*, November 1948, p.13–14.

Van der Kiste, John. 'Two Imperial Heirs', *Royalty Digest*, October 1995, pp. 110–114.

Unpublished Sources

Burnell, Jennifer. 'The McCraes of Guelph: Urban and Rural Development in Nineteenth Century Guelph'. Urban History Project, University of Guelph, 1992.

Dagg, Elizabeth. 'A Race of Passionate Men: The Lives of John McCrae and Norman Bethune'. B.A. Thesis, University of Guelph, 1993.

INDEX

292